SERMONS OF THE CURÉ d'ARS

The Pulpit from which St. John Vianney preached.

Sermons of the Curé d'Ars

For the Sundays and Feasts of the Year

by
St. John Marie Vianney

Re-typset and edited from
the 1901 Wagner edition by:

MEDIATRIX PRESS

MMXVI

The Sermons of the Curé d'Ars
For the Sundays and Feasts of the Year

ISBN: 978-1-953746-50-4

Reprinted from:
Sermons for the Sundays and Feasts of the Year
Joseph F. Wagner and Co. 1901.

Translated from:
Sermons du vénérable serviteur de Dieu,
Jean-Baptiste-Marie Vianney, Curé d'Ars.
Paris : V. Lecoffre, 1883

© Mediatrix Press, 2016
Post Falls, Idaho

This work may not be reproduced for commercial purposes in either electronic or physical format without permission of the publisher.

Printed in the United States of America.

Table of Contents

Preface to the Mediatrix Press Edition. xi

A Table of Synopses. xiii

TWENTY-SECOND SUNDAY AFTER PENTECOST. 1

TWENTY-THIRD SUNDAY AFTER PENTECOST. 9

TWENTY-FOURTH SUNDAY AFTER PENTECOST. 17

LAST SUNDAY AFTER PENTECOST. 25

FIRST SUNDAY OF ADVENT
        THE LAST JUDGMENT. 33

SECOND SUNDAY OF ADVENT
        THE ETERNAL TRUTHS. 41

THIRD SUNDAY OF ADVENT
        FEAR OF MAN. 49

FOURTH SUNDAY OF ADVENT. 57

SUNDAY IN THE OCTAVE OF CHRISTMAS. 67

THE EPIPHANY
        CALLED TO THE FAITH. 73

FIRST SUNDAY AFTER EPIPHANY
        RELIGIOUS PICTURES IN THE HOME. 79

SECOND SUNDAY AFTER EPIPHANY
        THE GLORY AND THE POWER OF THE HOLY NAME. 85

THIRD SUNDAY AFTER EPIPHANY
        THE HOLY FAMILY. 91

SEPTUAGESIMA SUNDAY
 ON ENVY. 97

SEXAGESIMA SUNDAY
 THE WORD OF GOD. 103

QUINQUAGESIMA SUNDAY
 THE ENEMIES OF OUR SALVATION.. 109

FIRST SUNDAY OF LENT
 TEMPTATIONS. 115

SECOND SUNDAY OF LENT
 THE DEATH OF THE SINNER.. 121

THIRD SUNDAY OF LENT
 INDULGENCES. 125

PASSION SUNDAY
 "REPENTANCE". 131

PALM SUNDAY. 137

EASTER
 PASCHAL JOYS. 141

LOW SUNDAY
 " EASTER CONFESSION". 149

SECOND SUNDAY AFTER EASTER
 ON PERSEVERANCE.. 155

THIRD SUNDAY AFTER EASTER
 TRIBULATIONS. 161

FOURTH SUNDAY AFTER EASTER
 THE PROGRESS OF CHRISTIANITY. 167

FIFTH SUNDAY AFTER EASTER
 PRAYER.. 173

SIXTH SUNDAY AFTER EASTER
    THE FOLLOWERS OF CHRIST SHOULD
    GIVE TESTIMONY OF HIM............................ 177

WHIT-SUNDAY
    CHILDREN OF THE HOLY GHOST AND
    CHILDREN OF THE WORLD.......................... 183

TRINITY SUNDAY
    THE HOLY EUCHARIST................................. 189

SECOND SUNDAY AFTER PENTECOST
    HOLY MASS.. 195

THIRD SUNDAY AFTER PENTECOST
    THE MERCY OF GOD................................... 201

FOURTH SUNDAY AFTER PENTECOST
    HOPE.. 207

FIFTH SUNDAY AFTER PENTECOST
    THE SECOND COMMANDMENT..................... 213

SIXTH SUNDAY AFTER PENTECOST............................ 217

SEVENTH SUNDAY AFTER PENTECOST
    ON FALSE AND TRUE VIRTUE...................... 223

EIGHTH SUNDAY AFTER PENTECOST
    THE PARTICULAR JUDGMENT....................... 229

NINTH SUNDAY AFTER PENTECOST
    THE SOUL... 235

TENTH SUNDAY AFTER PENTECOST
    RASH JUDGMENT....................................... 241

ELEVENTH SUNDAY AFTER PENTECOST
    DETRACTION... 247

TWELFTH SUNDAY AFTER PENTECOST
    THE FIRST COMMANDMENT. 253

THIRTEENTH SUNDAY AFTER PENTECOST
    ABSOLUTION. 259

FOURTEENTH SUNDAY AFTER PENTECOST
    THE LOVE OF GOD. 265

FIFTEENTH SUNDAY AFTER PENTECOST
    THE NATIVITY OF THE BLESSED VIRGIN. 271

SIXTEENTH SUNDAY AFTER PENTECOST
    HUMILITY. 277

SEVENTEENTH SUNDAY AFTER PENTECOST
    CHARITY. 283

EIGHTEENTH SUNDAY AFTER PENTECOST
    LUKEWARMNESS. 289

NINETEENTH SUNDAY AFTER PENTECOST
    INTEMPERANCE. 295

TWENTIETH SUNDAY AFTER PENTECOST
    EXTREME UNCTION. 299

TWENTY-FIRST SUNDAY AFTER PENTECOST
    ANGER. 305

TWENTY-SECOND SUNDAY AFTER PENTECOST
    THE SOUL OF MAN THE IMAGE OF GOD. 311

SERMONS FOR THE FEAST DAYS OF THE YEAR

FEAST OF ALL SAINTS. 315

ALL SOULS' DAY. 323

FEAST OF THE IMMACULATE CONCEPTION
     SANCTIFYING GRACE, THE MOST PRECIOUS GIFT...... 333

THE NATIVITY OF OUR LORD
     GOD WITH US.................................... 339

NEW YEAR'S EVE.. 349

NEW YEAR'S DAY: THE CIRCUMCISION OF OUR LORD
     THE TRANSITORY AND THE ETERNAL. 357

THE FEAST OF ST. PATRICK
     THE GLORIOUS VIRTUES OF ST. PATRICK.............. 361

THE FEAST OF THE ASCENSION. 367

CHILDREN'S FIRST COMMUNION
     HOLY COMMUNION A MEMORIAL OF
     THE LOVE OF JESUS TOWARD US. 373

TWO JUBILEE SERMONS................................... 381

ASSUMPTION OF THE BLESSED VIRGIN MARY
     THE GLORIES OF MARY. 393

Preface to the Mediatrix Press Edition

E ARE VERY PLEASED to offer the Sermons of the St. John Vianney, the Curé d'Ars, complete and unabridged from the 1901 Wagner edition. We have completely re-typeset this work while maintaining the original spelling and wording. We also found the need to make some editorial changes to the presentation, most specifically, removing the synopses from the 1901 edition and placing them into their own table of synopses. The editor of the 1901 edition had done this only half way.

Moreover, the editors of the original edition found that they did not have enough sermons from St. John Vianney to complete the entire liturgical year, so they added sermons from preachers at that time, which make up about 5 of the total sermons. These can be distinguished from the saint's sermons by the fact that their names are placed at the end.

We hope this new and unabridged edition of the 1901 Sermons will be of profit to all those who read them and strive by them to live a fully Christian life.

Ryan Grant
Post Falls, ID

A Table of Synopses

TWENTY-SECOND SUNDAY AFTER PENTECOST
Ill-gotten goods a curse. Nothing more reasonable or just than to give to God what belongs to God, and to your neighbor what belongs to him. Nevertheless unrighteousness is very common and restitution just as scarce.
Ill-gotten goods never bring advantage;
How we can injure our neighbors;
How, and to whom you must make restitution.
 Ill-gotten goods a curse. St. Paul: he who tries to get rich by unjust means will soon fall into evil ways. St. Augustine, Zacharias, King Achab and Jezabel.
Many of you, my friends, are thieves. The many ways of thievery.
Restitution indispensable. Make restitution while you are able, do not delay it.

TWENTY-THIRD SUNDAY AFTER PENTECOST
No one can serve two masters. God and the world utterly opposed to each other. To please the one is to become the enemy of the other. The Saints an example. Three classes of people: those entirely for and of the world, those entirely devoted to God, and those who would like to serve both, God and the world. A description of these last ones. They lead a miserable, inconsistent life. How they act. The vanity of the world recognized in the hour of death. Do not put off the return to God until too late.

TWENTY-FOURTH SUNDAY AFTER PENTECOST (page 16).
Seek first the Kingdom of God. Although we are all convinced that we are created for the sole purpose of serving God, still very few of us strive earnestly to do this. Reason, many consider the service of God difficult.
 I. His service is easy;
 II. If we serve God, we shall find peace for our souls and rest for our hearts.
I. Joy, pleasure and happiness for this life and the future found in the service of God. Poverty, sufferings, and trials, contempt, so many means for happiness, if borne patiently and for God's sake. The various ways in which we can make our lives a continual service of God.
II. Those who serve the world on the path to perdition. There is but one means of salvation, the service of God. The evil ways of the godless. When in need of assistance, the world will not give it. The difference between the death of the godless and the death of the just.

TWENTY-FIFTH SUNDAY AFTER PENTECOST
A Happy Death. Death a cause of alarm for the sinner, a cause of joy for the just.

I. *The advantages of a happy death.*
II. *The means to obtain it.*

I. *Whether we may expect to die happily or not depends upon the life we are leading. St. Jerome. St. Paul. St. Gregory. St. Ludivina. To lead a good life follow the footsteps of Jesus Christ. Prayer, good deeds, suffering. Example of the saints. Innocent I., St. Lawrence, St. Augustine. The three crosses on Calvary. The just has no cause to fear death.*

II. *Three means to insure a happy death: A holy life, true repentance, union with Christ. Isaias. St. Jerome. The Holy Ghost. Peter Damian. As the life, so the death. Do not hope for a miraculous conversion. Abimelech. Saul and the Amalekite. How the Christian prepares for death.*

FIRST SUNDAY OF ADVENT
The last Judgment. Not a god, clothed with our weakness, come to redeem the world, but a God in power and majesty, a judge in righteous wrath, will then appear. St. Luke. We shall be judged, this is certain, and we shall be judged without mercy. God preceding His visitations by signs. The destruction of Jerusalem. The signs preceding the day of judgment most terrible. The things that will come to pass. How you will be judged. Excuses vain and useless. Not the merciful God, now ever ready to forgive, will judge us, but the just God, the revenging God. Never lose sight of the fact that some day you will be judged according to your merits, without mercy or forbearance.

SECOND SUNDAY OF ADVENT
The eternal truths. The Holy Ghost assures us that we shall never sin if we contemplate them earnestly. Death certain, it may befall us at any moment. Nor can we take any goods of this world along with us into eternity. Behold, how Jesus Christ wishes to save us. Four things to be contemplated: The brevity of life, death, judgment, eternity. Remembering these four things, we should be fortified in the service of God, and in bearing the trials of this life. Example: the Saints. The many graces received from God for the salvation of our souls and how do we use them? Happy the one who hears and obeys the voice of God.

THIRD SUNDAY OF ADVENT
Fear of man. Nothing more honorable or glorious than to confess to the name of Christian, nothing more despicable than to be ashamed to confess Jesus Christ. To deny God means to become a slave of Satan.
 I. *How the fear of man offends God;*
 II. *How those who fear the world's criticism betray a weak and narrow mind.*
 I. *I will not speak of haters of religion, like Nero, Voltaire, Ingersoll, etc. They meet their fate by dashing to pieces on the immovable rock of the Church. Nor will I refer to those who are afraid of showing openly their enmity, but who, secretly, antagonize everything holy and sacred. I will speak about ourselves, and our fear to fulfil our*

religious duties before the world. When are we guilty of this? Eating meat on forbidden days, for fear of ridicule; listening to and seemingly approving of indecent talk, etc.

II. Three reasons why those who practice their religion are criticized because they are considered hypocrites, from hatred of religion, or envy. The injustice of ridiculing others on these pretenses. The foolishness of fearing this ridicule. Raise your eyes to the crucifix and you will not be wanting in courage.

FOURTH SUNDAY OF ADVENT

Penance. The punishment due for our sins. Difference between the Sacrament of Baptism and the Sacrament of Penance. Temporary punishment either in this life or in purgatory. Therefore

I. We are not exempt from the obligation of doing penance, even after our sins are forgiven;
II. How we can do penance in this life.
I. The Sacrament of Penance explained. How it is received worthily. One condition of receiving it worthily is: satisfaction, which means doing penance. Sins remitted but not the punishment. Examples: Adam, David, penances of the early Church.
II. How penance must be done. The various ways of doing penance.

SUNDAY IN THE OCTAVE OF CHRISTMAS

The Threefold Love of St. John. John the "disciple whom Jesus loved." A model for our imitation. The love of St. John was
 I. A pure love;
 II. A faithful love;
 III. A fruitful love.
I. A pure love. John pure and innocent of heart. The preference of our Saviour for him on account of his purity. Privileges bestowed on St. John. Is our love pure?
II. A faithful love. John faithful when the other apostles fled, when even Peter denied his master. St. John at the cross. How does our love compare with this?
III. A fruitful love. His love manifested in the services of his master, in preaching the gospel, in suffering for Christ's sake. Let us follow his example.

EPIPHANY SUNDAY

Called to the Faith. The Magi signifying how the mercy of God called us to the knowledge of true faith. The Magi kings an example of ready obedience to God's call. How they disregarded and overcame all difficulties that would keep them away from their God. The sacrifices they made. Their persistence. Who of us would show such resolution, such persistence, in seeking God and our salvation? The offerings of the Magi Kings and their meanings. We, to whom was given the precious gift of Faith, do we appreciate it sufficiently? Is not the example of the Magi Kings a lesson and a reproach for us?

FIRST SUNDAY AFTER EPIPHANY
Religious Pictures in the Home. The house of God, the temple, the Preferred abode of our Lord. Jealous for its dignity and sacredness. The temple, the church, should also for us be the place where we prefer to be. But as our duties and obligations do not leave us much time to spend in church, let us make our homes temples of God. Religious pictures the means. Sacred pictures help us to raise our thoughts from the visible to the invisible. Religious pictures in use from the earliest ages of the Church. The crucifix to hold the place of honor. Pictures of the saints. These pictures, however, should not only be a decoration, but a continuous appeal to your hearts.

SECOND SUNDAY AFTER EPIPHANY
The Glory and the Power of the Holy Name. On this Sunday we celebrate the festival in honor of the Holy Name of Jesus. The name of Mary, and names of the Saints, dear to us, but above all a name that calls for the greatest reverence and love is the name of Jesus. We should cherish this holy name.
I. On account of its glory and excellence; and
II. Because of its wonderful power and abundance of grace.
I. God Himself chose the name which His Son should bear upon earth, and announced this name through an angel. The name Jesus means Saviour, Redeemer, and Mediator. In this name is contained the entire life and death of Our Lord, all His miracles, His teachings; in fact, everything that He did and still does for us. This name is a name of honor, a reward received by Our Lord from His Heavenly Father.
II. The power of the holy name set forth by Our Lord Himself. Miracles worked by the apostles by name. Reverence and love to the Holy Name rewarded by Our Lord.

THIRD SUNDAY AFTER EPIPHANY
The Holy Family. Family life in a disturbed and wavering condition. For this reason the Holy Father draws our attention to the example of the Holy Family. The institution of the family, what it is, what it should be, the reason of its ruin, the means of its restoration. The family the most ancient institution. Threefold mission of the family: the care of the material life, of the spiritual life, and of the supernatural life. The care of the spiritual life neglected. The establishing of a family in our times not given the serious thought it ought to receive. Frivolity in many marriages. God's blessing can not attend them. God's curse often follows them. The impiety of our times due to family life without religion. To preserve the Christian family from ruin, to bring about reform of the ungodly ways of the world, God must come back into the family, the Holy Family of Nazareth must be our model and example.

SEPTUAGESIMA SUNDAY
On Envy. Envy:

I. *Disgraceful;*
II. *Injurious.*
I. What is envy? Vexation and displeasure at the happiness and success of our fellow-men, and satisfaction at their misfortune. No other vice carries its disgrace so publicly on its face as envy. It has no excuse. Envious man even more malicious than the envious devil. Envy is practically finding fault with God's providence.
II. Envy one of the seven deadly sins. A source of other sins. No vice produces more harm than envy. Cain and Abel. Joseph and his brethren. Saul and David. Daniel. The Pharisees. Envy crucified our Saviour. Envy has no regard for the most sacred of bonds. Examples in your daily experience. Holy Scripture on envy: Prov. xiv. 30. Ecclus. xxx. 26. Gal. v. 21. St. John Chrysostom.

SEXAGESIMA SUNDAY
The Word of God. if we rightly understood what precious gift the word of God is, with what love and reverence we should listen to it. The dissemination of faith the work of the word, joined with grace. Excepting Christ's death, and Baptism, there is nothing in our religion to be compared to the word. Many of the blessed never received the Sacrament of Penance, or Holy Eucharist, or Confirmation, or Extreme Unction. But the word of God as necessary for our salvation as Baptism. Many lost because they would not hear the word of God, or despised it. The word of God and its power. The parable of the seed. Are you among those that yield good fruit?

QUINQUAGESIMA SUNDAY
The enemies of our salvation. The tempest described in today's gospel the picture of the life of a Christian. Our soul the little ship. Our emotions the waves. Two things especially dangerous to the soul. The great number of enemies eager to work its ruin, and our disregard of the dangers that surround us. Our real enemies not those who do injury to our body, or temporal welfare, but those who do injury to our soul. Interior enemies. Pride, envy, rancor, etc. Exterior enemies. Worldly possessions. Seducers, etc. What must we do to escape our enemies?

FIRST SUNDAY OF LENT
Temptations. Our Saviour permitted the devil to tempt Him for our consolation and example. Temptations necessary, for they teach us to know ourselves. St. Augustine. We are inclined to rely too much on ourselves, and too little on our Lord. St. Peter. How little it sometimes takes to cause our fall. Temptations necessary to remind us of our weakness. The devil tempts most of all the elect. He does not have to trouble about the wicked. Some snares of the devil for the zealous in the service of God: fear of the world's criticism, extraordinary scruples. The fact that you are greatly beset with temptations no cause for worry; on the contrary, it is a sure sign that you are on the right path to heaven.

SECOND SUNDAY OF LENT
The death of the sinner. The terrible threat in today's gospel. How can a Christian, who believes in his religion, who has all means of grace at his command, run the risk of such terrible death? What it means to die a bad death. The world deplores those who meet with sudden, or violent deaths. But these are not bad deaths, unless they overtake a person in sin. A death in sin a bad death. The Holy Ghost. Antioch. The end of a sinner. Voltaire. Reform while there is time.

THIRD SUNDAY OF LENT
Indulgences. Those who by a good confession have driven the devil from their hearts must be careful lest he return. To guard against this, the Church offers us certain means. Penances. Indulgences.
I. What is understood by indulgences;
II. From whence are they obtained;
What is necessary to gain them.
 The Church has power to grant indulgences. What is an indulgence. Indulgences in the early Church.
II. Indulgences obtained from the overflowing merits of Jesus Christ and the Saints.
 Conditions necessary to gain an indulgence. Let us make abundant use of this means of grace.

PASSION SUNDAY
Repentance. The words of St. Augustine. A contrite heart sure of regaining the friendship of God. What true repentance should mean may be learned by a contemplation of the abhorrence of our Lord for sin, the torments which He had to suffer to gain pardon for our sins, the blessings which we lose by sin, and the evil consequences of sin. To move you to true repentance not the example of the Saints, not the despair of the damned in hell; no, the bitter passion of our dear Lord alone suffices. How you can tell whether or not you are truly repentant. The qualities of true repentance. True repentance a grace obtained by prayer.

PALM SUNDAY
Behold, thy king cometh to thee. The triumphal entry of Jesus into Jerusalem. Jesus a King, not only over nature and man, but also over Satan. As Jesus held His triumphal entry in Jerusalem, welcomed by the admiration, the loyalty and devotion of the city, so should He hold entry, in the Holy Eucharist, into our hearts.

EASTER
Paschal Joys.

SYNOPSES

I. Why this day is such a joyful one;
How we ought to give expression to our jubilation.
I. Remembrance of the gloom of Holy Week first cause of joy. Resurrection second cause. Today He proved Himself the true God: third cause.
Practical expression of our joy: Parents, arise from your sleep of sin. Children, arise. All arise from the grace of sin and put on a new man. As Good Friday was followed by Easter Sunday, so shall our sorrow be turned into joy. The risen Lord a cause of hope for us. The hope also of the Church.

LOW SUNDAY
Easter Confession. Paschal tide days of joy if good confession and communion cleanse us from sin. Reason of Lenten season. Yearly confession. Requirements of a good confession. Delay of confession for a whole year a bad sign. True repentance. How yearly confessions are made. Coldness in accusation a sign of want of contrition. Firm purpose of amendment.

SECOND SUNDAY AFTER EASTER
On Perseverance. Wherein perseverance consists.
I. Obedience to the promptings of grace;
II. Avoiding bad company;
Prayer.
Frequent use of the Sacraments.
I. How promptings of grace are obeyed. Exterior graces. Conversion of Peter and Matthew. Advice of Moses.
II. Avoid occasion to sin. Bad company.
Prayer.
Reception of Sacraments. Why Sacraments strengthen us. They must be received with proper disposition.

THIRD SUNDAY AFTER EASTER
Tribulations. Suffering the lot of a good Christian. A means to atone for our sins. Examples. Suffering a misfortune from a worldly point of view. Means to bear up with our crosses. Iob. God chastises like a good father. The knife of the physician. Suffering due us. Trials for the just.
(For the rest of the sermons a synopsis will be found prefixed to each of them.)

FOURTH SUNDAY AFTER EASTER
Heresy and Unbelief contradicting each other in reproaching the Church; the one claiming the Church is making new doctrines; the other complaining that she isn't. The Church truly progressive, without changing her doctrines.
I. The Holy Ghost causing progress in knowledge of the teachings of Christ. The Apostles did not fully understand the words of Our Lord until the Holy Ghost taught

them. *Progress in Christian Practice. Progress through the learning of the Fathers of the Church, through Councils and the Popes.*
II. *The Holy Ghost causing progress in the practice of Christ's teaching. Christian charity. The evangelical counsels. Fasting. The Church not an enemy of progress.*

FIFTH SUNDAY AFTER EASTER
Introduction. Christ's promise that everything we shall ask the Father in His name we shall receive. In His words to the Apostles we are commanded to pray. Prayer the source of all good. What it means to pray.
I. *Without prayer, impossible to be saved. Prayer means of perseverance. Examples. Our own experience. Conversion the result of prayer. Prayer ensures the pardon of God. Prayer prevents sinning. Those in hell damned because they did not pray. Heartfelt prayer a great delight.*
II. *How and when to pray. Vain excuse that you have no time to pray. Prayer the communication with God. The graces obtained by prayer. Method of praying constantly. Mental prayer. Follow the example of the saints.*

SIXTH SUNDAY AFTER EASTER
—*The struggle between the King of heaven and the prince of darkness. Christ won victory over hell and founded His Church to continue the struggle to complete His victory. His words to the Apostles: "You will give testimony of me," also apply to us. We must give testimony by leading a Christian life. We must imitate Christ in our will, our words, and our works.*
I. *The will of Christ. His example in submitting His will to the will of the Father. How Christians should imitate His example. Many, however, do not give testimony of Christ in this respect, but act like the heathens.*
II. *The words of Christ. He had no words but those of mercy and consolation. Has your speech been of this description? Is the speech of many Christians not rather giving testimony of satan?*
III. *The works of Christ. St. Bernard's conception of Jesus. He practised His teaching. If Christians would practise their faith the whole world would soon be Christian. Love of body, comfort, and pleasure stronger than our faith. Exhortation.*

WHIT-SUNDAY (PENTECOST)
Introduction. Whit-Sunday one of the great feast days in memory of our Redeemer. Christmas, Easter, Ascension. "I will send you the Comforter, the Holy Ghost." The Holy Ghost not only to guide Mother Church, but each individual soul. Children of the Holy Ghost and children of the world.
I. (a) *A child of the Holy Ghost—one that avoids grievous sin. Especially the sin of impurity. Purify your souls by penance.*
 (b) *A child of the Holy Ghost adorned with numerous virtues. The principal virtues.*
 (c) *A child of the Holy Ghost fond of prayer. The Apostles assembled in prayer when*

the Holy Ghost descended upon them.
II. (a) Children of the world in direct contrast.
(b) The hearts of children of the world attached to worldly goods.
(c) Children of the world strive after worldly pleasures. Not all enjoyment, however, forbidden. The difference.
(d) Children of the world the lukewarm Christians.
(e) Children of the world those that indulge in frivolous and sinful speech. Exhortation.

TRINITY SUNDAY
This earth not our true home. Our consolation the fact that Our Lord dwells among us. We possess Him in both His divine and human nature. He is even nearer to us than He was to the first Christians. Let us consider:
   I. The great mercy of God manifested in the Holy Eucharist.
   II. Our duties toward this great Sacrament.
I. The presence of God the happiness of the just and the unhappiness of the sinner. Adam. Cain. The omnipresence of God a great benefit. King David. The Holy Eucharist one of the three great mysteries, the other two being the Incarnation and the Passion. In creation we see the power, the wisdom, the providence of God; in the Holy Eucharist His infinite love.
II. What must we do to repay this love? Reverence in His presence. In sacramental processions. Gratitude for benefits received, reparation for insults offered to Him. The two disciples knew Him not, yet they burned with love for Him. How great ought to be our love who know Him present! Consider the time before the Blessed Sacrament as the happiest of your life, for there you obtain forgiveness and the grace of perseverance.

SECOND SUNDAY AFTER PENTECOST
Man as creature and as offender owes God sacrifice. This fact acknowledged by the sacrifices of the Old Law. They were insufficient. Jesus Christ the adequate sacrifice. This sacrifice perpetuated in Holy Mass.
I. What a great good fortune it is for us to assist at Holy Mass.
II. With what disposition we should assist.

I. What is Holy Mass? The same sacrifice as that offered up on Calvary. Greatness of the merits of this sacrifice. Effects of this sacrifice. Holy Mass the most propitious time for us to obtain graces.
II. Institution of Holy Mass on Holy Thursday. To unite oneself with the priest best manner of hearing Mass. The three parts of Holy Mass: 1. From beginning to the offertory; 2. From the offertory to elevation; 3. From the elevation to the conclusion. In the first part remember your trespasses, in the second offer yourself up to God, in the third prepare yourself for Holy Communion. Examples: 1. The publican; 2. The good thief; 3. The centurion. Conclusion.

THIRD SUNDAY AFTER PENTECOST
The mercy of Christ toward sinners a distinct characteristic of his earthly life. The parable of the good shepherd. The parable of the woman who lost a penny. Our Lord applying both parables to Himself.
I. *The greatness of God's mercy toward sinners.*
II. *What we must do on our part to merit it.*
I. *The mercy of God demonstrated by His patience. Example: The deluge. His compassion proved throughout the history of the Old Law. His giving His only Son to redeem us. The mercy of the Son. Examples: The woman at Jacob's well; Mary Magdalen; Matthew; Zachaeus; the adulteress; His weeping over Jerusalem; the prodigal son.*
II. *Conditions by which we obtain mercy, (a) Prayer and confidence; (b) Listen to His voice; do not misuse His patience, (c) Gratitude shown by earnest conversion. Conclusion.*

FOURTH SUNDAY AFTER PENTECOST
God deserving to be loved, even if there were no heaven to hope for nor hell to fear. How much more reason for us to love Him since He promises eternal reward. This eternal reward should instil in us the virtue of Hope, by means of which we may overcome all difficulties. Though unworthy of this reward, the merits of Jesus Christ give us cause to hope. Meaning of the word hope. God demands that we have hope and confidence in Him. The providence of God for those that put their trust in Him. Hope our consolation. Job. Confidence in Christ; in the Blessed Virgin. Examples.

FIFTH SUNDAY AFTER PENTECOST
Misusing the name of God a dreadful crime. But this sin, in spite of its enormity, very common. The various sins against the second commandment:
   I. *Blasphemy and swearing.*
   II. *Imprecations and curses.*
   III. *Swearing falsely, or perjury.*
Distinction of these sins necessary for the penitent confessing them. The Holy Ghost, as also Jesus Christ, warning against these sins. Punishments threatened.

SIXTH SUNDAY AFTER PENTECOST
Abyss of love of God shown in Holy Communion. When the Redeemer clothed Himself in our flesh, He hid His divinity. In Holy Communion His great love for us induces Him to hide also His humanity. The Holy Eucharist the greatest of the Sacraments. How few there are who appreciate the magnificence of God's grace in this Sacrament.
   I. *The sublimity and importance of this Sacrament.*
   II. *The effects and blessings of Holy Communion.*

I. Christ's presence productive of grace. St. Elisabeth, Simeon, Zachaeus, St. Peter, Lazarus. In Holy Communion Our Lord not only enters our house, but our hearts. Little appreciation shown by many Christians. The command of the Church.
II. Effects of Holy Communion. 1. Intimate union with Jesus Christ. 2. Receiving the source of all grace. 3. Weakening of our inclination to sin. 4. Holy Communion a pledge of our salvation.

SEVENTH SUNDAY AFTER PENTECOST
Good and bad Christians known by their works. A false and superficial virtue will manifest its true nature. I. A Christian should not be contented with the performance of good works; he should be careful how to perform them. II. It is not enough to be virtuous in the eyes of the world; we must be so in our hearts.
I. Good works must proceed from the heart. St. Gregory. Our actions should be only the medium to express our intention. Our works must be perfect, unselfish. Hypocrisy. Jeroboam. The poor widow's mite. Perseverance.
II. Have you the true virtue? Conclusion.

EIGHTH SUNDAY AFTER PENTECOST
The thought of judgment fills us with fear. Death comes unexpected and we may be called for judgment when least expected. Leading a good life the proper preparation.
I. What account will be exacted from us at the judgment?
II. How we should make our preparation for this judgment.
I. There are two judgments—particular and general. The particular judgment taking place immediately upon death. An exact account will be demanded of the gifts with which we have been endowed, 1. In nature. 2. In grace. The witnesses of the judgment. If such strict account will be demanded of the gifts and graces, how much more severe will we be judged for sins committed?
II. The judgment takes place in the very moment of death. This thought, and the knowledge of the severity of the judgment, should inspire us with fear and caution us to make preparations. Even the saints dreaded judgment. What must we do to prepare ourselves. Let us lead a good life.

NINTH SUNDAY AFTER PENTECOST
Jesus weeping over Jerusalem because He foresaw the loss of so many souls. I. What a soul really is. II. Our obligation toward our soul.
I. The value of a human soul. God alone knows its beauties and perfections. The soul an image and likeness of God. The destiny of the soul. The soul filled with desires which can not be gratified in this world. The soul capable of the love of God and also of serving Him. God giving His own flesh and blood for the food of this valuable soul.
I. Care to be taken not to lose this soul, if God Himself wept at the thought of its loss. He deplored the loss of souls also in His prophets. Amos. Jeremias. Christ in all His sufferings had but one object: the saving of our souls. The value of our souls also

demonstrated by the work of the devil Therefore, the knowledge of the value of your soul should prompt you to save it.

TENTH SUNDAY AFTER PENTECOST
Rash judgment the result of our pride, which makes us overlook our own faults, and leads us to despise and judge others. Rash judgment is so great a sin, that Christ warns us against it expressly, in the parable of today's gospel. Definition of rash judgment. Pride and envy the prime causes. Examples: Cain, Esau. One guilty of this sin is unhappy. Charity in judging our neighbors a great virtue. Example. Appearances deceitful. Those condemning others on appearances following the example of the judges of the chaste Susanna, and of the persecutors of Christ. Rash judgment sometimes of serious consequence. God Himself did not judge Adam unheard. Judith, Joseph and Potiphar. Our own experience tells us that many times people are judged wrongly on appearances. Be careful, therefore.

ELEVENTH SUNDAY AFTER PENTECOST
Detraction a very common sin, although one of the most vicious and one of the most harmful. It brings the saddest consequences in its train. The different ways in which we may become guilty of detraction, and other sins often caused by it. Definition of detraction. Calumny. Exaggeration of faults. Making known the faults of others without good reason. Disparaging the good actions of others. Detraction by significant silence. Pretended pity. Tale bearing. How we should act when slandered or calumniated. How slanderers must accuse themselves in confession.

TWELFTH SUNDAY AFTER PENTECOST
Our eternal salvation depends upon our observance of God's commandments. God rewards already in this life those who are faithful to Him. The Happiness of those who obey the laws of God, and the Unhappiness of those who do not. Examples from the Old Testament. Adam, David, Solomon. In the New Testament we are exhorted to observance of the commandments in the words and parables of Jesus Christ. How God takes care of His faithful servants. Elias. The widow of Sarepta. Daniel. Exhortation.

THIRTEENTH SUNDAY AFTER PENTECOST
The sacrifice of our Lord on the Cross made these words efficacious. The priest the dispenser of graces by giving Absolution. He is bound by laws, and must give or withhold Absolution according to these laws. The confessor's position one of greatest responsibility. He must, therefore, proceed with the greatest care.
I. What Absolution is, and to whom it must be given or withheld.
II. One of the principal reasons why it must be withheld.
I. Man, having lost God, can again find Him in Absolution. Definition of Absolution. Conditions on part of the penitent. The priest at times obliged to refuse or postpone

Absolution.
II. Some of the reasons why Absolution is withheld. One of the principal reasons is insufficient knowledge of the Holy Truths of Religion. The essentials of Religion, which every Catholic Christian must know. Not only in words but in meaning.

FOURTEENTH SUNDAY AFTER PENTECOST
The love of God necessary to possess eternal life. Not by words, however, but by deeds we must express our love of God. The consciousness that there is no real happiness but in God, shared by all men, just or sinner; therefore even sinners are desirous of loving God, but their pretended love is but in words. In order to know in what the true love of God consists, and how to know whether we have that true love, let us consider:
I. What God has done for love of us.
II. What we should do for love of Him.
I. God created man that he should love and serve Hint. He planted into the heart of man a craving for something supernatural, not to be satisfied with anything earthly, so as to induce man to seek his happiness in God. God the worthiest object of our love. Consider what Jesus Christ has done for us. His life and death. After His death the institution of the Blessed Sacrament. How do we return this love?
II. "Whosoever loves me, keeps my commandments!" It is therefore easy for us to know whether or not we have the true love. How do we observe the commandments? If we love God we should (1) often think of Him; (2) offer everything up to Him; (3) suffer for His sake.

FIFTEENTH SUNDAY AFTER PENTECOST
The greatest praise of Mary contained in the words "Of whom was born Jesus". The Church regards Mary as her Mother, her Protectress, and her powerful Helper against her enemies, and therefore celebrates the happy day upon which she was given to the world. Let us join the jubilation of the Church, and in order to better understand her joy, let us contemplate why the Blessed Virgin is considered:
I. The model of perfect virtue.
II. The mediator between God and mankind.
I. The testimony of the Holy Ghost about the virtues of Mary, proclaimed by the prophets and patriarchs. Her example followed by the Saints. God Himself, in Paradise, the first One to announce her coming. Mary the beautiful sun that dispersed the darkness of sin. Her birth, like the birth of her divine Son, lowly.
II. All graces given to man pass through Mary's hands. She intercedes for sinners. Mary also a rampart against the assaults of the enemy. To obtain Mary's protection it is not enough to praise her, we must also imitate her virtues. Her humility, her modesty, her purity, her patience, her love of God. Her death.

SIXTEENTH SUNDAY AFTER PENTECOST

The necessity of humbling ourselves. The parable of the Pharisee and the Publican. Humility most pleasing to God.
I. *Humility a virtue most necessary.*
II. *Our reasons for practising this virtue.*
I. *Humility as necessary for our salvation as the sacraments of Baptism and Penance. Pride produces every sin, humility every virtue. Nothing so pleasing to God as this virtue. Children loved, by our Saviour because they are humble. The Blessed Virgin owes her great exaltation to this virtue. Christ mentions humility first in the Beatitudes. Humbleness also pleasing to men. Humility the foundation of all other virtues. In what humility consists. Exterior and interior humility. Exterior humility: (1) Avoiding to praise ourselves, (2) hiding our good deeds, (3) feeling no pleasure when praised by others, (4) avoiding disputes, (5) not feeling sad when despised by others, (6) not excusing our faults. Interior humility: (1) thinking little of ourselves, (2) not minding if others know our faults, (3) satisfied if others surpass us in good qualities or wealth.*
II. *We should be induced to practise humility (1) by the consideration of God's glory, (2) by the example of Jesus Christ, (3) by our own wretchedness.*

SEVENTEENTH SUNDAY AFTER PENTECOST
Charity a most necessary virtue. It is a virtue by reason of which we love God and our neighbor. The love of God necessary for our salvation; we must be ready to abandon everything for the love of God. Examples: the Saints, the Martyrs. The love of our neighbor. Who is our neighbor? All men, even our enemies. How do we know if we have true charity? The qualities of charity. When charity enters our hearts it brings all other virtues with it. St. Paul: the greatest virtues without charity are of no avail.

EIGHTEENTH SUNDAY AFTER PENTECOST
These words a warning to lukewarm Christians.
I. *How a lukewarm Christian is recognized.*
II. *The means to avoid that condition.*
I. *By lukewarm Christians are not meant those who entirely neglect to approach the Sacraments. Nor those who strive to serve two masters, God and the world. What is a lukewarm soul? The difference between a good and a lukewarm Christian.*
II. *To which do you belong, to the bad, the good, or the lukewarm? If lukewarm, what means must be used to escape that dangerous condition?*

NINETEENTH SUNDAY AFTER PENTECOST
Drunkenness a great sin. A disgrace in the eyes of men. Conversion of the habitual drunkard most difficult. Many people prone to make light of this vice, and excuse the same. To undeceive these people, I will show
  The enormity of this vice.

The folly to advance excuses for the same.
It is beyond the power of mortal man to describe the full extent of the havoc wrought by this vice. We are able to see, however, that great evil results from intemperance. We cannot be indifferent to the loss of good name, health, and salvation. The degradation of man by drink. The Holy Ghost tells us the drunkard should learn moderation from the beasts. What disgrace to human nature, if the beast is held up to it as example. This sin is not one that abates with advancing age. Drunkards not easily reformed. Disadvantages of the drunkard in social life. Ruin of his soul. The Council of Mayence holds that the drunkard transgresses all the ten commandments. Some excuses advanced to justify excesses. Sociability. Some claim they can drink a great deal without getting intoxicated. Business. Reform. The means.

TWENTIETH SUNDAY AFTER PENTECOST
In the same manner as our Lord during His human life was ever ready to help and heal the sick, so does He still mercifully hasten to their assistance, in the Sacrament of Extreme Unction. Of this Sacrament I will explain today:
I. That it is really a Sacrament of the Church of Christ.
II. What its effects are upon the sick.
I. St. James a witness to the fact that this Sacrament was instituted by Jesus Christ. Tradition. The Council of Trent.
II. The effects of this Sacrament: 1, Increase of the sanctifying grace; 2, alleviation of suffering; 3, improvement in the condition of the patient; 4, fortitude; 5, pardon of sins.

TWENTY-FIRST SUNDAY AFTER PENTECOST
The ungratefulness of the servant, who, having had his own debt remitted by a gentle master. Hew into passion when his fellow servant could not pay what he owed him. The irascible man likely to forget what God has done for him. In order to let you understand the enormity of the offense offered to God by anger, I will show you:
I. Why anger offends God.
II. How anger leads to other sins.
I. The trivial expressions of impatience and irritability are not meant by anger, although they also are sins, and may lead to more grievous things. There is a holy anger, which finds its source in the pious zeal of the soul for the glory of God. Examples: Moses, Our Lord. Sinful anger. Its pernicious effects. Anger in a home makes this home a hell. The bad example to children. Children made cripples by parents in fits of passion.
II. Anger the cause of swearing and cursing. The children learn cursing, and thus this vice of swearing is in some families passed from generation to generation. What should we do to avoid the sin of anger?

TWENTY-SECOND SUNDAY AFTER PENTECOST

Christ's words should remind us that our soul hears the image of God and therefore give unto God that which is God's, that is your soul.
I. The soul is God's image in nature by its faculties of reason and will.
II. And God's supernatural image by sanctifying grace.
I. Man is a creature, but a creature after God's likeness. The difference between man and animal, by reason and will. How the likeness of God is often disfigured and destroyed. Where such distorted images of God may be found.
II. The supernatural image of God also often destroyed in men. They are frequently not the image of God, but the image of the devil. Give to God the things that are God's. Man is God's creation and property. Therefore give yourselves entirely to God and you will be saved.

FEAST OF THE ASCENSION

Our Lord promising great reward to those who, for love of Him, suffer persecution. This promise causing the fortitude of the martyrs. Magnitude of the reward considered.
The Happiness surrounding the Saints. Vision of God. Companionship of the Angels. No fear of loss. Gratification and content. Happiness in proportion to mortification. Hence various degrees in joy.
What to do to gain this bliss. General obligations. Duties of wife, of children, of men. Exhortation.

CHILDREN'S FIRST COMMUNION

Introduction. The act which you are about to perform the most holy upon earth. Angels, and all those present, rejoice with you. You are pure now—will you remain so! So that you may be better guarded against sin I will show you the great love of Jesus in this Sacrament.
I. Jesus, for love to us, present in this Sacrament, in His divinity and humanity.
(a) As the Lamb of God who takes away the sins of the world. Golgotha and Holy Mass. Satisfaction for the sins of the world. The Son of God mediator between God and mankind. Behold, this Lamb of God comes to you today:
(b) As our help and consolation. The Church His abode, the tabernacle His throne. "Come unto me all you who are sorrowful and heavily laden; I will refresh you." In all afflictions He the refuge of Christians. Take also your troubles to Him.
(c) As the food for our souls. The table of God. The bread of angels. The Son of God our food.
II. Jesus humbling Himself for love to us. Benefaction measured by the effort required. Our God and Creator abandons His majesty and glory and takes the form of bread.
III. What does Jesus expect from us in return? Too often receives ingratitude. Exhortation. Renewal of baptismal vows. Blessing.

TWO JUBILEE SERMONS
First Sermon
The indulgences of the Jubilee the culmination of divine mercy, the removal of the last barrier preventing our entrance into heaven. The Jubilee indulgence has its origin in the Jubilee year of the Old Law. The Christian year of Jubilee celebrated for more than 400 years, the particularly solemn Jubilee at the beginning of a new century, however, celebrated for 600 if not more years.
I. What does the Jubilee grant us?
   (a) The Jubilee indulgence. What is an indulgence? Sin and its punishment two distinct things. Two ways to wipe out temporal punishment: by penance or purgatory, and by indulgence. Objections to the Catholic doctrine of indulgences. Proof of this doctrine. Practice of the early Church. Christ our model. St. Paul.
   (b) The source of indulgences, the merits of the Redeemer and of the saints. The power of the Church to dispose of these merits. If the Church can remit eternal punishments, why not temporal punishments? Satisfaction by proxy.
   (c) The Jubilee indulgence a plenary indulgence distinguished by great solemnity, great power, great authority.

Second Sermon
What does the Jubilee require of us? We must be in the state of grace, we must duly perform the prescribed works of penance. Our conversion must be sincere. Further conditions. Exhortation.

ASSUMPTION OF THE BLESSED VIRGIN MARY
The glories of Mary. Her humility the cause of her exaltation. Mary raised to such a degree of glory, of power, and of honor that not even the angels can realize it, only known to God. Our reason, therefore, insufficient to comprehend her exaltation. She is the Daughter of the Father, Mother of the Son, and Spouse of the Holy Ghost. Her presence on earth, after the death of her divine Son, needed, to encourage and to guide the Apostles. The last moments of her earthly life. Her death caused by her great love and desire for her divine Son. How we should imitate her in life and death.

TWENTY-SECOND SUNDAY AFTER PENTECOST

"Render, therefore, to Caesar the things that are Caesar's; and to God the things that are God's."—St. Matt. xxii. 21.

TO GIVE to God what belongs to God and to your neighbor what is his due—nothing can be more reasonable and more just. If all Christians would follow that path there would be none of them in hell, but they would all meet in Heaven. "Oh! I wish," says the great St. Hilary, "that God would make the people ever remember this command. But, oh! how many are deceived! They pass their life in cheating some and stealing from others." Yes, my friends, nothing occurs more seldom than restitution. The prophet Osee is right when he says that unrighteousness and larceny cover the earth and are like the deluge which destroyed the world; unfortunately many are guilty, many persons do not follow this law. Oh, my dear Lord! how many thieves will be revealed by death! Now, my dear people, to deter you from this path I will show you that, firstly, ill-gotten goods never bring any advantage; secondly, how we can injure our neighbors, and thirdly, how and to whom you must make restitution for what does not belong to you.

I.

Ill-gotten goods will never enrich anybody. On the contrary they will be a curse. Oh, my God! how blind is man! He is perfectly convinced that he is only for a short moment in this world; every minute he witnesses the departure of those who are younger and stronger than he; in vain; it does not open his eyes. The Holy Ghost may urgently remind you through the mouth of holy Job that he came naked into the world and will take nothing out of it, that all these riches which he is striving for will leave him at the moment when he least expects it; all this does not lessen his avarice. St. Paul says that he who tries to get rich by unjust means will soon fall into evil ways, and more than that, he will never see the face of the Lord. That is so perfectly true that a person who has gained possession of anything by fraud or roguery will never be converted unless it be by a miracle of grace. Listen to what St Augustine says to those who have appropriated the goods of others:

"You may," he says to them, "go to confession, do penance, and cry over your sins as much as you want to, God will never forgive you if you do not make restitution when you can. All your confessions and your communions will be sacrileges which you heap one upon another. Return what does not belong to you or you must make up your mind to burn in hell. The Holy Ghost forbids us not only to take and desire the goods of our neighbor, but he does not even want us to look at them, as the mere sight may induce us to stretch out our hands for them."

The prophet Zacharias says that the curse of the Lord rests upon the house of a robber until it is destroyed. And I say to you that goods obtained by fraud or trickery will not only bring you no advantage, but will also be the cause of your losing all you have obtained in a rightful way, and that they will shorten your days. If you doubt it, listen to me for a moment and I will convince you.

We read in Holy Scripture that King Achab, who wished to enlarge his gardens, went to a man named Naboth and told him that he wished to buy his vineyard. "No," said Naboth, "it is the inheritance of my forefathers and I wish to keep it." The King was so excited over this refusal that he became quite ill. The Queen came to him and asked him what was the cause of his sickness. The King said that he was sick because he wanted to enlarge his gardens and Naboth had refused to sell him his vineyard.

"Well," said the Queen, "where is thy power? Do not trouble. I will get you the vineyard."

She procured at once several persons, who, paid and bribed by her, testified that Naboth had blasphemed the name of God and also of Moses. The poor man defended himself and insisted upon it that he was innocent. It was no use—they would not believe him; they dragged him away and stoned him to death. When the Queen saw him stricken down she hurried to the King to tell him that he could have the coveted vineyard, because he who had been so bold as to refuse him the ownership of it was dead. Upon hearing this, the King, who had recovered, rushed like a madman, to take possession of the vineyard. The unfortunate man did not think that God was there to punish him. The Lord called His prophet Elias and commanded him to tell the King that on the same spot where the dogs had licked up the blood of Naboth they would lick up his own blood, and that none of his children would reign after him. The Lord sent his prophet also

TWENTY-SECOND SUNDAY AFTER PENTECOST

to Queen Jezabel to announce to her that as a punishment for her crime she would be devoured by dogs.

It came to pass as the prophet had predicted. The King was killed in battle and the dogs licked up his blood. When the new King, Jehu by name, entered the city, he saw a woman sitting at a window of the palace. She had arrayed herself in her royal robes, hoping to make an impression and gain the heart of the new King. They told him it was Queen Jezabel. Upon hearing this he commanded that she be at once thrown out of the window, and horses and men trampled upon her. When night came and they went to bury her, they found only a few pieces of her body; the dogs had eaten the rest.

"Thus," exclaimed Jehu, "has the word of the prophet been fulfilled." King Achab left seventy sons and descendants, all princes. The new King had them all decapitated and exposed their heads in baskets at the city gate, to prove by this terrible spectacle what misery the wickedness of parents may bring upon their children.

Another reason why we should be afraid to appropriate other people's goods is: that it will lead us into hell. The prophet Zacharias says that in a dream God had shown him a book, in which there was written that robbers and thieves will never see God, but be thrown into fire. And yet there are, my friends, many people who are so blind that they would rather die and perish forever than to return ill-gotten goods.

II.

If I was to make a thorough investigation of what you, my friends who are present here today, are in the habit of doing, I should probably find that many of you are thieves. You are surprised at this? Listen to me for a moment and you will see that I am right. If I commence a vigorous investigation I will find that the wage-earner is in debt to his employer and to the poor. He is in debt to his employer, and therefore obliged to make restitution, if he has taken more time to rest than was necessary, if he allowed by his negligence the property of his employer to perish or be taken away, if he gained his position by asserting that he could do certain work, well knowing that he would not be able to accomplish it. In all such cases he is bound to make restitution. He further robs the poor if he spends his money in gambling or in the saloon or in the purchase of unnecessary things. But, you will say, it is his own money, gained by his own labor. To this I reply that it certainly is his own, but yet he is at fault if he spends it in any such way. Perhaps his parents are so poor that they had to become objects of public charity; if he had saved his wages he would have been able to support them. There is many a wage-earner who spends his earnings in the purchasing of useless things, in saloons, in gambling places. If God sends him sickness or he meets with an accident, he must go to a public hospital and eat the bread of the poor, or wait until a charitable person extends a helping hand and gives to him what ought to go to his more unfortunate brothers. When such people marry they soon find themselves with their children in need. Why? Because they did not know how to save when they were young. Would you, dear sisters, have let vanity lead you as far as it did if you had thought of this? But the most unfortunate part of it is that you not only squander what you will need some day, but that you will lose your poor soul.

There is a sin that is the more deplorable by reason of its frequent occurrence: that is that children steal from their parents and the employed from their employers. Children should never take anything away from their parents under the pretext that they were not given enough. When your parents nourish you, clothe you, and give you an education, it is all they need to do. Besides, a child that steals from its parents is considered capable of anything. Everybody avoids it and despises it. An employee will sometimes say: I am not getting enough for my work; I must help myself. If you are not getting enough for your work, why do you remain with your employer? Did you know when you accepted the position, what your wages were going to be and what work was expected of you in return? And let those look out who have received goods which children have stolen from their parents or employees from their employers. If these things remain with them only for five minutes, or even if they do not know the value of them, they must, under pain of punishment, make restitution if the thief himself does not do it. And whoever has induced another person to steal is, if the thief does not do it himself, obliged to make restitution, even if he has himself derived no benefit from the stolen goods.

Thieving is most common in buying and selling. Let us go a little into details, so that you may recognize what wrong you are doing and reform. When you are asked whether the wares you are selling are good or fresh or of a certain quality, and you say they are, whilst you know they are not, then you commit a sin. Another time you have gained an undue advantage in giving or receiving change, and you let the person go without rectifying the mistake, simply because he has not noticed the error. Someone else will adulterate the goods he sells and represent them to be the genuine article. He will put sand in sugar, water in milk, and do other similar deeds, which all lead surely to perdition.

What, then, should parents do when they see their children with stolen goods? They should force them to return the same to those from whom they have taken them. Once or twice will be sufficient to correct their evil ways. An example will show you how careful you should be in this matter. A boy, when only about ten years old, commenced to commit small thefts, taking at first only things of small value, such as fruit, etc. Later he took larger objects and soon passed to burglary, during which he had the misfortune to commit murder. This naturally led him to the gallows. When his parents came to see him for the last time before the day of execution he exclaimed:

"Oh, unhappy father and unhappy mother! I wish I could let everybody know that you are the cause of my disgrace. If at the beginning you had stopped me from committing those small thefts, I should never have done that monstrous deed which is leading me to the gallows."

I told you in the beginning that nothing was more common than injustice and nothing so rare as restitution. There are few persons who have not something on their conscience in regard to this question. Where are those who make restitution? I really do not know, although, my dear friends, we are obliged, under pain of not seeing God to return ill-gotten goods.

III.

We do now, you will say, at least know in what way we can commit an injustice. But how and to whom must we make restitution? You wish to make reparation? Well, then, listen to me a moment and I will show you how. We must not be satisfied to return the half or three-quarters, but the whole, when it is possible, otherwise you might be lost. There are some who, without trying to find out how many persons they have injured, give alms and have Masses said, and then they think their conscience is all right. Alms and Masses are very good things, but the offering must be out of your own money and not with that of your neighbor. This money doesn't belong to you; return it to the rightful owner and then give your own if you wish to. Do you know what St. Chrysostom calls such almsgiving? The alms of Judas and the evil spirit. When Judas sold our Lord and saw that he was damned, he hurried to give the money back to the scribes, but they, although they were avaricious, would not take it; they bought a field with it in which to bury strangers.

You will ask, when one whom we have cheated is dead, to whom shall we make restitution? Can we not then keep it or give it to the poor? My friends, this is what you must do: if there are any children you must give it to them; if not, then to the relations or heirs; if there are no heirs you must go to your confessor, who will tell you what you had better do. Others say: I was unjust to someone, but he is rich; I have someone who wants it more than he. My friends, give this person something out of your own means, but return to your neighbor what you took from him. He will make a bad use of it! That is none of your business. Give him his own, pray for him, and then sleep in peace.

Ah! nowadays the people in the world are so avaricious, they are so grasping after the things of the earth, that while they never think they have enough, they try ever to outwit others in cunning and to dupe them. But remember, my dear friends, you must restore to those persons exactly what you have deprived them of or you will be punished. I don't know whether your conscience is at ease on this point. I doubt it. As I said before, the world is full of thieves and swindlers! The storekeeper cheats in weight and measure; he doubles the price of an article to an inexperienced person or induces him to buy more than he wants; masters steal from their help by not giving them their full wages; others by making them wait so long or deducting their pay while sick; servants rob their masters by not doing their work properly, losing property through their own fault; a workman lets himself be paid for work he hasn't done; saloons, those places of injustice, those gates of hell, that Calvary where Jesus Christ is unceasingly crucified afresh, those schools where Satan is the teacher and where religion and morals are destroyed—the saloon keeper, I say, steals the bread from wife and children by giving liquors to those drunkards who on Saturday night spend all they have earned during the week. Oh, my God! what will become of us? How many things will be investigated at the hour of death!

If your conscience troubles you, lose no time in seeking a confessor. He will remit to you your debt. If you don't want to make restitution you will find a thousand excuses to show that others have wronged you and that you are not able to do it just now. Ah, my friend, I am not sure that God will be satisfied with your reasoning. If you give up some of these vanities, this gambling, and visit the saloon less, you will do a great deal more work and soon be able to pay off some of your debts. Mark my words, if you do not strive your utmost to restore whatever you have taken from another, no matter what penance you do, you will be judged by God. Of this you may be sure! You will find some so blind that they say their children will make restitution for them after their death. No, dear friends, your children will do as you have done. Do you wish that your children should take more trouble about your soul than you do yourself? You will be damned—that is what will happen to you, if there be question of grievous matter. Tell me, have you made sufficient reparation for all the injustice your parents committed? You have taken good care not to; and perhaps your parents are lost because they did not make restitution in their lifetime, but confided too much in your good-will. But to be brief, how many of you now present were asked twenty years ago to have Masses said and to give alms for the repose of your parents' souls, and you have not done it? You never troubled about it at all! You prefer to enlarge your possessions, to visit pleasure resorts, to buy your children useless trifles.

Shall I speak to you about those who defer restitution till the hour of their death? I will give you two examples to show you that at the hour of death either you will not want to make reparation, or that, wishing to make reparation, you will not be able to.

(1.) You will not want to. They relate that the father of a large family being about to die, his children said to him:

"Father, you know that this property which you are going to leave us does not belong to us. It ought to be given back to the rightful owner."

"Children," said the father to them, "if I were to restore all that does not belong to me, then there would be hardly anything left for you all."

"Father, we would rather work for our living than to know that you were damned."

"No, my children, I will not make restitution. You don't know what it means to be poor."

He died like a reprobate. Oh, my God! how is man blinded by the sin of avarice!

(2.) I have said even if you wanted to make restitution at this moment you would not be able to do so. A missionary tells us of a father who, as he saw his end approaching, called his children to his bedside and said to them:

"My dear children, you know that I have cheated a great many persons. If I do not make restitution I shall be lost. Call a lawyer so that I may sign the necessary papers."

"What! Father, do you wish to dishonor yourself and your children by exposing yourself as a thief? Do you wish to bring us to poverty and cause us to beg our bread?"

"But, children, if I do not do this I shall be damned!"

Then one of his wicked sons said to him:

"Father, you are afraid of hell? Go on. One can get used to anything. In a week you won't mind it."

Now, my friends, what conclusion shall we come to after all this? How incomprehensibly blind is man! He loses his soul to leave his children a few acres of land or a house, and they, far from ever being grateful, ridicule him while he is in the midst of flames.

Let us conclude by saying we are foolish to think of amassing wealth which can only make us miserable while we are striving for its possession, while we have it, and also in eternity, where we must give it up. Let us be wiser, my dear children. Let us accumulate goods which will follow us into the next life and be our delight in the endless days of eternal glory, the blessing which I wish you all. Amen.

TWENTY-THIRD SUNDAY AFTER PENTECOST

"No man can serve two masters."—St. Matt. vi. 24.

JESUS CHRIST said to us, my dear friends, that we cannot serve two masters—*i.e.*, God and the world. You cannot, he says, please both God and the world at the same time. No matter how you may try, you will never succeed. The reason is this, my good friends; they are utterly opposed to each other in their thoughts, their desires, and their actions. What God commands is the very opposite to that which the world promises; the former forbids what the latter allows and favors; the world offers you pleasure, honors, and riches; God shows you only tears, repentance, and self-denial; the one leads you upon a—in appearance at least—flowery path, the other upon a thorny path. The one, which is the world, promises to let us enjoy everything we may wish for during this life (though it generally promises more than it can give); at the same time it hides from us the sufferings which await us during eternity. The other, which is Jesus Christ, does not promise us anything of all this, but merely tells us for our consolation that He will be with us and mitigate our sufferings: "Come to me all you that labor and are heavy laden, and I will refresh you. Take up my yoke upon you, and learn of me, because I am meek and humble of heart; and you shall find rest to your souls."

These, then, my dear friends, are the two masters who demand our whole heart. To which of the two do you wish to belong? All that which the world offers you is only for the present time; fortune, pleasure, honors, will terminate with our life. But if we follow Jesus Christ, who heavily laden with his cross calls us, we shall soon see that the hardships in His service are not as great as we think. He will lead us, and aid us, and console us, and after our suffering, which lasts but a moment. He promises us a happiness which will last as long as He Himself. So as to let you see this clearer, I will show to you, my dear friends, that it is impossible to please God and the world. Either all for God or all for the world; there is no middle way.

It is certain, my friends, that Jesus Christ, while knowing full well that many would retire from the world to devote themselves entirely to Him, that would choose the follies of the cross to spend their life, like His, in sighs, in tears, and in penance to become worthy of the reward which He has promised them, He knew at the same time that many would desert Him to devote themselves to the world, whose promises are never fulfilled and whose misery is carefully hidden. And that is the reason why He gave us only one heart, so that we could devote ourselves to one master. He tells us expressly that it is impossible to serve God and the world. So soon as we wish to please the one we shall become an enemy to the other.

You know, my dear friends, that the spirit of Jesus Christ is a spirit of the love of God. Now, how can you preserve this spirit when you join the company of those who will speak to you only of pleasures and honors, only to laud themselves and to boast of their pretended good qualities and of all they have done or not done? If you are in the company of such a one for any length of time you will become, without noticing it, as proud as he. If you hear somebody continually talk evil of his neighbor you will yourself, without noticing it, get a wicked tongue, which carries to every place, wherever you may be, destruction of peace. You know that Jesus Christ, whom you have chosen as your Master, wishes you to keep your heart as pure as possible; but when you associate with that reprobate who does nothing but think and speak of the filthiest and most shameful things, you will become just as bad as he is. You know that your Lord wishes you to love and respect your religion and all that regards your religion, but if you have frequent intercourse with an impious person who scoffs at everything, despises and ridicules the Most Holy, how can you love your religion and fulfill her commandments if these blasphemies are ever dinned in your ears? How can we go to confession to a priest if some godless man has whispered a slander against a priest into our ear and tried to persuade us that it was true and that all priests are thus?

Ah! my good friends, woe to him who follows the world! He is lost! If you wish to be saved you must necessarily flee this world, as otherwise you would think and act like the world and find yourself among those who have been cursed by the Lord.

If you have any further doubts about it, just remember what all the saints did: they considered the world and its pleasures a plague, from which they fled. What else was the reason that the deserts became peopled with so many persons who had before lived in towns and villages, but that they dreaded the world and fled from it for fear that they might become infected and become imbued with the spirit? Yes, my friends, let us flee from the world, or else we may perish with it. We must not be in accord with the world if we want to be saved. We must wage a continuous war with it; all the saints did that. We must renounce either heaven or the world.

To show you still better to which of the two parties you should belong, we will take a closer look at this world. It consists of three classes: the first is composed of those who are entirely for the world; the second are those who are entirely for God; and the last consists of those people who would like to belong to the world without ceasing to belong to God.

I said, my dear people, that one portion,—the larger, perhaps— is the one which is entirely for the world. To it belong all those who are content when they have suppressed every religious feeling and all thoughts of the life to come, who have done all they could to banish entirely from their mind the terrible thought of the judgment which will be theirs some day. They make use of their knowledge and oftentimes their wealth to draw as many people as possible to their way of thinking. They don't believe in anything, and they glory even in making themselves appear more godless and more profane than they really are, so as to better convince others not to believe the truths, but the falsehoods they have engendered in their hearts. Like Voltaire, who, at a banquet which he gave to his friends the unbelievers, rejoiced over the fact that of all those present, none believed in religion. And yet he himself believed in it, as was proved at the hour of his death. It was then that he eagerly called for a priest to help him to reconcile himself with his God. But it was too late. The good Lord whom he had reviled with such zeal, did to him as he had done to Antioch—He delivered him to the rage of the demons. But let us leave these infidels. You, my dear people, though you are not as good Christians as you ought to be, do not at least, thanks be to the Lord, belong to them.

But, you will ask me, who are those who belong now to God, now to the world? Let me explain, my good friends. Observe them, my dear listeners, from morning until night, from one year's end to the other. These people consider Sunday merely as a day of rest and pleasure; they remain in bed longer than on week-days, and instead of turning their heart to God, never give Him a thought. Some think of the amusements they will have on this day—the Lord's day; some, of the visits they will pay to friends. Some will even omit their few morning prayers, thinking it will be time enough to say them in Church before Mass. But they have so much to do before going to Mass so that they arrive at church long after the commencement of Mass. Or the meeting of a friend or anything else that might happen is sufficient to keep them away altogether. Still, to keep up the appearance and to be considered by their neighbors and friends as Christians, they do go once in a while, but with what feelings of unrest and weariness! The only thought they have is:

"Oh, Lord! How long is it going to last? It's too long. I don't think I can go again."

Others, again, don't like the Word of God as pronounced from the altar, the Word of God that has converted so many sinners. They must get out, they say, to get fresh air; they feel depressed, uneasy; and no sooner is the end of the service approaching than they eagerly make for the door even before the priest has had time to leave the altar, and they are again all smiles and merriment. They are too tired to return to Vespers and Benediction. If you ask them why they don't go to Vespers they say:

"Oh, we can't be in church all day. We have other things to do."

These are the people that belong to the world without realizing the fact. But wait. Let us try to make them understand better; only as they are deaf it is very difficult to make them listen to the Word of Life, and as they are blind too, it will be more difficult to make them see their unhappy condition. They have left off saying grace before and after meals or to say the Angelus. And if they do they do it just as a matter of habit, without giving a thought to our dear Lord and His blessed Mother.

Do you know, my good friends, what kind of people these are? They are people who have not lost their faith altogether, who would not wish to give up everything, for they even blame those who absent themselves entirely from divine service; only they do not have courage to break with the world and turn to the good Lord. These people don't want to be damned, but they also don't like to be under any restriction. They hope to be saved without taking much trouble about it. They think God is merciful and certainly did not create them only to destroy them; that He will forgive them in His mercy; that it will be time enough later on to devote themselves to God alone and to rid themselves of their bad habits. If they do think once in a while of the poor use they make of their life, they sigh and maybe some of them will even shed a few tears.

Oh, my dear friends, what a miserable life do those people lead who want to belong to the world without ceasing to belong to God! Let us go into the matter a little further, and you will soon see how inconsistent their way of living is. One moment you will hear them pray to God and perhaps do an act of penance; the next moment you will hear them curse and swear and take the name of the Lord in vain if something goes against their will. This morning you saw them attend Mass and join in the praise of the Lord, and on the same day you will hear them using the most blasphemous language. The same hands which took the holy water and asked God to cleanse them from all sins are used for all kinds of sinful ways; the same eyes which have looked upon the Lord in the Most Holy Sacrament look later in the day at the most indecent objects, and with great pleasure at that. Yesterday you saw a man do an act of charity to his neighbor; today you can see him try to cheat him. A moment ago a mother prayed for all kinds of blessings for her children; now she overwhelms them with all sorts of maledictions because they have done something to displease her. One moment she sends her daughters to church to confession; the next moment she lets them go to a dance. One day she will tell her daughter to be careful and beware of bad company, and the next she will let her be together with young men for hours at a time. Oh, my poor mother, you are of the world. You think you belong to God, but you are deceived. You belong to those of whom Jesus Christ has said: "Woe unto the world!"

Oh, poor world! How unhappy thou art! Continue in this way, and nothing but hell will be thy lot. Some would like to make frequent use of the holy sacraments, or at least once a year, but they need a very easy confessor. If their confessor does not find their heart and mind in the right dispositions and refuses them absolution, oh! then they are deeply offended and nothing is too bad to say of the poor priest, and yet they know in their own hearts that he cannot give them absolution in the state of sin they are in. Live on, O world! live on in this every-day manner, and you will see what you did not want to see. As if we could divide our heart into two parts! No, my friend: you either belong wholly to God or wholly to the world. You wish to make frequent use of the sacraments? Very well. Quit gambling, keep away from indecent shows, and quit the saloon. Today you are willing to approach the sacred tribunal of penance and to receive the Blessed Eucharist, the bread of angels, and in two or three weeks you spend the night in the company of drunkards who are crazed with liquor and, worse still, commit the most abominable acts of impurity. Go on, O world, go on! You will soon be in hell. There they will teach you what you should have done to reach heaven, which you have lost through your own fault.

No, my dear friends, do not let us deceive ourselves. We must sacrifice the world for Jesus Christ or we must sacrifice Jesus Christ for all that which we consider dearest on earth. Besides, there is not one among those attached to the world and who have tried to gain satisfaction from their animal and corrupt instincts—I say there is not one who has not been deceived and who did not regret at the hour of his death to have loved the world. Yes, my friends, that is the time when we recognize the vanity and perishableness of all things. We would recognize it now if we would only reflect upon our past life; we would see of how little value life is.

And you, my dear people, you whose growing years are already beginning to bend your heads upon your breasts, you who in your young days chased after the pleasures of this world and thought you would never become tired of them; you have spent many years in the pursuit of these pleasures: dances, gambling, saloons, vanity formed your whole occupation. You put off the return to God again and again. Then when you reached a maturer age you thought of nothing but of accumulating a fortune. And so you have reached old age without having done anything for your salvation. And now, when you have returned from the follies of your youth, when you have ceased your efforts to make a fortune—now, you think, is the time to do better. Don't believe it, my friends. The infirmities of age which are bending you down, your children who despise you—all that will be a new obstacle to your salvation. You thought you belonged to God, and you find out now that you belong to the world, that is, to those who belong now to God and now to the world and who receive their final reward from the latter. You know well enough now that you are deceived if you follow the world. Now, my friends, if somebody deceives us we do not trust him any more, and we are right; but the world deceives us all the time and yet we love it.

If we would only meditate a little more upon what this world really is, we would spend our life in keeping away from it as much as possible.

At the age of fifteen we say farewell to the pleasures of childhood; we stop running after butterflies and building houses of cards. At the age of thirty we say farewell to the boisterous pleasures of impetuous young manhood; what we delighted in so much begins to weary us. Yes, my friends, we say daily farewell to something in this world. We are like the traveler who delights in the beauties of the landscape through which he passes: as soon as he sees it he must leave it. It is the same with all our possessions and our friends to whom we have such an attachment. And finally we reach the shore of eternity, into which everything passes like into an abyss. Then, my friends, the world disappears forever from our sight, and it is then that we shall recognize how foolish we were in

TWENTY-THIRD SUNDAY AFTER PENTECOST

following it. And all that has been told us about sins we will then recognize as being only too true.

"Oh," we shall say, "I have only lived for the world. I have in all my actions only sought the approval of the world, and now all my possessions and my friends of the world are nothing to me! Everything has passed away from my hands. And now I must return to my Creator."

Oh, my dear people, how consoling is this thought for those who have during their life only sought their God! And what despair does it bring to those who have lost sight of their God and the salvation of their souls!

No, my friends, do not let us deceive ourselves. Let us flee, or else we may run the danger of being lost. All our saints have fled and despised the world all their lives. Those who were obliged to live in it lived as if they were not in it. How many of the real great ones have left this world to live in solitude! Let us look at St. Arsenius, who was struck with the idea how difficult it was to obtain salvation in this world, and forthwith left the Emperor's court to spend his life in the woods, to repent of his sins and do penance. Yes, my dear friends, if we flee from this world, at least as much as it is possible for us to do, we can not perish in this world.

St. Augustine gives us a good example of this. He tells us that he once had a friend, a young man, who led a perfectly good life.

One day he was in the company of his fellow-students, who did not like it that he always lived and acted differently from them. They urged him to go with them to the amphitheater, where there was a prize-fight among men. As our young friend detested such shows, he resisted with all his might. Finally they urged him so much, that he consented with the words:

"Very well. I will go with you, but only my body will be there standing among you. My mind and my eyes will not partake in this horrible spectacle."

So they led him forth, and, while the whole multitude went wild with barbarous delight, the young man took no part and kept his eyes shut. Would that he had also stopped his ears, for at a certain great noise curiosity got the better of him and he opened his eyes. That was sufficient to ruin him. The more he saw the more delighted was he, and after that there was no need of urging him to visit the place. He was only too eager to go there and to induce others to go with him.

"Oh, my Lord!" exclaimed St. Augustine, "who will lead him away from this abyss? The grace of God alone can do it!"

In conclusion, my dear friends, let me say to you: If we do not flee from the world and its pleasures, if we do not hide ourselves away as much as possible, then we run into our ruin and will be lost forever. If you want to belong entirely to God you must be prepared to be despised and rejected by the world. Blessed is he, my friends, who belongs to these, and who follows in the footsteps of the Lord with courage and carries his cross with patience. It is only by doing so that we may obtain the happiness of reaching heaven. Amen.

TWENTY-FOURTH SUNDAY AFTER PENTECOST

"Seek ye, therefore, first the kingdom of God and His justice, and all these things shall be added unto you."—St. Matt. vi. 33.

T. MATTHEW tells us that Jesus, finding Himself in the company of those who busied themselves about worldly things, said to them: Do not be so anxious about these things. "Seek first the kingdom of God and his justice, and all things else will be given you over and above." And He meant to imply by these words if they would be so happy as to strive their utmost to please God and to save their souls, their Heavenly Father would supply them with all that was necessary for their bodies. But you will say, how can we seek for the kingdom of God and his justice? How, my dear friends? Nothing is easier or more consoling: by being zealous in the service of God, which is the only means which we have to lead us to the noble and blessed end for which we were created. Yes, my friends, we all know it, even the worst of sinners are convinced that we are in this world solely to serve God and to keep his commandments. But, you will ask me, why are there so few who strive for this? My friends, the reason is this: Some consider the service of God as something too difficult. They imagine they haven't sufficient strength to undertake it, and if they did undertake it they would not continue it. It is just that, my dear people, which makes so many worthless Christians or that turns them away altogether; instead of listening to these consoling words of our Redeemer, who in His own words tells us that His service is easy, and that if we obey Him we shall find peace to our souls and rest to our hearts.

I.

Yes, my dear friends, whichever way we consider the service of God, whether by prayer or penance, or the frequent reception of the sacraments, by our love of God, and of our neighbor, or in our absolute self-sacrifice—yes, dearly beloved, in all these things we shall find only joy, pleasure and happiness for the present and the future, as you will soon see. Those who know their religion and practice it understand that the cross and persecution, contempt, suffering, poverty, and death itself are changed into sweetness, consolation and an everlasting reward. Tell me, have you ever pictured this to yourselves vividly? Certainly not! Nevertheless, it is, my dear friends, just as I tell you, and to prove it to you in such a way that you cannot doubt it, listen to Jesus Christ himself, who says: "Blessed are the poor, for theirs is the kingdom of heaven, and woe unto the rich, for it is very difficult for the rich to be saved."

You see, then, poverty, according to Jesus Christ's own words, will not make us unhappy, because the Redeemer says: "Blessed are the poor."

Secondly, the same with sufferings and trials, for Jesus Christ says: "Blessed are they that mourn, and that are persecuted, for the day will come when they shall be consoled but "woe unto the world and those who enjoy its pleasures, for a day will come when their joy will be changed into tears and everlasting sorrow."

Thirdly, nor contempt, for Jesus Christ says: "They reviled me, and they will revile you; they persecuted me, and they will persecute you; but be not cast down, but rather rejoice; for your reward will be great in heaven."

Yes, my dear friends, even in this world, he who is true to his God is far happier than the worldly man with all his luxuries. Listen to St. Paul:

"Yes," says he, "I am happier in my chains and my prisons, in contempt and suffering, than are my persecutors in their freedom, in their excesses, in their revelry. My heart is so full of joy that it can hardly contain it; it flows over on all sides."

Yes, indeed, my friends, St. John the Baptist is happier in the wilderness, forsaken by all human kind, than Herod on his throne, buried in riches and a prey to his shameful passions. Then look at David. Is he not happier in his flight from the wrath of Saul, although he has to pass nights in the forest, betrayed and forsaken by his dearest friends? For during this time he was united to his God and he placed all his confidence in Him. Was he not happier than Saul in the magnificence of his possessions and his sinful pleasures? David praises the Lord for lengthening his days and giving him time to suffer for love of Him, while Saul curses his life and is his own executioner. Why is this, my friends, but because the one is zealous in the service of God, while the other forsakes it? What conclusion do we draw from this, my beloved? None other than that it is neither goods, honors, nor vanities which make man happy here below, but an abiding faithfulness in the service of God, if we have the happiness to know in what it consists and conscientiously to practice it.

TWENTY-FOURTH SUNDAY AFTER PENTECOST 19

The wife who is unhappy in her married life is not so because of her husband's neglect, but because she has not faith, or because she does not practice what it commands her. Let her have a lively faith, and she will, as soon as she knows what the commandments are, not complain nor be unhappy. Oh, how happy would man be in this world if he knew his religion and had the happiness of practicing what it commands—if he would consider the good that is promised to him in the life to come. Oh, what power we have with God when we love Him and serve Him faithfully. Oh, my friends, look at one who is despised by men and who is not deemed worthy to be trodden upon. Such a one commands the will and the power of God Himself. Look at Moses, who caused the Lord to forgive three hundred thousand sinful men. Look at Joshua: at his order the sun stood still and the sun was motionless, a sight that was never seen before and may never occur again. Look at the apostles: because they loved God the evil spirits fled before them, the lame walked, the blind saw, and the dead were raised to life. Look at St. Benedict, who commanded the clouds to stand still, and they remained hanging in the air. See how he multiplied the bread, how he brought water forth from the rocks, and made the stones and wood as light as a feather. Look at St. Anthony of Padua who commanded the fishes to come out of the water and listen to the Word of God, and they obeyed him so well that they listened to his sermon. Look at St. John, who ordered the birds to cease singing, and they obeyed him. Look again at others, who without any human assistance walked on the waters. Now, on the other hand, look at the ungodly with all their great intellects and their sciences. What can they accomplish? Nothing! And why? Because they do not serve God. Oh, how powerful, and at the same time how happy is he who knows his religion and lives up to it!

Listen to me a moment, and you will see that to serve God in the midst of the trials of this life is consolation and happiness. For this purpose it is not necessary to give up your fortune or to forsake your parents and relations, so long as they do not lead you to sin. You need not spend your days in the wilderness, there to bewail your sins. No. A father and mother can serve God by bringing up their children as good Christians. A servant can very easily serve God and his master at the same time; there is nothing to prevent him; on the contrary, the work and the obedience which his master expects of him are an occasion of merit.

No, my friends, the service of God in all that we do does not necessitate any change, but, on the contrary, all we do will be done better.

We shall be more industrious and careful in fulfilling our duties; we shall be gentler, more cheerful, and kinder toward all; frugal in our eating, guarded in speaking, and less sensitive at losses and insults which we may have to bear. That is to say, my friends, when we remain faithful to God, we shall do everything better and behave like good and perfect Christians.

Instead of doing our neighbor a good turn from pride, or giving an alms so that we may be esteemed, we shall do these things only to please God and in satisfaction for our sins. Yes, I repeat, a Christian who knows his religion and practices it sanctifies all his works, without in any way changing what he does and without adding anything. All he does has merit for heaven. Now, my friends, tell me, if you had known how sweet and consoling it was to serve God, would you have lived as you have been doing all along?

Now I will ask you whether it is the outward form of religion which frightens you and seems so hard? Is it prayer, services, days of abstinence and fasting, the frequent reception of the sacraments, the love of our neighbors? Well, then, we shall see that there is nothing difficult in all these things.

First I ask, is it hard for you to pray? Is it not rather the happiest moment of your life? Do we not by prayer converse with God as friend to friend? Do we not thereby begin what we shall do with the angels in heaven? Is it not too great a favor for us, we who are so miserable, that the good God should tolerate us in His sacred presence and that He should console us? Did He not give us all that we have? It is, then, only just that we should adore Him and love Him with all our strength. Is this not the happiest moment of our lives, when we enjoy such ineffable sweetness? Is it hard every morning in our prayers to ask Him to bless our labors and business? Is it difficult to devote one day each week to Him? Should we not rather rejoice when this day comes, when we shall be told our duties which we have to perform toward God and man, when we are told how we should long for the goods of the next life, and how little everything else is in comparison? Do we not learn in the instructions the penalty for sin? Do we not feel determined not to sin any more, so as to avoid the sufferings which are represented to us? Oh, my God! how little does man know his good fortune!

Tell me, is it against your inclination to go to confession? But, my dear friend, is it possible to find a greater happiness than that in less than three minutes our eternity of misery should be changed into an eternity of bliss? Does not confession restore us to the friendship of God? Does not confession quench in us the remorse which is an unceasing agony to us? Does it not restore peace to our souls and renew our hope of heaven? Does not Jesus Christ at this moment appear to unfold to us the riches of His infinite mercy? Yes, my devout children, how many more of the damned would there be, and how far fewer saints, if we had not this sacrament? Oh, how the saints in heaven thank our blessed Lord that He has instituted this sacrament!

Tell me, my friends, does fasting, which the Church commands, appear to you to make the service of God hard? Well, the Church does not ask you to do more of it than you are able. If we consider it with the eye of faith, will it not seem to us a great happiness that we can, by such slight privations, escape the fires of purgatory, which are so severe? How many are there, my friends, who undergo much greater fasts for the sake of their health, and in consequence of their sensuality and gluttony?

Although we have said, my friends, that everything in our holy religion is full of consolation, which is certainly true, still we must add that we must do good to those who treat us badly; love those who hate us; protect the good name of our enemies; take their part when we see that others speak ill of them; and, instead of wishing them ill, we must ask God to bless them. Far be it from us to murmur when God sends us trouble and worry. We must thank Him for this, like King David, who kissed the hand that struck him. We must look upon sin as our deadliest enemy. Now, my friends, this it is which appears to us as the most difficult and repellent. But tell me, do we not seek in all this our happiness on earth and for all eternity? Ah! my friends, if we knew our holy religion and what joy one experiences when we practice it, how paltry would all else appear to us! How many saints have done more than God asked of them to reach heaven! They have told us that when once they had tasted the sweetness and consolation of serving God, it was impossible to forsake Him and to serve the world with its pleasures. The holy King David tells us that one day spent in the service of God is of more value than a thousand others which the children of this world spend in their luxuries and pleasures.

II.

Tell me, who would serve the world if they had the great happiness to know all the miseries to be found there by becoming a slave to our passions, as well as the torments which are prepared for eternity? Oh, my God! how blind are we if we lose so much happiness even in this life, not to speak of the next! And then the pleasures—or rather what has the appearance of pleasures— and joys mixed with such trouble and sadness. Look at the man who has made up his mind to amass a fortune; neither wind nor weather hinders him in his pursuit of money. He undergoes hunger and thirst, and very often is his life in danger, and he even will sacrifice his good name.

Would it not be better for us to spend more time in church than to waste hours going around gossiping about trifles? Would it not be more profitable to go to Vespers than to idle the time away at home while the praises of God are being sung?

Now, you will tell me: But one must do violence to one's self to serve God. Yes; but I tell you that you have less to suffer in following the cross than in serving the world and its pleasures, and I will prove it to you. You think, I suppose, that it is hard to forgive an insult; but tell me, which of these two loves the most—he who forgives quickly for the love of God or he who bears malice and hatred in his heart toward his neighbors, perhaps for years? Is there not a worm that gnaws at his heart and will not let him eat or sleep? While, on the other hand, he who forgives finds at once peace and happiness. Is it not better to overcome our passions than to satisfy them? Could we ever satisfy them? No, my friends, never. After committing a mortal sin you are led to commit another, without stopping to ask if it is enough. You are a slave, dragged hither and thither.

So that you may understand this better, we will take the case of a man whose whole aim in life is to pander to his passions. Alas! my friends, if that man could have seen, before he gave himself up to debauchery, what a life he would lead, could he have contemplated such an existence without shuddering? If you had told him. My friend, you have two alternatives to consider, either to overcome your passions or to be a slave to them. Both have their pleasures and their sufferings. There they are— choose between them. If you decide to be virtuous you will have to fight against temptations, and you must choose your friends among those who think and act as you do. You will read edifying books, which will help you on to love God; every day your love of Him will increase. You will pass your time profitably, and your amusements will be innocent ones which will refresh you, body and soul. You will fulfill your religious duties, not for the sake of appearances, but conscientiously. You will select a holy and learned confessor, who will lead you in the way of salvation, and you will faithfully follow his advice. That, my friend, is all you will have to suffer in God's service. Your reward will be a heart and soul at peace always. You will be esteemed by the good; you will prepare for yourself a happy old age, free from many infirmities which afflict those who were wild in their youth; your last moments will be peaceful and quiet. From whichever side you look at your life, there will be nothing to trouble you, but everything will contribute to rejoice you. Your crosses, your tears, and all your penances will be as so many ambassadors which heaven will send you as an assurance of eternal happiness and that you have nothing to fear. If at this moment you look at the future you will see heaven opened, ready to receive you. At last you will leave this world, like a holy and virtuous dove, hidden in the bosom of her beloved. You will have nothing to leave, but everything to receive. You will be for all eternity with God.

If, however, you neglect the service of God to follow the world and your evil ways, your life will be spent in desiring and seeking without ever being satisfied. No matter what you do, you will never reach the goal. You will have to begin by banishing from your mind all the good precepts of your childhood. You will not read any more those good books which nourished your soul and helped you to avoid the wickedness of the world. You will not mortify your passions any longer; they will lead you wherever they will. You will make a religion of your own; read bad books, which breathe only contempt for sacred truths, and you will tread the path which they point out. You will never recall the past when you practiced your religion and it was a pleasure to you to approach the sacraments. You will go so far as to deny everything and become more and more ungodly. You will give free rein to your passions and say that as everything ends with this life you will enjoy yourself while you can. Blinded by your passions, you will fall from one sin into another without knowing it. You will, in fine, sacrifice rest, fortune, health and honor, and even your life. I won't say your soul, because you don't believe that you have one. You will be the talk of the parish and regarded as a monster. People will avoid you and be afraid of you. You will suffer in body and mind, your health broken down, and a miserable old age will be yours. During life you forsook your God; now at your death the light of faith will glimmer again, which you had extinguished by your bad life. You have forsaken God and He will forsake you, and you will be delivered over to everlasting torments. Then you will feel the remorse of conscience which you have persistently stifled, and you will be powerless to stay the gnawing at your heart. Everything will be despair and perdition.

The world, which you so dearly loved, whose displeasure you were afraid to incur, for which you sacrificed your God and your soul, despises and rejects you. You obeyed your passions, and now when you stand in need of assistance, you will be left to yourself. Your only help will be despair. Still worse, you will die, and in falling into hell you will say, "The world deceived me;" but you will see your miserable state too late.

Now, my brethren, what do you think of all this? These are the pains and the joys of those who lead a virtuous life and of those who lead a life of sin. Oh, my dear friends, what a misfortune for those who only live for the world and who put on one side the salvation of their soul! Oh, what a great happiness, to seek only the love of God and the salvation of our soul! How peacefully our life passes! How many pains less in the service of God, and how many more joys! How much remorse of conscience we shall escape at the hour of our death! What agonies for all eternity avoided! Oh, my friends, what a change comes over one who is so happy as to seek God alone on this earth! If a husband or wife are unhappy in their family relations, persuade them to dedicate themselves to God's service, and you will see that their unhappiness will vanish and peace and concord reign between them. Yes, let us confess it, a person who practices his religion does not live for himself alone, but to do good to his neighbor.

Let us come to the conclusion, my dear friends, which we must bear in mind, that if we follow the world, and thereby satisfy our own will, we shall never be happy and never find what we are striving for, while, on the other hand, if we are faithful in the service of God, all our wants will be satisfied, or at least turned to joy and consolation, by the thought that we are working for heaven. What a difference between the one who dies after a wicked life and the one who dies after a good life! The latter has heaven for his portion; all his trials are at an end; his happiness, which he tastes beforehand, begins for him, never to have an end. Amen.

LAST SUNDAY AFTER PENTECOST

"Precious in the sight of the Lord is the death of his saints."
Ps. cxi. 15.

EATH, my dear people, is a just cause for alarm to the unrepentant sinner, who finds himself obliged to leave behind his pleasures. Bowed down with pain, tormented by thoughts of the judgment to which he must submit, devoured in advance by fear of the horrors of hell into which he will soon be thrown, he looks upon himself as abandoned by God and man.

On the contrary, death fills the good man who has lived in the light of the Gospel, and who has walked in the footsteps of Jesus Christ and has satisfied divine justice by true repentance, with joy and consolation. The righteous consider death as the end of their sufferings, their sorrows, their temptations, and all their wants. They consider it as the beginning of their salvation.

There is no human being, my dear friends, however abject he may be, who does not wish for and desire a precious death, and yet there are very few who take the means to obtain it. It is a blindness hard to be explained; but as it is my ardent desire that you may all die a happy death, I will encourage you to live in such a way that you may have reason to look forward to this happiness, by showing you, firstly, the advantages of a happy death, and, secondly, the means by which you may obtain it.

I.

If a person is at the moment of death possessed of a vicious habit, his soul will descend into hell; if, on the other hand, the soul is in a perfect condition, it will forthwith take its flight to heaven. If it falls to our lot to have to go to purgatory, we will surely find the path some day. All this depends upon the life which we have led. It is certain that our death will correspond with our life. If we have lived as good Christians and in the fear of the Lord, we shall die as good Christians and live with the Lord for all eternity. But if, on the contrary, we have lived for our passions, our pleasures, and excesses, then we shall without fail die in sin. Do not let us forget the fact which has converted so many sinners, that "where the tree falls, there it lieth forever." Death in itself is not so dreadful as it is generally supposed to be, my dear friends. It depends entirely upon ourselves to make it a happy, beautiful, and blissful one.

When St. Jerome was told by his friends that he was near death, he gathered all his strength and exclaimed:

"Oh, welcome and delightful message! Come soon, O death! How longingly have I awaited thee! Come and deliver me from all the troubles of this world! Come and reunite me with my Redeemer!"

And to those who surrounded him he added:

"My dear friends, not to fear death and to find it a consolation, one has only to walk in the path which our Lord Jesus Christ has pointed out for us and to mortify one's self continually."

What inexpressible joy a person experiences who was banished from home or led away into captivity, when told that he or she may return to their own country, to their families and friends! The same happiness awaits a soul which loves God and languishes in the ardent desire of seeing Him in heaven in the midst of the saints, who are our real family and friends.

Death, my friends, is to the just man what sleep is to the tired laborer who is glad of the approach of night, which will bring him rest after the hardships of the day. Death delivers the just man from the prison of his body, as St. Paul says: "Unhappy man that I am, who shall deliver me from the body of this death?" "Deliver me, my God," said the holy King David, "deliver my soul from the prison of this body. Who will give me wings like a dove, and I will fly and be at rest?"

Ah! our poor soul in our body is like a diamond in dross. St. Gregory tells of a poor man who, having been for a long time paralyzed in all his limbs, and who felt the end approaching, asked the people who surrounded him to sing some joyful songs to him. When he was asked how it came that his mind was in such a joyful mood, he replied:

"Because my soul will soon leave this body and be freed from its prison."

After they had sung for a few minutes they heard sweet strains of music as from the angels.

"Oh," said the dying man, "don't you hear the angels sing? Oh, let them sing! Oh, let them sing!"

And with that he died.

Who could comprehend the joy of St. Ludwina when she, after twenty-seven years of sickness, eaten up with cancer, exclaimed at the end of her suffering:

"What joy! All my sufferings are at an end! O precious death, make haste! I have longed for thee many days with all my heart."

How happy, then, is a Christian when he follows in the footsteps of the Divine Master!

But in what consists the life of Jesus Christ? Listen, my good friends. It consists of three things—namely: Prayer, good deeds, and suffering. You know that the Redeemer often withdrew from public life to pray and that He was always active in the salvation of souls. The thought of God should come as natural to us as breathing. During His life of prayer and good deeds Jesus Christ had to suffer much. Now poverty, now persecution, now humiliations, and then all kinds of harsh treatment. "My life," He says through His prophet, "is wasted with grief: and my years in sighs. My strength is weakened through poverty" (Ps. xxx. 11). Can the life of a good Christian be any other than that of a man who is nailed to the cross with his Master? The righteous man is a crucified man.

We find that the saints have found such happiness in their sufferings that they seemed to have ever longed for more. Contemplate the life of the great Pope Innocent I. He was covered with sores from head to foot, and yet he was not satisfied and sighed unceasingly for more suffering. He prayed to God daily for them.

"My God," he said, "increase my suffering, send me still more cruel diseases, if Thou wilt only give me new mercies!"

"Why," they said to him, "are you asking God to increase your suffering—you, who are already covered with wounds?"

"You do not know how great the merit of suffering is. If you could only conceive the merit of it, you would love to suffer."

St. Lawrence was put upon a gridiron, and the flames, which had before spared the three children in the furnace of Babylon, burned him mercilessly, and all he did was to ask them to turn him over on the other side, so that all the parts of his body might be equally glorified in heaven. This example, my dear friends, is a miracle of that grace which is so powerful in all those who love the Lord.

"Oh, how consoling it is!" says St. Augustine, "to die with your conscience at rest." "Tranquillity of soul and peace of mind are the most precious gifts we can obtain," says the Holy Ghost. "There is no pleasure which is comparable to the joy of an innocent heart." "The righteous," says the same teacher, "does not fear death, because by it he is reunited to his Master and put in possession of innumerable delights." Only see what joy the saints express when they are in the arms of death. "See," says St. Chrysostom, "the fearlessness and eagerness with which St. Paul goes back to Jerusalem, though he knew that nothing but harsh treatment awaited him: 'And now, behold, bound in the spirit, I go to Jerusalem, not knowing the things that shall befall me there. Only that the Holy Ghost in every city witnesseth to me, saying that chains and afflictions wait for me at Jerusalem. But I fear none of these things: neither do I count my life more precious than myself, so that I may consummate my course, and the ministry of the word which I have received from the Lord Jesus to testify the gospel of the grace of God.'" And when he saw his disciples crying the apostle added: "What do you mean, weeping and afflicting my heart? For I am ready not only to be bound, but also to die in Jerusalem for the name of the Lord Jesus."

Of course we are not as certain of being the friends of God as St. Paul was; but though we are sinners we must have confidence, if we have confessed our sins with sincere repentance and have striven to pray and do penance as much as lie in our power, particularly if our sorrow for our sins has been coupled with a deep love for our good Lord; if, I say we have done all this, then we may have confidence that our sins will be washed away by the precious blood of Jesus Christ, like Pharao's host was by the Red Sea.

My devout friends, there were three crosses on Mount Calvary: that of Jesus Christ, which is the cross of innocence; we cannot strive for that because we have sinned. Then there is the cross of the penitent thief, the cross of penance; this shall be our cross. Let us imitate this penitent thief who used the last moments to repent and who ascended from the cross directly to heaven. Jesus Christ Himself told him: "Today shalt thou be with me in Paradise." The last cross is that of the bad thief; let us leave that to those sinners who want to die in their sins. But we, my dear people, we may be sure, if we only desire it most sincerely, that we belong to those who will die the death of a Christian.

Tell me, why should a good Christian be afraid in his last hour? Is it on account of his goods, which he has considered of so little value during his life? Is he concerned about his body—that body which he must consider his cruel enemy that more than once brought him in danger of losing his soul? Would he trouble about the pleasures of the world? Certainly not, for he has passed all his life in sorrow, in repentance, and in tears. No, my dear friends, in all of these he misses nothing. Death separates him only from that which he has always hated and despised, from the sins of this world and its pleasures. In his passing away from this life he takes with him what he has loved most dearly, his virtues and his good deeds. He leaves all kinds of miseries to take possession of innumerable riches; he leaves the strife to gain peace; he leaves a cruel enemy, the evil spirit, to rest in the bosom of the best of fathers. Yes, his good works lead him triumphantly before God, who appears to him not as a judge, but as a tender friend who, after taking pity on his sufferings, desires above all to give him his reward. The prophet Isaias teaches us that our good works will make God's mercy open to us the gates of Paradise and determine our habitation in heaven. It is perfectly true that our good works will accompany us.

"Blessed," says St. John, "are the dead who die in the Lord, for their works shall follow them." Yes, my friends, our earthly possessions we leave behind, but our good deeds we shall take with us. The devout Christian will find all his good confessions and communions which he has made, all the virtues which he has practiced during his life. It is indeed a happy death, the death of the righteous. Listen to the prophet Isaias: "Tell the just man that he is blessed, for he will reap the reward of his works."

You will admit, my dear friends, that a good death is considered very precious in the eyes of all men.

II.

My dear friends, I know we all hope for a happy death, but to hope for it is not sufficient; we must work for it—this great happiness, this sublime happiness. Do you wish to know how to obtain it? Let me tell you in a few words. From among the means which we should employ to die a happy death I will select three which, with God's grace, will invariably lead us to a happy death. We must prepare ourselves for it (1) by a holy life, (2) by true repentance when we have committed sin, and (3) by a perfect union of our death with the death of Jesus Christ. As a rule, one dies as one has lived. This is one of the great truths which has been confirmed many times by Scripture and the holy fathers. If you live like good Christians you will be sure to die like good Christians; but when you live unchristian like your death will be of the same kind. The prophet Isaias says: "Woe to the ungodly, whose only thought is wickedness, for he will be treated as he deserves; in death he will be rewarded according to the works of his hands."

It is true, though, that sometimes, as by a miracle, a good end may follow a bad beginning; but this happens so seldom that as a rule, as St. Jerome says, death is merely the echo of life. If you are on the wrong path do you believe that it will be easy for you to return to the dear Lord? No. More likely than not you will perish in the weary path. But when, filled with the spirit of repentance, you begin to live a Christian life, then you will belong to those contrite souls who move the heart of the Lord and recover His friendship.

The Holy Ghost says to us: "If you have a friend, do good to him before his death." Now, then, my dear listeners, can we have a better friend than our own soul? Let us do for it all we can, for at that very moment when we shall wish most to do something for it we shall not be able to. Life is short. If you think you can postpone your conversion to the hour of your death you are blind, because you know neither the moment nor the place where you will die, perhaps without having any one near you. Who knows but what you may have to appear this very night, covered with sins, before the judgment seat of God? No, my friends, you must not do that. You must purify yourselves and be always ready to appear before your Judge. The following example will show you how one who postpones from day to day his return to God died as he had lived.

Cardinal Peter Damian reports that a monk had spent the best part of his life in intriguing and quarreling with his brethren. When he was on his death-bed they implored him to confess his sins, to pray to God for pardon, and to do penance with the firm resolution not to fall into the same sins again if his health should be given back to him. They could not get a word out of him. Some time after, when he had found his tongue again, he spoke to them, and of what? Of that which had formed the subject of his conversation during life—lawsuits and other quarrels. His brethren begged him to think of his soul, but it was all in vain. He fell asleep again, and died without having given the least sign of repentance.

Yes, my friends, as the life, so the death. Do not hope for a miracle, which God vouchsafes but seldom. If you live in sin you will die in sin. Many examples prove to us that after an evil life we cannot expect a happy death. We read in Holy Scripture that Abimelech, an impetuous and proud monarch, seized the kingdom which he was to govern conjointly with his brother, and had his brother put to death so as to reign alone. When he attacked a certain city the defender of it withdrew into a fortified tower, upon which he advanced for the purpose of setting it on fire. A woman who saw him from the city wall threw a stone, which split his head open. When the unfortunate monarch found himself mortally wounded, he called upon his shield bearer to draw his sword and kill him quickly, so as to save him the dishonor of dying at the hands of a woman.

What strange behavior, my dear friends! Was he the first prince who had been wounded in such a way? Why did he request his shield bearer to kill him? Because all his life long he had striven for this world's honor and glory. Saul was fighting a battle with the Amalekites. The fate of the armies was uncertain. He thought all was lost. He was wounded and expected every moment to be captured by the enemy. Leaning on his sword, he saw a soldier coming toward him. He called to him and said: "Come here, my friend. Who are you?"

"I am an Amalekite," was the reply.

"That is well. Do me a great service. Come and kill me. I am overwhelmed with pain and misfortune, but I cannot die. Come and kill me."

And why, my dear friends, did this unfortunate man want to die by the hand of an Amalekite? Was he the only king who ever lost a battle? We need not be surprised at it, for the holy fathers tell us that he was a king who all his life had given himself up to vice, and who was governed by envy, cupidity, and all other kinds of passions. Why did he die such a dishonorable death? Why? Because he had lived a dishonorable life.

You see quite plainly, then, my dear friends, that if we desire to have a happy death, we must live a Christian life and do penance for our sins. We must, by the grace of God, carry in our heart a profound humility and a lasting repentance that we have offended such a good Master.

A third way by which to prepare ourselves for a happy death is to offer our death in union with the death of Jesus Christ. When our blessed Lord is brought to a sick person the cross is also brought to him, not only to drive away the evil spirit, but far more that the crucified Saviour may serve the dying man as a model to prepare himself for death in the same way as our Lord prepared Himself.

The first thing Jesus did before he died was to take leave of His apostles. A sick person should do the same—that is, take leave of the world and all those who are nearest and dearest to him, and to occupy his mind solely with God and his salvation. When Jesus knew that His end was approaching he threw Himself upon the ground in the garden of olives and prayed fervently. A sick person should do the same when the hour of death is approaching— that is, pray fervently and unite himself in his death agony to the agony of Jesus. The dying man who wishes to make his sickness meritorious should accept death with joy, or at least with resignation to the will of his Heavenly Father, and think that we must die before we can see God, and that therein consists our whole happiness. St. Augustine says that he who does not want to die shows signs of impenitence.

Oh, my dearest friends, how happy is a Christian who has lived worthy of his name at that last moment! He leaves nothing but misery, to enter into possession of his heavenly inheritance. Happy separation which unites us with our highest good, our blessed Lord Himself! And this is what I wish you all, with my whole heart. Amen.

FIRST SUNDAY OF ADVENT

THE LAST JUDGMENT

"Tunc videbunt Filium hominis venientem in nube cum potestate magna et majestate."
"And then they shall see the Son of man coming in a cloud with great power and majesty."
—St. Luke xxi. 27.

NOT A GOD clothed with our weaknesses, hidden in the darkness of a wretched stable, housed in a crib, treated with derision and mockery, bowed to earth by the heavy burden of his cross; but a God who, clad in the glorious splendor of his great power and majesty, makes known His advent by the most terrifying manifestations, by the darkening of the sun and the moon, by the falling of the stars and by the upheaval of all creation. Not a Redeemer who comes with the meekness of a lamb to be judged by men whom He tries to gain over to Himself; but a judge in righteous wrath, to judge mankind with the awful measure of His justice. Not a loving shepherd, who tries to find His stray sheep and who pardons them when they have returned, but a God of vengeance, who will separate forever the just from the unjust, who will make the sinners feel His terrible vengeance and overwhelm the just with celestial bliss. O terrible moment, O fearful moment, when wilt thou arrive? O unhappy moment! perhaps in a few days from now we may observe the harbingers of this, for sinners, so terrible a day of judgment! O sinners, arise from the grave of your iniquities, appear before the judgment seat of God and suffer the treatment the sinner will have to undergo! The godless of this world like to deny the power of God, because they see the sinner pass unpunished through the days of his life; yes, they will even make the bold assertion that there is no God, that there is no hell; or, they say: "God does not take any notice of what we do here upon earth." Oh, but wait for the day of judgment; on this great day God will reveal His power and show all nations that He has seen everything and taken an account thereof.

St. Luke says that men will wither away for fear and expectation of what shall come upon the whole world. Oh, my friends, one could wither away for fear and die from fright at the thought of a misfortune which is a thousand times less than what is impending for the sinner and which is sure to be his fate if he persists in leading a life of sin.

My friends, if at this moment, when I am about to speak to you of the judgment to come, before which we must all appear to render an account of the good and evil we have done during this life and to receive thereat our final judgment, which will be either Heaven or hell, I say, if at this moment an angel was to appear and announce to you the message from God that in twenty-four hours by a rain of fire and sulphur the whole world would go up in flames; if you could already hear the distant rolling of the thunder; if the fury of the storm was beginning to tear down your houses, and if the lightning was growing so vivid that the earth was like unto a fiery ball; if hell was beginning to hurl forth the damned to fill the world with their screams and howls, and if the only way to avoid this misery would be to detest sin and repent, could you then, my friends, listen to all this without shedding streams of tears and imploring mercy? Would you not throw yourself down at the foot of the altar and cry for mercy? Oh, inconceivable folly of sinful man! It will then be too late to repent.

Yes, my brethren, we shall be judged; nothing is more certain. Yes, and we shall be judged without mercy.

We read in Holy Scripture that God, whenever He intended to send a scourge over the world, always preceded it by a sign, so as to strike terror into the hearts of the people and cause them to implore His mercy. The historian Josephus records that long before the destruction of Jerusalem there was visible in the sky a comet, in the form of a sword, which caused general consternation. Every one asked what is the meaning of this sign? Is it perhaps a great misfortune which God is going to send us? The moon appeared eight nights in the sky without showing any light; the people began to tremble for their lives, when all at once an unknown man appeared, who for three years without interruption passed through the streets of Jerusalem day and night, shouting: "Woe to Jerusalem! Woe to Jerusalem!" He was arrested and scourged to make him stop his lamentations, but nothing would deter him. At the end of the three years he called out: "Woe to Jerusalem! Ah! woe to me! At that moment a stone, which had been thrown at him from a slingshot, struck him and killed him instantly. Soon all the misfortunes which this unknown man had prophesied broke out all over Jerusalem. The famine became so terrible that mothers killed and devoured their own children. The city was captured by the enemy and levelled to the ground; the streets were covered with the dead, and blood flowed in streams; the few who escaped with their lives were sold into slavery.

As the day of judgment will be the most terrible and frightful day of all, the preceding signs will be so horrible as to strike terror into the innermost parts of the earth. Our Lord has said that on that fateful day the sun shall give no more light; that the moon will seem like a bloody mass, and the stars will fall from the heavens. Lightning and thunder will be so terrible that men will wither away with fear. The wind will become so violent that nothing will be able to withstand it; trees and houses will be torn away and carried far out to sea; the sea itself, lashed into fury by the storms, will rise higher than the highest mountains, and the terrors of hell will be open to the eyes of mankind; all creatures will try to hide themselves away from the presence of the Creator when they behold the crimes with which men have defiled and disfigured the face of the earth.

When then the earth is cleansed from the many crimes with which it was covered God will send down His angels, who will blow their trumpets at the four corners of the earth, and call to the dead: "Arise, ye dead, arise from your graves and appear anon before the judgment seat!" And forthwith all the dead, just and unjust, good and bad, the virtuous and the sinners, will be rejoined to their bodies; the seas will give up their dead, and the earth will bring forth all who have been lying in her bosom for all these centuries. After this upheaval the souls of the Saints, clad in their glory, will descend from Heaven, each of them to take possession of their earthly body. "Come," they will say to it; "come, thou companion of my sufferings, thou hast always striven to please God; thou hast sought thy happiness in suffering and in fighting. Come, ye blessed eyes which have closed so often at the sight of unclean objects for fear of losing the grace of God, come into Heaven, where you will see nothing but the beautiful things which are vainly sought for on earth. Welcome, my ears, which had such a horror of unchaste and slanderous words and conversations; be welcome in Heaven, where you will listen only to heavenly music, which will be your constant delight. Welcome, my feet and my hands, which were so often the means of bringing solace to the unfortunate; let us wander about in this beautiful Heaven, where we shall gaze upon our adored Redeemer who loves us so much. There we shall see Him who has lived in our hearts: there we shall see His hands, still reddened with blood, by which He has merited our great joy."

When the Saints have taken possession of their glorified bodies, they will look forward with rapture to the moment when God will reveal to the sight of the whole world all the tears, all the works of penance, all the good they have done. "Yea," Jesus Christ will say to them, "I want the whole world to behold the reward which I have prepared for you!"

But what a terrible and awful change is before us. I hear the trumpet call to the condemned to come back out of hell. Come, ye sinners, ye malefactors, ye tyrants, your God calls you who was so eager to save you; appear before the judgment seat of the Son of man. Come and stand forth, for all the wrong you have ever committed will be revealed in sight of the whole world. Then the angel will call: "Depths of hell, open your portals, belch forth the damned: their Judge is calling them." Oh, horrible moment! They will come forth from the depths, these miserable damned souls, and seek for their bodies in despair. Oh, horrible sight, at the moment when the soul enters its body the latter will feel all the terrors of hell. Oh, this cursed body and this cursed soul, they will revile each other thousands and thousands of times. Oh, thou cursed body, the soul will say, thou has drawn me and dragged me into the filth of impurity; thousands of years have I suffered and burned in hell. Come, ye cursed eyes that have so often taken pleasure in throwing impure glances at their own or the bodies of others; come down to hell, where you will see nothing but the most horrible monsters. Come, ye cursed ears that have so often delighted in listening to indecent words and conversations; come down to hell, where you will hear the howling and roaring of the devils for all eternity. Come, thou cursed tongue, thou cursed mouth; come down to hell, where you will get no other nourishment but gall. Come, thou cursed body, to whose cupidity I have given in so often, thou shalt forever be stretched out in a pool of sulphur and fire, which is kindled by the power and wrath of God.

Yes, my brethren, there the just and the condemned, after they have reoccupied again the body which was theirs during life, the body as we see it now before us, all will stand up before their Judge. See, there He comes, seated on His throne, blazing with glory, surrounded by all the angels, before Him His standard, the Cross! When the damned see their Judge, then they will cry out: "Ye mountains, throw yourselves upon us and hide us from the sight of our Judge; ye rocks, fall upon us and throw us back into the depths of hell! No! No! Come forth, oh, sinner, and give an account of thy whole life. Come forward, oh unhappy one, thou who hast offended the good God so greatly. Oh, my Judge, my Father, my Creator, where is my father, my mother, who have been the cause of my being damned? Oh, my father, my mother, it is through your fault that I am damned, it is you who have caused my destruction. Ah! who can estimate the misery of a condemned soul, who sees before Him his own father and mother resplendent in glory, destined for Heaven, and himself condemned to hell. These rejected ones will cry out, Mountains, bury us, we beg of you fall upon us; oh, ye portals of the abyss, open and hide us! Then the Lord will open up, as we are told by the Prophet Ezechiel, that great and wonderful book, in which the crimes of all men are recorded. Oh, what an enormous number of sins which have never been revealed to the eyes of the world will then become apparent! Oh, tremble, all ye, who have heaped sin upon sin for years!

But, you will say, what about all the good works we have done, were they all in vain? All those fastings, penances, almsgivings, the communions and confessions, do they not deserve any recompense? No; Jesus Christ will say to you, Your prayers were only idle babblings, your fasting hypocrisy, your almsgiving vain seeking for notoriety; I was never considered in any of your doings. Besides, I have blessed you with earthly possessions; I have blessed your work, I have given fruitfulness to your fields, I have enriched your children for the little good you have done. I have given you full recompense, as much as you could expect. But, He will say to us, your sins still live, and they will live forever before me. Depart, ye accursed, into eternal fire, which is for all those who have thought little of Me in life.

You see, my brethren, as the most distressing thing on that terrible day it will be made clear to us that God has spared no effort to save us; that He allowed us to participate in the boundless merits of His death on the Cross; that He gave us the privilege of being born in the bosom of the Church; that He gave us guardians of the soul to show us and advise us what to do to gain eternal happiness. He has given us the sacraments that we may regain His friendship as often as we have lost it; He has fixed upon no number of sins, which He is willing to pardon; if our return to Him is sincere we are sure of His forgiveness. He will wait for us for years, though we may live only to offend Him. He does not want to destroy, He would rather save us at any price if we will only let Him! We, ourselves, force him through our sins to pronounce the judgment of eternal damnation over us.

On earth the sinner will always have some excuse for the sins committed by him; he even brings his pride into the tribunal of penance, where he ought to appear only to accuse and humble himself. Some plead ignorance, others strong temptations; others again special opportunities and bad examples; every day you can hear the reasons which the sinners proffer to hide the hideousness of their crimes. Come now, ye proud sinners, and let us see how your excuses will be received on the judgment day; explain yourselves before Him who holds the torch in His hand and has seen, counted and weighed in the balance everything concerning you.

You did not know, you say, that this was a sin! Oh, unfortunate one, Jesus Christ will tell thee that if thou hadst been born amongst the heathen nations, who have never even heard of the true God, thou mightest offer thy ignorance as an excuse, but thou, a Christian, who had the happiness of being born in the bosom of the Church, who had grown up in the centre of enlightenment and who hast been preached to about thy own salvation, what about thee? Oh, unfortunate one, if thou didst live in ignorance it was thy fault, because thou wouldst not learn and make use of the instructions. Away, oh, unfortunate one, thy excuses only make thee more deserving of damnation. Away with thee to hell, there to burn in thy ignorance!

But another one will say, My passions were so strong, and very great was my weakness. Well, the Lord will say, after God showed you the great mercy to let you recognize your own weakness and your priest told you that you must be constantly watchful over yourself, mortify yourself, so as to become master of it, why did you behave just the contrary; why did you take so much trouble to satisfy the desires of your body and the promptings of your passions? God let you recognize your weakness and yet you fell at every step. Why did you not take refuge in the Lord and pray for grace to God? Why did you not obey the guardians of your soul who never failed to ask you to pray and ask for grace and strength, which you needed to overcome the devil? Why were you so indifferent to the Sacraments and approached them so seldom; those Sacraments which would have given you such strength to do good and avoid evil? Why did you despise so frequently the word of God, which would have led you to His habitation? Oh, you ungrateful, you blind sinners, why did you not use the opportunities which He gave you to make you strong, as so many others have done and are doing? What have you done to keep clear of sin? Away with you unfortunate ones, away, away with you to hell.

But, you will say, we have always had such bad examples before our eyes. Bad examples! What an empty excuse! If there are bad examples, there are also good ones. Why did you not rather follow the latter than the former? If you saw a young woman go to Church and receive the Sacraments, why did you not follow her rather than the one who went to dance halls? If a young man goes to church to pray to the Lord in the Holy Tabernacle, why did you not follow him rather than the one who went to the saloon? Say, rather, you sinners, that you preferred to wander on the broad path which leads to destruction than the narrow path which has been pointed out to you by the Lord. The real cause of your sins and your damnation is certainly not to be looked for in bad examples, or in opportunities, or your weakness, or in the want of grace; the real cause lies solely in the wickedness of your heart, which you have done nothing to suppress. Your fate is your own fault.

But, you will say, we have always been told that God is merciful. Certainly He is merciful, but He is also just. His love and mercy is at an end.

What conclusion shall we draw from all this, my friends? This: That we should never lose sight of the fact that some day we shall be judged without mercy, that all our sins will be revealed in the sight of the whole world, and that after the judgment day, if it should still find us tainted with sins, we should have to go to hell, there to suffer for them, without ever being able to extirpate or forget them. Oh, how blind we are, my brethren, if we do not use the short space of time which we still have to live through to assure ourselves of the heavenly Kingdom. So long as we are in this life we may hope for pardon, but if we wait too long it may be too late, and there may be no help for us. Oh, Lord, give me the grace that I may never lose the thought of this dreadful judgment day out of my mind, and do not let me fall into temptation, so that I may on that day hear the sweet words from the mouth of the Redeemer: "Come, ye blessed of my Father, possess ye the Kingdom which has been prepared for you from the beginning." Amen.

SECOND SUNDAY OF ADVENT

THE ETERNAL TRUTHS

"Memorare novissima tua et in aeternum non peccabis."
"In all thy works remember thy last end, and thou shalt never sin."
—Ecclus. vii. 40.

THESE TRUTHS, my brethren, must be very powerful and wholesome; for the Holy Ghost assures us that we shall never sin if we think over them earnestly. And, in fact, my brethren, who could attach themselves to the goods of this world, if they considered that in a short time they would no longer be here; that from Adam until today, nobody has ever taken anything away with him, or ever will do so? Would not anybody who was constantly thoughtful that he might die at any moment be always prepared for it? But, you will say, how is it that these truths, which have converted so many sinners, make so little impression upon us? Ah! my brethren, that is because we do not take them to heart sufficiently. Nothing is more likely to draw us away from ourselves and from the goods of this world, nothing so powerful to spur us on to bear better the sufferings of this life in a spirit of penance, than an earnest consideration of these truths. Behold, my brethren, how much Jesus Christ wishes to save us; at one time he appears to us as a poor child in the crib, lying on a handful of straw, which He moistens with His tears, again treated like a criminal, bound, pinioned, crowned with thorns, scourged, falling under the weight of the cross, and dying in martyrdom out of love for us. If this is not capable of moving us, drawing us towards Him, then He announces to us that He will one day come, clothed in the radiance of His glory and the Majesty of His Father, to judge us without clemency and without mercy; where before the whole world He will reveal the good and the bad which we have committed in the course of our lives. Tell me, dear brethren, if we rightly considered all this, should we require anything further to make us live and die like Saints?

According to my idea there are four points which determine the happiness of a Christian, namely: The shortness of life, the thought of death, the judgment, and eternity. What a joy for us, my brethren, when we think that in a short time we shall leave this world, where we are so tempted to offend God, who is such a loving Saviour, and has suffered so much for us. Ah, my brethren, can we with this thought in our minds cling to life, which abounds with so much misery? I say that the judgment, far from bringing despair to you, brings consolation. We find, not a severe judge, but a Father, a Redeemer. Yes, a Father who opens His sympathetic heart to us, to take us unto his fatherly bosom, who will, I say, take into account our tears, our penances and good works, as many as we have done during our life.

Dear brethren, how this thought ought to encourage us with all zeal to serve God, and with patience to bear all the weariness of life, of which we shall be forever free in heaven. Ah, my brethren, all the weariness of this world passes, it all lasts only for a time, whilst the reward endures for all eternity. Courage, cries St. Paul to us; we shall soon reach the end of our pilgrimage. But for a Christian, dear brethren, who has lost sight of his last aim, the matter has quite another aspect; the shortness of life is a trouble and a bitter thought which disturbs him in the midst of his pleasures; he does his utmost to keep this thought of death far from him. Everything that reminds him of it frightens him, doctors and remedies; everything is tried to keep away the thought that death is near. He is in pursuit of happiness on earth, but he deceives himself. Whilst this poor unfortunate man forsakes God, God forsakes him. He will be obliged at the end of his days to admit that he has spent his life seeking for a good which he never found. Outside of God, oh, so many sufferings, so much misery, and no consolation, no recompense! At his death he will cry out like that king we read of in the Old Testament, who, when he was about to leave all his possessions, complained: "Ah! must I then die, must I forsake my great possessions, my beautiful gardens, my flower beds, to go into a land where I do not know any one?" Ah, death, the consolation of the just, brings only despair to him; he must die, and he has never once given thought to it.

We are told in our catechism that at the moment of our death we shall be severely judged, and that all the good and all the evil which we have committed during our life will accompany us to the judgment seat. Were you not told, when you came here in your childhood, that after this life, which soon ends, another begins, which never ends, and which has in its train all measure of good or evil, according as we have acted well or badly? Answer! My brethren, if all these truths were engraved upon our hearts, could we be able to live without loving God, and doing everything in our power to avoid all these evils?

Ah! my brethren, how these truths caused the Saints to tremble, how they have converted sinners, and made the penitent perform works of penance and mortification! We read in history that St. Ambrose wrote to the emperor Theodosius, who had committed a sin, more from thoughtlessness than badness, "I have seen in a vision, with which God deigned to honor me, the following: 'As I saw you coming to church, I was ordered to close the doors, for your sins had made you unworthy to enter it.'" After reading these lines the emperor burst into tears; then he drove up to the door of the church, as was his custom, in the hope that the Bishop would yield on seeing his tears and his repentance. But the Bishop, far from yielding, commanded him, as he saw him approaching the church, that he should remain outside according to the order of God, for he was unworthy to enter into the House of Him whom he had not been afraid of offending, and that he should begin to expiate his sins. "Certainly," replied the emperor, "I am a sinner and unworthy to enter the House of the Lord, but God can see my repentance. David sinned too, and the Lord forgave him." "Very well!" replied St. Ambrose, "you have imitated David in sin, now therefore, imitate his repentance." Without making any answer, the emperor withdrew, tears streaming from his eyes, his heart breaking with sorrow, he laid aside his imperial robes, put on old and torn clothes, threw himself prone upon the ground, and gave himself up to the bitterness of his sorrow; his palace resounded with heart-breaking lamentations. He was not satisfied to confess his sins in the tribunal of penance, but announced them publicly, that through his humiliation he might draw down the mercy of God. But, you will ask me, what was the cause of so many tears, of such a great sorrow, of such exceptional works of penance? Ah, my brethren, it was the bare thought that God would one day call him to the judgment seat, where he would be judged without mercy.

Ah, my brethren! if these important truths were engrafted deeply in our hearts, could we live without working in such a way that the judgment of God which our sins have provoked might be mitigated? In fact, dear brethren, who could, at the thought that we are only in this world to save our souls, cheat his neighbor, or do him any injustice? Who would give himself up to the pleasures of this world, which are of such short duration, and so dangerous for our salvation, and thereby put on one side the important affair of his salvation? Who would dare to commit a grievous sin if he had before his mind the fact that a single mortal sin would send him to perdition? or who would, if he were so unfortunate as to have committed such a sin, remain in such a lamentable condition, where the hand of God might reach him at any moment, and not hasten to take refuge in the Sacrament of Penance, which is the one remedy that God in His mercy offers us?

Ah, my brethren, let us say rather who would not, if he pondered these powerful truths rightly, not live and die a Saint? "O my soul!" cried out a holy penitent, "think of thy sins, and these great truths. Never forget from whence you came, where you are going, from whom you have received your existence, to whom you must give your heart, which you brought into the world with you, and which you must take away with you on leaving this place of exile." Ah, my brethren, we have not thought about all this before; ah, we shall wait until our tears and repentance will be in vain. Let us turn away, my brethren, from what is transitory and perishable, and let us cling to that which is eternal and lasting. Let us say to all earthly things as the Saints did: No! No! I do not want you any more, as perhaps either you or I will not be here to-morrow; leave me the short space of time which is yet mine to employ in seeking the forgiveness of God. Ah, yes, I will live for God alone, because I despise all transitory things. Ah, how well the Saints understood the importance of these truths, and we can say that they occupied themselves with them entirely. We read in the history of the Church that a large number of Saints, penetrated with the nothingness of this world, and the greatness of the eternal truths, despised the world and forsook it, and shut themselves up in a convent, or in the wilderness, hiding themselves in the forest, so as to be better able to give themselves up to contemplation. And there, in dark and lonely caves, they occupied themselves, apart from the noise and tumult of the world, only with the practice of these irrevocable truths, penetrated by these great truths, with severity towards their bodies, which their love of God implanted in them. Prayer, fasting and scourging brought their bodies into a pitiable state. And so they passed their lives, which were only a long martyrdom. And when after twenty, thirty, forty or eighty years of penance, the end of their days came, they asked each other frightened and trembling: "Do you think, my friend, that God will have mercy upon our souls, and appease His wrath? That He will forgive us our sins? Do you think we shall find favor with this Judge, who will be without mercy?" Alas, who will be our advocate, to make the Judge more lenient? Ah, may we hope to partake of the happiness of the children of God! Yes, my brethren, we see that the holy penitents, who had the happiness of seeing what sin is, and how severely it will be punished by God in the next life, put no limit to their works of penance.

My dear brethren, St. John Climachus tells us that if the thought of eternity moved so many Saints to perform such extraordinary work of penance, what will our lot be, who are laden with sin, and not at all repentant? My God, how awful will be Thy justice to the poor sinners who have nothing to rely on! Ah, my friends, he continues, I have seen penitents in a place where no one could look at them or think of them without weeping. Everything there was so horrible that you could not see them without crying in sympathy. These exalted and holy penitents never saw fire or food; they lived on roots and hard bread, which they moistened with their tears.

Ah, my brethren, how do we find ourselves, compared to this? What would be our condition and our eternity if God expected as much from us? Ah, if we, not speaking of practicing these great works of penance, if we had at least the good fortune to abstain from sin, and to begin from today to love God, we might expect and hope for the same happiness. My God, how blind we are concerning our everlasting happiness? Ah, my brethren; tell me, had these great Saints whom we admire another Gospel to follow? Did they have another religion to practice? Had they another God to serve; another eternity to fear or to hope? No; certainly not, my brethren; but they had a faith which we have not, which, through the multitude of our sins, we have almost extinguished; but they worked zealously for the salvation of their soul, whilst we leave our poor soul without attention. But they meditated without ceasing upon the mighty and dreadful truths, the loss of God, the evil of sin, a happy or unhappy eternity, the uncertainty in regard to death, the awful abyss of the judgments of God, and the result, either a happy or an unhappy eternity, according as we have lived well or badly; whilst we on the contrary never think of these things. Only busy with earthly concerns, we leave God and heaven without thought. In a word, they lived as penitents and Saints, while we live in sin, and bound upon the pleasures of the world, without penance. O how great is the blindness of men! Who can ever understand it? To be put in the world, to love God and to save our soul, and then to live only to offend Him, and to make our soul miserable! What, my brethren, has been our life in reality up to this? And what have we been thinking about since we came to reason? To whom have we given our hearts? What have we done for God, who is our first and last aim? What zeal, and what ardor have we shown for the glory of God, and the salvation of our poor soul, which has cost Jesus Christ such bitter sufferings?

What have we got to offer him? What answer can we give to all His questions, when on the one hand He will hold up to us all the graces which He had lent us during our whole lives, and, on the other hand, the little use, or, rather the misuse, which we have made of it? Is it then possible that we who are in the possession of so many precious gifts, are still so lukewarm, so lazy, and so indolent in the service of God. Ah, my brethren, if some idolaters and heathens had received as many graces as we have, they would be great saints. If, my brethren, so many great sinners had been heaped with grace as we have, would they not, like the Ninivites, do penance in ashes, and chastise themselves? Let us remind ourselves, my brethren, of all that God has done for us since we came into this world. How many have died in your midst without having received holy Baptism? How many others, after having committed a single mortal sin, have been cut off by death and cast into hell? And from how many bodily dangers has the mercy of God spared us, while he preferred us to so many others, who in extraordinary ways lost their lives? How often has God, when we had the misfortune to sin grievously, pursued us with remorse of conscience, and good intentions? How many instructions, how many good examples were afforded us, to arouse us from our indifference for the salvation of our soul?

Tell me, dear brethren, what answer shall we be able to give to God for showing us such mercy if He asks us the amount of good fruit we have produced from it? Oh, what a disturbing thought, dear brethren, for a sinner, who misused everything and who did not know how to make use of anything. Listen, you ingrates, Jesus Christ will say to us. Were the practices of virtue which I recommended to you too hard? Were they not as easy for you as for many others? In what state do you appear before me? Did you not know that a day would come when I should be paid for all I had done for you? Very well, then, you wretch, give an account of everything that My mercy has done for you! Ah, my brethren, what answer shall we make, or rather what a disgrace for us! Let us, dear brethren, anticipate this by cooperating with the graces from now on, which the goodness of God still gives us today; I say today, because, perhaps, to-morrow perhaps God may forsake us, or we may be no longer in this world!

Yes, my brethren, He awaits us with open arms. He opens to us the wound of His divine Heart, to hide us therein from the severity of His

Father; He offers us all the merits of His death and Passion, in satisfaction for our sins. If our conversion is sincere, He takes it upon Himself to answer for us at the judgment seat of His Father, when we shall be called upon to give an account of our whole life.

Happy is he who follows the voice of His God who calls him! Happy is he, my brethren, who has never forgotten that his life is short, and that he may die at any moment, whom the thought never leaves that he is destined after this life for a happy or unhappy eternity, for heaven or for hell. O my God, if we would only think without intermission of our last end and aim, could we live in sin, could we forget the future, which once commenced will never end? Tell me, my brethren, do you believe in this eternity, you who have lived ten or perhaps twenty years in enmity with God? Do you believe in eternity, my brethren, you who enjoy other people's belongings? Ah, no; it is impossible; if you believed in it you could not live as you do. Tell me, O sinner, you who have concealed for so many years sins in confession and who have committed as many sacrileges, if you had the least spark of faith, would you not nearly succumb with horror at the thought of yourself, that you were not sure for one moment that you might be called upon to give an account of all your shameful deeds to a Judge who knows no mercy? Yes, my brethren, if we were only fortunate enough to ponder well what is before us after this life, which is so short, we should feel obliged to pass our lives in fear and trembling, working so as to accomplish the salvation of our souls. Happy is he, my brethren, who holds himself always in readiness! That is what I wish you all. Amen.

THIRD SUNDAY OF ADVENT

FEAR OF MAN

"Beatus qui non fuerit scandalizatus in me."
"And blessed is he that shall not be scandalized in me."
—St. Matt. xi. 6.

NOTHING, my brethren, is more glorious or more honorable for a Christian than to be allowed to bear the exalted name of a "child of God and brother of Jesus Christ." But nothing, either, is more despicable than to be ashamed to confess Him openly, that is, as often as the occasion presents itself. Where shall we find a meanness more culpable, and a perjury more presumptuous, than when anyone denies his creed, that he believes in Jesus Christ, after having, by the most sacred promises, pledged himself to follow in His footsteps, to give up his life if necessary for His cause and His honor; but who is so thoughtless that at the first opportunity he violates the promises which he made at the baptismal font? Ah, unhappy man, what are you doing! Who is He whom you deny? Ah, you will be faithless to your God, to your Redeemer, to become a slave of Satan, who deceives you and who will accomplish your ruin and your eternal misery! O cursed fear of man! how many souls dost thou cast into hell! But to show you how contemptible this is, I will point out to you: 1. How greatly fear of man offends God; that is to say, to be ashamed to do good. 2. How those who let themselves be moved by it betray a weak and narrow mind.

I.

My brethren, I will not speak of all those ungodly people who employ their time, their knowledge, and their miserable life, as far as in them lies, to destroy our holy religion. These unhappy people seem to live only to deny the merits of the death and passion of Jesus Christ. Some have employed their power and others their science to crumble away the rock on which Christ has built His church. But these fools are dashed to pieces on the rock of the church, which will live forever in spite of their attacks.

As a matter of fact, my brethren, how does the fury end of these persecutors of the church? Of a Nero, of a Maximin, of a Diocletian, and of so many others, who imagined that by force of arms they could exterminate it from the face of the earth? Just the contrary took place. The blood of the martyrs, says Tertullian, caused religion to bloom more beautifully than ever, and their blood seemed to be a seed which yielded a hundred for one. And in our own time, has the persecution of England for past centuries driven out the faith from Catholic Ireland? Has Luther succeeded in depriving the German Catholics of their faith? Windhorst, with his centrum party, has proven only a few years back what a bulwark the church was against the proud Bismarck, so that he had to go to Canossa and submit to the Holy Father. Unhappy man! what has this beautiful and holy religion done to you that you persecute it so, for she alone can give men happiness on earth? Ah! what tears and lamentations are there now in hell, where they see clearly that this religion, against which they raged, would have led them to heaven. But their repentance is useless because too late.

Look at those other impious men who work with all their strength to destroy our holy religion by their writings, a Voltaire, a Jean Jacques Rousseau, a Diderot, an Ingersoll, a Darwin, and so many others, who only lived to desseminate by their writings what the devil had instilled into them. Alas! they have worked a great deal of misery, they have ruined numberless souls and cast them into hell; but they could not destroy religion, as they believed—they were dashed to pieces on that rock. They did not crumble the rock away on which Christ had built His church and which must continue until the end of the world.

I will be silent, my brethren, about those other people, who, although they do not show themselves openly as enemies of religion, for they practice it a little outwardly, but from whose lips you hear now and then jeering remarks about the virtue and piety of those whom they have not the courage to imitate. Tell me, my friends, what has this religion done, which you received from your forefathers, who practiced it so faithfully before your eyes and who told you so often that it alone was capable of making men happy upon earth and that we should be unhappy if we forsook it? And whither, my friend, do you think that your half-hearted impiety will lead you? Alas, my friend, into hell, where you will have to bewail your infatuation.

I will be silent about those Christians in name only, who acquit themselves of their religious duties in such a miserable way that one could die of pity. Look at one of them at prayer—full of uneasiness, distracted, and without reverence. In church they have no devotion; divine service begins too soon for them and is over too late; the priest has not yet left the altar and they are already outside. It is no use to speak to them of the frequent receiving of the Sacraments; if they do go once in a while, they do so with such indifference that it is easy to see they do not know what they are doing. Everything which relates to the service of God is accomplished with most conspicuous dissatisfaction. O my God, how are souls lost for all eternity! O my God, how small is the number of those who will go to heaven, for there are so few who do what they ought to do to serve Thee.

But you will now say: Who are those who sin through fear of man? My brethren, listen to me for a moment and you shall learn. First I will say, with St. Bernard, that fear of man consists in this, that we are ashamed to fulfill our religious duties before the world. Yes, my brethren, to be afraid to do good for fear of being despised or ridiculed by some ungodly and ignorant men is a dreadful insult which we offer to the presence of God, before whom we find ourselves and who could indeed cast us into hell for it at any moment. What is the reason, my brethren, that these wicked Christians ridicule and jeer at your devotion? Ah, my brethren, the true reason is this—that they have not the courage to do what you do, and so you occasion them remorse of conscience; but you may be sure that in their hearts they do not despise you; on the contrary, they have a high opinion of you. If they want good advice or if they want to obtain a favor from God, then they run, not to those like themselves, but to those who, at least with words, they have mocked at. You are afraid to serve God, my friend, for fear of being made little of? But, my friend, consider who it was who died upon the cross! Ask Him if He was afraid of being despised and to die the most shameful death on this ignominious cross!

But why should we be afraid of the world? We know, of a certainty, that we shall be despised by the world if we please God. If you fear the world you cannot call yourself a Christian. You know that at the holy baptismal font, in the presence of Jesus Christ, you took a solemn oath that you would renounce the world and the devil, that you pledged yourself to follow Jesus Christ, who carried His cross laden with ignominy and contempt. If you are afraid of the world, very well; renounce your baptism and give yourself up to the world, whose displeasure you are so afraid of incurring.

But you will ask me, When are we guilty of fear of man? My friend, listen to me. One day you were at a table where meat was served on forbidden days, and you were asked to eat it, too; you were satisfied to drop your eyes and turn red, instead of saying, I am a Christian; my religion forbids me to eat it. You ate it with the rest, while you said to yourself, if I do not do as the others do they will make fun of me. Yes, indeed; and that would be too bad. Ah, you will make answer, I should cause more mischief if I was the occasion for all the bad jokes which would be made about religion than the wrong which I should commit by eating meat. Tell me, my friend, would you cause more mischief? If the martyrs had been afraid of all the blasphemies and oaths, then they would have been unfaithful to their religion. That is so much the worse for those who jeer at you for doing right. Ah, my brethren, let us say, rather, it is not enough that these other unfortunate men should, by their wicked lives, crucify Jesus Christ over again; you too, must be reckoned amongst them, so that Jesus Christ should suffer still more.

You do not know when you showed fear of man? At that time, when in company, when obscene words were dropped against the inviolable virtue of purity or against religion, and you had not the courage to find fault with anyone. You even perhaps, for fear that they might jeer at you, laughed with them. But you will tell me one is obliged to do this or one would be turned into ridicule all the time. You are afraid, my friend, of being laughed at? That was the kind of fear that moved St. Peter to deny his divine Master; but fear did not prevent him from committing a mortal sin, which he wept over his whole life long.

You do not know when you have shown fear of man? On that occasion when the thought came to you that it would do you good to go to confession, but you thought you would be laughed at and taken for a pietist. How often has this cursed fear of man prevented you from attending the instructions or the evening benediction? How often, when you were saying your prayers at home or reading a spiritual book, you have hidden it away as soon as you heard anyone coming? How often have you omitted your morning and evening prayers because you were with people who did not say any? And all that from fear that you might be laughed at.

Away with you, poor servants of the world, waiting for hell, into which you will be cast! There you will repent in vain the good which the world prevented you from doing. Ah, my God, what a sad life those lead who want to please the world and God! How you deceive yourself, my

THIRD SUNDAY OF ADVENT

friend. Apart from the fact that you will always lead an unhappy life, you will never attain your end—to please the world and God; it is just as impossible for you as to put an end to eternity. But in order not to discourage you I will advise you: give yourself either entirely to God or to the world; seek and follow only one Master, and when you have determined to do this, never more forsake Him. You remember the words of Jesus Christ in the Gospel: "You cannot serve God and Mammon." That is to say, you cannot follow the world and its pleasures and Jesus Christ with His cross.

It is true that fear of man does not prevent us altogether from performing good works. But of how many merits for good works does it rob us? How many persons go to church only out of fear of man, because they think that no one has confidence in them unless they now and then make an outward show of being religious; according to the maxim, where there is no religion there is no conscience! How many mothers only appear to take care of their children, so as to enjoy the esteem of the world! How many become reconciled to their enemies only because they are afraid to forfeit the good reputation which they enjoy! How many are careful in their speech and devout in church on account of the world! O cursed fear of man, how you spoil good works, which would take so many Christians to heaven, but instead of which it only casts them into hell!

But, you will tell me, it is very hard to keep our actions free from all worldly admixture. But, my brethren, we expect our reward for all this, not from the world, but from God alone; when I am praised by man I know certainly that I do not deserve it, because I am a sinner; when I am despised by man that is just as it should be for a sinner like I am, who has so often abused God by my sins; I deserve a great deal more. Besides, has not Jesus Christ told us, Blessed are those who are despised and persecuted? And again, who are they who revile you? Ah, poor sinners like yourself, who have not the courage to do what you do and who wish you would behave as they do so as to have a companion in shame.

But, you will tell me, one cannot help being affected by it! Do you know why they ridicule you? Because you are afraid of them and the slightest thing causes you to blush. They do not mock at your piety, but at your inconstancy and your indolence with which you follow your conscience. Consider the worldling, how courageously he follows his principle! Do they not glory in being abandoned, drunken, cunning and revengeful? Consider the shameless; are they afraid to spit out their filthy talk before the world? Why is this, my friends? Because they feel obliged to follow their master, the world; to think and strive to please him alone; in vain are they placed under hardships; nothing can deter them. Behold, my brethren, how it would be if you did this! You would neither fear the world nor the devil; you would only strive and wish for that which would please your Master, who is God Himself. Acknowledge that the worldling is more constant in making sacrifices to please his master, which is the world, than we are by the fulfillment of our duties to please our Master, who is God.

II.

Now we will consider this matter from another side. Tell me, my friend, why do you make fun of those who practice piety? Or, if you do not understand this exactly, of those who say more prayers than you do, who receive the Sacraments oftener than you do, and who flee the approbation of the world? For three reasons, my brethren: either you take these people for hypocrites, or you ridicule piety itself, or, finally, you are angry because they are better than you are.

First—To treat them as hypocrites you must have read their hearts and you must be thoroughly convinced that their devotion is false. Now then, my brethren, does it not appear natural that by observing the good works which others do, we should conclude that they proceed from a good and pure heart? Well, then, how absurd is your talk and your judgment! You see good behavior in your neighbor and from that you infer that his inner man is worthless. Here, we say, is good fruit; certainly the tree which bore it must be of a good kind; and we judge rightly. And when it is a question of judging men from the good they do, you say, on the contrary, there is good fruit, but the tree which bore it is worthless. Now, my brethren, you are not so blind and so unreasonable as to judge so foolishly.

Secondly—I say you make fun of piety itself. No, I am mistaken; you do not make fun of this person because he prays often and reverently; no, not on that account, because you pray yourself (at least, if you do not you neglect one of your first duties). Do you despise him because he receives the Sacraments more frequently? But formerly you went to Sacraments oftener; you were seen at the confessional and also at the altar rail. You do not find fault with these persons because they fulfill their religious duties better than you do; they are perfectly convinced of the danger in which we stand of being lost and therefore of the necessity of having frequent recourse to prayer and the Sacraments, so as to remain in the grace of God, because after this life there are no more means of salvation; we shall

THIRD SUNDAY OF ADVENT 55

be found there either good or bad for all eternity.

No, my brethren, it is not that which troubles us in the person of our neighbor, but because we have not the courage to imitate him we do not want to feel the shame of our negligence; we would much rather induce him to imitate our disorder and our indifference. How often do we not say, What is the use of these long faces? Why remain so long in church, and go there so early in the morning? etc. Ah, my brethren, the life of a person sincerely pious is a continual reproach to our lax, indifferent lives. It is very easy to understand that humility and modesty itself are a reproach to our haughty lives, which cannot bear anything, which would like everyone to praise us and to like us. There is no doubt that their meekness and kindness to everybody mar our violent passion and our anger; it is very true that their modesty and retirement condemn our worldly and scandal-giving life. Is it not this alone which makes us uneasy in our neighbor's person? And what makes us angry when we hear other persons spoken well of, whose good actions are thereby made known? Yes, without doubt, their devotion and their reverence in church condemns us and arouses distrust towards our utterly frivolous life and an indifference for the salvation of our soul. But if you want to learn something about the blindness of those who ridicule others, who fulfill their duties as Christians better than they do, then listen to me for a moment.

What would you say of a poor person who envied a rich one if that poor person was not wealthy simply because he did not want to be? Would you not say to him: My friend, why do you speak badly about this person—because he is rich? It is your own wish if you are not so rich, and even richer, than he is. In the same way, my brethren, why do we defame those who are more retiring than we are? It depends entirely upon ourselves to be just the same, or even more so, if we wish it. Those who are more godly than we are do not prevent us from being just as pious, or even more so, if we wish.

You see then, my brethren, that those whom you derided did not deserve it? You must never cease to thank God that there are some good souls to be found in your midst, to mitigate the anger of God, or we should be soon annihilated by the justice of God. But, all things considered, you cannot say that a person who says his prayers well, who tries to please God alone, is kind and obliging to a neighbor, who knows how to help him in his necessity, who forgives willingly when offended, that such a person behaves badly, but quite the contrary. Such a person is in reality worthy of praise and to be thought well of. Whilst you were slandering that person, you were not thinking of what you were doing. At any rate, you say to yourself, he is happier than I am. Wait a moment, my friend, and I will tell you what you ought to do: instead of insulting and making fun of him, you ought to try with all your strength to imitate him; you ought to join him every morning in prayer and in all his good works which he does through the day. But to do all that he does, one must do violence to one's self and make sacrifices. There is a great deal to be done.... Not so much as you think: is it so hard to say your morning and night prayers? Is it extraordinarily hard to listen to the word of God with reverence and to ask God for the graces which are so especially necessary for you? Is it so hard not to go out during the sermon? On the Sunday not to work? Not to eat meat on forbidden days, to despise infidels, who will certainly be lost?

If you are afraid that you will not have the courage, raise your eyes to the crucifix, on which Jesus Christ died, and you will see that you will not be wanting in courage. Look at the innumerable martyrs, who, out of fear for the salvation of their souls, endured so much. Are they sorry now, my brethren, that they despised the world and the maxim, "What will the world say?"

I conclude, my brethren, by saying how few persons there are who really serve God faithfully. There are some who do their utmost by force of arms to exterminate religion, as the pagan kings and emperors did; others try to make it despicable by their ungodly writings, and, if it were possible, to annihilate it; others deride it in the person of those who would like to practice it, and finally there are those who would like to practice it but are afraid of doing so before the world. Ah, my brethren, how small is the number of those who get to Heaven, for it only consists of those, who, without ceasing, and courageously fight the devil and his servants and who despise the world and its ridicule! As we, my brethren, await our reward and our happiness from God, why do we love the world, which we pledged ourselves to hate and to despise, to follow Jesus Christ alone, by carrying His cross all the days of our life? Happy is he, my brethren, who seeks God alone and despises all else. That is the happiness which I wish you all. Amen.

FOURTH SUNDAY OF ADVENT

"Facite ergo dignos fructus poenitentiae."
"Bring forth therefore fruits worthy of penance."
-Luke iii. 8.

HIS, my brethren, was the sermon which the holy Precursor of the Redeemer preached to all those who sought him in the wilderness, to learn what they should do to attain eternal life.

Bring forth, said he, real fruits of penance, that your sins may be forgiven you, that is to say, whoever has sinned, has no other remedy but penance, even for those who obtained forgiveness in the sacrament of penance, there is still a punishment due, which must be atoned for, either in this world, by suffering, and all the other tribulations of this life, or in the flames of purgatory. This, my brethren, is the difference between the Sacrament of Baptism, and that of Penance; in the Sacrament of Baptism, God forgives us without requiring anything from us; on the other hand in the Sacrament of Penance, God remits our sins, and gives us grace on the condition that we undergo a temporary punishment either in this life, or in the flames of purgatory; so that man shall be punished for his contempt and abuse of grace. When God wills that we should do penance, so that our sins may be forgiven us, He demands it only to preserve us from relapsing into sin, so that by remembering what we have had to endure for our sins which we have confessed, we shall not dare to return to them again. God desires that we unite our works of salvation with His, and that we contemplate how much He has suffered to make our works meritorious. Ah, my brethren, let us not deceive ourselves; without the Passion of Jesus Christ, all that we might have done would have been valueless to atone for the least of our sins. I will now show you, my brethren:

(1) That we are not exempt from the obligation of doing penance even when our sins are forgiven; (2) by what means we can satisfy divine justice; or to make my words clearer, I will show you in what satisfaction consists, which is the fourth condition which we must fulfil, to receive the

Sacrament of Penance worthily.

I.

You all know, my brethren, that the Sacrament of Penance is a Sacrament, which our Lord Jesus Christ instituted for the forgiveness of sins committed after Baptism. The distinguishing marks of this Sacrament, consist in this: that the Saviour of the world shows us the greatness of His mercy, for there is no sin which this Sacrament does not remit, no matter how numerous or how fearful they may be; so that every sinner is sure of forgiveness, and of being reinstated in the friendship of God, if he, on his part, makes the necessary preparation which this Sacrament demands. The first obligation is that we must know our sins, the number of them, and the circumstances which either aggravate them or change their nature; so as to attain this knowledge, we must pray to the Holy Ghost. He who in making his examination of conscience does not pray for enlightenment to the Holy Ghost, runs the chance of making a sacrilegious confession.[1] The second condition is to declare your sins distinctly as the catechism says, without exaggeration and without excuse, that is to say, as we know them ourselves; this accusation will only result as it should do, if we have beseeched God to give us the necessary grace; without which it is impossible for you to accuse yourself as you ought to, so as to obtain the forgiveness of your sins. You must then beg of God for this grace, and examine yourself before Him as often as you go to confession. The third condition, which this Sacrament demands, to obtain the forgiveness of your sins, is repentance, that is to say, sorrow for past sins, joined with a sincere intention of not committing them again, and a firm determination, to avoid everything, which might cause us to fall into the same sins again. This repentance comes from heaven, and is only produced by prayers and tears. Want of repentance has damned many men.

Many weep over their sins, but at heart they are not really contrite. We tell our sins as if we were relating an indifferent story, because we

---

[1] This view of the venerable Cure of Ars is in its general sense too strict and is not believed in by the moralists. The French editors remark that it would be more correct to say that a person who does not pray to the Holy Ghost for enlightenment is in danger of making a sacrilegious confession by weakness of memory, the cunning of the devil, the deceit of our passions, or by human respect, vanity or superficiality.

have not contrition, and we do not change our lives. We have the same sins, and the same faults, once a year, every six months, every month or three weeks, or probably every week, we are always going the same way; there is no change in our manner of living. Whence come all the evils, which cast so many souls into hell, if not from want of contrition? and how can we expect to obtain contrition if we do not pray to God for it, or in praying for it, to almost wish that we might not get it. If you do not notice any alteration in your way of living, that is to say, if after so many confessions and communions you are not better; then turn over a new leaf, so that you may not discover your misfortune when it is too late.

When by the grace of the Holy Ghost we have recognized our sins, and have properly confessed and repented of them, there still remains (so that these three things should have the desired result), a fourth requisite to be complied with, namely: that we make satisfaction to God and our neighbor. We must make satisfaction to God, for the offences we have committed against Him by sinning, and to our neighbor, for any injury we may have done him in soul or body.

In the first place, I want to impress upon you that God from the beginning of the world, when He forgave sin, still, on account of His justice, demanded a temporal satisfaction. His mercy forgives us; but His justice must be appeased by a penance which equals the sin committed; after having been forgiven, we must punish ourselves, by chastising our bodies which have sinned.

Look at Adam, who was assured by God Himself of the forgiveness of his sins, and who, notwithstanding, did penance for nine hundred years, and penance that would make one shudder. Consider David, to whom the Lord announced the forgiveness of his sins through the prophet Nathan, and who undertook such a severe penance that his feet would not support him any more; his sorrow for his sin was so profound that his palace resounded with lamentations and sobs. He said of himself, that he would descend into the grave weeping, that his contrition would not leave him until the end of his life; so copious were his tears that he said of himself, I will moisten my bread with my tears, and I will water my couch with my tears. Look at St. Peter; for one sin, which he committed, and which the Lord forgave him, he wept such plentiful tears during his whole life that his cheeks were hollowed out. What did St. Magdalene do after the death of the Redeemer? She buried herself in a wilderness, and wept and did penance for the rest of her life. And yet God had certainly forgiven her, for He said to the Pharisees, that many sins were forgiven her, because she had shown such an heroic act of charity.

But why do we go back so far, my brethren! Look at the penances which were imposed in the early ages of the church. If anyone called on the name of God in haste—alas, how often is that not the case, even with children, who hardly know their prayers—they were made to fast for seven days on bread and water. He who worked on Sunday, even for a short time, had to do penance for three days. If any one omitted to fast for one day during Lent, he had to fast for seven days. If anyone spoke slightingly of their Bishop or Pastor, or turned their instructions into ridicule, he had to do penance for forty days, and so on. Why all this? In order to appease the justice of God? All to satisfy the divine justice for our sins? How can we do this? You will find that there is nothing easier. The first is the penance imposed by our confessor, which constitutes a part of the Sacrament of Penance. The second is prayer; the third is fasting; the fourth is almsgiving, and the fifth is indulgences. These are the easiest, the most complete, and the most practical penitential works. Therefore, the penance, which the confessor gives us, before he absolves us, we must accept cheerfully and gratefully, and perform it as soon as we can, otherwise our confession or the sacrament is incomplete. If we think we might be unable to do it we ought to give the Priest our reasons humbly; if he is satisfied with them, he will change it. But there are penances which the Priest cannot change, and he dare not. Penances, which have for their aim the sinner's improvement; for example, forbidding the drunkard the saloon, the young girl the dance, or a young man going around with a person who is the occasion of sin for him; a restitution made for an injustice committed, or for some one who for a length of time has lived a negligent life, to go frequently to confession. It must be clear to us that the Priest cannot and must not change such penances. But when we have reasons for asking for our penance to be changed, at least we ought, unless it is quite impossible to do so, to ask the same Priest, because another confessor would not know the reason why the penance was imposed. You find your penances tiresome or hard, my brethren, but without cause. Compare them with the pains of hell, which you have deserved by your sins. O how joyfully would a poor lost soul perform the penance imposed upon you, and a much severer one until the end of the world, if at this price he could come to the end of his punishment.

II.

Now, my brethren, if we accept our penance with joy and with the firm intention of doing the same as well as possible, we liberate ourselves from hell, just as if God released the lost soul which we just mentioned.

I say that we must perform the penance imposed upon us by our confessor. To neglect this would be a sin. Tell me, my brethren, would it not be presumptuous to neglect to do our penance, and to expect the forgiveness of our sins? That is against sound reason; that would be to expect payment where no work was done. What, my brethren, are we to think of those who do not perform their penance? For my part I think this: If they have not received absolution they are of the number of those who do not want to be converted, for they shun the means which, in this case, we must employ; when they come again to confession, the Priest will have to withhold absolution. If the penitent has received absolution, and has neglected to perform his penance, he commits thereby a grievous sin, if he had mortal sins to confess. But I am speaking only of those who neglected their penance altogether, or left undone a considerable part of it, and not of those who, perhaps, forgot it, or were not able to do it at the appointed time. Further, I wish to state, that one must say their penance entirely, at the time appointed, and with devotion. I say: entirely. Nothing at all must be omitted of what has been given us to do; on the contrary, we ought to add more to the penance imposed on us by the Priest. St. Cyprian says, the penance must equal the fault; because the remedy must not be less than the evil. But, tell me, dear brethren, what kind of penances are laid upon you? Ah, a few Our Fathers, one or two Litanies, some almsgiving, slight mortifications. Tell me, does all this bear any comparison with our sins, which deserve torments that never end?

Yes, my brethren, we must punish and chastise that which has been the cause of our sin. This is the right means to employ to spare ourselves the punishments and chastisements of the next life. It costs us certainly a great deal to overcome ourselves; but we cannot escape from this, as long as we live, and God is satisfied with so little. If we wait until after death, then, my brethren, it will be too late, then all is over; nothing will remain to us but sorrow for not having done this. If we feel averse to do penance, let us, my brethren, raise our eyes to our amiable Redeemer. Let us contemplate what He has done, what He has endured to satisfy His heavenly Father for our sins. Let us take courage by the example of so many glorious martyrs, who delivered up their bodies joyfully to the torturers. Let us inspire ourselves, my brethren, with the thought of the devouring flames of hell, which the poor souls have to endure on account of their sins, which were, perhaps, less than ours. If it does cost you an effort to overcome yourself, you will, my brethren, receive the eternal reward which your penitential works have deserved.

We can make satisfaction to the justice of God by prayer, and also by offering up all our actions, by lifting up our heart to God from time to time during the day, and saying: My God, Thou knowest that I work for Thee; Thou hast condemned me to this, to make satisfaction to Thy justice for my sins. My God, have mercy on me, for I am a poor sinner who has so often revolted against Thee, my Redeemer and my God. I desire ardently, that all my thoughts, all my desires, all my actions shall have for their single object to please Thee. It is also pleasing to God, when we think of our last end, particularly of death, judgment, and hell, which is reserved as a dwelling place for sinners.

Thirdly, I say we can satisfy the justice of God by fasting. Now by the word fasting[2] is meant everything that is calculated to mortify the body or the soul; for instance, for the love of God to bear patiently contradictions, insults, contempt, wrongs, when we know that we have not deserved them; to give up a visit, for instance, a journey to see our parents, our friends, at home, and many other things of a like nature which would give us pleasure; kneeling longer than usual, so that our body which has sinned shall suffer for it.

I have said that we can satisfy the divine justice by giving alms. There are several kinds of almsgiving: some which have reference to the body; for instance, to give food to those who are starving; to clothe those who want clothing; to visit the sick, give them money, make their bed, keep them company, give them their medicine at the proper time; all that has reference to the body. But the almsgiving which regards the soul is of much greater value. But, you will ask, how can we give spiritual alms? That happens, when you undertake to console someone who is in trouble, or who has just suffered a loss; you console them by your words full of

---

[2] The blessed author takes the word "fasting" not in its strict, but in a more extended meaning.

In its strict meaning fasting consists of the taking of one daily meal to which may be added a little refreshment in accordance with the mild rulings of the Church.

In its wider and more extended sense it means, as the author says, "everything which mortifies body or soul."

kindness and charity, whilst you remind them of the great reward which God has promised to those who suffer for love of Him; and you call to their mind that the sufferings of this world last only a short time, whilst the reward is an everlasting one. We give spiritual alms when we instruct the ignorant, that is to say, those poor persons who would go astray if no one took pity on them. Alas, how many poor persons there are of this description, who do not know what is necessary for salvation; who do not know the fundamental principles of our holy religion; who, in spite of their sufferings and other good works, will be lost.

Mothers and fathers, teachers and housewives, in what does your duty consist? Do you know them even superficially? I hardly think so. If you know them ever so little, you would be careful to see that your children knew what was necessary for their religion, so as to escape eternal damnation. How you would use every means at your disposal to teach them all that your duties as parents oblige you! My God, how many children are lost on account of this ignorance! through the ignorance of their parents, who, perhaps, because they themselves are not in a condition to instruct them, do not confide their children to those who are able to do so, but let them live on in this way, and thereby lose their souls for all eternity.

Masters and mistresses, what kind of alms do you give to your employees, who, for one reason or another, know nothing of their Religion? My God, how many souls go to ruin for whom employers will be responsible at the last day! I pay him his wages, you say, it is his affair to see that he is properly instructed; I only employ him to work for me, he does not even earn what I give him. You are mistaken; God has not only confided this poor child to you, to help you in your work, but also that you may help him to save his soul. What! an employer, a housewife, can live on peacefully, whilst they see that their servants are in a condition whereby they may lose their souls? My God! the loss of a soul touches your heart so little? Alas, how often housewives witness that their servants do not say any prayers, either morning or evening, and yet you say nothing to them. But that is not necessary; so long as they do your work you are satisfied. O my God, what blindness! who can comprehend it? I say: that a master or mistress shall look after the spiritual welfare of their servants with as much care as they do after their children's. God will ask an accounting at your hands, the same as in respect of your children. You take the place of their father and mother. God will call you to account for them.

Fathers and mothers, masters and housekeepers, do not forget this spiritual almsgiving which you owe to your children, to your servants. Besides this, you owe them the alms of your good example, which shall serve them as a guide on the way to heaven.

These are, my brethren, as I think, the most appropriate means to satisfy the divine justice for our confessed and neglected sins. You can satisfy the justice of God by bearing with patience all the wearinesses which you are obliged to bear; for example, sicknesses, weaknesses, troubles, poverty, fatigues of work, cold, heat, accidents which happen to us, as well as death.

Behold in all this the goodness of God, who has lent us the grace to make all our actions meritorious and powerful to save us from the punishments of the next life.

Fourthly, we have said, indulgences are a very effective means of making satisfaction to the justice of God; that is to say, to save us from the pains of purgatory. Indulgences are formed for us from the superabundant merits of Jesus Christ, the Blessed Virgin, and the Saints; they are an inexhaustible treasure, from which God gives us the authority to draw. So as to make my meaning clearer to you, listen: it is as if you owed a rich man, who wanted to be paid, twenty or thirty dollars; you, however, have nothing; at least it would take a very long time before you could pay your debt. And then the rich man would make you this offer: "You have nothing to pay your debts with; take from my cash box all you want to pay what you owe." God acts exactly in this way with us. We are not able to make satisfaction to His justice, He opens to us the treasure of indulgences, from which we can take as much as we need, therewith to satisfy the justice of God. There are partial indulgences which remit only a part of our punishment, and not all of it, for example, that which one obtains when one says the Litany of the Holy Name of Jesus, by which we gain an indulgence of three hundred days; or when we say the Litany of the B. V. M., for which there is an indulgence of three hundred days, and so on. We can gain indulgences by saying the Hail Mary, the Angelus, by making Acts of Faith, Hope and Charity, by visiting the sick, or teaching the ignorant. And then there are the plenary indulgences, which remit all the punishment due to sin; after we have confessed a great number of sins there may remain, in consequence of the same, although the sins are remitted, an almost endless number of years to go through in purgatory; if, then, we gain entirely a plenary indulgence, we shall be as free from purgatory as a child who dies right after Baptism, or as a martyr who has just given up his life for God.

Indulgences of this sort can be gained by being a member of the League of the S. S. Heart of Jesus, every first Friday of the month, and on the feasts of the S. S. Heart and the Immaculate Conception, besides many other occasions on the usual conditions of confession and communion. O how easy it is, my brethren, for a Christian, if he makes use of the graces which God offers him, to escape the pains of the next life. But I must add, that to partake of such blessings we must be in the state of grace, confess, and receive Holy Communion and say the prayers prescribed by the Holy Father in church; only for the way of the cross is confession and communion not necessary. But we must always be free from mortal sin, have a great horror of all our venial sins, and a firm determination not to commit them any more. When you are in this disposition, you can gain them for yourself, or for the poor souls in purgatory. Nothing, my brethren, is easier than to make satisfaction to the divine justice of God, as we have so many means to attain this end, so that it will be the fault of our negligence if we have to go to purgatory.

After we have made satisfaction to God, we must make satisfaction to our neighbor for the wrong which we have done him, in soul and body. I say for the wrong that we have done to his body, that is to say to his person, by speaking of him in an abusive and contemptuous way, or by insulting him by our malicious actions. If we have had the misfortune to offend him by our abusive talk, we must ask his pardon, and become reconciled with him. If you have assailed the honor of your neighbor, for instance, by speaking ill of him you are obliged to speak of his good qualities, as you have spoken about his bad ones. If you have calumniated him, you must seek out all those persons in whose presence you have spoken falsely about him, and tell them that all you said about your neighbor was not true; that you are very sorry about it, and that you beg them not to believe it. If you have wronged him in regard to his soul, that is far more difficult to make good; however, you must do what you possibly can, or you will not obtain forgiveness from God.

You must examine your conscience carefully, whether you have not given your children or neighbors scandal. How many parents, masters, and housewives give scandal to their children and servants? How often are they not heard swearing, and perhaps even blaspheming? How often have you been seen working on Sundays? You must also examine, whether you have sung improper songs, or read bad books, or given bad advice; for example, by saying that somebody should take revenge, or abuse his neighbor. You must also examine whether you have not borrowed articles from your neighbor and neglected to return them; whether you have not forgotten to give an alms which was given to you for that purpose, or to make an offering for the repose of the souls of your parents. If you want to obtain the forgiveness of your sins you must not have in your possession anything belonging to your neighbor, which you must return and are able to do so; if you have injured his reputation, you must do everything which lies in your power to restore it again without blemish; you must be reconciled to your enemies, you must speak to them, as if they had only done you good their whole lives. You must only keep in your heart that charity which a good Christian must have for everybody. You must accept your penance with the firm intention of doing it as well as you possibly can, saying it with devotion and thanksgiving to God who is so good, and who is satisfied with so little; and striving to make the hardships of your state serve as a penance; we should gain all the indulgences that we can, so that after death we shall have had the happiness of having made satisfaction to God for our sins, and to our neighbor we shall have made satisfaction for the wrong we have done him, so that we may all appear with confidence before the judgment seat of God. May God grant us this blessing! Amen.

SUNDAY IN THE OCTAVE OF CHRISTMAS

"Peter, turning about, saw that disciple whom Jesus loved following, who also leaned on His breast at the supper"
John xxi. 20.

F THE TWELVE APOSTLES, Holy Writ calls the Apostle John "the disciple whom Jesus loved." To him is given the title of honor, "apostle of love and favorite disciple of the Lord." His father was Zebedee, and his mother was Salome, who were nearly related to the Blessed Virgin Mary. The Saviour called him whilst he was busy on the shores of Lake Genesareth, mending his fishing net. John no sooner recognized the call of his Lord than with his brother James "they immediately, leaving their nets, followed him" (Matt. iv. 22). As an apostle, John became worthy of the love of his Lord to such a degree that Jesus was transfigured before Him, with Peter and James, and he was allowed to lean upon His breast at the last supper. Our Saviour exhibited a special love for him, but he also loved his Lord and Master with the entire love of his virginal heart. On account of his great love for Jesus, St. John is a model for our imitation. As St. John loved the Saviour, so ought we, dear Christians, to love our divine Saviour. But if we ask in what the love of St. John for Jesus consisted, the answer is:

That the love of St. John for Jesus was:
I. A pure love,
II. A faithful love,
III. A fruitful, practical love.

We will take this threefold love of the holy Apostle as the subject for our consideration today; with the intention that we also may attain to a love like this for our divine Saviour.

I. The love of St. John for Jesus was pure love. When St. John was called to be an apostle, he was pure at heart and unblemished by the concupiscences of the world, he shone with virginal innocence and purity. Now he had, as an apostle, the great happiness of being able to remain in the immediate vicinity of the Saviour for three long years. His eyes beheld the Lord, his ears heard the words of the King of Virgins, and he went everywhere as disciple and friend with Him who was purity and virginity itself. Who can describe the happiness which St. John enjoyed in the company of his Lord and Master! He loved Jesus with the pure undivided love of his innocent heart, and he was loved in return by the Lord; indeed, of all the Apostles, he was the most beloved. The chief reason, however, why our Saviour loved him with such preference was on account of his purity. When pure, virginal souls associate with one another their innocence and purity is thereby increased. In what a high degree must not this have been the case with St. John, who for three years was permitted to associate with Jesus! He beheld in Jesus his God and his Saviour, the Beloved of his heart. The Saviour Himself acknowledged the tender love which John entertained for Him, for, in that solemn hour when He instituted the Most Holy Sacrament of the altar, He allowed him the privilege of taking the place of honor at His side, and of leaning upon His breast. Jesus acknowledged this pure love of St. John's when He confided to him, and to him only, His beloved Virgin Mother as a sacred bequest, in those words full of meaning: John, behold thy mother: woman, behold thy son. It is, indeed, my dear Christians, a great bequest, an exalted privilege, an especial mark of distinction for John. And this privilege only became his on account of the pure love which united him with the Saviour. This is why it fell to him alone to protect and console the Blessed Virgin Mary, the Mother of God; for this reason it was, that she, the Mother of God, became his mother, and he was her son. The pure and chaste disciple of love should take the Virgin Mother to himself, his chaste eyes should keep guard over her, his chaste ears should hear her wishes, his pure hands should serve the Queen of Virgins.

Dear brethren! In view of this pure love of the Apostle John towards Jesus, we must ask ourselves: In what does our love towards Jesus consist? Is it as pure and undefiled as that of St. John's? Or is our heart and our love divided? Do we love creatures more intimately than we do the Creator? God alone is the God of our hearts. He must then, also, be the only pure love of our hearts. And if we love a creature, we must love that creature for the love of God, and love our God and Saviour the most and above all things. Let us, then, so order our love that we may imitate St. John in his love for Jesus!

II. The love of St. John for Jesus was also a faithful love. He preserved his love in such a way that nothing, no danger, no fear could weaken it;

in fine, he remained the disciple of love of his Lord, in the cross and passion, as on Mount Thabor, so also in the garden of Olives, and on Mount Calvary. Sorrowfully, in his love and faith, he followed his beloved Master to the Mount of Olives; there he was a witness of His bloody sweat, there he saw Him betrayed by Judas Iscariot and taken prisoner, and loaded with chains. Most of the Apostles fled with fear and trembling; only Peter and he, the faithful disciple of love, remained and kept their Master company. And when even Peter began to waver, and denied the Saviour, St. John alone remained faithful and steadfast. He was never confounded in his Lord, he never forsook the Friend of his soul, his love was stronger than death. For this reason he accompanied Jesus on the way of His passion, and stood at last, as the faithful loving friend, under the cross of his well-beloved Master. Who can enter into his feelings and picture to himself what he suffered in his noble heart, when he heard his beloved Lord nailed to the cross, and saw Him hanging for three long hours wounded and in agony? He endured all this and abided it in faithful love. My dear Christians, contemplate St. John in his love of Jesus! That is real, true love, which no trial could weaken, which no fear could break. That is the real, true love of a friend, which is not confounded in the beloved friend, but remains devoted to Him even when He is calumniated, despised, reviled and persecuted. Dear brethren! are we devoted to our Lord and Saviour in faithful love? We are Christians, we are Catholics; can we, though, say in all the stations and circumstances of our life, with truth: Jesus, for Thee I live; Jesus, for Thee I die; Jesus, I am Thine, living or dead? Are we devoted to Jesus in faithful love, when suffering and trouble, trials and want, sickness and pain overtake us? And when it is a question of professing our holy faith, of announcing our Catholic convictions, even when we may thereby expect insult and ridicule, neglect, and even temporary disadvantage, did we stand by Jesus in faithful love, by His teachings, by His Holy Church, as St. John did? O, how many Christians do we find, unfortunately, who are wavering, even faithless, when it is a question of showing true love in the service of Jesus.

The love of the Holy Apostle John for Jesus was, finally, a fruitful, practical love. The sacred fire of divine love burned in his heart until his death, and his whole life was love and a manifestation and proof of love in the service of his Lord and Master. No sooner had the joyful news reached the Apostles that the Lord had risen from the grave, than he hastened with Peter to the grave, but John made greater haste than Peter, for he came sooner to the grave. The love of Jesus lent wings to his steps, he was burning with longing to convince himself that his beloved Master had risen.

After the Feast of Pentecost in Jerusalem, he began, like the other Apostles, to practice his apostolical teachings. Who could depict with what zeal St. John announced the joyful message of salvation, and how he sought to win souls to the holy faith; or with what heroic courage he endured ignominy and pain for the sake of Jesus? For Jesus and His holy Church and for the salvation of souls he was at all times untiringly active. It was Peter and John who were the first to be dragged before the council, and were scourged and imprisoned for having preached of the crucified and risen Saviour. They were forbidden to speak to the people about Jesus; he, however, answered with Peter in these heroic words: "We must obey God more than men." And he rejoiced to suffer ignominy for the name of Jesus. See, my dear Christians, how St. John proved his love of Jesus, by word and act; how fruitful and practical it was. In the second persecution of the Christians, under the Emperor Domitian, St. John, then an old man of eighty-five years, was dragged to Rome; he was chaffed, scoffed at and derided, cruelly scourged, and thrown into seething oil before the "Latin gate"; finally, he was banished by the Emperor to the island of Patmos. But he bore all this ill-treatment and suffering in steadfast faithfulness, he bore it all for love of his divine Master. How zealous St. John always was, and how active to inflame the souls of men with love for God, with love for Jesus Christ, the Son of God! He is the most zealous preacher in praise of divine love, and he wishes to fill all men with this love. "Let us love God," he cries out, "for He has first loved us," and "God is love; he who abides in love abides in God, and God in him. He who does not love, abides in death." When he was an old man of nearly a hundred years, and not able to walk any longer, nor to preach any more, he had himself carried to the assembly of the faithful and exerted all his strength, as the Apostle of the love of Jesus, to exhort the faithful thus: "My little children, love one another. For this is the commandment of the Lord; he who does this does enough." "O Saint, whose mouth was consecrated to the love of God only," says rightly a pious writer of St. John. "O precious heart, which was all love; O life, which only breathed love; O messenger of salvation, whose last words reminded us of the love of God and our neighbor!" May our love for God be fruitful, my dear Christians, by occupying itself with works of charity! Our love of God shows itself in an especial manner fruitful when we keep the commandments of God and the Church and when we fulfil faithfully the duties of our calling. For the Saviour says:

"He who has my commandments and keeps them, he it is who loves Me."

How perfect, my dear Christians, is the love which St. John exhibited and practiced towards Jesus, his divine Master. It is a pure love, it is a faithful love, it is a fruitful, practical love. And now certainly we understand why it is that Holy Scripture, in speaking of St. John, says with emphasis: "He is the disciple whom Jesus loved." Tell me, dear Christians, could the holy Apostle have greater praise lavished upon him than this, that Jesus loved him? O that this praise might be our portion, too! May our divine Saviour love us also! And this happiness, dear Christians, will be granted to us, if we, after the example of St. John, love Jesus with a pure, faithful and practical love; in short, if we keep the commandments of God. For the same holy Apostle says: "By this, do we know that we are children of God, if we love God, and keep his commandments." Amen!

THE EPIPHANY

CALLED TO THE FAITH

"We have seen His star in the East, and are come to adore Him."
Matt. ii. 2

THIS IS A BLESSED and memorable day for us, my dear brethren, on which the mercy of the Redeemer called us in the person of the Magi, from the darkness of unbelief, to the knowledge of the true faith. The Magi came at dawn of day to worship and to acknowledge the Messiah in our name, as their God and Redeemer. Yes, my brethren, they are our forefathers, and our models in the faith. Happy are we, if we imitate them faithfully, and follow in their footsteps. The holy Pope Leo calls out in an ecstasy of love and gratitude: "O angels of the heavenly city, lend me your glowing love, to thank Almighty God for being called to Christianity and eternal salvation." "Let us, my brethren," says this great saint, "celebrate joyfully the beginning of our blessed hopes. But let us be faithful to our calling, after the example of the Magi: otherwise we should have great cause to fear, that God might chastise us as He did the Jews, who were His chosen people. From the time of Abraham until His coming, He led them by the hand, and showed Himself everywhere their protector and liberator; and thereafter He rejected them, and thrust them from Him, because they despised His graces." Yes, my brethren, this precious gift of faith will be taken from us, and given to others, if we do not make a practical use of it. Now, my brethren, do we wish to keep this precious legacy in our midst? Let us follow faithfully in the footsteps of our fathers in the faith.

So as to obtain a feeble idea of the magnitude of the grace of our call to Christianity, we have only to consider what the coming of the Messiah was to our forefathers. He was their God, their Saviour, their Light, their Hope.

As soon as they became aware of the appearance of the star, they at once, without asking any questions, made preparations to seek out their Redeemer. So powerfully did they feel impelled, so ardent was their desire to arrive at the place towards which they were attracted by the star, and towards which grace called them, that they did not delay a moment. Ah, my brethren, how very far indeed are we from imitating them! For how many years has God been calling to us by His grace, by inspiring us with the thought of renouncing our sins, and of making our peace with Him? But we are still deaf and stiff-necked. Oh, when will that blessed day come, on which we shall do as the Wise men did, and leaving everything give ourselves to God?

Secondly, I say, my brethren, that their faithfulness to their calling was strong; they overcame every difficulty and hindrance which stood in their way, so as to follow the star. And what sacrifices they had to make! They had to leave their country, their palaces, their families and their kingdom, or in other words, they had to leave everything which was most dear to them in this world. To part from them, they underwent the fatigues of a long and troublesome journey, and all this of a very cold season of the year: everything seemed to stand in the way of their undertaking. How much ridicule did they not have to put up with from their equals, and even from the people? But no! Nothing daunts them from undertaking this important journey. You see here plainly, my brethren, that the merit of the true faith consists in this, that we sacrifice all that which we love best, to obey the voice of grace which calls to us. Ah, my brethren, if we were called upon to make the same sacrifices as the Wise men did, to win heaven, how small would be the number of the elect! But no, my brethren, if we only do as much for eternal as we do for temporal affairs, we shall be sure to gain heaven. Look at the miser, how he labors day and night to gain money, and to hoard it up. Look at him who is addicted to drink: he works hard the whole week, and then spends his earnings on Saturday night in the saloon. Look at those young people on pleasure bent! Distance is no object to them in the pursuit of pleasures which they find to their cost are mixed with much bitterness. Now, in all these things, you can see for yourself, many sacrifices are required; but nothing hinders them and they all reach their goal: some by deception, others by cunning.

But, my dear brethren, how do we act, when it is a question of our eternal salvation? Almost everything seems impracticable to us. We must admit, my dear brethren, that we are in a condition of lamentable blindness, because all our actions are performed for this miserable world, and we are not willing to undertake anything for our eternal salvation.

Thirdly, my brethren, let us consider what degree the persistence of the Wise men attained. On their arrival at Jerusalem, the star which had guided them on the journey, disappeared. They imagined without doubt that they had reached the place where our Saviour was born, and they thought that the whole of Jerusalem was beside itself with joy at the birth of its Redeemer. What astonishment, how surprised they were, my dear brethren. Jerusalem not only exhibits no signs of joy whatever, but it does not even know its Redeemer is born at all. The Jews are so surprised to see how the Wise men came to worship the Messiah, that the Wise men wondered why such an event was announced to them at all. How little hope these circumstances afforded their faith! Was it not rather calculated to deter them from their journey, and to cause them to return home secretly, for fear that they might become the laughing stock of all Jerusalem? Ah, my brethren, the greater number of us would have done this, if our faith had been so severely tried. It was not without a meaning that the star disappeared: it happened so that the Jews, who kept their eyes shut from such an event, might be called back to the faith; it was left to strangers to show them their blindness.

But all this only served to strengthen their resolution, instead of causing them to waver in it. Will the three holy kings allow themselves to be frightened after the brilliancy of that light has vanished? Will they, my brethren, give up? O no! We should; undoubtedly much less would dishearten us. They betake themselves elsewhere: they take refuge with the theologians, for they knew that the prophecies which designated the place and the time of the Messiah's birth were in the custody of these theologians. Fearlessly they enter Herod's palace, and ask him where the new-born king of the Jews is, and they explain to him without fear that they have come to adore Him. Although the king was offended at this speech, he was unable to prevent them from undertaking this significant journey; they wanted to find their God at any cost. What courage, my brethren, what steadfastness! O my brethren, how different is it with us, who are afraid of the least ridicule? The thought of "what will the world say" prevents us from fulfilling our religious duties, and from frequently receiving the Sacraments. How often have we not been ashamed to make the sign of the cross, before and after meals? How often has not the fear of men caused us to dispense with the days of fasting and abstinence, for fear of being observed, and taken for a good Christian? What a contrast, my brethren! O what confusion will be ours, if the Redeemer on the Day of Judgment compares our behavior with that of the Wise men, our forefathers in the faith, who would sooner forsake and sacrifice all things, than to resist the voice of grace, which called them.

Let us see how great was their constancy. The theologians told them the prophecies announced that the Messiah would be born in Bethlehem, and that the time had come. They no sooner received this answer, than they set out for that town. Might they not expect that it would happen to them, as it had happened to the Blessed Virgin and St. Joseph, namely, that the crowd of people would be so great that they would find no room? Could they possibly doubt but that the Jews who had waited four thousand years for the coming of the Messiah, would hasten in great multitudes to prostrate themselves before the crib and acknowledge Him as their Redeemer and their God? But no, my brethren; no one stirred; they were living in darkness, and they remained in it. A true picture of the sinner, who continually hears the voice of God, calling him by the voice of his shepherds, that he must renounce his sins, and be converted, instead of which he only plunges deeper into sin, and becomes more and more hardened.

But let us return to the three holy kings, my brethren. They set forth alone from Jerusalem. How prompt they are! O what faith! Will God let this go unrewarded? No, certainly not. Almost immediately on leaving the city, that same light, the wonderful star preceded them, and seemed to take them by the hand so as to conduct them to that poor dwelling place of poverty and want. It stood still as if to say: Here is He whose presence is sought by you.

Here is the expected One. Approach and behold Him. It is He who was conceived from eternity, and who is just born. He has taken a human body, which He will sacrifice, to save His people. Do not let the marks of poverty make you shrink back. He is bound in swaddling clothes; but He is that One who hurls the lightning from the heights of heaven. His look makes hell to tremble, because they behold in Him the avenger. These holy kings feel at this moment their hearts burning with love within them, they throw themselves at their Redeemer's feet, and moisten the straw with their tears. What a sight for kings to behold! An infant lying between two lowly animals, in a manger, and they acknowledge Him to be their God, and Redeemer. O what a precious thing is faith! Instead of being startled at the aspect of poverty, it touched and edified them. Their eyes never tired of gazing on the Redeemer of the world, the king of heaven and earth, the Lord of all things, in this condition. The astonishment which filled their hearts was so overpowering, that they gave to God all that they had, all that they could give Him. At this moment they consecrated themselves to God, for they no longer desired to be masters of their own person. Not contented with this gift, they offered Him their entire kingdom. According to Oriental custom, which presents gifts to great princes, they brought Jesus the richest products of their country, as an offering; namely, gold, frankincense and myrrh, and through these gifts they gave expression to their idea of the Redeemer by recognizing His Divinity, His boundless dominion, and His humanity. His divinity by the frankincense, which belongs to God alone; His humanity by the myrrh, which is used for the embalming of bodies; and His sovereignty by the gold, which was the ordinary tribute paid to a sovereign. But the feelings which filled their hearts were expressed far more by their offering: their glowing love was revealed by the gold, which is a symbol of love; their tender devotion was prefigured by the frankincense; the oblation which they gave to God of their mortified hearts was represented by the myrrh. How we must admire the virtuousness of these three Oriental kings, my brethren! God, who knew the state of their hearts, must have said, as He did say in the course of time, that He had not found such ardent faith in all Israel! In fact, the Jews had the Messiah in their midst, and they took no notice of Him; the Wise men, although far away, hastened to seek Him, and to acknowledge Him, as their God. The Jews treated Him afterwards as the greatest criminal that the earth had ever seen, and crucified Him at last, just at the time when He was giving irrefutable proofs of His divinity; whereas the Wise men, although they saw Him lying on straw, in the most poverty-stricken condition, prostrated themselves at His feet, worshipped Him, and acknowledged Him as their God and Redeemer. O, what a precious treasure is faith! If we were fortunate enough to appreciate this fact in the right way, what care should we not take to preserve it!

Whom shall we imitate, my brethren, the Jews, or the Wise men? What do we see in the greater number of Christians? Alas, a feeble and tepid faith; and how many are there who have not even the faith of the devil, who believes that there is a God, and who trembles in His presence! It is very easy to convince ourselves of this. See, my brethren, God dwells in our churches, where we talk, and look about us, where we do not perhaps even kneel down, when He shows us the highest degree of His love, namely, at Holy Communion, and at benediction. Do we believe that there is a God? O no, my brethren, or if we do believe it, it is only to offend Him. What use do we make, my brethren, of the precious gifts of our faith, and of the means of salvation which we find in the bosom of the Catholic Church? What connection is there between our manner of living and the sanctity of our religion? Can we say, my brethren, that our life corresponds with the precepts of the Gospel, with the example that Jesus Christ has given us? that is to say, do we love poverty, humiliations, and contempt? Do we prefer Christianity above all honors, and everything which this world possesses and desires? Do we entertain that respect, that longing, and that zeal to draw all the graces we can from the Sacraments, which our Lord so lavishly bestows upon us? Let us examine ourselves on this question, my brethren. Alas! how numerous and bitter are the reproaches which we must make to ourselves regarding these questions!

Ought we not, at the sight of so much unbelief and ingratitude to be seriously afraid, that Jesus Christ might take from us the precious gift of faith, as He did from the Jews, and plant it in another nation, where a better use will be made of it? Why did the Jews cease to be God's people? Was it not because they misused His graces? Take care, St. Paul exhorts us, that if you do not remain steadfast in the faith, you will be rejected and cast away like the Jews.

Imitate therefore the Wise men. If you hear the word of God, listen immediately; be strong in your faith in spite of difficulties, and never allow it to waver, but preserve it constantly; so that you, with the Wise men, will have the grace of beholding your God face to face in the hereafter—a blessing which I wish you all. Amen.

FIRST SUNDAY AFTER EPIPHANY

RELIGIOUS PICTURES IN THE HOME

"Did you not know that I must be about my Father's business?"
Luke ii. 49.

DID YOU not know that I must be about My Father's business? With these words Jesus wished to make Mary, His Mother, who had sought Him sorrowfully, understand that the place where he preferred to be was the house of God, the Temple. The heart of the Divine Saviour was full of tenderest love for the Temple of Jerusalem; with holy anger He was zealous for its dignity and sacredness, for one day He drove out of it those who bought and sold therein, and how He wept over the sad destiny which was to fall even upon the Temple by the descent of the Divine punishment over that stubborn and blinded Jerusalem, at the lamentable destruction of the city of David! We, also, beloved, must, after the example of our Saviour, be occupied with the things that are our Father's, and we must be filled with love for the house of God, which is the Church; it should be for us the place where we like best to pass our time; but as during the week the duties of our state and calling will hardly allow us time to spend an hour or two in Church, to pray there, and to seek for advice, consolation and strength, it ought to be the endeavor of every zealous Christian to make his home like a church, a temple of God, so that he may there be able to occupy himself with the things of his Father's. But how can we possibly make our home a Temple of God? I reply: The great means toward this end are religious pictures. The sermon of today will prove this to us.

Man, who is a creature composed of a body and a soul, requires perceptible objects to represent to him the unseen, or, in other words, he needs sacred pictures. From the visible our human thoughts rise up to the invisible; by that which is visible we are reminded of that which is invisible; by the natural of the supernatural. That is why, from the very earliest ages, Christians made pictures of the Divine Saviour, of the Mother of God, and of the angels; in some instances they even made pictures of the doctrines of faiths, such as the doctrine of the Blessed Sacrament. These visible pictures were the ladder on which their mind and heart ascended to the invisible God, and to the truths which He had revealed to them. After they had adorned their places of Divine worship with religious pictures of this kind, they did the same in their dwellings. To decorate the houses with religious pictures is a custom as old as Christianity itself, for the true Christian has always considered his home as nothing less than a Temple of God, and the religious picture as a means to extend and preserve the spirit of Christianity in the home.

In the sitting room, my dear Christians, the place of honor should be given to the crucifix. The cross is the sign through which the Catholic Christian, in an especial manner, professes his belief, and the crucifix in the parlor is a public profession of faith that those dwelling there are Catholics. For it is not enough that we believe in our innermost hearts; no, we must still more show our faith publicly, and we must never be ashamed of it before anyone. Our Divine Saviour says: "He who confesses Me before men, I will acknowledge him before my Father in Heaven, but he who denies Me before men, I will also deny him before My Father in Heaven." Let us, then, make a place of honor for the crucifix in our home, and confess freely and frankly before all the world our Catholic belief! Or ought we to be ashamed to hang the crucifix in our rooms,, and instead hide it away in some out-of-the-way corner? We decorate the walls with the pictures of celebrated persons, with the pictures of parents, children and relatives; indeed, in some places, there are even to be found pictures which are repulsive and altogether improper. But the picture of our God, of our Redeemer and Saviour, the sign of the Cross, to which we owe our salvation—ought a Christian to be ashamed to have these pictures in his rooms? No, anyone who would be afraid to publicly profess his faith in the Crucified One is not worthy of the name of Christian; such a family does not deserve the name of Catholic. I know of a certain place, dear Christians, where, in the midst of fields and meadows, there stands on an eminence a newly built dwelling- house, which almost resembles a lordly manor. On this spot there stood formerly an old house, over the threshold of which was fastened a large crucifix. When the parents of the present owner died, and he got married, he had the old building torn down, and built a new one. There were people who said to him: "You are surely not going to take that crucifix from the old house, and put it up over the door of the new house—it wouldn't look well at all."

What answer did the man make? "Under the sign of this crucifix my parents lived and worked, and God blessed them, for they became well-to-do, and I shall do just the same with my family. We shall live and work under the sign of the Cross, so that the blessing of God, which we enjoyed in the old house, may also fall upon the new one." And as a matter of fact the blessing of God has descended upon that house, in the most visible way, and remains with that family to this hour. And the blessing of God will flow down over every house where people live and work under the sign of the Cross. For all the members of the family know that when they look upon the crucifix in the right way it teaches them to pray to God, to have confidence in God in times of trouble; preserves them from haughtiness in times of good fortune; teaches them, not only to care for temporal things, but also for those which are eternal; and the family which understands this language of the Cross, and which orders its life according to the language of the Cross, such a family converts its house into a church and is blessed by God. As the crucifix in the parlor and the bedrooms leads the dwellers of the house to God, so in like manner do the pictures of the Saints teach them, in mute and yet eloquent language, encourage them, to do good and to avoid evil. Let us take, for instance, dear Christians, the picture of St. Joseph. Is it not an everpresent example and a constant motive for the father of the house, to be a father to his family, as St. Joseph was to his? Does it not recall to the father's mind his exalted dignity? Does it not admonish him of his responsibility for every member of the family confided to his care? Does it not make him zealous, like St. Joseph, to conscientiously care for the souls and bodies of those subject to him? And Mary's picture? What can the mother not learn from it? Was not Mary the best of all mothers who ever lived on earth, and should not every mother endeavor to imitate her? Does not Mary's picture tell the mother that her greatest blessings, her children, are a gift from God which she must therefore bring up for God and with Him? And in her many motherly sufferings, does not Mary's picture on the wall strengthen the mother's heart to bear her sufferings courageously, as a true Christian woman should? And the children, do they not find the most instructive models in the practice of a virtuous life, of obedience, innocence, piety, and the fear of God, and industry, in the pictures of Christ, of His Saints, which adorn the sitting and bedrooms? Cannot the mother give her children the best religious instruction, and the most practical education, by often telling them about the lives of those Saints, whose pictures hang around the rooms, and so lead them on to follow their example? Yes, truly, the pictures of Christ and His Saints, utilized in this way, convert the house into a Temple, into a Church, and God's blessing will rest on that house and on all those living in it.

Of course, religious pictures of themselves will not make a family good; only when they are contemplated and used in the manner which I have just described—then they are a practical help to true Christian sentiment, and to a true Christian way of living in the family. But if it should so happen that in the sitting and bedrooms, the pictures of Christ and His Saints on the walls are put to shame, and have to shut their eyes and ears, then certainly it would be far better to remove these pictures. We should then do as a certain landlord of an inn did once. One day several men were sitting in an inn, and they, as unfortunately is too often the case, used very doubtful and improper language. When the landlord of the inn heard their conversation, he went up to the wall and removed a crucifix which was hanging there, with these words: "Come away out of this, O Lord, for you cannot remain in such company!" And he carried the crucifix into another room. The men immediately stopped their improper conversation, and they knew that, for the future, if they wanted to use such language, they would have to patronize another inn. How often, dear Christians, we ought to remove the crucifix from our rooms, and say also: "Come away out of this, O Lord, for you cannot remain in such company!" But when the members of a household realize that they are living under the shadow of a crucifix, they will not offend against this sacred token by committing sin; then the crucifix will be a means to help them withstand sin and temptation, and their house will be a house of virtue, a house like a Temple of God.

Dearly beloved, in some parts of Europe the corner-shaft of a farm house is called "God's pillar." This is made out of the largest oak tree which the farmer can procure. Before this pillar is put in position, the master carpenter gives the command: "Hats off, and say three 'Our Fathers!'"

When the building is completed and the household things are arranged, they bring into the room where the (so-called) chief pillar stands, the crucifix and a small altar, with pictures of the Saints. That is why it is called "God's pillar." Here the members of the household, surrounded by pictures of a better world, are reminded that they are not only upon earth to work in the sweat of their brow, and then to die, but that they have an exalted destiny.

Dear Christians, let our house rest upon the pillar of God; let the mightiest and most powerful support of our house be the crucifix; let us give it the place of honor in our home! If the Cross is the profession of faith of the family, if the family are induced by it and the other religious pictures to prayer, to the conscientious fulfillment of their religious duties, to bring up their children in the right way and to be industrious; if, indeed, the family hang these religious pictures on the walls, not only as a decoration, but let these pictures appeal to their hearts, and follow their advice, then the house is really firmly built on God's pillar, it is God's Temple; then you can say of this family, in the words of our Saviour: "Where two or three are gathered together in My name, there am I in the midst of them!" Amen.

Rev. A. A.

SECOND SUNDAY AFTER EPIPHANY

THE GLORY AND THE POWER OF THE HOLY NAME

"He humbled Himself, becoming obedient unto death, even the death of the Cross. For which cause God also hath exalted Him, and hath given Him a name which is above all names."
Phil. ii. 8-9.

EARLY BELOVED in the Lord! On this Sunday we celebrate in an especial manner the festival in honor of the Holy Name of Jesus, that Name which is, for every Christian, the noblest and dearest, the holiest and the most consoling. By honoring and loving the Name of our Saviour, we show our respect and love for Him who bears this blessed Name. In this sense we honor and praise the names of the Saints whose memory will never die, but will always be honored by God and men; we think with joy of their exalted and heroic virtues, their living and steadfast faith, their self-sacrificing love for their neighbor, their untiring zeal to help their fellow men to that true happiness and salvation which comes from God alone—yes, truly the names of the Saints, and, above all, that of the Queen of Saints, and the names of all God's elect, are dear to us, and we pronounce them with reverence and love; indeed, it would be a sin not to do so.

But there is a Name which is above all other names, a Name which we must always pronounce with the greatest reverence, with the most blissful happiness and the tenderest love; and that is the Name of Jesus. And why do we all cherish in our hearts so profound a respect, such love and devotion for this Most Holy Name? First—On account of its glory and excellence, and then (second) because of its wonderful power and abundance of grace.

Let us make this the subject of our meditation in the Name of Jesus: "Who humbled Himself, becoming obedient unto death, even the death of the Cross. Wherefore God also hath exalted Him, and hath given Him a name which is above every name."

I.—Beloved in the Lord! No one is able to explain the great mystery revealed on earth by Christ, the Incarnate Son of God. According to the expression of St. Paul, the Apostle, in his letter to the Colossians, this mystery, which the Apostle says is Christ Himself, has been hidden from all eternity in God. When in the fulness of time it was revealed, it received a name which showed us distinctly, in the light of faith, the great and wonderful signification of the Incarnation of the Son of God and our redemption. God, the Eternal Father, wished to choose the name Himself which His well-beloved Son should bear upon earth, and He announced this name to the world by an angel from Heaven. For, commissioned by God, and sent by Him, the archangel Gabriel brought the message to the Blessed Virgin Mary: "Behold, thou wilt conceive in thy womb and bear a Son, and His name shall be called Jesus." And the angel said to Joseph: "Joseph, son of David, fear not to take unto thee Mary thy wife, for that which is conceived in her is of the Holy Ghost. And she shall bring forth a Son, and thou shalt call His name Jesus, for He shall save His people from their sins" (Matt. i. 20-21).

And, again, as we have heard on the Feast of the Circumcision of Our Lord: "And after eight days were accomplished that the Child should be circumcised His name was called Jesus, which was called by the angel before He was conceived in the womb" (Luke ii. 21).

The name of Jesus, therefore, was not given to our Saviour by man or angel, but by God Himself. This most holy Name was from all eternity hidden with the mystery of the Incarnation in the bosom, in the heart, of the Father, and descended at the same time with the fulfillment of this mystery from Heaven, so that we men might express in a worthy manner our respect and our gratitude for what the Son of God, in His human nature, out of His incomprehensible love for us, had done and suffered for our salvation. "Thou shalt call His name Jesus, for He shall save His people from their sins" (Matt. i. 21); but not only His chosen people, but all mankind, as the Apostle St. John says, so as to bring together all the dispersed children of God, to be made one here upon earth and one in Heaven. "Jesus Christ," says this same Apostle, "is the propitiation for our sins; and not for ours only, but also for those of the whole world" (I. John ii. 2). As St. Paul says, Christ Jesus is the only Mediator between God and man. The name of Jesus means, therefore, Saviour, Redeemer and Mediator, and reminds us of all that the Son of God accomplished here upon earth to redeem us and to make us eternally happy. It reminds us of His entire earthly life, from His birth, until His death, of all the steps that

He took, of the miracles that He worked, of all the sick that He cured, of all the dead that He raised to life, of the sinners whom He forgave, of the Sacraments which He left in His Church—in a word, of everything which the Incarnate Son of God did, and still does, not only to render us happy here upon earth, but also to make us happy and to bless us for all eternity. The name of Jesus is, therefore, for us the dearest and the most glorious name.

Our Saviour merited this name for Himself. It is the name of honor, which belongs to the Son of God, who died upon the Cross to save the fallen world. This name is the reward, the price of victory, which He received from His Heavenly Father; the praise and the renown which He will receive forevermore from the grateful Christian world. This is taught and proclaimed to us by the great Apostle of the people, in the most thrilling words, when he says of Christ: "He humbled Himself, becoming obedient unto death, even the death of the Cross. Wherefore God also hath exalted Him, and hath given Him a name which is above every name, that in the name of Jesus every knee should bow of those that are in heaven, on earth and under the earth; and that every tongue should confess that the Lord Jesus Christ is in the glory of God the Father."

And, behold, as it was said, so it has come to pass. The name of Jesus was placed over the head of the crucified Saviour on Golgotha; *Jesus Nazarenus, Rex Judaeorum* (Jesus of Nazareth, King of the Jews), but now it shines over heaven and earth, to the glory of God the Son. All the angels and saints in heaven pronounce this glorious Name with indescribable jubilation and rapture. All the faithful on earth praise the Name of their greatest Benefactor with the most profound reverence and intense gratitude. The suffering souls in purgatory sigh with ardent longings as often as they think of this Holy Name, and their desire is to praise and glorify this Holy Name with all the elect in heaven. Who amongst us would dare to utter this Most Holy Name with indifference or without circumspectness? No, O Jesus, how could we possibly be guilty of such an offense against Thee! With the most profound reverence, and ardent love, we will forevermore preserve Thy Glorious Name in our hearts, and give utterance to it with our tongues. And we will also call upon it with the most complete confidence.

II.—For this reason, beloved Christians, listen to a few words on the wonderful power of the Name of Jesus. In the first place, it is the Saviour Himself who assures us of the wonderful power of His divine Name, for

He says of those who believe in Him: "They shall cast out devils in My Name, they shall speak new tongues, they shall pick up snakes, and if they drink anything poisonous, it shall not harm them. They shall lay their hands upon the sick and heal them."

Of the power of His Name, Jesus says, further, that every prayer offered up in His Name shall be heard. "Verily, verily, I say unto you," He says to His Disciples, "if you ask the Father anything in My Name, He will grant your request. Hitherto you have not asked for anything in My Name, but pray, so that you may receive, that your joy may be perfect."

Holy Scripture and the traditions of our Holy Church teach us the innumerable times that the Lord has kept this His promise, and how powerful and full of blessing is His Holy Name.

Peter and John, in the early days of the Church, went up into the Temple to pray. A man who had been lame from his birth was sitting at the door of the Temple, which was called "the beautiful", and he begged an alms of the Apostles. Peter felt himself possessed of treasures which surpassed all the wealth of this earth, and, fortified by our Saviour's promises, he spoke to the lame man: "Look at us!" The latter did so, in the hope of receiving something from them. But Peter said to him, "I have neither gold nor silver, but what I have that I will give thee: In the Name of Jesus Christ, the Nazarene, arise and walk!" And the lame man jumped up and went with them into the Temple to praise God.

St. Paul had arrived at Philippi, the capital of Macedonia. He went through the streets of the city toward a house of prayer. On the way he was met by a servant girl, who was possessed by an evil spirit. The Holy Apostle took pity upon the unfortunate girl, and, confiding in the Lord's promises, said to the evil spirit: "I command thee, in the Name of Jesus Christ, depart out of her!" And the devil immediately departed out of her.

A goblet full of poison was handed to the Apostle St. John; he uttered the Name of Jesus over it, and the poison did not harm him.

Endowed with the power of the Holy Name, the Apostles went out to convert the world. Not only did they work numberless miracles, but, also, those who believed in their words performed miracles in the Name of Jesus. At the sound of this Divine Name, the temples of the pagans collapsed. Before it the spirits of darkness fled. Through this victorious Name the teachings of Jesus were disseminated over the face of the earth. In this Name the Church carries on her divine mission every day until the end of the world; in it she teaches, prays, blesses and consecrates. But, my dear Christians, each and every one of us can experience in ourselves the wonderful power and effects of this consoling Name. Yes, O Christian soul, if you call upon the Name of Jesus with devotion, you will most certainly obtain all things necessary for your salvation. This Most Blessed Name will give you advice in difficulties, courage in dangers, fortitude and strength in temptations, perseverance in good, consolation and joy, in trouble and suffering. When the Apostles of the Lord were scourged at Jerusalem, they rejoiced that they were accounted worthy to suffer ignominy for the Name of Jesus.

The more devoutly we reverence and call upon the Name of Jesus, the more will our Saviour show a tender and perceptible love toward us. "My Jesus," says St. Augustine, "so soon as I begin to utter Thy Name, I perceive an unearthly sweetness in my mouth, and an amazing change of heart." "The Name of Jesus," says St. Bernard, "is as honey in the mouth, a sweet sound in the ears, and a joy to the heart." How sweet and consoling is the Name of Jesus, in all the pains and sufferings of this changeable life, but it is sweetest of all at the hour of death. With the Name of Jesus on their lips, the Saints of God breathed forth their souls. Jesus was their last prayer, their last sigh. "Lord Jesus, receive my soul!" This is how St. Stephen prayed when they were stoning him to death, and so he died in the Lord. "Jesus, my love!" sighed the holy martyr Ignatius, Bishop of Antioch, as they led him to his death, to be torn asunder by the wild beasts. When they ordered him to deny the Name of Jesus, he replied, quietly and firmly: "I will never cease to utter His

Name. And if you could prevent me from pronouncing it with my mouth, you could not efface it from my heart." Confessing the Most Holy Name of Jesus, and whilst pronouncing the same most fervently, the holy Bishop died the glorious death of a martyr.

Grant to us, also, O Jesus, that Thy ever-blessed Name may be to us as long as we live, and especially at the hour of our death, our consolation and our hope, and in heaven our eternal joy and blessedness. Amen.

Rev. H. N., D.D.

THIRD SUNDAY AFTER EPIPHANY

THE HOLY FAMILY

BELOVED in the Lord! Our Holy Father stands on a watch-tower and looks down upon his children with enlightened eyes. He is aware of the melancholy fact that family life is in a disturbed and wavering condition. For this reason he draws our attention toward the Holy Family at Nazareth, and calls upon all the faithful of the entire world to join the Society of the Holy Family, which he has inaugurated. In plain words, we will now consider: the foundation of the family, what it is, and what it should be, the reason of its ruin, as well as the means of its restoration. May God bless my words at the intercession of the Mother of God and St. Joseph!

The family is the most ancient institution which God founded in Paradise, when He called the first pair of human beings into existence. The first blessing which God gave was for the well being of the family. With family life the history of the world commences. In the course of centuries many dynasties have been established and mighty kingdoms founded; they lasted for a short while, and have disappeared. An institution, however, which has not been destroyed by the many revolutions of time, is the family; generations come and go, but family life remains. It outlasts everything, until, finally, the whole of humanity will at the end of time be divided by God into two great families; God's family in heaven, and the devil's family in hell. As it was the commencement, so will family life be the end of the world's history. In the little word family there reposes happiness and peace for some, and likewise for the greater part of mankind, at the same time, however, also misery and curses, heaven and hell.

The family received from God a threefold mission: The care of the material life, the spiritual life and the supernatural life. We will today, in particular, consider closer the two last questions, because by the very fact of this great duty being neglected the ruin of the family must follow in consequence, bringing with it a miserable eternity for parents and children.

It is, of course from a natural standpoint, understood that when man is born into the world, he should receive all the bodily care possible which the state of life will allow. Protection and attention in health and sickness are indispensable to him. The benevolent, loving and inventive care of a family, how it beautifies and makes easy man's path through life! In his old age he longs for this family, and he would wish to close his eyes in its bosom.

But, with the material care alone, the problem of family life is not solved; man does not attain the goal by strength and height of body. He requires as a thinking being, provided by God with a free will, spiritual care also, instruction in that which is good, so that he can fulfill his mission and attain his object. He was created not only for this earth, but, also, for a higher everlasting life; he must find one day his bliss in God. For this reason it is, above all things, necessary that he should know the means that are indispensable for him to this end—and that is the knowledge of the commandments of God, or, in one word, Religion. But how is it in most families with this, the most important thing of all? God says: Strive first after justice, and all things else shall be given you. How seldom is this divine command observed? Prayers have been forgotten, and the church is only known from the outside. Ought we to be astonished if the peace of God has disappeared from the hearts of parents and children; if the hands, instead of being clasped in prayer, are lifted up for acts of violence; if blasphemous curses are uttered?

The foundation of many families takes place often in grievous sins. Therefore, I cry out to you, beloved Christians, that: Christ must come hack again into the family! The Holy Trinity cannot give its blessing to a modern marriage which is not contracted filled with the spirit of the Holy Family at Nazareth. People enter into matrimony without the necessary preparation. They neither take counsel with God nor the Church; they are occupied with the dowry, and arranging everything as well as they possibly can; for the Church, the hearts of the young couple can find no time. So long as there is a suitable maintenance, everything else is of minor importance. Whether their life partner is of the same religion as themselves, or whether he knows anything at all about religion, is a matter which does not interest them. They receive the Sacrament of Penance and the Holy Eucharist unworthily, and enter the married state with a threefold sacrilege upon their souls. They discover only too soon in their wedded life that, not true love, but passion; not happiness, but, instead, a material and spiritual misery, has come to stay with them.

Just look around in the homes of so many newly married couples. In the houses of the wealthy, what luxury; in the apartments of the middle class, what extravagance; even in the rooms of the poor, how many wants have been gratified of which our simple ancestors knew nothing! But we look in vain in most families for any signs of Christianity. The holy water font which formerly was to be found in every room is hardly ever seen nowadays. The pictures of Christ and His Blessed Mother have had to make way for worldly and indecent representations. We seek in vain for a crucifix. The literature corresponds with the prevailing spirit of the household. The Catholic press is entirely ignored; it is inconvenient to have the mind led to serious subjects, to be reminded of the transitoriness of all things earthly, and of the reward beyond. Ungodly novels and magazines, dulling to the souls, inimical to religion, and newspapers which stupefy our moral sense, are the mental food. Do not tell me that these are only exterior signs; they affect the heart. At any rate, by considering these things, we learn to know the prevailing spirit of the household. Where are the morning and night prayers, which formerly were said in common by every family? Or, where this is not possible, do the children ever see their parents kneel down to say their prayers? How do they keep Sundays and Holy days?

To all this I hear the simple answer: We have not time for all this, but the good will is not wanting. In reply to this I must draw attention to the crowded liquor saloons, theaters, and places of amusement; it does not look as if people had neither time nor money.

O dear Christians! You enter the married state without God, and you desire to remain in that state without Him. What is the result? These days of pleasure are followed too soon by days which are for the married couple hell upon earth. Those who will be married at any cost, will find themselves fearfully disappointed in the end. Those who seek money and pleasures by marrying, will very soon find out that though the money lasts, their hearts do not agree. Those who are dazzled by exterior perfections, will by daily interactions discover so many faults and weaknesses in their ideal, that all the perfections combined will be thrust into the background. In a word: those who enter the married state without God, will very soon find God's curse upon them, and they will consider themselves mutually deceived. As a matter of fact they have both been deceived by their passions.

And what is the consequence? Complaints, contradictions, coldness, indifference, perhaps curses and maledictions, from the same lips which formerly only spoke of love, this is their daily bread, and the bitter tears of repentance and sorrow which fall on the ruins of their conjugal happiness, is their daily portion. We are moved to compassion for these unfortunate creatures, who gave their all to the false, deceitful world, and had nothing left for God. We should, however, do them an injustice if we held them alone accountable for the origin of these lamentable conditions. The parents are accessory to their children's misery; they did not set them a good example, or bring them up for God. They seldom or ever discussed religious subjects with their children, but on the contrary excited in them a worldly spirit, helped them in their pursuit of pleasure, told them that wealth affords a life of ease, but that poverty brings unhappiness. They perceive, when too late, what a grievous mistake they have made. They looked forward to gratitude in their old age, but find only ingratitude; indeed, they live too long for their children. What a shame it is, when children become engaged, and the parents do not even know whether the prospective son or daughter-in-law is a Catholic or not. Fathers and mothers, if you wish to be contented and happy, and see your children happy, Christ must come back into your family again!

The reason why our times are so irreligious is on account of the unchristian families. Where the wrong was, there must be the remedy. All the authority of Church and state is useless if the family does not cooperate. Children are often great philosophers, they ask innumerable questions and seek for information. How sad it is when they are neglected spiritually, when they become ungodly, for want of their parents' good example and a religious training.

What must be done to preserve the Christian family from ruin and to raise up the ungodly, and reform the unhappy family life?

If we wish to see any improvement in the state community or family the family must in common with the Church educate the children in Christianity. It is true that the hope of a better future is founded on a good obedient youth. The home, therefore, must be in accord with the Church, that all harmful influences must be withheld from the souls of the children. Where there is true piety in the household, purity of morals reigns supreme, and every agreeable virtue finds a home therein. I turn to you, dear parents, and implore you: To imitate the Holy Family of Nazareth!

Christian fathers and mothers, if you wish to have pious, good children, you must first of all yourselves be God-fearing and lead good lives. As the tree, so will the fruit be, says an old proverb, and the divine word verifies this. A good tree brings forth good fruit, a bad tree fruit like itself. We know that now and then, even in good Christian families, there are to be found degenerate sons or daughters, but the rule is as our Saviour says in the above words.

What are the means to renew the family life in the spirit of Christ and the Church? I answer: Keep the commandments of God, and follow the infallible teaching which God has placed in that haven of salvation, the Holy Catholic Church, so that you may walk in the right path which leads to the inheritance of the Saints. If you wish, Christian married people, to imitate St. Joseph and the Blessed Mother of God, you must sanctify yourselves; you must practise the virtues which shine out to us from the life of this most holy couple. Matrimony is a great sacrament, as St. Paul says, but only in Christ and His Holy Church. Husbands, love your wives, as Christ loves His Church; wives, be subject to your husbands, in love and obedience, and care for one another; bear with patience your imperfections—it is not always possible to overcome them of our own strength. Do not forget daily prayer, keep holy the Sundays and Holy days, and receive frequently, being well prepared, the Sacraments. Show by your course of life, by your example, that you are thoroughly penetrated with Christianity and that you make a practical use of it daily. When it is possible, say in common the morning and night prayers, and grace before and after meals. Tell the children about God and His saints. During the holy time of Lent, speak to them of their suffering Saviour, during Paschal time of His glorious resurrection, during Christmas time of His birth. You will see what a profound impression it will make on the minds of your children.

O what a happiness to grow up in the bosom of a truly Christian family! It requires care, a great deal of care conscientiously to fulfill the obligations of a father or mother. The parents are a mirror to their children; and the children constantly look into this mirror. Be careful therefore that only the good, and what is worthy of imitation is perceptible in you and graven upon your hearts. What a consolation it is for you if you can say: I am the father, the mother of a pious child, pleasing to God and man. Watch particularly over your children when they have grown up. Do not allow them to associate with irreligious persons. Be sure to employ Christian servants, for many a child has been eternally lost, on account of bad servants. How many hearts have been poisoned in their youths by obscene writings. Do not permit anything of the kind to be brought into your house. Bring up your children simply, withhold all luxury from them, discourage a too great desire of pleasures, and let them learn only that which is good, useful, and practical. See to it, that in their childhood, as well as when they are older, they frequent the Sacraments regularly.

Christ must come back into the family!
Christ must remain in the family!

Let this be your motto. Then, with the help of God, a devout, chaste generation will spring up to the joy of the parents and of the church. When the time comes for your children to make their choice for life, the divine blessing will descend upon them, and with unpolluted hearts they can join hands for life. Such good, well brought up children, will at last be the support and consolation of your old age.

Christian husband! imitate St. Joseph by beginning your day's work with God, and ending it for Him. Cherish those belonging to you as the holy foster father did Jesus, and be their faithful protector. Christian wife! follow in the footsteps of the ideal of all womanhood, the Blessed Mother of God; in joy and sorrow she will be your advocate at the throne of her Son. And you, dear children, be as pious as the twelve-year-old Jesus, and like Him be subject and obedient to your parents, as the Saviour was to His parents for thirty long years. Help your parents in their labors as the Redeemer helped his foster father.

We will all make our hearts like unto the Heart of Jesus.

Let us often say the ejaculatory prayer: "Jesus, Mary! Joseph! enlighten us, help us, save us!"

Christ must come back into the family! Then God will make you partakers of His blessing, then will true happiness reign amongst you! (Let us say today and every day the act of consecration to the Holy Family. With this we will conclude our instruction today.) I will pray for you that God may bless my words, at the intercession of St. Joseph and the Blessed Mother of God. Amen!

Rev. A. M, O.S.F.

SEPTUAGESIMA SUNDAY

ON ENVY

"Is thy eye evil, because I am good?"
Matt. xx. 15.

WHY DID the laborers murmur, who were sent first into the vineyard, that their fellow laborers who were set to work later than they received the same pay as they did? They had no right to ask for more than their day's wages which they had agreed upon with the lord of the vineyard, and which they received. Did they suffer any wrong, because the others were paid as much as they were? Would they have received more if the others had been paid less? Why then did they murmur at the Master, and show their indignation at His action? You may guess the reason, dear brethren, and reply that it was because they were envious. If they had not been possessed by envy, they would have praised the Master as a kind and generous Lord, and congratulated their fortunate fellow laborers.

What a hateful and abominable thing envy is!

Every one who has not lost all feelings of morality considers envy as a most disgraceful vice, and yet this vice is not as rare as people think. There is no end to envy in the world. Even amongst ourselves, envy is not a stranger. Indeed, there is not a man upon earth who has not to be upon his guard to close his heart to the vice of envy, to keep down every emotion of envy within him. For this reason I wish to warn you today against envy, to show you, (1) how disgraceful and (2) how injurious envy is.

If we recognize how bad and pernicious a vice is, then we shall detest and avoid it.

I. It is not a very difficult task to show the hideousness of envy. We have only to explain what envy is, to make its disgracefulness understood. What is envy? None other than a certain sadness and trouble, a vexation and displeasure at the happiness and success of our fellow men, and a certain joy and satisfaction, pleasure and elation at the unhappiness and misfortune of others. To envy our neighbor, means to grudge him his good fortune, and to wish him evil. In the Orient there is said to be a bird which stays in its nest sad and troubled when the weather is fine and the sun shines, but when it is stormy it flies gaily and joyfully about This extraordinary bird is an image of envy. It resembles exactly those envious persons who in the same manner are sad when the sun of good fortune is shining on their fellow men, but on the contrary are joyful and delighted when the storm of misfortune breaks over them. Is anything further necessary to prove the hideousness of envy? Is it not a shame to be vexed at the well-being of our neighbor, at which we ought to be glad, and to feel pleased when misfortune overtakes our neighbor, when we should be sorry? Every vice is disgraceful; but none of them carry their disgrace so publicly on their forehead as the vice of envy. Other vices have even a pretext with which at least they can be apparently explained; but where will you find an excuse of envy?

The impure person may say he has been violently tempted, sensuality made him blind, the dangerous occasion caused him to fall; the thief may say that want and hunger misled him; the revengeful person may say that he was overcome by anger; but the envious person, what excuse can he or will he make? None; nothing but his disgraceful malice. Envy is pure malice, a true child of hell. Yes, envy is the devil's sin. If there are envious men, it is a sad proof that the devil has gained influence, power, and dominion over men, otherwise there would be no envy amongst them. When man came from the hand of God, he knew not what envy was. It is natural for man to rejoice with the joyful, and to be sad with the sorrowful. In the heart of man, as it was formed by God, there is to be found pity and charity, a brotherly interest in the weal or woe of his fellow creatures. If there are men who betray their human nature, and who rejoice at those things which cause good men to grieve, it is evident that these men are under the devil's influence, whose concern it is to pervert what God has ordained, and to ruin that which God has made.

I will even venture to say that the envious man is more malicious and behaves more disgracefully than the envious devil. Why is this? The envious man vents his poison on his own kind, and the devil does not do that. The devil burns with envy toward man. Human happiness distresses him, human misery delights him, but the other devils do not excite his envy. Yet men envy one another; envious men rage against their own flesh. Is not every man our brother, and does not our enemy belong as we do to the same family of God? How can the happiness of a brother vex a brother, or the unhappiness of the one be the delight of the other? I will show you envy from another point of view, from which it will appear no less disgraceful. Envy not only consists in a diabolical malice toward our fellow men, but it is also a heinous crime against God. To envy our neighbor's happiness means to murmur at the dispensations of Providence and at God's government of the world. The envious laborers in the vineyard, of whom the gospel speaks, murmured at the father of the family, and in like manner do all envious persons. Even if they do not grumble in just so many words, envy is practically a complaint against God. The envious person grudges his neighbor the good fortune that befalls him. But is it not God who has granted it to him? It is a subject of vexation to the envious that his neighbor's undertaking has succeeded, that his business is prosperous, that a joyful event has taken place. But does not every good gift come from God, who is the success of every enterprise, allows business to prosper, and brings about that joyful event? Envy therefore, is a censure, a disapprobation of divine Providence. The eye of the envious one is evil, because God is good. According to this reasoning, God ought not to rule the world according to the decrees of His love and justice, but in accordance with the diabolical wishes of the envious, dispense His gifts and His chastisements. How malicious, and what a crime envy is! This vice, however, is not only shameful, but also injurious, not only malicious but also ruinous, as we shall discover in the second part.

The destructiveness of envy is even easier to demonstrate and to recognize than its baseness.

It is not without reason that we find envy amongst the seven deadly sins. It is the source of innumerable other sins. The evil is boundless which has its origin and root in envy. Envy is in reality the origin of every sin, because on account of the devil's envy sin came into the world. Holy Writ, the history of mankind, and daily experience prove that there is no vice which creates more evil, or produces more harm than envy.

What was the cause of the first murder that was committed? Did not the wicked Cain slay his brother Abel out of envy? Did not Jacob's sons sin against their brother Joseph out of envy? Was it not envy that caused the enraged Saul to hurl his spear at David? Was it not envy which caused Daniel's enemies to cast that great prophet into the lions' den? Did not the Pharisees and the elders conspire to put to death the Son of God; did they not crucify the divine Saviour from envy? How many crimes have occurred in the history of the world, all of which had their source in envy!

Envy has occasioned divisions in the Church, produced heresies, originated wars, armed brother against brother, laid countries waste, pillaged cities, separated families, and brought them to ruin. Envy knows no bounds. It regards neither the bonds of friendship nor of blood. It incites the child against his father, as in the case of Absalom; brother against brother, like Cain; friend against friend, as with Saul; it causes men to forget the greatest benefaction, and to hate the kindest of benefactors, as was the case with the Pharisees toward our divine Saviour. Envy occasions a great host of sins; ingratitude toward God, even blasphemy; hatred and enmity toward mankind, very often a deadly hatred, an irreconcilable enmity; calumny, defamation of character, tale-bearing, desire of revenge, and of persecution: all these are the daughters of envy, verily a hellish crew, worthy of their hellish progenitor. It is hardly necessary to have recourse to Holy Scripture, or to history, to prove the disastrous effects of envy. It suffices to draw your attention to daily experience, and to your immediate surroundings, where the havoc worked by envy is everywhere apparent. Ought not the evil fruits of envy to be a motive for us to strive to banish this devilish vice from our hearts? So as to encourage you still more in this resolution, I will show you, in conclusion, how injurious this vice of envy is for the envious man himself. Envy certainly causes a great deal of misery in the world, but it produces the greatest havoc in that man who fosters it, and who is controlled by it. No vice punishes itself so severely as envy does. For this reason the holy fathers called envy a just vice, not because it was just in itself, but because it is itself its own punishment; by its own torture it chastises itself, and in a way exercises justice upon itself. As the worm eats the wood, to which it owes its existence, so envy gnaws at the heart of the man who admits it. And when it has taken up its abode in our hearts, it soon shows itself in our outward bearing, for it takes the glow of health from the cheek of the envious, and reveals its presence in our interior, by sickly pale cheeks and hollow eyes. Envy gnaws at the heart as the rust does at the iron, it enfeebles the body like a lingering fever, tortures the soul, destroys the peace of our mind, and fills man with dejection and sadness, and banishes all peace and gladness from the soul.

"Soundness of heart is the life of the flesh; but envy is the rottenness of the bones" (Prov. xiv., 30). "Envy and anger shorten a man's days" (Ecclus. xxx. 26). The way in which envy is generally portrayed is very appropriate. It is represented as an old woman, bearing in her hands snakes and torches, with long sharp finger nails, pale of countenance and emaciated in body. Envy is represented as a woman, because it is a vice of a weak, unmanly, effeminate spirit; as an old woman, because it is as ancient as the world itself; with snakes and torches in the hands, because it stings and exudes poison like the snake, and kindles the torch of hatred and discord everywhere; with long sharp nails, because it preys upon itself and others; with a pale countenance and emaciated body, because it pines away through constant vexation and ill-humor; and finally the woman eats up her own heart, because envious persons shorten their lives and hasten themselves to an early death. "Envy and anger shorten a man's days" (Ecclus. xxx. 26). Besides the torture which the envious prepare for themselves in this life, a still greater one awaits them in eternity. Perhaps you believe that the envious may be saved? St. Paul names envy amongst those works of the flesh which close the kingdom of heaven to us (Gal. v. 21). Let us not be surprised at this. Eternal blessedness is the reward of love, the hope and portion of those who love God and man. The envious person, however, loves neither God nor man. If he would work miracles, says St. John Chrysostom, or even if he preserved his chastity, or fasted, slept on the ground, and resembled the angels in their virtues, so long as he was polluted with envy, he would remain a lost man. It is utterly impossible for us to escape that fire which is prepared for the spirit of malice, if we do not liberate ourselves from this passion.

Spare yourselves, therefore, the torments of the envious in this world, and their chastisement in the next. Banish from your heart this shameful and destructive vice. Let charity reign amongst you, and do not envy one another any more. Rejoice with the joyful, and mourn with the sorrowful. Take a sincere interest in the weal or woe of your fellow man. Grant to every one the good which belongs to him, even to your enemy; and do not refuse your sympathy to any unfortunate person, not even to your enemy. And thus you will fulfill the law of the Lord: "Thou shalt love thy neighbor as thyself" (Mark xii. 31). Let us beseech God to preserve us from the vice of envy, and to fill our hearts with His holy love. Amen.

SEXAGESIMA SUNDAY

THE WORD OF GOD

"Blessed are they who hear the word of God, and keep it."
Luke xi. 28.

MY DEAR BRETHREN, we read in the gospel that the Redeemer of the world said such wonderful and astonishing things in His sermons to the people, that a woman in the multitude raised her voice and cried out, "Blessed is the womb that bore thee, and the paps that gave thee suck;" but Jesus Christ answered immediately, "Yea rather, blessed are they who hear the word of God, and keep it." Perhaps it seems to you, my brethren, that Jesus Christ teaches us that he who hears the word of God with the earnest wish to profit by it, is more pleasing to God than he who receives Him in Holy Communion. Yes, without doubt, my brethren, we have never really understood what a precious gift the word of God is. Ah, my brethren, if we rightly understood it, with what reverence and love should we not listen to it! Let us not deceive ourselves. The word of God must of necessity bear within us either good or bad fruit. The fruit will be good if we are well prepared to receive it, namely, by a real desire to profit by it and to do everything that it prescribes. It will be bad if we hear it with indifference, or perhaps with distaste and disesteem. This sacred word will enlighten us and show us how to fulfil our duties, or it will blind us and make us stiff-necked. So as to prove this more clearly to you, I will show you how great is the word of God.

So as to impress upon you the exalted worth of the word of God, I will specify that the entire extension and progress of the Catholic religion is the work of the word, joined with grace which is always with it. Yes, my brethren, we can even say that, excepting the death of Christ on Mount Calvary, and Baptism, our holy religion gives us nothing that can be compared to the word. How many persons are there not in heaven who never received the Sacrament of Penance? How many others who have never received the Blessed Sacrament? How many there are in heaven who neither received Confirmation nor Extreme Unction? As far as instruction in the word of God is concerned, it is as hard for us, when we have arrived at the age when instruction is necessary for us, to get to heaven without instruction, as it is without Baptism. We shall find out at the day of judgment that the greater number of Christians who are lost were damned because they did not know their own religion.

Let us ask the souls of the lost Christians why they are in hell. They will all avow that the cause of their damnation was either that they would not hear the word of God or that they despised it. But, you may ask, what effect has the sacred word upon us? I say that it resembles that pillar of fire which guided the Jews when they were in the desert, which stood still when the people should stand still, and moved on when they were to move on, so that the people had only to follow it faithfully, to be sure of not taking the wrong road on their way. Yes, my brethren, it does the same in regard to us. It is a bright torch, which enlightens us, and guides us in all our thoughts, undertakings, and actions. It enlightens our faith, fortifies our hope, inflames our love of God and our neighbor. It describes to us the majesty of God, the blessed end for which we were created, the goodness of God, His love for us, the value of our soul, the sublime reward which is promised to us. At the same time, it depicts for us the gravity of sin, the sorrow which it occasions God, the misery into which it will plunge us in the next life. It brings us face to face with the judgment which threatens sinners, and we shudder at the awful picture which it conjures up. Yes, my brethren, this word determines us to believe all the most mysterious truths of our holy religion, without indulging in subtile inquiries, for it confirms our faith.

Tell me, are we not all of the same opinion, that after a sermon our hearts are touched and full of good resolutions, while those who despise the word of God reject and despise all those means of salvation which God has given us? Tell me, my brethren, of what did the patriarchs and the prophets, Jesus Christ Himself and His apostles, as well as all their holy followers, avail themselves to strengthen and spread our holy religion, if it was not the word of God? For instance, what did Jonas do when the Lord sent him to Nineve? None other but announce the word of God, by telling them that within forty days the place would be destroyed! Was it not this sacred word which changed the hearts of the inhabitants of this large city, who, from being great sinners, became great penitents? What did St. John the Baptist do to make the Messiah, the Redeemer of the world, known? Did he not preach the word of God? What did Jesus Christ Himself do when He passed through the cities and places where He was always surrounded by a crowd of people, who followed Him as far as the desert—what other means did He make use of but this sacred word, to instruct the people in that religion which He was going to found? Tell me, my brethren, what made all the great ones of this world forsake their possessions, their parents, and all their comforts? Was it not because they had heard the word of God, which opened the eyes of their soul, and showed them the short duration and the perishableness of all created things, and persuaded them to acquire eternal goods, as, for example, a St. Anthony, a St. Francis, a St. Ignatius?

Tell me, who can make children understand to honor their father and their mother, and to consider them, indeed, the representatives of Almighty God? The instruction which they receive in Sunday-school from those who have charge of their soul, whereby the great reward which they may expect if they are good, obedient children is impressed upon them. What kind of children are those who despise their parents? Alas, my brethren, how many wicked, ignorant children are there not, who, in consequence of their ignorance, are unchaste and disorderly, and who often bring their parents with sorrow to the grave! What causes a neighbor to be kind to his neighbor, if it is not the instruction which he heard where it was made clear to him how pleasing to God is the love of our neighbor? Or, at another time, when he heard the terrible condition of the sinner described who falls into the hands of the living God? Listen for a moment, and I will give you a proof of this, which will convince you.

It is related that a French army officer happened to be stationed in a place where a mission was being held by a certain Father Bridaine. Curious to hear the priest who had such a great reputation and whom he did not know, he entered the church, where Father Bridaine was just depicting in awful colors the state of a soul steeped in sin, the blindness of the sinner who remains in his sins, and pointing out how easy it was to give up a sinful life by means of a general confession. The soldier was so touched at this, his remorse of conscience was so great, or, rather, it was so unbearable, that he made the resolution at that moment to make a general confession. He waited for the missionary at the steps of the pulpit, and told him that he desired to confess the sins of his whole life. Father Bridaine treated him with the greatest kindness. "Father," said the officer, "I will do all that you will tell me to do. I have the greatest desire to save my soul." He made his confession with the greatest piety and contrition which could be expected of a converted sinner. He admitted, indeed, that it seemed to him as if a heavy burden was taken off his conscience each time he accused himself of a sin. His confession ended, he left Father Bridaine, and wept tears of bitter repentance. The people were astonished to see this soldier shedding so many tears, and they asked him the cause of his trouble. "Ah, my friends, how sweet it is for me to shed tears of love and gratitude, I who have lived so long at enmity with God! Oh, how blind is man who does not love God and who lives at enmity with Him, while God loves him so tenderly!" The soldier sought Father Bridaine in the Sacristy, and declared, in the presence of the other missionaries, that he had never in his whole life experienced such unalloyed happiness as he did at that moment when he was in the state of grace: "My Fathers, I do not think that my sovereign, whom I have served for thirty-six years, can be as happy as I am. I do not believe, in spite of all the pleasures which surround his throne, that he can enjoy the contentment that I do after having laid down the dreadful burden of my sins by repentance, and having made the firm resolution to do penance for them. I would not exchange my happiness for all the wealth and the pleasures of this world." With these words he pressed Father Bridaine's hand, and begged him to pray to God for him that he might have the grace to be a true penitent all his life long.

Now, my brethren, what was the cause of this soldier's conversion? None other than the word of God, which he understood, and which found his heart docile to the call of grace. Ah, how many Christians would be converted if they were so happy as to listen to the word of God with a good intention! What good thoughts and good resolutions would be awakened in their hearts! How many good works for heaven would be accomplished!

He who is not moved by the word of God is lost, unless a miracle should happen, which very seldom does. O my God! who could believe that any one could display such indifference at the thought of such endless misery! Meanwhile, before we proceed any further, we will examine into the condition of most of this congregation. You know that sin reigns in your hearts; and you know that, so long as this sin reigns there, you can expect nothing else but an eternity of misery. O my God, this thought alone should frighten us almost to death! Ah, God saw beforehand how few would profit by this word of life, when He spoke the following parable in the gospel:

" The sower went out to sow his seed. And as he sowed some fell by the wayside, and it was trodden down, and the fowls of the air devoured it. And some fell upon a rock, and withered away. And some fell among thorns, and the thorns choked it. And finally, some fell upon good ground, and yielded fruit a hundred fold."

You see, my brethren, that Jesus Christ shows us that, of all the people who hear the word of God, only a fourth part derive profit from it. It would be a good thing if, among every four persons, there should be one to profit by it. Oh, that the number of good Christians was greater than it is! The apostles were astonished at this parable, and they asked Him to explain it to them. Jesus Christ then explained it to them:

The heart of man is like unto a field, which brings forth fruit according as it is either well or badly cultivated. The seed, Jesus Christ said to them, is the word of God. It falls by the wayside, when those that hear it do not change their lives, or make the sacrifices which God asks of them, so that they might become good and pleasing to Him. They will not forsake the company or the places where they have so often offended God; others, again, are restrained by a false fear of man, which causes them to waver in all the good resolutions which they formed when they heard the word of God. The seed which fell among thorns are those who hear the word of God with joy; but it produces no good results in them: they hear it gladly, but they are not willing to do what it commands. The seed which fell upon the rock are those who have a hard and stubborn heart, who hear the word of God to find fault with it and to abuse it. Finally, the seed which falls on good ground are those who ardently desire to hear it, and who embrace every opportunity which God gives them to profit by it as much as possible, and only in these hearts does it yield abundant fruit. And these fruits are: To retrench their worldly life, and to practise all those virtues which a Christian should so as to please God and to save their soul. You see from the words of Jesus Christ how few persons there are who derive any benefit from the word of God, as, among four parts, only one part yielded fruit.

Now, my brethren, you wish to be that fourth part. Listen, then, with great desire to the word of God; put aside all sin, the world with its pleasures, your inordinate desires and passions; form good solid resolutions, and put them in practice at the first and every opportunity offered afterward, and rest assured you will bear fruit a hundred fold. Amen.

QUINQUAGESIMA SUNDAY

THE ENEMIES OF OUR SALVATION

"And behold a great tempest arose in the sea, so that the boat was covered with waves."
Matt. viii. 24.

THIS IS the picture of the life of the Christian upon earth. Our soul, subject to thousands of passions, and exposed to thousands of temptations, is, indeed, like unto a little ship, covered by the waters, and never for one moment safe from shipwreck. Who, then, my brethren, would rest contented in view of the dangers which expose us to eternal damnation? Who among us, my brethren, would not feel the necessity of watching unceasingly over every emotion of his heart, that is to say, over all his thoughts, his words, and his actions, and to make sure whether they are bent toward pleasing God or pleasing the world? But a great many of us seek in all their doings only to please the world. And what is the consequence, my brethren? Nothing else but that the devil can as easily lead us into hell as a mother can lead a young child wherever she wills. Yes, a Christian who wishes to please God and to save his soul meets with two things which are liable to perplex him: First, the great number of enemies which surround him, and the eagerness with which they bring about his ruin; and, secondly, the carelessness and contentedness with which we live on among these many dangers, and to which we are continually exposed. Now, to teach you how to watch and pray, I will show you what enemies we should fear and avoid most.

Our real enemies are not those who damage our good reputation, who rob us of our earthly possessions, or who even try to take our lives. These are only tools which Divine Providence uses to sanctify us, by giving us the opportunity to practise humility, meekness, charity, and patience. If the salvation of our soul is dear to our heart, we shall, instead of hating and complaining about those who caused us these troubles, love them the more. Naturally, it is hard for a Christian whose heart is set upon earthly goods to be deprived of his possessions. An ambitious man must naturally feel sensitive at seeing his good name attacked. Without doubt, it must be terrible for a man, who always lived as if death would never be his portion, to feel its approach. And yet, my brethren, all these are not real enemies. On the contrary, they will be the cause of our reaching heaven, if we accept them in a Christian spirit. If you, now, want to know which are the enemies we ought to fear, I will explain them to you, and I ask your undivided attention.

Our real enemies, my brethren, are those who make it their object to rob our poor soul of its innocence, to deprive it of grace, to kill it in the sight of God, and to cast it into hell. Oh! how terrible and frightful are such enemies. And as dangerous as they are, just so numerously we find them about us. Yea, we carry them within ourselves; and this fact should impel us to be constantly upon our guard, as death alone can entirely free us from them. And it is these invisible enemies which we have to fear the most.

Let us contemplate, at first, that foolish self-esteem which pervades most of us. How proud we are of our little merits, our possessions, talents, and our family, and how ready we are to look down upon others! How anxious we are to equal our superiors in the stations of life, and to leave that station to which we really belong! And how often do we pride ourselves that our work is better than that of anybody else! Observe, then, my brethren, this invisible enemy, who persecutes you unceasingly and causes your wrongdoing.

How proud we are when we have a little more than our neighbor, can dress a little better than he! How ready we are to boast of these little worldly advantages! If a poor man addresses us in the street begging for alms, we pass proudly by him, not even giving him the recognition of a denial. We treat him as if he was an entirely different being to ourselves. Do you see, then, my brethren, how filled we are with pride? And, again, how sensitive we are of the way in which we are treated by our neighbors! A word misunderstood, a slight joke at our expense, a cold greeting—how all that offends us, and how bitterly we complain of these little unpleasantnesses, and how we hate those people who have inflicted them upon us! O my Lord! what pride! What self-love! Look at this man who has come into possession of a fortune. How high he holds his head, and how eagerly he tries for recognition from those who would have no communication with him before, and how ready he is to drop all his friends of former days! Remember how sad you are and full of trouble, if your neighbor prospers in his business more than you do in your own, if he gains an advantage which you have missed; but if, on the contrary, trouble comes to him, and he is hemmed in by embarrassments, how delighted you feel and glad in your hearts! Do you see, my brethren, how you are persecuted by this spirit of selfesteem and envy?

We do not like to meet a person who has, perhaps without any intention of doing so, offended us. We like to believe ill of her, and like to hear other persons speak ill of her. We feel a great satisfaction when an occasion offers to anger her. Observe, then, my dear Christians, this feeling of hatred, this desire for vengeance, this bitterness which prevails among us and devours us!

Do you wish to know, my brethren, how deeply we are attached to this life and the goods of this world? Is not our mind filled day and night with temporal affairs, occupations, and business transactions? Are you not always busy thinking how to make money, and is not your conversation taken up entirely by that one subject? Do you not continue these thoughts of your worldly affairs in your prayers, and do you not even bring them into the house of God during the holy sacrifice of the Mass? How often have you not thought during Mass over matters which you had to accomplish afterward, about people whom you were going to see on business affairs! How willing you are to travel miles for the purpose of gaining a few dollars, and yet how unwilling to walk a few steps for the purpose of doing good to your neighbor or attending to your religious duties! It is necessary to mention here the habit of most people to inquire curiously into the affairs of their neighbors and to criticize them, to meddle in other people's affairs. Do you recognize, in this, my dear friends, that secret enemy, who causes discord among neighbors and brings unhappiness into families?

Do you know, then, my brethren, why we know so little of these secret enemies? For the simple reason that we shut our eyes and ears, so as not to see them or hear of them. To learn to know them thoroughly, you have only to look into your own hearts. There is their hiding-place, and of a great number of them, too. I have mentioned to you only a few of the most conspicuous; but the more you examine your heart, the more of these secret enemies you will find. Our poor heart is like the great ocean, which contains a multitude of fishes of all kinds and sizes. In a like manner, our heart contains a multitude of evil inclinations, some stronger than others, which are all liable to cause our ruin, if we do not suppress them with great care. These are the enemies that live within us. It is impossible for us to get away from them. Our only salvation is in fighting them.

Having told you of our interior enemies, it now remains to speak to you of our exterior enemies. Pay attention, that you may learn to know, and, with God's grace, to conquer them. Let us, first, state that these exterior enemies go hand in hand with our interior inclinations. Yes, my brethren, everything has been created by God for the use and service of man, and will tend to his salvation or ruin, according to what use he makes of them. Look at this poor man, who on account of his poverty should be sure of getting into heaven. But what does he do? He grumbles, complains, and envies the rich, speaks ill of them, and calls them cruel and tyrannical. The sufferings and mortifications which God sends him as so many blessings, goad him on to despair. On the other hand, look at the rich and the well-to-do. Instead of being thankful to God for the abundance which He has given them, and making proper use of it by helping the poor in their spiritual and temporal wants, what do they do? Their riches make them proud and haughty, and cause them to live in entire oblivion of the necessities of their soul. Thus we meet enemies in every station of life that must be subdued by fierce combat. Here our ears have to listen to calumnies: there our eyes meet with bad examples. No matter whether we are awake or asleep, drink or eat, we are surrounded with the snares of the devil, and must ever be ready to fight temptations, even by the most innocent amusements, or in company with the most virtuous persons; yes, even during the most sacred functions and during our prayers. What distractions and what pride! How often do we not think ourselves better than our neighbors! What excuses do we not make, when we confess our sins, so as to appear less guilty than we really are! How often do we not go to some strange priest to confession, so as not to have to be too much ashamed of ourselves! Ah! and what sacrileges at Communions! What regard for, and fear of, the opinion of our neighbor! O my brethren! these are a few of the snares in our path of life, and there are many others. The devil, who is bound to cause our ruin, is constantly about us, and ever ready to catch us in his net. Yes, my brethren, he makes use of everything to lead us into sin.

Now, my dear friends, you know some of the enemies of our salvation. Judge for yourselves whether they are to be dreaded; but judge rather more by the misery they have caused you, and the bad condition in which they have so often left you. Let the years of your life pass through your mind, and convince yourselves that, since the early days of your youth, you have been the victim, the slave, and the unfortunate plaything of the devil, the world, and your own passions. O my brethren! who could count all the evil thoughts which the devil instills into man's mind? Be convinced, then, that he who works really and truly for the salvation of his soul, will soon recognize the truth of what St. John says: "For all that is in the world, is the concupiscence of the flesh, and the concupiscence of the eyes, and the pride of life." We carry the seed of vice within us, and every one of us may be tempted and seduced by his own evil inclinations; everything about us may give us cause for sin. If we would fully understand the dangers to which we are constantly exposed, we would live in constant fear of ruin. Yes, my brethren, in all we see and hear, in everything we do and say, we are ever drawn toward evil. When we are at our meals, we are tempted by gluttony and intemperance. At the time of recreation, we are tempted by frivolity and vain speech. When we work, we do so mostly from avarice, profit-seeking, envy, or even vanity. When we pray, we have to beware of carelessness, distraction, disinclination, and wearisomeness. If we meet with suffering or affliction, we are only too ready to grumble and complain. Praise makes us proud. Fault-finding makes us angry. It was all this which made our greatest saints tremble, and populated the desert with hermits, caused copious tears, innumerable prayers, and penances. Of course, the saints, though they lived in the wilderness, did not remain free from temptations, although they were free from the many bad examples which surround us constantly and are the ruin of so many souls. But we see, my brethren, that they were ever watchful and prayed fervently, while we poor deluded mortals live cheerfully and carelessly in the midst of so many dangers for the salvation of our soul. O my brethren! who will escape all these dangers? Who will be saved? Brethren, I say that nobody could live who would keep all these dangers constantly before his eyes. He would die of fear. But what should give us strength and consolation is the thought that we may have recourse to our dear Father in heaven, who will never allow us to be tempted beyond our strength, and who will always help those to victory who come to Him with confidence and prayer. Watch and pray, therefore, and you will conquer. Amen.

FIRST SUNDAY OF LENT

TEMPTATIONS

"Then Jesus was led by the Spirit into the desert, to be tempted by the devil."
St. Matt. iv. 1.

DEARLY BELOVED BRETHREN, we must not be surprised that Jesus chose the desert as the place where He went to pray, for He loved solitude; nor ought we to be surprised that He was led there by the Holy Ghost, for the Son of God could have none but the Holy Ghost as His guide. But that He was tempted by the devil, and taken about on several occasions by the spirit of darkness, we would not dare to believe, if Jesus Himself had not told us so through the mouth of St. Matthew.

Yes, my brethren, instead of being surprised at these facts, we ought to rejoice over them, and be extremely grateful for them to our Saviour, who only wished to be subjected to these temptations so as to show us how to gain victory over them. How fortunate we are, my brethren! Since the Saviour, in His tender love for us, allowed Himself to be tempted, all we need do to gain victory is to desire to be victorious. That is the great advantage which we can gain from the temptations of the Son of God. What, then, is the subject of my discourse today? It is this: That temptation is necessary for us, because it teaches us to know ourselves.

I said that it is necessary for us to be subjected to temptation, for the reason that we must learn to know that in our own selves we are nothing. St. Augustine tells us that we ought to be thankful to God just as much for His protecting us in temptations as for His pardoning our various transgressions. If we have frequently the misfortune to be caught in the snares of the devil, we must look for the cause of this misfortune in the fact, that we rely too much on our own principles and ideas, and too little on our dear Lord. This is only too true. So long as nothing goes against us, so long as all our wishes are fulfilled, so long we are inclined to believe that nothing could cause us to fall; but we forget our own nothingness and our miserable weakness; we make the most fervent promises, and say that we would rather die than fall into temptation. An excellent example of this fact is furnished us by St. Peter, who said to our Lord: "Though all men shall be scandalized in Thee, I shall never be scandalized." To show how insignificant a being man is when he relies upon himself alone, the Lord did not use as a medium a king or prince, but merely the voice of a servant-maid. One moment St. Peter was willing to give his life for the Lord, and the next he denied all knowledge of Him; yea, was even willing to swear to it.

O my Lord, what are we not capable of when left to ourselves! There are people who, according to what they say, seem to envy the saints, who took such heavy penances upon themselves. These same people think that it would be easy to do as much as these saints. When they read the life of a martyr, they say that they would be willing to suffer as much for the honor and glory of our dear Lord. What is the suffering of a moment, they say, in view of the eternal reward!

Now, what does God do to bring us to a knowledge of ourselves, to make us conscious of our unworthiness? He allows the devil to approach us. Look at that Christian, who envied those saints who were living on roots and herbs, and who made the heroic resolution to chastise his body with the same hardships; but, lo! a slight headache, the prick of a needle, causes him to break out in loud lamentations. Here he was ready to undergo all the penances the anchorites inflicted upon themselves, and there he is in despair over a little mishap. Look at that other one, who wishes to appear to be willing to devote his whole life to the service of God, no matter what torments he might have to encounter. And, behold, a calumny, a slander, yea, even only a cold reception or a slight wrong with which he meets, brings forth in his heart such a feeling of hatred of revenge and of dislike that he will not even look at his neighbor, and tries in every possible way to demonstrate what is uppermost in his heart. O my brethren, how little are we, and how wrong it is for us to rely upon our fine resolutions!

You see, then, my friends, that temptation is necessary to convince our mind of our unworthiness, and to prevent pride from becoming master over us. Now, you may think that the people who are the most tempted, are the drunkards, the slanderers, the unchaste, who wallow in the mire of their shame, or perhaps the misers. No, my brethren, these are not the people who are tempted the most. On the contrary, the devil may even try to restrain them, for fear that they may not live long enough to do evil and help cast souls into hell by their bad example. St. Augustine teaches us that the devil does not tempt such people particularly: he rather despises and neglects them.

But, you will say, who is it that is most tempted? I will tell you, and please give me your whole attention. It is those who are willing, with the grace of God, to sacrifice everything for their poor soul, who are willing to renounce all those things which are generally striven for with great eagerness in this world. It is not only one devil who tempts them, but there are millions of them who try to ensnare them.

The first temptation, my brethren, which the devil prepares for those who have begun to be more zealous in the service of God, is the fear of man. They are afraid to show themselves. They shun those persons whose society they formerly frequented. If they are told that they have changed very much, they are ashamed! The question, "What will be said of me?" haunts them so, that they have no more courage to do good before the world. If the devil is unable to win them over through the fear of man, he excites in them extraordinary scruples. They are afraid that their confessions were not good; that their confessor does not understand them; that they are working in vain; that they will be lost anyhow; that they would gain just as much if they did not take any trouble.

Why, my brethren, is a person not tempted as long as he lives in sin and never thinks of his soul's salvation, while, on the other hand, as soon as he changes his life, that is to say, as soon as he desires to give himself to God, hell is let loose upon him? Listen to St. Augustine: "This is the behavior of the devil toward a sinner: He acts like a jailer who has several prisoners shut up in his prison. He leaves them quietly alone, because he has the key in his pocket, and he is convinced that they can not break out. This is his behavior toward a sinner who does not think of leaving his sins: He does not trouble himself to tempt them. He would consider it as so much lost time; because he not only does not dream of letting them go, but he loads them with more chains. It would be so unnecessary to tempt them, he lets them live in peace, if one in mortal sin can have any peace. He hides their condition from them as much as possible until their death; but then presents to them the most frightful image of their life, so as to throw them into despair. But a person who has decided to change his way of living, and to give himself to God, that is quite another matter." While St. Augustine lived in the state of sin, he hardly knew what it was to be tempted. He thought he was in peace, as he relates of himself; but, from the moment that he wanted to turn his back upon the devil, he had to struggle with the devil until he nearly lost his breath; and this continued for five years. He shed the bitterest tears, and performed the most severe penances. "I struggled with him," he says, "in my imprisonment. At one moment I thought I was victorious; the next day I was defeated. This cruel and stubborn fight lasted five years. Then," he says, "God gave me the grace to triumph over my enemy."

These, my brethren, are the struggles which God permits His saints to undergo. Ah, my brethren, how much are we to be pitied when we are not violently tempted by the devil! According to all appearances, we are friends of the devil. He lets us live in a false peace. He lets us slumber under the pretense that we have accomplished so much good, that we have given alms, and that we have practised less wickedness than others. In fact, my brethren, ask any frequenter of the saloons if the devil tempts him. He will answer simply: "No; he does not bother me in the least." Ask the vain girl what struggles she has? She will tell you smilingly that she has none; that she does not know what it is to be tempted. You see, then, my brethren, this is the worst of all temptations: Not to be tempted; that is the state of the soul which the devil has prepared for hell. If I might say so, he is careful not to tempt them for fear of recalling their past life and causing them to think of their sins.

I said just now, my brethren, that it is the greatest misfortune for a Christian not to be tempted, for we have good reasons for believing that the devil looks upon him as his own property, and that he awaits only the moment of his death to plunge him into hell. Nothing is easier of comprehension. Look at a Christian who works ever so little for the salvation of his soul. Everything that surrounds him incites him to evil. He can not even open his eyes sometimes without being tempted, in spite of all his prayers and works of penance. And an old sinner, who has perhaps been wallowing in sin for twenty years, will tell you that he is not tempted. Well, so much the worse for you, my friend, so much the worse! That fact alone ought to make you pause, that you do not know what it is to be tempted; for to say that you are not tempted is as good as to say there is no longer a devil, or he has lost his power over Christians. "If you have no temptations," says St. Gregory, "then the devil is your friend, your guide, and your shepherd. If he now permits your life to flow on in peace, he will at the end of your life draw you down into the abyss." St. Augustine says that the greatest of all temptations is not to be tempted; for such a one is abandoned by God, and delivered over to his passions, and will be lost.

I have said that temptation is necessary for us, to preserve us in humility and distrust of self, and to oblige us to take refuge with God. We read in history that a Superior said to a hermit who was violently tempted by the devil, "My friend, do you wish me to ask God to deliver you from these temptations?" "No, Father," answered the hermit; "for they have the effect of keeping me continually in the presence of God, because it constantly necessitates my taking refuge with God, that He may stand by me in my struggles." Meantime, my brethren, we can say that it is one of the surest signs that we are on the path to heaven, if we are tempted, no matter how humiliating the temptation may be. There remains only one thing for us to do, and that is to fight courageously, for temptation is the time of harvest, as the following example will prove. We read in the lives of the saints that a certain saint was so troubled by the devil during a long term of years that she looked upon herself as lost. God appeared to her for her consolation, and disclosed to her that she had gained more in these particular years than at any other time in her life. St. Augustine teaches that everything which we do without overcoming temptation is of very little value. Instead of being discouraged, therefore, we must, on the contrary, thank Almighty God, and fight courageously, because we are sure of the victory, and because we are certain that God will not give way to the devil, and that He will prepare for us the crown of glory which I wish you all. Amen.

SECOND SUNDAY OF LENT

THE DEATH OF THE SINNER

"And you shall seek me, and you shall die in your sin."
St. John viii. 21.

THIS IS A TERRIBLE THREAT, my brethren, and the more terrible because it will surely be fulfilled. As Jesus Christ said to the Jews: "What have I not done for you, you ungrateful people! But there will come a day when you will seek me, and you will not find me, because I will flee, and you will die in your sins." A terrible, but just punishment.

How can a Christian, overwhelmed with God's graces during his whole life, resist the qualms of conscience, and remain in sin! A Christian, who knows without doubt that every mortal sin he commits will bring him into hell! A Christian who knows full well that God Himself offers him every means for conversion, if he would only desire to be converted. A Christian, I say, who has everything at his disposal: God's ministers, who implore him not to remain in that deplorable condition, who pray for him, who offer him the most effective remedies for the healing of the wounds with which sin has afflicted his heart; and who, in spite of it all, remains obdurate, and plunges every moment into more mischief. A Christian who goes so far in his frivolous ways, as to utter cutting sarcasm against the charitable ministers of the Lord, who are only too willing to help him save his poor soul from sin and hell. Is it not just that such a sinner should perish, that God should desert him—him whom the Lord has treated with kindness so long, and to whom He has offered the merits of His own passion! Yes, brethren, it is just, that such a one should perish in his sins, that Jesus Christ, whom he has despised, should leave him to despair and to the power of the devil. "Depart, unfortunate one," exclaims Amos, the prophet, "thou shalt perish in thy sin, as thou wouldst not obey when the Saviour called thee." Oh, how dreadful is the death of a sinner, and yet how many die that death! Oh, if I could only inspire you with dread of such a death, so that you may avoid it! For this purpose, I will try to describe to you the last moments of a sinner, who refuses to be saved, who is full of despair at the thought of his sins, as well as on account of his contempt of God's graces, and of the torments which will be his portion for all eternity.

Now, let me explain to you what it means to die a bad death. If one dies in the flower of his age, having been blest with the best of health, happily married, endowed with all the world's goods, and leaves a loving wife and a family of children, that is no doubt a cruel death. King Ezechias exclaims: "Must I now, O Lord, die in the prime of my life?" and the kingly prophet prayed to God not to let him die. Others say that to die by the hands of the executioner is a cruel death. Still others are of the opinion that a sudden death, for instance, by lightning or drowning, or any other fatal accident, is a bad death; others, again, consider that dying in an epidemic of infectious disease, is a great misfortune. But I tell you, my brethren, that there is nothing evil in all these different ways of meeting death, provided you have made your peace with God. What matters it if you die in the prime of life; such a death does not make you appear any less in the eyes of God. Nor is it in itself a bad death to die at the hands of the executioner, so long as you are well prepared. Many martyrs have died that death: St. Simeon died by a stroke of lightning, and St. Francis de Sales died of a stroke of apoplexy. To die of pestilence can neither be considered a sad death; both St. Roch and St. Francis Xavier died such a death. What makes the death of the sinner dreadful is his sins. It is sin, accursed sin, which tears him to pieces and devours him at that terrible moment. Wherever he turns he sees nothing but sin, graces despised, and, raising his eyes to heaven, what meets his gaze? God, in His just anger and wrath, ready to cast him away. And if he casts his eyes down into the depths, O terror! there is nothing but raging hell, waiting to devour its victim. Alas for the poor sinner! he would not recognize divine justice during life, and now he not only recognizes it but finds it lying heavily upon him. During life he was always bent upon hiding his sins, or to belittle them; at this moment they appear before him as clear as day. He now sees clearly what he ought to have seen long before, but what he refused to see; he would bemoan his sins now, but alas! it is too late! During life he despised God, and now God despises him, and leaves him to utter despair.

Listen, you hardened sinners, who wallow in the mire of unchastity, without a thought of how to extricate yourself from it; you, who never dream that God may desert you as He has deserted so many who were less guilty than yourselves. "Yes," says the Holy Ghost, "the sinners will, at the very thought of their vices, gnash their teeth in their last hour, and a fearful terror will seize them; their vileness will become clear to them. Oh, how they will break out in lamentations, these miserable creatures! Oh, what good have they derived from their vaunted pride, their idle vanity, from all the pleasures and delights they partook of in sin? All is gone; they have not a spark of good, and must succumb under the weight of their own baseness. This happened to the unfortunate Antioch, who fell from the chariot and had his whole body dashed to pieces. He felt an excruciating pain in his intestines, as if they were being torn out of him; worms gnawed at him, and his body emitted an offensive odor. Suddenly his fate became clear to him, as it does to all sinners when it is too late. "Yes, I know," he cried out, "these are the evil deeds I committed at Jerusalem; they devour me, and crush my heart."

His body was racked by the most terrible pains, his mind cast down by direst misery. He called for his friends in hope of finding consolation in them, but no. God who alone can give consolation, has deserted him. "Oh, my friends," he cries out, "I am cast into a terrible doom. I can not sleep, nor rest for a single moment. My heart is drowned in sadness. I am filled with anxiety and misery! Thus must I die, and in a foreign land! O Lord, have mercy on me! I will amply repair all the wrong I have done in Jerusalem; all I have taken I will restore. I will become a Jew, and observe the law of Moses, and confess openly my belief in God Almighty. O Lord, have mercy on me!" But his sickness grew worse from day to day, and God, whom he had despised all through his life, did not listen to his entreaties; he had to die in his sins. He had been a blasphemer and, therefore, his most earnest prayers were not heard, and he was cast into hell.

It is a sad, but just punishment which thus meets the sinner, who, after despising all the graces which were offered him during life, receives no longer any grace, which will be of benefit to him. And yet, how great is the number of those who die in such a way! How many of the children of this world are blind, and have their eyes opened only at the moment when it is too late for them to obtain forgiveness for their sins? Yes, brethren, he who lives in sin will die in it. If you live in sin, do you not wish to be delivered from it? If you say no, you will perish; you will die the death of a notorious French philosopher, named Voltaire. His death will be your portion. You will see that God, whom you despised, while he was continually offering you His love and graces during your life, will suddenly turn you over to a just judgment, at the moment when you are at last willing to return to Him.³ To remain living on in sin with the idea that some fine day you may reform, is nothing but a devil's snare, by which he has ruined many a soul, just as sure as he thus will ruin yours. Voltaire, in his last illness, was a terrible example of a sinner who dies with a guilty conscience. He tries to abandon his wicked ways, and begs God to forgive him his many sins. He counts upon divine love, which is infinite, and is fortified by this thought. He will send for the same priests whom he has vilified and mocked at during his whole life. He will go down on his knees, confess his sins, and flatters himself to be able to accomplish the great work of reconciliation with his Creator; but he is very much mistaken. God has deserted him. Look at him! Death comes before he can receive that last help. The poor, unfortunate creature finds himself surrounded by terrors. "Woe to me," he cries, "I am deserted by God and man." Yes, miserable man, nothing but hell can be thy portion. Listen to Voltaire, how he cried to God, he who had uttered so many blasphemies against his Creator, his religion, and the servants of the Lord. "Jesus Christ, Son of God," he cries, "who died for the sins of all men, have mercy on me!" But, alas! a century of wickedness has tired divine patience. God has cast him away, he is now nothing but a victim of divine wrath, destined for everlasting fire. The priests whom he had despised for many years, how he longs for them, but they are not there. There he lies in convulsions and terrors of despair. He shakes and trembles, and all the calumnies which he has belched forth almost through a life-time, take vengeance upon him. His wicked companions, for fear that after all the Most Holy Sacrament might be brought to him, remove him to a lonely place in the country, and leave him there, a prey to his despair.

Despair is a torment of hell, and in life a foretaste thereof, and whosoever lives the life that leads up to it, can not but be delivered to the same in eternity. My brethren, take heed, therefore, now; refuse not to become reconciled to God, especially in this holy season of Lent; the servants of God, His priests, are ready to receive you, to give back to you the peace with your conscience, the peace with God, and living in this peace you need not fear despair, but carried on by confidence and hope, all will end in love never to be extinguished. Amen.

---

³Note.—The author must here he understood that true conversion is lacking, for otherwise God would not refuse pardon even to the most wicked sinner.

THIRD SUNDAY OF LENT

INDULGENCES

"When the unclean spirit is gone out of man ... he saith: I will return into my house, whence I came out."
St. Luke xi. 24.

HE GOSPEL of today tells us how great the anger of the devil is against those who, by means of a good confession, have driven him from their hearts. They must be constantly watchful of the emotions of their hearts, for fear that the devil might induce them to commit the same sin again, which would put them into a worse condition than they were in before they went to confession. With the intention of guarding us from this evil, the Church gives us penances, when we confess our sins. These penances have a double purpose: first, to give satisfaction to divine justice for our sins; and, secondly, to keep us from committing the same sin again. Yet we must be aware, brethren, that there will always remain some suffering for us to go through, either in this life or in purgatory, even if we have performed the penances ever so well, because they do not begin to compare with our sins. Because, however, my dear brethren, the dear Lord wishes us, as soon as possible after our death, to partake of the bliss of His Holy presence, He offers us, through His representatives on earth, a very easy and efficient means to avoid these sufferings after death. This means, my brethren, are the indulgences, which we may gain, so long as we are on this earth. These indulgences are an alleviation, or a complete remission of such penances incurred by the sinner which he would have to perform either in this life or in purgatory. But so that you should better understand the value of indulgences, I will show you:

I. What is understood by indulgences.
II. From whence are they obtained.
III. What is necessary to gain them.

I.

I will not stop to prove to you, my brethren, that the Church has the power to grant indulgences; it would simply be losing precious time, for you all know that Jesus said to the Apostle Peter, and through him to his successors: "And I will give to thee the keys of the kingdom of heaven. And whatsoever thou shalt bind upon earth, it shall be bound also in heaven: and whatsoever thou shalt loose on earth, it shall be loosed also in heaven." (St. Matt. xvi. 19.) Which power He also conferred at some other time upon all Apostles. We see that the Apostles themselves granted indulgences, and the Church has not only the power to impose upon us penances for our sins, but she can also shorten the time of suffering we have to undergo in purgatory. You know, brethren, that there are two kinds of sins, venial and mortal sins. Mortal sin deserves eternal punishment; it is one of the dogmas of the Church that we shall be damned if we have the misfortune to die in mortal sin, without having obtained pardon for it. Irreverent Christians may say to you, that God is not as wrathful as the priests say He is, but that does not alter the fact. After having duly confessed our sins, there still remains for us to undergo punishment for them, either in this or the next world. Then, when we weigh the burden of our sins with the amount of penance, which is laid upon us in expiation of them, there seems to be no comparison between the two. Something has to be done, therefore, which may aid us in giving satisfaction to Divine justice. It is true, that the troubles of this life—sickness, vexation, slander, loss of worldly possessions, may help us toward expiating our sins, if we are prudent enough to offer up all those troubles to God for that purpose.

Since the foundation of the Church a penance of a certain amount and character has been imposed upon the sinner, according to what was considered necessary for satisfying Divine justice. When, in the early days of the Church, a sinner wished to become reconciled to God, he appeared before his Bishop, barefoot, in ragged clothes, and ashes upon his head, and confessed his sins in public; he then had to pass through the different degrees of penance. After a sinner had confessed and repented his sins, he was obliged to remain kneeling outside the door of the church, because he was not considered worthy to enter the sacred portals, and he begged the faithful, while they passed him, for their prayers in his behalf. When he had passed this first degree, which was often of long duration, he entered upon the next, the degree of the weeper. In this degree their remorse and

THIRD SUNDAY OF LENT 127

self-abasement was so heartrending as to make the passer-by burst out in tears; they did not hesitate to confess their sins publicly, so as to gain the favor of the faithful, and their prayers. After this degree, they were allowed to take a place near the door of the church, where they could hear the instructions given to the congregation, but as soon as these were ended, they had to retire and were not allowed to join in the prayers of the faithful. After a further term of penance they were allowed to participate in the sacrifice of Holy Mass up to the time of the Gospel, when they had to leave, still being considered unworthy of being present at the sacred mysteries. But before they left, the whole congregation prayed for them, while they themselves lay prostrate upon the floor. At the end of all this penance, they received solemn absolution, after which they were allowed to take part in all the prayers and in the holy sacrifice of the Mass, but even then they were not allowed to receive communion for a considerable time. During the whole time of penance they had to keep away from all public functions and ceremonies, and had to live in retirement, to live on bread and water several days each week, and to give alms, all of these being means to give satisfaction to Divine justice. For the irreverent mentioning of the name of the Lord, even when done thoughtlessly, they had to live on bread and water for seven days, and if the sin was repeated, for fifteen days. For a blasphemy against God, the Blessed Virgin, or the Saints, they had to remain kneeling before the church, barefoot, with a rope around their neck, and had to fast for seven Fridays on bread and water, during which time they were not allowed to enter the church. For working on Sunday they had to live on bread and water for three days; for unnecessary traveling on Sunday, seven days, and so forth.

You see, then, my brethren, how the Church in those early times acted toward those who wanted to be saved. Today, as you know, she no longer imposes such hard penances, although our sins are no less wicked and offensive to God. See, then, my brethren, how good God is, and how much He desires our salvation. He gives us indulgences, in place of penances, which we do not have the courage and strength to carry out.

II.

But from whence are these indulgences obtained which bring us so much good? Listen well, O brethren, and keep what you learn well in mind, for he who understands this matter thoroughly can not help but praise the Lord and derive the greatest possible benefit for himself. What happiness for us that we are enabled to save for ourselves, by a few prayers, hundreds of years of suffering in the next world? Now, let me tell you that these indulgences are obtained from the overflowing merits of our Lord Jesus Christ, of the Blessed Virgin, and of the Saints who have suffered more and did more penance than was necessary for the expiation of sin. This is the inexhaustible treasure which the Church divides among her children. And I tell you, further, that these indulgences are the remission of punishment, which we would have to undergo for our sins, even after they have been pardoned in the Sacrament of Penance. To make you understand this more fully, we must learn the relation between offense and punishment: offense is the wrong which we do to God, when we sin, and for which we deserve punishment. And to cleanse ourselves gradually of these sins, which have been forgiven to us in the Sacrament of Penance, we gain indulgences, because, after confessing our sins, we ought to do more penance than our confessor imposes upon us, if we wish to avoid the pains of purgatory. We are told in Holy Writ, that the saints, though they were sure of forgiveness, received the obligation from God to do penance, as, for instance, David, Mary Magdalen, St. Peter, and many others.

How fortunate are we to possess in the indulgences such an easy means for escaping the torments of purgatory, which seem so terrible and long. Yes, my brethren, a sinner who had the good fortune to obtain a complete plenary indulgence at the moment of death, would appear before God entirely free of sin. He would stand before God as pure and innocent as if he had just been baptized; he would be as ready to be received into heaven as the Holy Martyrs were upon their death. Yes, my brethren, in regard to the blotting out of temporary punishments, there is no difference between baptism, martyrdom, and a plenary indulgence in the full meaning of the word. O precious grace, so little known, and if known so little appreciated by the greatest number of our fellow Christians!

How many souls there are in purgatory today, and who will remain there for years and years, because they did not make use of the benefits of indulgences!

III.

After the doctor knows the illness of which his patient is suffering, he prescribes certain remedies to cure him, and at the same time he states how they are to be applied, for without this precaution the remedies might become more injurious than useful. And so it is with the means which we must employ for the cure of our soul. I know well that there are many persons who will hear all this with proud disdain, and a certain doubtfulness. Well, we must pity them. They are those poor blind persons who imagine that they can see clearly and distinctly, and all the time their eyes are closed by sin. If, in spite of all the graces which God in His goodness gives them, they intend to go to perdition, let them alone. The time will come when they will say to us lamenting: "How happy are you to have used these graces." Let us seek the light of faith, let us make use of all the means which God in His goodness offers us, so as to make sure of heaven.

You may ask, "What must we do to gain an indulgence?" The first condition is, my brethren, that you should be in the state of grace; secondly, you must do the works and say the prayers authorized by the Holy Father, and have no inclination to any, not even wilful venial sin. This is all that is necessary, and you must admit that our good Mother Church has certainly made it easy for her children to make use of this precious means of salvation. So much more reason, and even obligation for us to make the greatest use of indulgences, and so much less excuse if we refuse this great benefit to our immortal soul.

Therefore, my brethren, as we all have offended God, and perhaps grievously, and as we have not, and of ourselves can not, give perfect satisfaction, let us make use of this easy means of gaining indulgences to render to God what is God's, and He, seeing our good will, will surely give us sufficient strength to overcome the devil if again he should attempt to attack us, and things will not be worse, as in the example of today's Gospel, but better, which good grace and fortune I wish you all. Amen.

PASSION SUNDAY

"REPENTANCE"

"Woe me, for I have sinned so much during my life."
Confessions of St Augustine.

THUS SPOKE St. Augustine, when he thought over his past life, which he had spent incessantly in the abominable vice of impurity. As often as the thought occurred to him, his heart was torn and devoured by repentance. "Oh, my Lord," he exclaimed, "I have lived without loving Thee; oh, my Lord, how many precious years have I lost! Deign, O Lord, I implore Thee, to efface from Thy memory my past faults!" Oh, precious tears, O salutary contrition, which made of such a great sinner so great a saint! Oh, how quickly does a really contrite heart regain the friendship of God! Ah, would to God that every time we let our sins pass before our mind's eye, we could say with the repentant St. Augustine: "Ah, woe is me. I have sinned much during my life; have mercy on me, O Lord!" How soon would we alter our mode of living! Yes, my brethren, let us all who are here present, confess with the same fervent repentance and sincerity, that we are great sinners who deserve to experience the full wrath of God. And let us praise God's infinite mercy, who gives us abundantly of His treasures to solace us in our misery. If our sins have been ever so great, and our life has been ever so dissolute, we are sure of His pardon, if we follow the example of the prodigal son and throw ourselves with a contrite heart at the feet of the best of fathers. Now let me show to you, my Christian friends, that our repentance must have this quality before it can procure for us pardon for our sins: The sinner must, in consequence of his repentance, hate his sins sincerely, and detest them.

To make you fully understand what repentance, *i.e.*, the pain which our sins should cause our conscience, means, I would have to show you on the one hand the abhorrence which the Lord has for them, and the torments which He had to suffer to gain pardon for them from God the Father, and on the other hand the blessings we lose by committing sin, and the evils which we bring down upon ourselves in the next world; but no man will ever be able to understand this fully. Where shall I lead you, my brethren, to show you this repentance? Into the solitude of the desert, perhaps, where so many saints spent twenty, thirty, forty, fifty, or even eighty years of their lives, bemoaning faults which were no faults in the eyes of the world. No, your heart would not be moved by such as these. Or shall I lead you to the entrance of hell, so that you may hear the woeful cries and howls, and gnashing of teeth, which is caused by the repentance of their sins; but though bitter and hard to bear, their pain and repentance is useless. No, my brethren, you would not learn here the real repentance which you should feel over your sins. Oh, if I could only lead you to the foot of the cross which is still reddened with the precious blood of our Lord, shed to wash away our sins! Oh, if I could only lead you into that garden of sorrow, where our Lord shed for our sins, not ordinary tears, but blood, which flowed forth from all the pores of his body! Oh, if I could only show Him to you laden with the cross, staggering along the streets of Jerusalem, at every step He stumbles and is driven on by kicks. Oh, if I could only lead you to Mount Calvary, where our Lord died, for the sake of our salvation. But even if I could do all that, it would be necessary that God should give you the grace of inflaming in your heart the burning love of a St. Bernard, who broke out in tears at the mere sight of the cross. Oh, beautiful and precious repentance, how happy is he who harbors thee in his heart! But to whom am I addressing myself: where is he who feels it in his heart? Alas, I do not know. Is it to that head-strong sinner who has abandoned his God and neglected his soul for twenty or thirty years? No, that would be like trying to soften a rock by pouring water over it. Or to that Christian who has neglected missions, and ceased prayers, and despised the admonitions of his spiritual adviser? No, that would be like trying to heat water by adding ice to it. Or, perhaps, to those persons who feel satisfied if they make their Easter duty, and then, year in and year out, continue in the same sinful course of living. No, those are the victims which are fattened to serve as food for the eternal flames. Or to those Christians who go to communion every month, and fall back into their sins every day? No, for they are like the blind, who do not know what they do, or what they ought to do. To whom shall I address myself, then? Alas, I do not know. Oh, my Lord, where shall I look for it, where shall I find it? Yes, my Lord, I know whence it comes and who bestows it. It comes from heaven, and Thou dost bestow it, O Lord. Oh, my Lord, we implore Thee, bestow it upon us, the repentance which crushes and devours our heart; this beautiful repentance which disarms God's justice and changes an eternity of misery into eternal bliss. Oh, beautiful virtue, how necessary thou art, and how seldom to be found! And yet, without it there can be no pardon, no heaven, and more than that, without it all is in vain: penance, charity, alms, or anything else we might do to gain the eternal reward.

But you may ask, "What does this word 'repentance' mean, and how can we tell whether we have it or not?" My brethren, if you will listen to me, I will explain to you how you can find out whether you have it or not, and if you have it not, how you may obtain it. Now, if you ask me what repentance is, I tell you that it is an anguish of the soul, and a detestation for past sin, and a firm resolve never to sin again. Yes, my brethren, this is the foremost of all conditions which God makes before pardoning our sins, and it can never be dispensed with. A sickness which deprives us of speech, may dispense us from confession; a sudden death may dispense us from the necessity of giving satisfaction for our sins during life, but with repentance it is different. Without it, it is impossible, absolutely impossible, to obtain forgiveness. Yes, my brethren, I must say with deep regret that the want of repentance is the cause of a great number of sacrilegious confessions and communions, and what is still more to be regretted is the circumstance that many do not realize what a sad state they are in, and live and die in it. Now, my friends, if we had the misfortune to conceal a sin in confession, this sin is constantly before our eyes like a monster which threatens to devour us, and it causes us to soon go to confession again, so as to free ourselves from it. But it is different with repentance; we confess, but our heart does not take part in the accusation which we make against ourselves. We approach the Holy Sacrament with as cold, unfeeling, and indifferent a heart as if performing an indifferent act of no consequence. Thus we live from day to day, from year to year, until we approach death, when we expect to find that we have done something to our credit, only to discover nothing but sacrileges, which we have committed by our confessions and communions. Oh, my God, how many Christians there are who will discover at the hour of their death nothing but invalid confessions! But I will not go further into this matter, for fear that I may frighten you, and yet you ought really to be brought to the verge of despair, so that you may stop immediately, and improve your condition right now, instead of waiting until that moment when you will recognize your condition, and when it will be too late to improve it. But let us continue with our explanation, and you will soon learn, my brethren, whether you had the repentance in all your confessions, which is so absolutely necessary for the forgiveness of sin.

I said that repentance is an anguish of soul. It is absolutely necessary that a sinner weep over his sins either in this world or the next. In this world we can wipe out our sins by repentance, but not in the next. We should be very grateful to our dear Lord that the anguish of our soul is sufficient for Him to let it be followed by eternal joy, instead of making us suffer that eternal repentance and those awful tortures which would be our lot in the next life, that is, hell. Oh, my God, with how little art Thou satisfied!

Now, let me tell you that this anguish of soul must have four qualities; if either one of these qualities is wanting, we can not obtain forgiveness for our sins. The first quality is that it must come from the bottom of the heart. It need not necessarily show itself in tears; they are good and useful, but they are not essential. It is a fact that when St. Paul and the penitent thief turned to God, it is not reported that they wept, and yet their anguish of soul was sincere.

No, my friends, you must not rely on tears alone. They are often deceiving, and many persons weep in the confessional and fall back into the same sin at the first opportunity. The anguish of soul which God demands of us, is like the one of which the prophet says: "Rend your heart and not your garments. A sacrifice to God is an afflicted spirit; a contrite and humbled heart, O God, Thou wilt not despise." Why does God require that our heart should feel this anguish? Because it is in the heart where we commit our sins. "It is the heart," says the Lord, "where all bad thoughts, all sinful desires, originate." Therefore, if our heart is guilty, the heart must suffer, or God will never forgive us. The second quality of this anguish which we must feel over our sins, is that it must be supernatural; that means, that the Holy Ghost and not natural causes must call it forth. To be troubled about a sin one has committed because it would exclude us from paradise and lead us into hell, is a supernatural motive, of which the Holy Ghost is the originator, and will lead to true repentance. But to be troubled about a sin because of the shame of which it will be the consequence, or the misfortune it will cause us, that is merely a natural sorrow, which does not merit pardon. It is perfectly plain, then, that the anguish of soul caused by our sins, must arise from our love of God and our fear of His chastisement. He who, in his repentance, thinks only of God, feels a perfect repentance, which, from its very inception, purifies the sinner even before the reception of absolution. But he who only repents of his sins merely on account of the temporal punishments which they will bring with them, has no proper repentance, and is not justified in expecting forgiveness of his sins. The third quality of repentance is that it must be unlimited, that is, the anguish it calls forth must be greater than any other sorrow, as, for instance, at the loss of our parents, or our health, or in general at the loss of anything that is dearest to us in this life. The reason why our sorrow must be so great, is because it must be equivalent to the loss it will cause us, and the misfortune it will bring us after our death. Imagine, then, how great an anguish ought to be ours over a sin which deprives us of all the glories of heaven, alienates our dear Lord from us, and casts us into hell, which is the greatest of all misfortunes. But, you may ask, how are we to know whether we possess this true repentance? Nothing is easier. If you have real repentance, you will neither act, nor think, as you did before, and you will change your mode of life completely; you will hate what you have loved and you will love what you have despised and avoided. For instance, if you had to confess that in action and speech you were of a hasty temper, you would hereafter be remarkable for your gentleness of behavior, and your consideration for all. You need not trouble yourself whether you have made a perfect confession, as errors are easily committed, but the consequence of your confession should be that the people say of you: "How he has changed; he is not the same man. A wonderful change has taken place in him!" Oh, my Lord, how rare are the confessions which cause such a great change!

The fourth and last quality is that repentance must be comprehensive. We see in the lives of the saints, in regard to the comprehensiveness of repentance, that we can not receive pardon for one sin, even if we have properly repented the same, if we do not feel the same repentance for all our sins.

History furnishes us with an example which shows us how absolutely necessary the saints considered this anguish over our sins, to obtain forgiveness. One of the papal officers fell sick. The Holy Father, who had a high esteem of his bravery and sanctity of life, sent one of his cardinals to express his sympathy, and to give him general absolution. "Tell the Holy Father," said the dying man to the Cardinal, "that I am very thankful to him for his tender regard, but tell him also that I would be infinitely more thankful to him if he would pray to God to obtain for me the grace of a true repentance for my sins. "Oh!" he cried, "what good is anything to me if my heart does not break with anguish at the thought that I have offended so good a God. Oh, Lord, if it be possible, make the repentance over my sins equal to the offense which I have given you!"

Examine yourselves, oh, my friends, and see how rare such a repentance is. Alas, it is as scarce as a good confession! Yes, my brethren, a Christian who has sinned and wishes to obtain pardon, must be so minded that he would rather suffer the most cruel tortures than fall back into the sin which he has just confessed.

And this disposition is obtained by prayer—earnest, fervent prayer. "Create a clean heart in me, O God: and renew a right spirit within my bowels. Cast me not away from thy face, and take not thy holy spirit from me," etc. (Ps. 1. 12.) Joined to this repentance will naturally be a firm resolve not to commit the sin again; and this is the contrite and humbled heart which God will not despise, but receive again as its child, and restore to him all the privileges of a child of God, and heir to the Heavenly Kingdom which I wish you all. Amen.

PALM SUNDAY

"Behold, thy King cometh to thee, meek."
St. Matthew xxi. 5.

Y DEAR CHRISTIANS, as we have just learned from today's Gospel, the Saviour celebrates today His triumphal entry into Jerusalem. Many times had the people of the Holy Land, when they were witnesses of His deeds and miracles, tried to bestow upon Him extraordinary honors; several times His enthusiastic admirers went so far as to announce their intention of proclaiming Him king, but Jesus had always managed to avoid their intended demonstrations of respect and admiration. This was particularly the case, when in the most miraculous way He procured in the desert food for a multitude of many thousands of hungry people. But today we see to our astonishment, that the Saviour Himself makes arrangements for a solemn entry into the Holy City.

And what time did He choose? The time of the Paschal Feast. Every Jew on earth, who had the means, made it a point to celebrate this feast, the memorial festival of their delivery from Egypt, at the place where stood the Ark of the Covenant, that once led them safely through the river Jordan into the Holy Land. And as the sons of Israel, in spite of their captivity in Assyria and Babylon, in spite of the persecution from the pagans, and in spite of their being scattered all over the earth, remained participating in the blessing of Abraham, they were to be found in Jerusalem at Paschal time by the hundreds of thousands.

This enormous multitude of people could see for themselves on this day on which Jesus held His triumphal entry, that the words of the prophet Zacharias were being fulfilled: "O daughter of Jerusalem, behold thy King will come to thee meek." (Zach. ix. 9.) A true king he entered, not like a conqueror, but meekly, like a prince of peace.

A true and real king made his entry, and why should we not call Him king, who had proved His supremacy over nature and man in such an unmistakable manner? The tempest roared upon the sea, the frail boats were in danger of sinking, and their occupants cried out in terror: "Lord, save us, we perish!" And He arises, calls them "of little faith," and commands the wind to abate, and the waves to calm down. Where sickness, even in its most terrible aspect, seeks and finds its victims, there He stops its progress. He heals the leper, gives sight to the blind, makes the lame to walk, and causes the paralytic to carry home his own bed.

Since original sin, the evil spirit had been master over nature and man. Nature does not supply any longer the temporal wants of the rational creatures of God, unless it is forced to it. And it has gone so far that man created in the image of God has become a tool in the hand of the arch-enemy. But as soon as Satan, the enemy of mankind, perceives the Saviour, he is overcome by fear, though he may try to still practice and hold on to his sovereignty, yet he will have to let go of his prey, and retire before the King, who is even master of the evil spirits.

All this was known before Jesus entered Jerusalem; thousands of witnesses had announced the miracles He had performed. Then came the rising of Lazarus. Consider! one of the best known and most highly esteemed Jews, a friend and follower of Christ, had died. The Saviour was not in time to be present at His friend's last moments. He did not arrive in Bethany, where Lazarus lived, until three days after he had been buried. Martha, the sister of Lazarus, tried to restrain our Lord from viewing the remains, because they had been buried so long and emitted a strong odor of decay. The Saviour insisted upon visiting the grave of His friend, and many hundreds of the better class of citizens of Bethany, many of whom had come from Jerusalem, accompanied Him. And what is their experience? Jesus simply called upon Lazarus to rise from his grave, where he had been entombed for four days. Jesus is master over the decay already set in; He can command nature to interrupt its work, and, therefore, He must be master over the whole world of creation. The miracle was not to be denied, and many became converted on the spot. The news of this great deed of Jesus Christ spread like lightning, and involuntarily many thousands in Jerusalem asked themselves: "Who is he, who has command over death and the grave? He is human, but he must be endowed with divine power; he is surely sent from heaven, and if he says of himself that he is the Messiah, it surely must be so."

All those who followed sincerely the promptings of their heart, saw in the approaching Saviour the long-promised Messiah, the Son of David. For them he was the king, whose coming the prophet had told of; for had he not obtained victory over everything man had been subjected to heretofore? Had He not shown Himself master over all creatures, over nature, and the evil spirit? A true King, the King of Zion, entered this day into Jerusalem. But He was not a king like the earthly potentates are; His triumphal entry was quite different from what the entry of one of the princes of this earth would have been. The prophet says: "Thy King cometh to thee meek." We know the triumphal processions of the days of old; the victorious warriors, or the leaders of the people appeared in gorgeous, gold-laden chariots, or upon fiery steeds; the spoils of victory were borne before them, and they were followed by the vanquished foe, laden with chains and bent with sorrow; great treasures, the fruit of victory, were exposed to the gaze of the multitude, and the Kings themselves (the ideals of ah enthusiastic and pleasure-loving populace) were received with frantic shouting and applause. How did the King of Zion appear? Where are the conquered treasures, the vanquished foe, the chained captives? Where is the gorgeous chariot, the prancing steed? All this is wanting: the King, who celebrated His triumphal entry this day, was seated upon an ass, which His devoted followers had covered, not with gold-embroidered blankets, but with their outer garments. In this triumphal entry, pride, ambition, and avarice are not represented, but humility, meekness, mortification, and self-denial: in one word, unselfishness. The King, who enters Zion, has resigned everything temporal. He was born in poverty, and remained in poverty all His life. He has earned nothing but the love of those whom He has assisted, and of the noble minds who were able to understand Him. He has no friends in the houses of the rich, but all the more in the dwellings of the poor; no adherents among the pleasure-seekers, but thousands among the poor and castaways of this world. And these form His following on this day. Not upon command, not from idle curiosity, but from love and veneration they stream forth from all sides. As soon as they gain sight of Him, the glorious, the Godlike, an indescribable cry of jubilation resounds in the air; they show their admiration in their own peculiar way; they break off branches of palms and olive-trees, and strew them upon His path; they spread their garments before Him, as a token of their reverence, and they call out joyfully: "Hosanna! Hail to the Son of David! Blessed is he who comes in the name of the Lord!" And in this way the King of Zion takes possession of His kingdom. What, then, does the Gospel of today teach us? The Saviour enters likewise here in glorious majesty, but at the same time poor and meekly, whenever He approaches us with His grace in the Sacrament of the Holy Eucharist. The Church recalls it, when she says before the consecration, "Blessed is he who comes in the name of the Lord! "Let us give Him the same reception which His friends gave Him in Jerusalem. Let us present to Him all we have, and let us spread under His feet, not only our earthly possessions but also our worldly ideas and longings, so that the Lord may have a triumphal entry into our hearts. Amen.

Rev. S., D. D.

EASTER

PASCHAL JOYS

"You seek Jesus who was crucified; he is not here; he is risen."
Matt, xxviii. 6

DEARLY BELOVED in the Lord! This is the day which the Lord has made, let us rejoice and triumph with Him. The Church meets us today with this joyful announcement, adorned as a bride. The dawn of day has brought us a beautiful, a great day of rejoicing. As we came to the sepulchre with the holy women, the angels greeted us with this joyful message: "You seek Jesus of Nazareth, who was crucified: he is risen, he is not here." This is the joyful message from heaven which resounds loudly and joyfully from north to south, to the uttermost ends of the earth. How this glad message should resound in songs of triumph and flood the heart with joy unspeakable. The heavens behold Him, the glorious risen One, and the sky covers itself with the loveliest azure; the sun in the firmament beholds Him, and it shines with the brightest, most perfect light, the favored earth and its inhabitants behold the glory of the risen Saviour, and they too rejoice. The whole world today joins in that glorious hymn of praise of St. Ambrose, "Almighty God, we praise Thee; O Lord, we praise Thy works; for this is the day which the Lord has made, let us rejoice and triumph with Him." We shall hear today:

I. Why this day is such a joyful one.
II. How we ought to give the right expression to our jubilation united to the words of the Gospel of the feast which says: "You seek Jesus of Nazareth, who was crucified: He is risen, He is not here."

May the risen Saviour bless our meditation.
I. 1. Beloved brethren, if you wish to know the true reason of our Easter joy, let us look back to the last days of Holy Week and represent to

ourselves in a vivid manner what happened to Jesus of Nazareth in those days at Jerusalem. All these events are fresh in our memory; we were, during Lent, led by the words of the preacher to follow our Saviour in His passion. We beheld Him trodden upon like a worm; we saw Him drag His rack to the place of execution; we heard the dull strokes of the hammer which fastened His hands and feet to the cross; we saw the cross lifted up with its precious burden; briefly, we were witnesses in spirit of the awful agonizing death of our Saviour, of whom even Pilate said: "What shall I do with Jesus, who is called the just man?" To her just and deep sorrow the Church wishes to give expression by exterior signs of mourning; therefore the house of God, and the sanctuary within it, the Altar, were surrounded with a deathlike stillness, the tones of the organ and the sound of the bell were silenced, the bare cross alone attracted to itself every eye, and filled our hearts with sadness. But, dear brethren, our mourning is now turned into joy. The seal of the grave is broken; He who reposed therein is living; He whom we saw die upon the wood of the cross, as the outcast of mankind, He has proclaimed His divine dignity; neither seal, nor grave, nor stone, nor lock could withstand Him; He is risen! Just as the newly awakened life in the Spring unfolds itself in a thousand buds and blossoms, touching our hearts powerfully, in like manner does every Christian soul feel itself strangely moved and touched when on Easter morning we hear the Easter bells ringing out to the cottage as to the palace the glad tidings which the angel brought from heaven: "He is risen, He is not here! Alleluia, Jesus lives!"

2. Jesus lives! At this announcement the earth rejoices, and it opens the grave of Him whose death upon Golgotha caused it to shiver and tremble at its base; Jesus lives! At this message heaven is joyfully agitated, and sends one of its angels to break the seal which the hatred of his enemies had placed upon their victim even after His death, to roll away the heavy stone and announce to the holy women: "You seek Jesus of Nazareth: he is risen, he is not here." *Resurrexit sicut dixit.* What joy for the poor disciples, who had fled in all directions when He was made a prisoner! Jesus lives! What glad tidings for us, beloved brethren; what joy and delight for us who are baptized in the name of Jesus, who believe in the teaching of Jesus; for us, who may live in the blessed hope that we too may one day rise again to a better life! When the Man of Sorrows, His struggle and His sufferings ended, cried out to the world with a loud voice those mighty words, "It is consummated," when He bowed His head and gave up the ghost, the sun was obscured; it did not want to behold that

dreadful spectacle; the earth was shaken mightily, its graves opened, and the dead arose. Today, however, one grave is opened, and from it has arisen a sun which will never be obscured, which will never set, a sun which, like unto the sun of springtime, creates new life. This new sun is the Crucified One, the Son of God, God Himself, blessed for all eternity. He it is in whom the words of the Apostle are fulfilled: "Because he humbled himself and was obedient even unto death upon the cross, therefore has God exalted him, and given him a name which is above all other names."

3. When the star of Jacob arose, when the Word was made flesh, the kingdom of falsehood and darkness was doomed to defeat. Already the cradle song, which the angels sang to the incarnate Saviour, "Glory to God in the highest!" was a solemn hymn of praise which announced in advance the glory of this day. The *Gloria in Excelsis* of that most beloved night is supplemented in glorious manner by the glad tidings of the heavenly messenger on Easter morn, who said: "You seek Jesus of Nazareth: he is risen, he is not here." But the truth which the Son of God brought from heaven, His divine teaching, was not to be proclaimed without a struggle; the light illuminated the darkness, but the darkness could not comprehend. The only begotten Son of the Father was calumniated as the poor Son of the carpenter, the Messiah sent from heaven was mocked as the Galilean, His words of charity were branded as the work of hell. When He said that He had come to found a kingdom which was not of this world, He was denounced as a seducer of the people, and an enemy of Caesar. Thus, my brethren, falsehood struggled against truth, and it seemed as if His enemies were really triumphant in victory when Jesus hung bleeding upon the cross. His enemies appeared sure of victory, when they said to the crucified Saviour in derision, "If thou art Christ, descend from the cross. Thou didst help others, now help thyself," and He made no reply to these words, but bowed His head and died. And still more, He was laid in a grave like an ordinary mortal, the grave itself being guarded and sealed.

Now, according to human calculations, everything was over and at an end; the world seemed to conquer. Whence, dear brethren, should that mustard seed which this incarnate God now lying in the grave had thus planted obtain its strength to grow and expand into a great tree whose fruit should bless all the races of the earth? Whence should the timid disciples have obtained the courage to proclaim to the world that this Crucified One is the true God, and to preach His Gospel to every creature?

Tremble not, little band of disciples, for the miracle has already taken place! The earth is jubilant with joy, heaven sends forth its messengers, the grave is empty, the hero is awakened, the Saviour is risen! Because He arose from the grave through His own almighty power, because He has built up again the temple of His body in three days, He has proven the glory of His divinity and placed the seal of completeness upon the work of redemption. If Christ had not risen again, says the Apostle, our faith would be vain! On Good Friday, when the earth trembled and the rocks were split open, we struck our breasts with the centurion and said, "Verily, He was the Son of God," we may therefore all the more cry out joyfully beside the empty grave on Easter morning, "He that is risen is the Son of God, He is the Messiah, He is the lamb of God that takes away the sins of the world." Is this not the day that the Lord has made? Should we not rejoice in Him and be glad? Let the chords of the organ peal forth in sweetest harmony, let the bells ring out in thrilling tones, let the song of triumph resound, The Saviour is risen! Alleluia, Jesus lives. Neither seal nor grave, stone nor rock, could withstand Him. "You seek Jesus of Na2areth: he is risen, he is not here."

II. 1. We have heard that we have every reason to rejoice from the bottom of our hearts on this ever memorable day, and to approach our risen Redeemer with joyous Alleluias. But this is not all, we must be active also, and make a practical use of today's celebration. Christ died for us, and He has given us an example that we should tread in His footsteps. As Christ is risen, so shall we arise and enter upon a new life. I call upon you, therefore, Christian parents, in the words of the Apostle: "Arise, and walk in the way in which thou shouldst go." You promised one another before God's holy altar mutual fidelity and help, that you would bear one another's burdens in peace, and that you would bring up your children in the fear of the Lord. How have you kept this promise? Is the throne of harmony erected in your home, and dispensing blessings upon you? Are you a good father and mother to your children, do you feed the flock confided to you in green pastures, and do you lead them, as a good shepherd should, to the source of living waters? Or are you, fathers, bad examples to your sons, and you, mothers, unnatural mothers to your daughters? Arise from your spiritual death, fortify anew the throne of peace, approach the Altar of God and renew your conjugal vows. Bring up your children as good Catholic parents should do, assist the teachers and those who have charge of their spiritual welfare in this difficult task, then, and then only, will you have a happy Easter; then Easter joys and Easter blessings will gladden you and your family.

2. Christian sons, Christian daughters, arise from the grave! We grown-up people, who have no longer the good fortune of seeing father and mother with us; we who can now only kneel at their graves and speak to them in spirit, how we envy you, dear, happy children, especially on this day, when it is such a joy to celebrate Easter in the family circle. And now, I ask you, beloved sons and daughters, whether you know how to appreciate this great happiness of possessing your father and mother, Or whether you, O frivolous son, grieve your good father by your sinful ways, and by your extravagance; and you, proud daughter, do you cause your mother to shed tears at your behavior, and at your disobedience? Well, then, today arise from the grave of sin and give your good parents an Easter joy by making the firm resolution of walking in that path which will bring you blessings in this life and in the life to come. The risen Saviour is the friend of children, He will extend His hands in blessing over you today, you will live long, and everything will be well with you upon earth.

3. Well may we apply to ourselves the words of the Apostle: "Man who is of the earth, is earthly." Now, if we have been in the past slaves of the flesh, and if our thoughts and actions were earthly, this is Easter; let us throw out the old leaven so that we may become a new dough. Then the words of the Apostle will come true: "If thou art risen with Christ, seek ye therefore the things that are above, not that which is upon earth." But in reality, to seek and to find that which is above, we must not only arise from the grave of sin, cleanse our hearts from every sin, but we must purify them from the old leaven. When Christ arose from the grave He left the burying sheets behind; so should we at our spiritual resurrection leave in the graves the fetters of our old habits; we must break with the old life and walk in a new one; we must put off the old man and put on the new man, which is created in holiness and justice. And so it must be with thee, O sensual man; let me say also of you, he is risen, he is not here, no longer there where he has so often sinned. We must be able to say: "He is risen, the miser, he lingers no more with his treasures, which the rust and moth will eat away; he no longer kneels at the altar of Mammon; he has become the father of the poor." He is risen, must be said of the drunkard, the gambler, he is not here, behold the place is empty where formerly he sat till far into the night playing and drinking, whilst his poor wife and

hungry children suffered want at home. And this is what ought and must be said of all sinners: they are risen, they are not here, the grave of sin is empty, they are leading a new life. O then indeed we shall all spend a blessed and happy Easter, a day of gladness, a day which the Lord has made.

PERORATION

III. Christ is raised from the dead to die no more. He is exalted high above principalities and powers and majesties, and He sits at the right hand of the Father. His words, spoken to the disciples of Emmaus, are true: "Ought not Christ to have suffered these things, and so to enter into his glory?" If then, dear brethren, crosses and sufferings come upon us, let us, too, kneel in the garden of olives; let us drain the chalice of suffering to the dregs on Golgotha, let us look up with courage and holy zeal. Good Friday was followed by a joyful Easter morn for the incarnate God, and we, too, shall enjoy a day of rejoicing, for if we suffer with Christ we shall also be glorified with Him. Our cross will be for us Jacob's ladder, upon which we shall ascend from earth to heaven, where there shall be no more weeping, no more pain, but where eternal joy, eternal peace, and eternal rejoicing will reign.

2. The glorified risen Saviour bears in His hand, instead of the reed, a flag of victory, upon which is written, "I am the resurrection and the life; whosoever believes in me shall live, though he were already dead." My brethren, what a consoling word! We can exclaim with jubilation: Death, where is thy sting? Death is defeated; now we may face death with confidence and say with Job: "I know that my Redeemer liveth, and that he will raise me up at the last day." Dry thy tears, then, poor wife, thou who art weeping at the heavy loss of thy children's provider; weep not, poor husband, at the early death of thy wife; children, mourn not the loss of your parents, who have left you orphans. My brethren, let us not weep and mourn for our beloved dead, like those who have no hope. We have a hope in the risen Saviour, that He will one day send His Angels to call us from our graves; we shall see one another again; we shall rejoice, and our joy no man shall take from us.

And if in our days we look sorrowfully into the future, and if the enemy presses hard upon our mother, the Church, she, too, our Church, will arise from the grave of oppression. That this will be the case every century testifies; the deeper they dig her grave, the tighter they seal and close it, the more gloriously has she ever arisen from the grave, and the more victoriously does she unfurl her flag. Her founder, who rose from the grave today, has said: "The gates of hell shall never prevail against her." And this founder proclaims joyfully to the redeemed world today: "All hail, Conqueror of Golgotha, Conqueror like unto none other! Alleluia!"

Let us, therefore, dear brethren, celebrate this Easter festival with glad, jubilant hearts; let us, at the empty grave of the Redeemer, the Prince of Peace, extend to one another the hand of pardon. He calls to us indeed: Peace be unto you! Let us break the bonds of sin, let us live in God, let us swear fidelity anew today to the victorious flag of Jesus Christ, let us stand fast in the faith! Then, yes then, we shall one day arise gloriously; we shall be transformed, and we shall possess the kingdom which has been prepared for us from the beginning. God grant it! Amen.

LOW SUNDAY

"EASTER CONFESSION"

"Now the Pasch, the festival day of the Jews, was near at hand."
St. John vi. 4.

MY DEAR PEOPLE, the blessed time in which many Christians renounce sin and the devil and take refuge under the sweet yoke of the Redeemer, has come. Would that we had lived in the happy days of the first Christians, who looked forward to the Paschal feast with holy joy. O fair day of salvation and mercy and grace, what has become of thee? Where are those holy, heavenly joys which formed the happiness of the children of God? Yes, my dear people, this time of grace may harbor for us either salvation or utter destruction; it leads to our salvation if we cooperate with the graces which are offered to us in this most precious time, and it will cause our destruction if we do not partake of these graces or even despise them. We are now in Easter-tide, also called Passover; in other words, it signifies the transition from the death of sin to the life of grace. By this explanation of the word Pasch (Easter) you will be able to judge for yourselves whether you have a right to feel satisfied, particularly those among you who, in sullen obedience to the wording of the laws of the Church, are content with a single confession every year and the subsequent Easter Communion.

Why, my dear people, has the Church instituted the holy season of Lent? You will answer that the holy time of Lent has been instituted for the purpose of giving us an opportunity to prepare ourselves worthily for the celebrating of Easter, a time in which our dear Lord seems to dispense His graces in a greater measure than at any other time, and during which we are constantly urged to stir up our conscience and free ourselves from sin. Yes, my friends, that much you have learned in your catechism; but if I would ask even a child what sin is committed by him who neglects to fulfil his Easter duty the child would simply answer, "a mortal sin"; and upon a further question, "how many mortal sins are needed to cast man into hell"? the answer would be, "one single sin for which we have not obtained forgiveness"! Well, then, my friends, are you going to fulfil your Easter duty? If not, you commit a mortal sin. I have heard people say: "Well, if I am sent to hell, I shall not be alone, at all events." If it is all the same to these people whether they are saved or damned, let them find consolation in that. If the idea that they will have plenty of company in their misfortune eases their mind, why should they trouble themselves about anything? But, poor soul, what dost thou say to such thoughts of the sinful body in which you are imprisoned? How many tears wilt thou have to shed in eternity? Jesus Christ has done so much for thee, and thou wilt be separated from Him forever!

Now, let us see how it stands with the confession and communion of those who are satisfied with attending to this duty once a year, so that we may learn whether they live with a clear conscience or not. If for a good confession nothing would be necessary but to enumerate one's sins, ask God for forgiveness, and perform some little act of penance, then sin, which the catechism describes as such a terrible monster, would not be anything so awful after all; nothing would be easier than to regain the lost grace and to follow the path which leads to heaven, and of which Jesus Christ Himself says, that it is so difficult to follow. Listen to the words which He addressed to the youth who asked Him what good he should do to have life everlasting, and whether the way that leads into heaven was hard. What did the Lord answer? "The path," he said, "is narrow, and very few tread it; and even of those who follow it, very few reach the goal." Yes, indeed, my dear people, some of you, after having lived through a whole year without fear or trembling, occupied only with worldly cares, pleasures, and pursuits, without having done anything toward your spiritual improvement, and toward the acquisition of virtues, here you come several weeks after Easter, very reluctantly, recount your sins as if you were reading from a story-book, and say a few prayers. And that is all. After it is all over, you go your old way and do exactly what you have done before. When Easter comes round again you act in the same way over again, and so on until death. And then you expect God to set aside justice, and give you His grace! You may rest assured, my friends, that such confessions are fruitless, if nothing worse.

To make you more fully convinced, let us now, my dear friends, go a little deeper into this matter. If our confession is to reconcile us with God, we must detest our sins from the bottom of the heart; we must be repentant, not because we have to tell the priest things which we would rather keep concealed, but because we have offended God; because we have remained in sin so long and have despised the many graces by which God tried to draw us away from our sins. This it is, my friends, which should break the icy crust around our hearts, and draw the tears from our eyes. Then, if we are really and truly penetrated with sorrow for our sins, then we will hasten to repair the damage done, and return as quickly as possible to our dear Lord. If you had a quarrel with a dear friend, would you not, when you found out that you were in the wrong, try everything to be reconciled to him as soon as possible? Or, if your friend found himself in that position, would you not expect him to do the same? And if he neglected to do so, would you not come to the conclusion that it was immaterial to him whether you were friends or the contrary? Now, this comparison should be perfectly clear to you. Is it possible for anyone who has committed a sin through weakness, thoughtlessness, or wickedness to remain long in that state of sin if he feels a true repentance? Would he not immediately take refuge in the sacrament of penance? If, instead of doing this, he remains for a whole year in the state of sin, and finds even the holy season of Lent inconvenient to free himself from it; if, when Easter comes round, he still waits until the last Sunday or two before he rushes from sin to the table of the Lord, and approaches Holy Communion indifferently, what good do you think will it do him?

No matter how long the Paschal time might be prolonged, some would wait until the last day before doing their duty. If the Church would say that we must go to Communion at least once in ten years, they would wait ten years; and if the Church had no law at all on the subject, they would wait until their dying day. Because neither repentance for the offense offered to God nor the love for God drives these people to Communion at Easter-tide, but merely the observance of the letter of the law and the idea that they will be able to say that they have fulfilled their Easter duty. But the fact of the matter is that they have merely added another sin to those with which their souls are laden. If you had real repentance in your heart, would you keep those sins for a whole year upon your conscience? If you had really the intention of leading a better life, would not a change in your mode of life, even the smallest, be observable?

I will not speak of those unfortunates who, for fear that they will be refused absolution, confess only half their sins, or who cover a shameless life with the mantle of virtue, and approach in that state the Holy Sacrament. They eat and drink damnation to themselves, and deliver themselves over to the devil.

I hope that all this does not apply to you, my friends, but I must repeatedly draw your attention to the fact that a single confession each year cannot be satisfying to your soul. Let me tell you what is necessary for a good confession, and you will be convinced that a confession once a year can not be satisfactory. To obtain forgiveness, your confession should be sincere and humble, accompanied by a real sorrow for the offense given to God and the firm resolution not to sin any more in the future. In my opinion, it is very difficult, almost impossible, to bring all these conditions to confession if you go only once a year.

What is a Christian who makes a confession of his sins at the feet of the priest? He is a sinner, who throws himself before his God with repentance in his heart like one accused before his judge, and who says: "O Lord, I am a malefactor, not worthy to be called Thy child. I have led a life contrary to the commandments of my faith. I have had nothing but aversion for everything appertaining to religious duty. Sundays and holidays of obligation were for me only days of pleasure and dissipation. In short, I have done nothing worthy of Thee. I shall be lost, I shall be damned, if God has no mercy on me." This, my dear brethren, is the feeling of a Christian who has an abhorrence of his sins in his heart.

Now, tell me, do those who are satisfied to remain in sin for fully twelve months, and to whom Easter comes only too soon, do those people, I say, confess like that? O God, Thou knowest the yearly confessions of those unfortunate ones who attend to their duty with great reluctance. Do they act like a malefactor covered with sins, and filled with repentance for their offenses offered to God? Do they accuse themselves and deem themselves unworthy of the pardon for which they ask? No; they come to tell a story, and they tell it badly, because they dissemble, and try to appear as innocent as possible. Such a one does not lose his temper, but he accuses a neighbor of having excited him; he has missed Mass, but he accuses the company he was in of preventing him to attend it; he ate meat on Friday, but he would not have done it if he had not been induced by others to do so. Husband accuses wife, the wife her husband; brother accuses sister, sisters their brothers. At the Confiteor they accuse themselves, saying, "through my fault," and a minute later they excuse themselves and accuse others. No humility, no sincerity, no repentance! Such is the demeanor of those who go to confession only once a year. The priest can tell perfectly well from the way they act that they are not in a proper condition to be entitled to absolution. But if he wishes to give them more time for proper preparation, so as to protect them from the danger of committing sacrilege, they grumble, and say they have no time to come again; that they could not prepare themselves any better, and if this particular priest would not give them absolution they could go to other priests who were not so particular.

I must admit that there are some who try with all their might to examine themselves thoroughly, and to mention all their sins as much as possible, but they do so with such indifference, such coldness, and such insensibility that it breaks the poor priest's heart to listen to them. There is no sigh, no tear, no emotion to show the contrition and the pain they should feel in their heart for having committed such sins. The priest is obliged to assume that they feel more than they show, to consider them worthy of absolution. We all know that tears and sighs are not infallible signs of repentance and conversion. It occurs only too often that many bemoan their sins in the tribunal of penance, and are no better Christians afterward than they were before; but at the same time it is very suspicious if people tell you with coldness and indifference of occurrences which should call forth bitter tears, and should well nigh break their hearts. If they really have any feeling of contrition in their hearts, why should there not be any outward manifestation of it? It is only too probable that the emotion which is lacking in their words is also lacking in their hearts, and that the sorrow over their sins is no greater than they show outwardly. They are the Christians who, after Easter, lead no better lives than they did before, and are not a whit more careful to avoid sin.

If, my dear friends, the regret over having offended God is to be considered genuine, it must include the sincere intention not to sin any more. If this intention is really sincere, it should determine us to avoid sin, to give up all thoughts of revenge, and detest all sins of impurity, and to try hard to exterminate all our passions and bad habits. How can your determination not to offend God any more be considered sincere if, after your confession, you lead the same kind of life that you have led before; if you frequent the same society in which you have been tempted so often? You have had the same intention of leading a better life when you went to confession last year, but what efforts did you make to carry out your intention? None! And why? Because you did not really and sincerely intend to lead a better life; your confession was a deception, your repentance a sham. What did you accuse yourself of last year? Was it not intemperance, lewdness, pride, passion, and neglect of divine service? And what did you accuse yourself of this year? Was it not the very same you had to confess before? And what will you have to accuse yourself of next year, if you are alive? The same sins over again.

All this happens, my dear friends, because you have no real desire to lead a God-fearing life; you have gone to confession merely because it is the custom, and because you want to be able to say that you have fulfilled your Easter duty, while, as a matter of fact, you go to confession every year, only to add more sins to your old ones. You are not aware of how the devil deceives you. If he would advise you instead of going to confession once a year, not to go at all, he would frighten you, and you would not believe him. But he is contented to let you remain in your own bad habits, and to rule over you in that way. Do you doubt my words? Then examine your life, and see whether you have improved, or whether you have at least avoided a few of the sins which you have confessed year after year.

Hence, dear brethren, be not satisfied with a confession once a year, for if you are in the state of sin you run the risk of perishing in it, and being lost forever. The same fate will meet you if, from fear or shame, you have concealed a sin, or if you have made your confession without true repentance and the firm resolution to do better, or if, after years and years of confessions, you do not find an improvement in your mode of life. To those who do not go to confession even at Easter I have nothing to say; if they insist upon going to perdition, that is their own affair. Let us bemoan their misfortune, and pray for them as it is the duty of every true Christian. Let us pray to God that we may not be stricken with the same blindness. Let us resist courageously the world and the devil, and let us sigh unceasingly for our real home—heaven—and for our glorification and eternal salvation! Amen.

SECOND SUNDAY AFTER EASTER

ON PERSEVERANCE

"He that shall persevere unto the end, he shall be saved."
—Matt. x. 22.

HE DIVINE SAVIOUR says: "He that fights and perseveres to the end of his life, without being overcome, or, when he has fallen, rises up again and perseveres, he shall be crowned." That is to say, he will be saved—words, dearly beloved, which produce in us fear and trembling when we reflect upon the dangers which beset us on every side, upon our weakness and the multitude of enemies by which we are surrounded. Let us not be surprised at so many saints forsaking parents, friends, possessions, and pleasures, that some should hide themselves away in the dark forests, others bewailing their sins in the clefts of rocks; others, again, shut themselves up in a solitary cell, to mourn there for the rest of their lives, far from the noisy world, and to occupy themselves with fighting the enemy of their salvation, fully convinced that heaven is only for those who persevere.

Now what is it "to persevere"?

"To persevere," my friends, means to be ready to make any sacrifice: rather to lose our wealth, our free will, our liberty, yea, even life itself, than to offend God. But what does it mean "not to persevere"?

"Not to persevere" means to relapse into our old sins, not long ago confessed, to frequent that bad company again which led us into sin; this is of all evils the greatest, because we thereby lose God, draw down His wrath upon us, estrange our soul from heaven, and make it ripe for hell. So as to help you to realize this properly, I will tell you the means which you must use to preserve the graces which you have received during this holy Paschal time. They are these four:

    I.—Obedience to the promptings of grace
    II.—The avoidance of bad company
    III.—Prayer
    IV.—The frequent use of the Sacraments

I. The first means to advance perseveringly on the way to heaven is to obey faithfully, and make use of the inspirations of grace which God gives us. All the saints have attained to their blessed lot only through obeying faithfully the voice of the Holy Ghost, and the damned owe their miserable state only to the fact that they have despised these inspirations. This alone ought to prove to you how precious these stirrings of conscience are, and how necessary it is to obey them. But you may argue, "How are we to know whether we have obeyed these inspirations of grace, or resisted them?" If you do not know how to recognize this, then listen to me for a moment, and I will explain it to you. First of all, I say that grace consists in the suggestions to our thoughts that we should avoid evil, and do good. Let us consider a few particular cases, so that you may understand this thoroughly. In the morning when you rise, turn your thoughts to God, give Him your heart, offer up your work to Him by kneeling down to say your prayers. If you do this at once and with a good will, you obey the promptings of grace; if you do not do this at all, or else if you do it badly, you do not obey them. You feel a desire to go to Confession, so as to overcome your faults and not to remain in your former condition, because had death overtaken you, you would have been lost eternally. If you obey this divine prompting you are faithful followers of the inspiration of grace. But if you leave these incentives unnoticed, for instance, to give alms, to do works of penance, to hear Mass, then you resist them.

In this way, beloved, we obey or resist grace. All this is a question of interior grace.

Exterior graces are, for instance, good reading, conversation with pious men who point out to us the necessity of changing our mode of life, of serving God better, of the remorse which we shall feel at the hour of death, or good examples which convert us. Also instruction by which we discern the means which we must employ to serve God, our duties toward Him, toward ourselves, and toward our neighbor. Observe well that your salvation or damnation depends upon this.

We know from the Gospel that all the conversions which Jesus made during His life were founded on perseverance. You know, beloved, how Christ converted Peter. It is mentioned that the Saviour looked at him, and that Peter wept over his sins; and his conversion assures us that he remained in the state of grace, and sinned no more. How was Matthew converted? We know that Christ met him and told him to follow, and

Matthew followed Him. What makes his conversion appear to us to be true is the fact that he never returned to his office as a collector of taxes; from that moment he never forsook Jesus. He persevered in grace and turned his back upon sin forever. A holy Bishop said to his flock: "If you were to give all your possessions to the poor, let your body be flayed, and your blood be shed; if each one of you was to suffer as much as all the martyrs put together; if your skin be torn off like St. Bartholomew's, or if you be sawed to pieces like Isaias, or be roasted on a slow fire like St. Lawrence; if you had not perseverance, that is to say, if you would relapse into sins again, and if death should surprise you in this state, everything would be lost. Who among us will be saved? Those who have fought for forty or sixty years? Possibly, dear brethren. Those whose hair turned gray in the service of the Lord? Possibly, dear brethren, but if they are wanting in perseverance they are as uncertain of their salvation as Solomon, of whom the Holy Ghost said that he was the wisest king upon earth, but of whose salvation we are very much in doubt, although he imagined himself perfectly sure of it.

"He that shall persevere unto the end, he shall be saved." Ought we not to tremble, dear brethren, we who fall every moment? There will be no heaven for us unless we are more steadfast than we have been heretofore.

How often do we not torment ourselves thinking whether we shall be lost or saved? Useless scruples! Listen to Moses, who, when he was dying, had the twelve tribes of Israel assembled, and said to them: "You know that I have loved you tenderly—that I have sought nothing but your happiness and salvation. Now that I am going to give God an account of all my actions, I must tell you the following, and you must not forget it: 'Serve God faithfully; remember the many benefits which He has lavished upon you; never separate yourselves from Him, no matter what it may cost you. You will have enemies who will persecute you, and strive all in their power to make you forsake God. Take courage, therefore; you are sure of the kingdom if you remain faithful to God.'"

Ah, my brethren, if even saints were all their lives afraid of not persevering, what will become of us who are without virtue, without confidence in God, laden with sins, and who are careless of the snares which the devil sets for us? We go about blindly among these numerous dangers, we sleep quietly in the midst of a crowd of enemies, who are all bent upon our destruction. But you will say: "What are we to do so as not to be overpowered?"

II. My friend, you must shun the occasions which have been the cause of your fall. You must take refuge in incessant prayer, receive frequently and worthily the Sacraments. If you do this, if you take this path, you will be sure to persevere; but if you do not take this precaution, no matter what penance you may lay down for yourself, you will go to perdition. I say you must fly by the occasions of sin.

Where did you learn these improper songs, and those ungodly manners, which cause you innumerable bad thoughts and desires? Was it not in that bad company? Who taught you to judge so rashly? Was it not the society of that slanderer who talked uncharitably of his neighbor? Where did that habit originate by which you sin and lead others to sin through improper looks and actions? Was it not by frequenting the society of that unchaste person? Why do you no longer receive the Sacraments? Is it not because you associate with that ungodly person whose aim it is to rob you of your faith by representing to you that what the priest says is exaggeration? Who tells you that Religion has only one good purpose, and that is to keep the young in bounds; but that only ignorant people allow themselves to be influenced by it; that those better informed simply laugh at it? Let me tell you, by the way, that these wise people hold these views no longer when they are on their deathbed. Would such doubts arise in your mind away from this society? Never!

III. Prayer is indispensable in order to obtain perseverance in the Divine Grace received in the Sacrament of Penance. By prayer you can do all things; you turn, as it were, the Divine Will, if I may say so. Without prayer you are incapable of doing anything. This alone should prove to you the necessity and the power of prayer. All saints began their conversion by prayer, and through prayer they persevered. All the damned were lost because they neglected prayer.

The prayer which I recommend to you as being powerful with God, which obtains many graces for us, which urges Him to grant what we ask, this prayer is composed of remorse and hope. Remorse at the sight of our unworthiness, and the dishonor which we have offered to God and His graces. We must acknowledge that we are unworthy to appear before Him, unworthy to ask Him for His graces, because we have already received so much from Him, and have continually repaid Him with ingratitude, for which reason we should fear every moment for our salvation. Penetrated with grief for having offended so good a God, let us shed tears of contrition and thanksgiving from penitent hearts. Mind and heart should be profoundly humbled at the thought of our infinite baseness, and of the sublimity of Him whom we have offended, and who in spite of all this permits us hope and grace.

I say prayer must be composed of despair and hope. Hope in the greatness of God's mercy, in His desire of making us happy, and in what He has done to merit heaven for us. Animated with this consoling thought, we can turn to Him with the greatest confidence. We should say with St. Bernard: "My God, that which I ask of Thee I have not deserved, but Thou hast merited it for me. If thou dost hear me, I thank Thy kindness and mercy." What does a Christian do, filled with these dispositions? Penetrated with feelings of the most fervent gratitude, he forms the firm resolution never again to offend his God who comes to meet him with His graces. This is the prayer, dear brethren, which is so necessary for us to obtain forgiveness and the precious gift of perseverance.

IV. As fourth and most important means, we must frequently receive the holy Sacraments so as to preserve sanctifying grace. A Christian who makes use of prayer and the Sacraments is to the devil what a soldier on horseback, equipped with weapons, is to a defenseless enemy, who flees at the very sight of him. Should he, however, get off his horse, and lay aside his weapons, the enemy will fall upon him, throw him to the ground, and overpower him. While he was armed, the sight of him alone seemed to crush his enemy.

The devil said to St. Theresa that on account of her great love of God, her frequent reception of the Sacraments, he could not breathe in the places where she had been. Why? Because the Sacraments gave her strength to persevere in the grace of God. There has never been a saint who kept away from the Sacraments and still preserved the friendship of God. In the Sacraments they gained the necessary strength to resist the devil, and not to be overpowered by him. The reason is this: when we pray to God He lavishes innumerable graces upon us, to fortify us and to give us courage. He Himself comes to destroy our enemy. As soon as the devil is aware of His presence, he casts himself in despair into the abyss. This is the principal reason why the devil strives his utmost to prevent us from receiving the Sacraments, and incites us to profane them. Yes, dear brethren, when any one receives the Sacraments frequently the devil loses his power over him.

However, we must make a distinction. I am speaking of those who receive the Sacraments with the right dispositions, who have a real horror of sin, who gladly avail themselves of all the means which God offers them to avoid a relapse into sin. Christians who go to confession one day, and the next day fall again into the same sins, I do not include them, nor those who confess their sins without contrition and without detestation, who repeat them every time as if they were telling a story, who make not the slightest preparations; who, without examining their conscience, tell just of what sins they happen to think; who approach the Lord's table without having examined into the recesses of their heart, without having obtained the grace to recognize their sins, without feeling the proper repentance, and without any resolution of not sinning again. All these persons work out their own perdition. Instead of fighting against the devil, they range themselves on his side, and bury themselves in hell.

What are we, then, to conclude from all this?

That we should promptly obey the incentives of grace, never fail in our prayers, and with proper dispositions receive the Sacraments. If beloved brethren, we carry out this resolution, if we remain faithful to it to the end, there shall be fulfilled in us the words of Christ: "He that shall persevere unto the end, he shall be saved." This I wish you all. Amen.

THIRD SUNDAY AFTER EASTER.

TRIBULATIONS

"Amen, amen, I say to you, that you shall lament and weep, but the world shall rejoice."
St John xvi. 20.

WHO, my beloved Christians, could listen without trembling to the address of the Redeemer to His disciples before His ascension into heaven, wherein He tells them that their life would be a series of tears, suffering, and bearing of the cross, while the rest of the world would rejoice and make merry? Not as if the people of the world did not also have their troubles, because sorrow and consternation are the natural consequence of a bad conscience, and a disorderly life finds its own punishment in a troubled heart. The lot of the good Christians is entirely different from this: they must make up their minds to suffer and weep in this life, but their suffering and their tears earn for them a joy and a pleasure which are unlimited in extent and duration. On the other hand, the children of the w6rld, after a few moments of enjoyment, mixed with much bitterness, follow the path which leads toward the eternal fire. "Woe unto you," says Jesus Christ to them, "woe unto you who think of nothing but rejoicing, for your joys shall bring forth eternal sufferings in the abode of my justice." "Ah, blessed ones," He says to the good Christians, "blessed are ye who pass your days in tears, for the day will come when I myself shall be your consolation." I will now show you, my dear Christians, that the cross, poverty, contempt, and suffering is the lot of a Christian who wishes to save his soul, and who tries to be pleasing to God.

You must either suffer in this life or give up the hope of seeing God in heaven.

Let me tell you, that from the moment that you are numbered among the children of God you must take upon yourself the cross, and never lay it down until the moment of your death. When Jesus Christ speaks to us from heaven He never fails to remind us that we can only merit it by carrying the cross, and by suffering: "Take up thy cross and follow me, not for a day, a month or a year, but for thy whole life." St. Augustine says: "Leave the pleasures and amusements to the children of the world; but you, who are the children of God, weep with the children of God."

Sufferings and persecutions are of the greatest avail to us, because we can find therein a very efficient means to make atonement for our sins, since we are bound to suffer for them either in this world or in the next. The sufferings in this world are not unlimited, neither in intensity nor in duration: the merciful God chastises us on account of His great mercy toward us; He allows us to suffer for a time, only to make us happy for all eternity. However great our sufferings may be in this world, He touches us only with His little finger, as it were; while in the other world the tortures and punishments which we have to go through are dictated by His great power and wrath. There it will seem that God wanted to exhaust His whole power to avenge His offended majesty. There our torments will be infinite in severity and duration. In this life our sufferings are mitigated by the consolation and help which our holy religion offers us, but in the other world there is no consolation, no mitigation; on the contrary, there everything drives to despair. Oh, how blessed is the Christian who spends his whole life in tears and tribulation, as thereby he prevents the greatest misfortune that can befall him, and procures for himself everlasting joy. Job, the holy man, tells us that life is but a continuous misery. Let us go into particulars. Let us go from house to house, and we will find planted everywhere the cross of Christ. Here it is the loss of earthly possessions, the result of an injustice, which has thrown a whole family into misery; there a sickness, which holds a person on a bed of suffering; there it is a wife who eats her bread in tears and sorrow on account of a drunken, brutal husband. There, again, we meet poor old people who have been thrown upon the charities of this world by their ungrateful children. Here is a man bowed down with sorrow and shame because he has been accused of misdeeds which he never committed. And, again, there is a house filled with lamentations over the loss of a father or mother, or a child.

Thus our mortal life seems poor and miserable, considered from a human standpoint; but if we consider our life from the standpoint of our religion, we shall soon be convinced that we are miserable only so long as we brood over, and complain about, our troubles from a human view of things.

Why are you so apt to consider yourselves unfortunate? Because you are thinking of those whose circumstances in life are better than your own. The poor man, in the misery of his poverty, instead of thinking of those who, on account of sickness, or, perhaps, having been put into prison or the poor-house, are worse off than himself, lets his thoughts dwell upon the mansions of the rich and their earthly possessions and pleasures. The sick man, instead of thinking of the tortures suffered by those condemned by the just judgment of the Lord to eternal punishment, directs his thoughts only to the few lucky ones who have never had the misfortune of being poor or sick. That is the reason, my dear friends, why we consider our sufferings unbearable. But what is the consequence? The consequence is that our grumbling and complaining deprives us of all the merits which we might gain in heaven through our sufferings: on the one hand, we bear them without consoling ourselves with the thought that they open to us the hope for forgiveness; on the other hand, we increase our sins by our impatience and grumbling, instead of diminishing them by offering up our suffering in atonement for them. It is our impatience, our want of submission under the will of God, our want of confidence in Him, which make us so unhappy, and which are the cause of augmenting our sins instead of diminishing them, by offering up our sufferings in atonement. How unfortunate and full of despair is the life of him who forgets for what purpose God has sent him a cross to bear!

But you will say to me: "We have heard these sentiments expressed hundreds of times; they are merely words, not consolations; we say the same things to those whom we see suffer." But I say to you, my friends, look up, look up to heaven. Withdraw your hearts from the mire of this life into which it has sunk; tear asunder the clouds of mist which hide the heavenly reward from you, which you may obtain by means of your sufferings here below. Lift up your eyes and see the good Father, who holds ready for you a glorious mansion in His dominions. God chastises you only to heal the wounds which you, poor sinner, have inflicted upon your own soul. God sends you the suffering only to crown you with everlasting glory.

If you wish to know, my dear friends, how to take up the cross, handed to you by the Almighty or by your own fellow beings, let me cite to you as an example, how Job took up his cross, how he never got discontented even at the loss of his numerous possessions and family, nor when the fire from heaven destroyed his flocks, nor when the thieves drove away the rest of his cattle, nor when a terrific cyclone destroyed his house and buried his children, but devotedly exclaimed: "Alas, the hand of the Lord lieth heavy upon me!"

There he had been lying on a dunghill for years, covered with sores, without help or consolation, deserted even by his own wife, who, instead of consoling him, only mocked at him with the words: "Why don't you pray to thy God for death, so that you may be delivered from all this misery; seest thou not how thy God, whom thou hast served so faithfully, how he tortures thee?" And he merely said to her: "Thou hast spoken like one of the foolish women; if we have received good things at the hand of God, why should we not accept the evil?"

But some of you will say, "I can not understand why God should visit us with such calamities; He, who is love itself and who loves us with an infinite love." You may as well ask me: "How is it possible that a father can chastise his own child, or a doctor give his patient bitter medicine?" Do you think it would be better to let this child live unrestrained than to lead it through punishment back to the path of virtue, and thus into heaven? Do you think that the physician should let his patient die rather than give him bitter medicine? How blind we are if we reason like that! God must chastise us, and if we are without cross, then we may be sure that we do not belong to the number of His children. Jesus himself said, that the kingdom of heaven would only be for those who suffer and fight until the end. And does He not always speak the truth? Contemplate the lives which the saints have led, look at the way which they have pursued; from the moment they ceased to suffer they feared that the Lord had deserted them, and that they had lost Him forever. "My God, my God!" cried out St. Augustine, in tears, "spare me not in this life, but let me suffer much. Show me Thy mercy only in the other life, and I am contented."

Most people who are afflicted with sufferings say: "What have I done to the dear Lord, that He should send me so much misery?" And I answer: "God sends you this affliction, because thou hast indeed done evil, my friend. Take all the commandments, one by one, and see whether you have not sinned against each and every one of them. Let all the days of your sinful life, since the innocent days of your childhood, pass muster in your memory, and then you will not ask what evil you have done, that God should so chastise you. Are the bad habits into which you have sunk for so long a time to count for nothing? And what about your pride? Do you think it is right that you should expect everybody to bow before you because you happen to have a few acres of land more than another, which may likely be the cause of your damnation? Have you forgotten that cupidity which keeps you forever in a state of dissatisfaction; what of that self-love, that vanity, that hasty temper, that thirst for vengeance, that intemperance, that jealousy? Have you forgotten your criminal neglect of the Blessed Sacrament, and all those religious obligations you should have performed for the benefit of your soul? Does your forgetfulness of all these and other facts make you less guilty? And if you are guilty, should not the justice of God punish you? Tell me, my friend, what penance have you done to atone for your sins, what fasting, what mortification? Where are your good works? When, after so many sins, you have not shed a tear, after so much avarice you have not given the smallest alms, after so much pride you will not suffer the least humiliation; when, after your flesh has served the evil one, you will not hear of penance, then heaven must step in and impose that penance which you did not practise yourself.

Oh, how blind we are! We would wish to do evil without being punished for it, or, in other words, we would rather that God was unjust. Indeed, O Lord! let the sinner lead a life of ease; do not lay Thy hand too heavily upon him; let him fatten like a beast of sacrifice, destined for that eternal punishment, where he will have time to make satisfaction to Thy justice; spare him in this life; he wants to have it so. He may do penance in the eternal fire, penance without merit, penance without end. O my Lord, do not let this misfortune befall us! "O my God," exclaimed St. Augustine, "increase my misery and my suffering as much as Thou wilt, only mete out to me Thy mercy in the life to come."

"Yes," says another one, "this is all very well for those who have committed these grievous sins, but I, thank the Lord, have never done anything of the kind." Such a person, therefore, believes that because he thinks that he has not committed these sins he need not suffer. But I say, that it is for the very reason that such a person tries to do right that God will send him trials and permit that he be mocked at, despised, and his piety ridiculed, because God wants to try him by sending him sickness and tribulations. Look at Jesus Christ, the true model of your life, and see whether He lived a single moment without suffering, and, in fact, suffering so much that the human mind has not yet been able to fathom it. Why did the Pharisees persecute Him and try continually to ensnare Him, so as to have a reason for condemning Him to death? Did they do it because He was thought wrong? Not at all; they did it because His miracles, His poverty, and humility condemned their pride and evil deeds. If we look through Holy Writ we see that from the beginning of the world suffering, reproach, and mockery was the share of the children of God—that is, of those who strove to lead a God-fearing life. Who, indeed, will deride and reproach those who fulfil the duties of their religion but a poor, miserable outcast from hell, who has been sent upon this earth for the purpose of trying to draw others into the abyss, which is his dwelling-place for all eternity. Let me give you a few examples. Why did Cain slay his brother Abel? He slew him because he could not induce him to do wrong, as he did himself. Why did Joseph's brothers throw him into the cistern? Because his God-fearing life was a reproach to their own dissolute way of living. What caused the persecutions of the Apostles, who were continually imprisoned, tortured, and maltreated, so that their life from the death of our Lord on was a continuous martyrdom? They all had to die in a most cruel and painful manner. And what had they done that they should suffer all that? They had sought only the honor of the Lord and the salvation of souls. If you are reproached, derided, mocked at, persecuted, though you have done nothing wrong, so much the better for you. If you have had to undergo no suffering in this world, how will it stand with you before the Lord on the day of Judgment?

If you are persecuted and ridiculed and injured, though you have done nothing wrong, you are, indeed, on the right way to heaven. What did the Saviour say? "Take up thy cross and follow me; they have persecuted me, they will persecute you; but be not discouraged, rather rejoice, for great is your reward in heaven. He who is not ready to suffer all things, even to lose his life for love of me, is not worthy of me." Amen.

FOURTH SUNDAY AFTER EASTER

THE PROGRESS OF CHRISTIANITY

" I have yet many things to say to you, but you can not bear them now."— John xvi. 12.

MY DEAR BRETHREN, among the reproaches charged against the Church by her enemies there are two which contradict each other. Heresy reproaches her with making new doctrines, and that for this reason she is no longer the Church of Christ. Unbelief, on the other hand, reproaches her with exactly the opposite, and finds fault because she steadfastly holds to the doctrines of her origin; that she must, therefore, be obstinate and an enemy to progress. Both are unjust reproaches. For it is not the Catholic Church which has departed from the teaching of Christ. She has added nothing new, but heresy has rejected many of the teachings and means of grace of Christ, which she continues to preach. The Church is not an enemy to progress, but she is an enemy to a return into the darkness of paganism, of vice, and of the gross ignorance of religious things, which she would countenance if she turned her back upon the light of the Gospel, if she rejected the teachings of divine revelation, as unbelief wants her to do. That the Church knows of a progress is taught by her divine founder Himself in today's Gospel in these words: "I have yet many things to say to you, but you can not bear them now. But when He, the Spirit of Truth, shall come, He will teach you all truth." The progress of the Church is ordained in these words in so far as:

I. *The Holy Ghost will bring about that the teaching of Christ shall be ever better known and understood,*

II. *The Holy Ghost will cause an ever-increasing influence of Christianity upon mankind.*

These two points shall be the subject of our consideration. May the

Holy Ghost enlighten us and guide us deeper into the holy truths of faith.

I. "I have yet many things to say to you, but you can not bear them now." Thus speaks the Saviour to the Apostles. But why could they not bear them then? The Apostles themselves gave the answer. For in spite of the presence of Jesus and of His divine teaching, they still showed, until the Ascension of the Lord, a disposition which was so worldly as to render them incapable of fully comprehending the divine mysteries. They even asked, shortly before the Lord's Ascension: "Wilt thou at this time restore again the kingdom to Israel?" (Acts i. 6.) They could even then relinquish the hope for a powerful earthly kingdom of the Messiah. That they should recognize and renounce such fallacies was to be the work of the Holy Ghost within them. As a practical result of the descent of the Holy Ghost upon them, they immediately received the essential knowledge of the nature of the Messiah's kingdom, promised by Jesus, as well as of the necessity of His passion and death, which was before so difficult for them to understand. Jesus had spoken of the one fold, into which He would also lead all his other sheep. (John x. 16.) Upon more than one occasion He had repeated this, in particular when he spoke of those who should come from the east and the west and sit down with the patriarchs (Matt. viii. 11), as also in the parable of the great supper (Luke xiv. 16); and yet it required, even after the coming of the Holy Ghost, a particular revelation to Peter in the story of the clean and unclean beasts (Acts x. 11) to induce him to receive the heathens into the Church without their passing through Judaism.

And as with this teaching, so it was with many others. The Apostles only attained to a full comprehension of the same through the Holy Ghost. Although Jesus had spoken repeatedly of three Persons in one Godhead, as, for instance, in His many promises of sending the Holy Ghost, and in His command to go and baptize (Matt, xxviii. 19), the Apostles were certainly wanting at that time in the knowledge of this mystery, as we find it defined by St. John in the beginning of his Gospel in the words: "For there are three that give testimony in heaven; the Father, the Word, and the Holy Ghost: and these three are one." (I. John v. 7.)

Jesus speaks here and there of the rejection of Judaism, its sacrifices and its customs; even the prophets, like Malachias, had already done this, and yet we see the Christians of the first Christian community still visiting the Temple. Only by the widespread growth of Christianity and its more visible formation did the Christians forsake this habit. All these and similar matters are referred to in the words of our Lord, that the Apostles could not bear them, that for them they then had no understanding. But they were there to receive it, and they did receive it through the operation of the Holy Ghost after the departure of Christ. They arrived at a better understanding of the teachings of Jesus, and this was some of the progress of Christianity.

But this progress was not to end with the death of the Apostles; it was to continue throughout the centuries. Revelation ceased more or less with the Ascension of the Lord. But a much clearer knowledge and an ever-increasing development of these doctrines took place. It is absolutely unjust, it is even calumny against the Church, to reproach her with formulating new doctrines of faith. What she has done was and is only to demonstrate more clearly and to bring more plainly to human comprehension the revealed truths. How brilliantly was this accomplished, for instance, by the voice and the pen of the Holy Fathers of the Church. Although they were not the voice of the Church, yet the voice of the Church, in speaking through general councils and the Popes, agreed almost invariably with the voice of the Fathers of the Church. How enlightening was such an explanation of the divine revelation, as opposed to the teachers of heresy, who appeared as early as the end of the first century. The necessary condemnation by the Church of their heretical teachings brought a more detailed statement of the true teaching with it, and the Church gladly availed herself of the cooperation of the inspired Fathers of the Church. The existence and the qualities of God, His relations to the world through creation and redemption, the most holy Trinity, divine grace and its relation to our free will—these are all subjects which are taught in divine revelation, but in consequence of the magnitude of its mysteries for our poor and imperfect understanding they underwent many misstatements at the hands of heretical teachers and their adherents. To protest against this, and to proclaim the truth in opposition to them, and to define it as far as possible in human language, that was the work of the Holy Ghost in the office of instructor of the Church. This was accomplished through all the centuries up to the overthrowing of the heresies of modem times by the councils of Trent and of the Vatican in Rome. In the ever-clearer definition of the truth consists the progress of Christianity; it is the fulfilment of the promise: "But when he, the Spirit of truth, shall come, he will teach you all truth."

II. And still in another sense Jesus could say, "I have yet many things to say to you, but you can not bear them now," namely, in reference to the influence of the teaching of Jesus upon conduct and morals. Here, also, we speak of progress of Christianity. Jesus gave an intimation of this influence by the parable of the leaven. But in what manner this parable should be fulfilled the Apostles certainly had a much better conception a few years after the Ascension of the Lord than at the time when they heard it. They understood, then, how, before the coming of the Holy Ghost, they had not been able to hear what Jesus had yet to say to them but had not said.

The commandment of exercising charity was already known to them from the Old Testament. How often, besides, had not Jesus impressed it upon them. But what great fruit this great commandment was to bear through the Holy Ghost they had yet to witness. How greatly the Apostles, enlightened by the Holy Ghost, were influenced in all things by Christian charity is shown in their letters.

The many precepts they give therein upon the mutual obligations of married people, parents and children, masters and servants, those high in authority and subjects, are all founded upon charity. How severely James censures the pride and luxury of the rich; how Paul impresses upon the members of his community the obligation of supporting their needy brethren in the faith by taking up collections for them. We admire, also, the voluntary sharing of property in the Christian community at Jerusalem; and we see therein a development of Christianity as the Apostles understood it, while before they had a very imperfect idea of all these things. The evangelical counsels were recommended by Christ and practised by the Apostles according to the words of St. Peter: "Behold, we have forsaken all things and followed thee." And the observance of the evangelical counsels by the numerous religious orders of our own days, to the immeasurable benefit of the Church and of mankind, is a visible sign of the progress of Christianity which the Apostles could not comprehend when Jesus said to them: "I have yet many things to say to you, but you can not bear them now." Then again let us consider fasting. How completely it is founded upon the teaching and example of Jesus. But its practise, its extension, and its restrictions, regulated and ordered to suit time and place, and to suit the ability and conditions of mankind, is the prerogative of the Church, under the guidance of the Holy Ghost.

We might mention many subjects upon which we could make the same observations. But you will admit that what we have said is amply sufficient to make it clear that, though the Catholic Church is unchangeable in her doctrines of faith and morals, she is in no way the enemy to the right sort of progress. Let us be firmly convinced on this point. Not a word of divine revelation has been rejected or changed by the Church; we will neither reject, nor be deprived of, a syllable of it. But for progress away from heresy and unbelief, which are a step backward from light into darkness, we are grateful. We willingly commit ourselves to the guidance of the Church, wherein the Holy Ghost fulfils the promises of Christ: "But when he, the Spirit of truth, is come, he will teach you all truth, he shall glorify me; because he shall receive of mine, and shall shew it to you." (John xvi. 13, 14.) Let us allow ourselves to be conducted by the hand of the Church through this Holy Spirit ever deeper into the truths of faith; there we shall find contentment and joy, until faith is at last changed into the vision of God face to face. Amen.

FIFTH SUNDAY AFTER EASTER

PRAYER

"Amen, amen I say to you: If you ask the Father anything in my name, he will give it you."
John xvi. 23.

THERE can be no greater consolation for us, my dear people, than the promise which Christ gives us in today's Gospel, namely, that everything we shall ask of the Father in His name we shall receive. But, more than that, He was not satisfied with giving us the permission to ask for our necessities in His name; nay, He even demands it of us, begs it of us. He says to His Apostles: "Hitherto you have not asked anything in my name. Ask and you shall receive; that your joy may be full." This teaches us that prayer is the source of all the good and all the happiness we can hope for on this earth. Therefore, if we find ourselves poor or without enlightenment and grace, we may be sure that we can find the reason in the fact that we do not pray or that we do not pray properly. It is with sorrow that I must tell you, my friends, that a great many people do not know what it means to pray. To make you understand the great deal of good which we may obtain by prayer, I will show you that all misfortunes which oppress us on this earth are caused by the fact that we do not pray or that we pray badly. To induce you, my dear people, to pray often, and to pray properly, I will show you:

I. *Without prayer it is impossible to be saved*
II. *How and when we should pray.*

I. To show you the power of prayer and the graces which it brings down upon us from heaven, I need only tell you that by prayer alone the elect obtained the grace of perseverance. Prayer is to our soul what the rain is to the soil. Fertilize the soil ever so richly, it will remain barren unless fed by frequent rains. You may perform good works as much as you like; if you do not pray frequently and pray properly you will not be saved, for prayer opens our mind's eye and shows our soul the magnitude of our misery and the necessity of divine assistance. The Christian confides solely in God and not in himself. Yes, indeed, my friends, prayer has given perseverance to the saints. What was it that caused them to make such sacrifices, to leave their earthly possessions, their relatives and friends, and the commodities of this life, and to retire into the woods, there to pass the remainder of their earthly existence in bewailing their sins? It was prayer, my friends, which inflamed their hearts at the thought of God; it was prayer which awakened in them the ardent desire to please God and to live solely and alone for Him. Look at St. Mary Magdalen. What was her occupation after her conversion? Was it not prayer? Look at St. Peter. But why go so far back? Let us look at ourselves, my friends. Do we not, from the moment that we neglect our prayers, lose all taste for heavenly affairs, and is not our mind continually occupied with worldly subjects? As soon as we seek recourse again to prayer, so soon do we feel a longing for heavenly things. Yes, my friends, if we are so fortunate as to be in a state of grace, we will always seek for divine help in prayer.

Furthermore, my friends, I maintain that the conversion of all sinners is due to prayer, some extraordinary miracles, which happen but seldom, excepted. Remember what St. Monica did to obtain the conversion of her son; how she knelt before the image of the Crucified One, wept and prayed; how she implored saintly men to help her in her prayers. And, again, look at St. Augustine himself: how he wept and prayed when the desire to be converted had entered his heart. Yes, my friends, though we may be ever so laden with sins, if we seek refuge in prayer, and pray in the right way, we may be perfectly sure of the pardon of God. Ought we not to be amazed, my dear people, at the unceasing efforts which the devil makes to keep us from prayer and to lead us into evil, knowing, as he does, how powerful a weapon prayer is against his snares, and that God in His goodness will not refuse anything that is asked of Him in prayer? Oh, how many sinners might abandon sin if they only had recourse to prayer!

Again I say, my good friends, that the lost in hell were damned because they did not pray, or because they did not pray properly.

From that we may draw the conclusion that if we do not pray we make ourselves miserable for all eternity, and that if we do pray, and pray properly, we assure ourselves of our salvation. The saints were so convinced that prayer was absolutely necessary for their salvation that they did not feel contented to pray during the daytime, but they spent whole nights in prayer. Why, my good friends, do we feel such an aversion for this sweet and consoling practise? It is because we do not pray properly, and therefore do not feel the delight which the saints experienced. Indeed, my dear people, a heartfelt prayer is like a sweet-smelling oil spread over our soul, which will make us feel the eternal bliss the saints partake of in heaven. The truth of this you will find confirmed in the life of St. Francis of Assisi, who often, when he prayed, rose to such a height of ecstasy that he no longer knew whether he was still on this earth or enjoyed the company of the saints in heaven. One day in church such ardent feeling seized upon him that he exclaimed aloud: "O Lord, I can bear it no longer!"

But, you may say, that all this is very well for those who know how to pray and who know nice prayers. My dear friends, neither long nor nice prayers are considered by our dear Lord, but prayers which come from the innermost heart, and are uttered with great reverence and a real desire to please God.

II. I say that prayer is the lifting up of the heart to God. Or, rather, it should be like a pleasant confidence, such as might exist between a child and his father, or between friend and friend. To depict this happiness more plainly to you, let me ask you to imagine the dear Lord taking one of his poor creatures in His arms and showering all kinds of blessings in abundance over him. Need I say any more, my friends, how you should pray, or why prayer is of such vast benefit and so necessary for us?

What, then, should we think of those lukewarm Christians who say they have no time to pray. No time to pray! Poor, deluded beings! What is of more value—to try to please God and save your soul or to do your daily share of toil. No time to pray! Suppose God had let you die during the night, would you do your work today? Or if God had sent you a protracted sickness, would you then be able to perform your daily labor? Oh, what blindness! Such people deserve that God should let them perish in their blindness. We deem it sufficient to devote a few moments to Him, to thank Him for the graces which we receive from Him every moment of our lives. You say you are too busy, but do not forget, my friends, that your principal business in life is to please God and save your soul. If you do not attend to your work yourself, somebody else will take your place and do it; but if you lose your soul, who will save it for you?

But you may ask, "What profit do we gain from praying so continually?" as I ask you to do. This is the answer, my friend: Through prayer, the cross which we have to bear through this life seems less heavy to us, we are more easily relieved from sufferings, we think less of this life, and our mind is directed more to the mercy of God. Prayer strengthens our soul against sin, awakens in us the desire for repentance, and gives us a delight in practising the same; it makes us feel and understand how much sin must offend our dear Lord. In short, prayer makes of us friends of God, enriches our souls, and assures for us eternal life. Is it necessary, my dear friends, to say any more to induce you to spend the days of your life in close communion with the Lord by practising constant prayer! If we are imbued with the love of God prayer will come as natural to us as breathing. But it is not sufficient to pray in haste or to just devote one solitary moment to a hasty prayer. God wishes us to spend in prayer a time sufficiently long to beg for the necessary graces, to give thanks to Him for benefits received, to sigh over our transgressions and to implore His pardon.

But you may ask, "How is it possible to be constantly praying?" My dear people, there is nothing easier than that. All that is necessary to do is to occupy our minds from time to time, while we are working, with God, by making now and then an act of charity, to prove to Him that we love Him because He is goodness itself and deserves to be loved; or an act of humility, in so far as we deem ourselves unworthy of His graces which He imparts to us unceasingly; or, again, an act of confidence, by recalling to our mind that though we are laden with sin He loves us and longs to make us happy. Or at other times we should think of the Suffering and Passion of Jesus Christ, we should contemplate Him in the Garden of Olives bearing His cross, His being crowned with thorns, and of His crucifixion; or some other time of His birth, His flight into Egypt; or, again, of death, the judgment, hell and heaven. Or we might say a little prayer in honor of our guardian angel, and for one thing we should never omit to say the Angelus when the bells call. All this will keep awake in our mind the thought of our final destination, remind us that in a short time we shall no longer be of this earth, and warn us not to remain in sin, for fear that death may surprise us and find us unprepared. You see, my friends, how easy it is to pray constantly; all the saints did this very same thing. All we have to do is to follow in their footsteps, so that after this short life we may join them in heaven, in the everlasting bliss and adoration of God. Amen.

SIXTH SUNDAY AFTER EASTER

THE FOLLOWERS OF CHRIST SHOULD GIVE TESTIMONY OF HIM

"And you shall give testimony, because you are with me from the beginning."
John xv. 27.

When two kingdoms are at war with one another it is easy to distinguish the soldiers of either party by their arms, their uniforms, and their flags. A violent struggle has been going on since the beginning of the world between the King of heaven and earth and the prince of darkness as to which of them the human race should belong. Christ, the Redeemer, by His death and resurrection, has won the victory over hell. Before He entered gloriously into heaven as a conqueror, leading with Him the souls of the just of the old law, as the first-born of His victory, He founded His Church upon earth as His kingdom, in which we should continue to combat against hell, and by His power we should and could complete the victory. Therefore He says to His Apostles, the generals of His kingdom, "You will give testimony of me," and Holy Writ says of them, "With great power did the Apostles give testimony of the resurrection of Jesus Christ, our Lord." (Acts iv. 33.) The words of Christ apply also to us. We are all obliged to give testimony of Him, not by sermons and miracles, as the Apostles did, but by our life, by the imitation of Jesus; for as we have all become members of His body, and have received from Christ the name of "Christians," we are obliged to lead a life worthy of this Chief, not to bring disgrace upon His Holy Name, but so to live that in our life the Christian can be distinguished from the non-Christian. This is our testimony of Christ. I will now speak on this subject. In the Canticle of Canticles, the divine Bridegroom says to the soul that loves Him: (Cant. viii. 6): "Put me as a seal upon thy heart, as a seal upon thy arm." We bear this seal of Christ when we imitate Him:

I. In our will.
II. In our words.
III. In our works.

I. 1. David expresses what the will of our Redeemer was in these words, which the Holy Ghost permits Him to speak (Ps. xxxix. 8-9): "In the head of the book it is written of me that I should do thy will: O my God, I have desired it, and thy law in the midst of my heart." But Christ says of Himself (John vi. 38), "Because I came down from heaven, not to do my own will, but the will of him that sent me," and (John iv. 34) "My food is to do the will of him that sent me"; and the Apostle extols Him, saying (Phil. ii. 8): "He humbled himself, becoming obedient unto death, even the death of the cross." When He descended from the glory of heaven upon earth He sacrificed Himself to the will of His Father. "Thou willest, O my God," He said, as it were, with complete resignation, "that I should be born in a desolated stable; that I should shed my blood at the circumcision; that I should flee before Herod; that I should bear the burdens and the troubles of this earthly life for three and thirty years. Thou wiliest that I should be betrayed, despised, spit upon, buffeted upon the cheeks and scourged, crowned with thorns, nailed to the cross, and suffer the most cruel of deaths. My God, I will it also. I am ready to suffer these and still greater afflictions."

2. Now, dear Christian, behold and act according to this model in thy dispositions. When a thousand disappointments beset you, say, too, "My God, I will it! "When poverty afflicts you, when the calumniator's tongue wounds you, when false friends deceive you, when sickness visits you, when bodily pains torment you, with invincible patience imitate Christ, and say, "My God, I will it!" You must have these dispositions, this will; then the life of Christ is your model and you give testimony of Him.

3. How have you acted up to the present? Examine yourself and acknowledge how different your dispositions have often been to those of the Lord. Ah, how many ambitious people there are whose whole thoughts and actions are directed toward the acquisition of honor, recognition, offices, and dignities! How many avaricious people who ponder night and day how to increase their mammon! How many world lings who think continually of their pleasures! How many revengeful souls who will not forget the insults they have endured! Is this giving testimony of Christ? Do not the heathens do likewise, who give testimony of satan?

II. 1. Of what kind are the words of Christ the Lord? Peter once said

(John vi. 69), "Thou hast the words of eternal life," for all His words were directed to the honor of God, the extirpation of sin, the growth of virtue, and the salvation of souls. Consider this in the seven last sacred words which He spoke from the cross in the midst of His death-agony. First He prayed to the heavenly Father, "Father, forgive them, for they know not what they do." (Luke xxiii. 34.) These are words of mercy and reconciliation. To the penitent thief He said, "This day thou shalt be with me in paradise "(Luke xxiii. 43)—words of blessed promise. He addresses these words to His Blessed Mother, "Woman, behold thy son!" and to His disciple, "Behold thy mother!" (John xix. 26.) What consoling words! In the moment of abandonment He cries out, with entire submission and confidence in God, "My God, my God, why hast thou forsaken me?" (Matt, xxxvii. 46.) His desire to suffer still more and in the highest degree for the sake of our salvation is proved to us by His cry, "I thirst" (John xix. 28), "It is consummated" (John xix. 30). He says, full of joy, that He has completed our redemption, and He recommends His soul with resignation into the hands of His Father: "Into thy hands I commend my spirit." (Luke xxiii. 46.) Now, dear Christians, look at this model and act accordingly in thy words. Whatever you speak must be to the honor of God, and to thine own and thy neighbor's salvation. Speech is given to us, as a servant of God says, to praise God, to the edification of our neighbor.

Have your conversations been of this description, dear Christian? Ah, how different have they often been from the Lord's! If we go into the houses and palaces of the rich and powerful, what talk, what conversations are there in vogue? What words do we hear in the halls of learning, in the assembly of the leaders of the people? In the streets we meet the indications of sensual pleasures, in the stores it is vanity; at home, in the workshops, too often, unfortunately, it is unbelief and blasphemy. Where is the place in which reputations are not blasted, slanders, blasphemies, oaths, and especially where improper conversations have not found a home, in our days? Even family life is no longer pure, and words are dropped into the ears of innocent children that poison their souls. Dear Christians, is this giving testimony of Christ? Do not the heathen do likewise, who give testimony of satan?

III. 1. Let us consider, in conclusion, the works of the Lord. St. Bernard describes them to us thus: "Under the name of Jesus I picture to myself a man humble and meek of heart, kind, temperate, chaste, merciful—in short, distinguished in every virtue and holiness." Our Lord's own teaching is witness that He was perfect in the practise of all the works which He taught. He says, "Blessed are the poor in spirit," and from His birth in the stable until His death upon the cross He was Himself the poorest, "for He had not where to lay His head." "Blessed are the meek," He says, and He forgives not only the wrong done to Him, but he rewards it with the richest of benefits. "Blessed are the sorrowful;" He expiated our sins by His whole body, and wept over them tears of blood. "Blessed are they who hunger and thirst after justice;" but His food was to do the will of His Father. "Blessed are the merciful;" He heaped good deeds upon His enemies. "Blessed are the peacemakers;" He made peace between God and man. "Blessed are those who suffer persecution for justice sake;" He bears hatred and persecution on account of His teaching until His death.

2. But how do we perform our works? Do you not love your body and your comfort inordinately, and adhere so obstinately to the maxims of the world that you are almost ashamed to be a Christian? Or you love sin, allow your vices to become habits, and have even laid aside all feelings of shame therefore, or you only think of that which is earthly, and live on like the unreasoning animal, constantly pursuing pleasures and sensuality. Unhappy Christian, is this the way to give testimony of Christ? Do not the heathen do the same, who give testimony of satan? Is it any wonder that heretics and unbelievers are not converted when they see that Catholics and Christians are worse than they are?

3. Therefore, my dear Christians, behold, and behave according to the model that is shown to you. It is your duty to imitate the teaching and the example of the Redeemer and to practise diligently Christian perfection. You must serve God and reflect night and day upon His laws; you must crucify your flesh with its wicked desires; you must not be overcome by adversity, nor dazzled by happiness. It is your duty so to practise the Christian virtues that even unbelievers shall admire them, and say that they are not able to reach to such a high perfection. If this could be said of all Christians, surely the whole world would soon be Christian!

Do not delay, dear Christian, to conform your life to the life of Jesus Christ, and thereby to give testimony of Him. Hear how the Apostle exhorts you (II. Cor. iv. 10): "Always bearing about in our body the dying of Jesus: that the life also of Jesus may be made manifest in our bodies." By mortification you must make your life a copy of His life. Your eyes should not be overcurious, nor your mouth without shame, nor your sensual desires ungovernable, as the heathens are; your conduct must not correspond with the life of the rich glutton. On the contrary, all those who see your retirement and your modesty must acknowledge that you are not only in name, but in deed and truth, a Christian, a follower of the Crucified One, and an heir of the kingdom of heaven. Amen.

WHIT-SUNDAY

CHILDREN OF THE HOLY GHOST AND CHILDREN OF THE WORLD

"Know ye not that you are the temple of God, and that the spirit of God dwelleth in you?"
I. Cor. iii. 16.

FROM the beginning of the ecclesiastical year, which you, dear Christians, know commences with Advent, the holy Catholic Church has celebrated glorious festivals in honor of our divine Saviour. First of all was the holy feast of Christmas, when the faithful rejoiced that the Redeemer had come down from heaven to deliver us from sin and eternal damnation; after that we celebrated the joyful feast of the Resurrection, and we sang with the risen Saviour joyful alleluias because His bitter passion and our redemption was accomplished; and, finally, a few days ago, we saw our divine Saviour return to His heavenly Father, from henceforth to take possession of His throne of glory for all eternity. But there the same Jesus, who in this world had done so many such unutterably great things for us, was not unmindful of our soul's salvation: He kept His word, which He had spoken to His Apostles, and also to us—the word, "I will send you another comforter," another deliverer, "the Holy Ghost," and this Holy Spirit will not only rule over the holy Church founded by Him, but, according to the words of my text, He will enter into every soul and enlighten and guide them in the way of salvation; in Him we shall live, walk, and work for heaven.

But do all men who have received the Holy Ghost cooperate with Him for heaven? In other words, are they all true children of the Holy Ghost? Unfortunately I must say that many men, although they have received the Holy Ghost, are not children of the Holy Ghost, but children of the world. I consider it, therefore, necessary to show you whereby we can recognize:

I. Who is a child of the Holy Ghost, and
II. Who is a child of the world.

I. Without doubt, dear brethren, that Christian is a child of the Holy Ghost who avoids all grievous sins, for the Holy Ghost can only dwell in a soul which is disunited from grievous sin; He is that purest Spirit in whose eyes sin is an abomination. Therefore St. Paul writes, "Grieve not," that is to say by sin, "the Holy Spirit of God." (Eph. iv. 30.) Sin turns the abode of the Holy Ghost into an abode of satan. St. Gregory writes, therefore: "The sinner's heart is the devil's workshop, but not the dwelling of the Holy Ghost." It is especially the sin of impurity, whether committed by unchaste thoughts, words, or works, which drives the Holy Ghost out of our hearts, and closes against Him, the entrance to our souls. "The sensual man," writes St. Chrysostom, "can not receive the grace of the Holy Ghost." And Holy Writ says, in expressive words, that on account of this sin the Holy Ghost can not remain in man. "My spirit," we read, "shall not remain in man forever, because he is flesh" (Gen. vi. 3); in other words, because he is addicted to the lust of the flesh.

For this reason, dear Christians, if through a sinful life you have lost the Holy Ghost, strive by penance to purify your soul again from sin, so as to receive the Holy Ghost into your heart again. St. Peter exhorts us to do this in the words: "Do penance, and be baptized every one of you in the name of Jesus Christ, for the remission of your sins: and you shall receive the gift of the Holy Ghost." (Acts ii. 38.) Reflect upon what you have lost through sin, namely, that you lire no longer a child of the Holy Ghost. Let us do penance, that we. may obtain the heavenly treasure again!

Without doubt, I say further, is the Christian a child of the Holy Ghost if his heart is adorned with numerous virtues. As our divine Saviour in Holy Communion enters only into a virtuous heart, and that the Christian before receiving the same should excite feelings of virtue, even so the Holy Ghost will only dwell in those souls which are adorned with these virtues; in such a soul He has an abiding dwelling place. Just as the oil keeps the light burning, and the flame is extinguished when the oil is all used, just so is the Holy Ghost—the light and fire of the soul—preserved within us by virtue and good works. St. Augustine, therefore, in a sermon on the feast of Pentecost, tells his listeners: "The promises of our Redeemer have been fulfilled; our Lord Jesus Christ is ascended into heaven, and the Holy Ghost has come down from heaven; there remains for us, in order that this double event be fulfilled in us, to preserve within us by a virtuous life the Holy Ghost who has descended, and by leading such life to follow Jesus Christ, who has ascended. And this virtuous life of ours should consist in a firm faith, in the hope of God's mercy, in the love of God and our neighbor, in humility, in being at peace with our neighbors, and in piety and the fear of God, especially in purity of heart and chastity. Where these virtues are found in the souls of Christians, there we find the true children of the Holy Ghost.

Finally, dear Christians, I say, a sure mark of a child of the Holy Ghost is borne by that one who is a child of prayer, especially when he often prays to God for the gifts of the Holy Ghost. Our divine Saviour demands such a prayer from us when He says: "If you, then, being evil, know how to give good gifts to your children, how much more will your Father from heaven give the good Spirit to them that ask him?" (Luke xi. 13.) The Apostles serve us with an example that the heavenly Father grants the Holy Ghost and His gifts to those who ask Him. He promised the Holy Ghost to them with these words: "And I will ask the Father, and he shall give you another Paraclete, that he may abide with you forever." (John xiv. 16.) What, therefore, did the Apostles do when they returned to Jerusalem after the ascension of Jesus into heaven from the Mount of Olives? They adjourned to an upper room where they lived, and they all united together in prayer with Mary.

And being assembled there in the same manner, in prayer, on the feast of Pentecost, suddenly there came a sound from heaven as of a mighty wind coming: and it filled the house where they were sitting, and there appeared to them parted tongues, as it were of fire; and it sat upon each of them; and they were all filled with the Holy Ghost, and they began to speak with divers tongues, according as the Holy Ghost gave them to speak. (Acts ii. 1, 2.) Should we, dear Christians, pray less than the Apostles did for the Holy Ghost and His gifts? Our holy Church imitates the Apostles in invoking God for the Holy Spirit. Through the entire week of Holy Pentecost she prays by the mouth of the priests, "Come, Holy Ghost, and visit the souls of Thy servants." She sings that beautiful hymn, *"Veni Creator Spiritus"* (Come, Creator Spirit), that He may descend into the souls of the faithful, and enlighten them by the word of God. Pious Christians have always prayed to the Holy Ghost for His seven gifts. A pious abbot named John cried out to his listeners in a sermon We will beseech God to grant us His Holy Spirit that He may fructify and refresh our hearts with the rain and dew of His grace." Yes, we will pray frequently for his sublime grace, and with heart and voice repeat after St. Augustine those beautiful words: "Breathe perpetually, O Holy Ghost, Thy holy work within me, that I may think upon it; move me, that I may do it;

persuade me, that I may love Thee; strengthen me, that I may hold Thee fast; keep me, that I may not lose Thee!" Truly, those who pray thus possess the Holy Ghost, and are indeed true children of the Holy Ghost!

II. I say, dear Christians, that the children of the world stand in direct contrast to the children of the Holy Ghost.

The children of the world, dear Christians, are manifestly those men to whom the world is everything, to whom the world and all that it offers is of more consequence than heaven—I might say, to whom the world is their God. To them belong those men who are attached with their whole hearts to transitory things; who make only the one effort to accumulate the treasures and wealth of this world, to become possessed of them. Tell me, is it conceivable that such efforts could proceed from a heart filled and animated by the Holy Ghost? Does the Holy Ghost not say in Holy Writ: "If riches abound, set not your heart upon them." (Ps. lxi. 11.) Can man, then, who has sold his heart wholly and entirely to the world and its treasures and possessions, say of himself that his exertions are holy and directed to heaven? Let the Holy Ghost, dear Christians, reign in your hearts, that he may turn them toward God and heaven, in heaven alone, where are true riches and treasures. "Seek first," that is to say, more than all earthly things, "the kingdom of God."

The children of this world are manifestly those persons who only strive after the joys and pleasures of this life. God has created us for heaven and its joys, "to the purchasing of salvation," as the Apostle writes. (I. Thess. v. 9.) At the same time, He has not forbidden us the enjoyment of worldly pleasures, for St. Paul says: "Rejoice with them that rejoice." (Rom. xii. 15.) But God has not created us that we should enjoy solely the pleasures of the world without thinking of heavenly joys, nor strive after them, much less that we should strive for them alone. "Seek first the kingdom of God." But, alas! how many people, how many Christian people, think only of joy, of pleasure, of the enjoyment of pleasures, and the lust of the world! How many seek these alone, and desire to enjoy them, without thinking of the joys of heaven, or longing for them! Worldly festivities with joyful meetings, with all the pleasures of the table; worldly pleasures with rioting and debauchery; worldly feasts with music and dancing; worldly festivities on Sundays and holy days: this is what occupies the attention of so many people— their hearts desire it, without ever being satiated. Pleasures, and still more pleasures, enjoyment on enjoyment: this is what so many people are striving for. Now tell me, dear

Christians, do not all these worldly pleasures and enjoyments generally bring grievous sins in their train? Do they not at least bury virtue beneath their pleasures, and are you not led thereby to eternal damnation? Can the Holy Ghost dwell and work in the hearts of such people, who only serve the spirit of the world?

The children of this world, I will say further, are manifestly those people who lead a tepid life, forgetful of God; in them the Holy Ghost can not be, for He is and lives only in the pious and God-fearing. Holy Scripture says of Simeon that he was God-fearing, and it adds these words: "The Holy Ghost was in him." (Luke ii. 25.) He was God-fearing, he was pious, as the Holy Scripture says of him. He came, as it says further on, "in answer to the Holy Ghost," and he had the grace to take into his arms the Infant Jesus, and he blessed God for this grace (Luke ii. 28.) Would Simeon have had this grace if the Holy Ghost had not dwelt in him, and if he had not led a pious, God-fearing life? Can we, then, say of lukewarm Christians that within them dwells the Holy Ghost, who instils in men the virtue of the fear of God and piety; may we say that of the lukewarm Christian who does not fear God, who does not lead a pious life nor visit the temple of God frequently, who neglects his morning and night prayers, who receives the Holy Sacraments either not at all or only once a year? No, I reply, he is a child of the world, he lives only for the world, he feels no desire to do good for heaven, and for this reason that it can not be said of him, as of the pious Simeon: "The Holy Ghost is in him."

In conclusion, those are the children of the world, and not the children of the Holy Ghost, who speak the language of the children of the world, and not the language of the Holy Ghost. But what language does the Holy Ghost speak? We see this in the holy Apostles. They are zealous to receive the Holy Ghost, who came down upon them in the form of fiery tongues, that they may speak for the holy faith; they preach virtue, they exhort to charity and peace, to mercy and justice, to chastity, and to a holy Christian life. But what is the language spoken by so many children of the world, over whom the Holy Ghost descended in the Holy Sacrament of Confirmation? I reply, they speak the language of the devil in derisive discourses on the holy faith; in unchaste conversations and stories; in curses and maledictions; in blasphemies against God and everything that is sacred to a Christian; in slander and seducing their neighbor to do wrong. The fiery tongue of the Holy Ghost, I might almost say, which descended upon them as it did upon the Apostles, even if invisibly, has been exchanged for the poisonous tongue of the devil, and for this reason they only speak the language of the devil, and not the language of the Holy Ghost.

O Christian, if your heart is so made that it only strives for the treasures and joys of the world; O Christian, if your heart is cold and lukewarm in the service of God; O Christian, if your tongue does not speak the language of the Holy Ghost, but the language of the devil, ah, then, be horrified at the unhappy state of your soul— the Holy Ghost does not live and operate in your heart! On this holy festival of the Holy Ghost, therefore, lift up your hands to God and pray fervently for your soul; "O my God, who hast enlightened the hearts of Thy faithful through the Holy Ghost, grant that henceforth I shall speak only in this same spirit of heavenly things, that I may pray and work only for that which is heavenly, only accumulate treasures and merits for heaven, so that I may be found worthy one day to reach there where Thou with the Holy Ghost rules on the throne of heaven for all eternity." Amen.

TRINITY SUNDAY

THE HOLY EUCHARIST

"I am a sojourner on the earth."
Ps. cxviii. 19.

THESE WORDS, dear brethren, point out to us the utter misery of this life, the contempt which we should feel for created and transitory things, and the longing we should be possessed of to be delivered from them, so that we may enter into our true home, which is not of this world. Meanwhile let us console ourselves, dear brethren, because we possess here among us a God, a Friend, a Consoler, and a Redeemer, who will ease our sufferings, who promises us in this place of hardships such great bliss that, with the bride in the canticle, we may exclaim: "Hast thou seen my Beloved, and when you see him, tell him that I languish with love." "How long, O Lord," exclaimed the holy king and prophet in his exceeding love and ecstasy, "how long must I still remain in this banishment and separation from Thee?" And see, dear brethren, how much happier we are than the saints of the Old Testament, we who not only possess Him in the immensity of divinity, but who have Him also as He was during the nine months in Mary's womb, and again as he was on the cross. More fortunate than the first Christians, who had to go fifty or sixty miles for the happiness of seeing Him: the church of every parish contains Him; any congregation can, if it so desires, enjoy His most sweet companionship. O happy people, what I wish to show you today is:

    I. How good God was in instituting the adorable Sacrament of the Holy Eucharist.
    II. What are our duties toward this Sacrament?

I.

    The very thing that constitutes the happiness of the just Christian causes, in my opinion, the unhappiness of the sinner. If you desire a proof of this, I will give you one: To a sinner who will not forsake his vices, the presence of God is a torture: he shuns the thought that God sees him, he hides himself and his evil deeds, he flees the light of day, he buries himself in darkness, he is suspicious of everything, the sight of a priest arouses his distrust, he fears and avoids it, and when after all he reflects that his soul is immortal, that there is a God to either reward or punish his deeds, then this thought tortures him, it gnaws at him unceasingly. Ah, sad indeed is the life of a sinner who lives on in his sins! It is in vain, my friend, that you strive to hide yourself from God's presence. You can never do it! "Adam, Adam, where art thou?" "Ah, Lord," he answered, "I have sinned, and I fear Thy presence!" Adam trembled in every limb, and he fled, that he might hide himself, and at the very moment when he thought that God did not see him he heard His voice: "Adam, thou wilt find me everywhere; thou hast sinned, and I was a witness of thy transgression, and my eyes were turned upon thee." "Cain, Cain, where is thy brother?" Cain heard the Lord's voice, and he fled like one in despair. But God followed him, and accused him with the words: "Cain, thy brother's blood cries for vengeance." Oh how true it is, that a sinner finds himself in continual fear and despair!

"Come, my children," says the holy King David, "I have something important to reveal to you: come and I will tell thee how good the Lord is to those that love Him. He has prepared a heavenly repast for His children, which bears fruit for this life. In every place we find our God: if we enter heaven, He is there; if we traverse the ocean, He is by our side; if we go down into the depths of the sea, He accompanies us." Our God no more loses sight of us than does a mother of her child that is beginning to walk. "My God," cried Moses, "show me, if it pleases Thee, Thy countenance, then shall I possess all things that I want." Ah, how consoling for a Christian is the blessed thought that God sees him, that God witnesses his sorrows and his troubles, that God is by his side! Ah, what is still better, that God presses him tenderly to His heart! O Christian people, how happy are you in the enjoyment of so many privileges which others have not! Am I not right when I say that the presence of God, which is such a torment for the sinner, is an endless happiness for the good Christian—it is heaven upon earth.

St. Bernard assures us that there are three mysteries upon which he can not meditate without feeling as if his heart would break with love and sadness. The first is the mystery of the Incarnation, the other that of the Passion and Death of Jesus Christ, and the third is the most adorable

Sacrament of the Altar. When the Holy Ghost speaks to us of the mystery of the Incarnation, He makes use of expressions which denote the magnitude of the love of God for men as boundless, for He says, "God has so loved the world," as if he would say, I will leave it to your imagination what love this is.

Listen how St. Paul expresses himself, in speaking of the mystery of the Passion of Jesus Christ: "God is infinite in His mercy and grace; but He appears to have exhausted Himself m His love toward us. We were dead, He has given us life. We were destined to be miserable for all eternity, and by His kindness and mercy He has changed our lot." Finally St. John says, in speaking of the love shown by Jesus Christ in the institution of the Holy Eucharist, "He has loved us unto the end;" that is to say, He has loved man during His entire life with a love that has no equal. Let us say, rather, that He loved us as much as He could love us. O divine love, how great art thou, and how little known!

Yes, dear brethren, when we contemplate all the things which God has made, heaven and earth and the beautiful order that reigns throughout creation, then everything proclaims to us an Almighty power which has created all things, a wonderful wisdom which rules over everything, a perfection in the highest degree which cares for everything with the same ease as if it had only one creature to occupy itself with; so the many wonders can only fill us with astonishment and admiration. But when we speak of the Most Holy Eucharist we can say that here is to be found the miracle of divine love for us, here His majesty, His grace, and His goodness shines forth in a most extraordinary manner. We can say truly that here is that bread which came down from heaven, the Bread of Angels, that is given to us for the nourishment of our souls. It is the bread of the strong, which consoles and lightens our sufferings. There is truly the subsistence of the traveler. "Whosoever," says the Saviour, "receives me, will possess everlasting life, and he who does not receive me, will die." "Those," said the Lord, "who take refuge in this sacred banquet, will awaken a source within them that will spring up into eternal life."

Has there been, or will there ever be, a nobler or more magnanimous love than that which He has shown us in the Sacrament of love? Must we not say, with the Council of Trent, that His generosity and His magnanimity have here exhausted all His treasures? Is there anything on earth or in heaven which can be compared to it? Has the tender love of a father or the liberality of a king toward his subjects ever reached as far as the love of Jesus Christ in the Holy Eucharist? Parents will their possessions to their children, but Jesus Christ gives us in His testament not temporal goods, but He bequeaths to us His most adorable body and His most precious blood. O, the good fortune of the Christian, how little it is appreciated! No, dear brethren, His love could have done no more than to give Himself to us; for when we receive Him, we receive Him with all His riches. Is this not really prodigality on the part of God to His creatures? Had God, dear brethren, left us free to ask of Him what we wanted, do you think we should have dared to place our hopes so high? "On the other hand," asks St. Augustine, "could God have been able to give us anything more precious than what He has given us?" Do you know, dear brethren, what induced Jesus Christ to condescend to be present in our churches by day and night? It was that we might be able to come to Him whenever we wanted to. O tender love of a Father, how great art thou! What, dear brethren, is more consoling for a Christian than to feel he adores a God who is really and truly present in body and soul. "O Lord," exclaimed the royal prophet, "a day passed in Thy presence is better than a thousand spent with worldly company!" What is it that makes our churches so sacred and so venerable? Is it not the presence of Jesus Christ? What an immense privilege we Christians enjoy!

II.

But, you will ask, what must we do to repay this love?

We must appear before Him with the greatest reverence, and when taking part in sacramental processions we should awaken within us the most profound respect, remembering that we are sinners and unworthy to accompany so holy and so pure a God. We have so often despised and offended this good Father, and yet He loves us, and promises us that He is ever ready to grant us His grace. What does Jesus Christ represent, dear brethren, when He is carried around the church in the procession? He is like a good and gracious king in the midst of His subjects, a kind father surrounded by His children, and a good shepherd gathering His sheep. What thoughts should fill our minds when we walk with our God? We should follow Him as the first Christians followed Him when He walked upon this earth and lavished His benefits upon the whole world. If we are so happy as to accompany Him with a lively faith, we are sure of obtaining all that we ask of Him. Do we not read in the Gospel that two blind men were seated by the roadside as Jesus passed by, and as they cried out, "Jesus, Son of David, have mercy on us!" He was touched with compassion, and He asked them what they desired. "Ah, Lord," they said, "grant that we may see!" And our Saviour gave them their sight.

We appreciate our God very little, we regard Him with indifference, the time passes slowly for us in His presence. Oh what a difference there is between us and the first Christians! They would have considered it the most blissful time of their life could they have spent days and nights in church, to sing the praises of the Lord or to weep over their sins; but nowadays it is very different. As a matter of fact, dear brethren, what indifference and even frivolity do we not often see in our churches.

As we are all created for God, and are unceasingly the recipients of His boundless mercy, we must prove our gratitude to Him, and be sorrowful when we observe how much He is subject to insults. We should behave like a friend who regrets the misfortune of a friend: this is a proof of sincere friendship. Whatever service a friend may render you, he can never do what Christ has done for us. Every good Christian must be grieved at the contempt which is so often shown Him, and must strive to make reparation to Him; and those Christians who have the good fortune of belonging to societies having for their object the adoration of Jesus in the Most Holy Eucharist, they are in an especial manner bound to do this. I say those "who have the good fortune," for can there be a greater happiness than to undertake reparation to Jesus Christ for the insults which are offered to Him in the Sacrament of His love?

We read in the Gospel that two of the disciples walked with our Saviour from Emmaus without knowing Him; when they recognized Him, He vanished. Beside themselves with happiness they said to one another: "How did it happen that we have not recognized Him? Were not our hearts burning within us whilst He was speaking on the way and opened to us the Scriptures?" We, my dear brethren, are a thousand times better off than those disciples who walked with Jesus without knowing Him. We know that our God and our Redeemer is really present in the Most Blessed Sacrament, and that He speaks to our hearts, and awakens good thoughts and good resolutions within us. "My child," He says, "why dost thou not love me? Why not give up this abominable sin which raises a barrier between us? Ah, my child, canst thou forsake me? Wilt thou force me to condemn thee to eternal punishment? Behold, my child, I will forgive thee thy transgressions if thou wilt repent of them!"

Oh how sweet it is, dear brethren, to enjoy the blessed conversation of the Redeemer!

Had you been so happy to taste this sweetness you would never leave Him any more. We need not be surprised that so many souls passed their lives, day and night, in His house—they could not tear themselves away from His presence. What conclusion, then, must we arrive at? We should consider those moments spent before the Blessed Sacrament as the happiest of our lives. Let us, sinners as we are, pray with tears and sorrow for the forgiveness of our sins and we shall certainly obtain it, and when we are forgiven, let us implore the most precious gift of perseverance. Let us say to Him in all earnestness that we would rather die than offend Him again! No, dear brethren, as long as you do not love God you will never be contented—everything will be a trouble to you, everything will weary you; but if you love God you will lead a happy life and be well prepared for death! A happy death, which will unite us to our God! O happiness, when wilt thou come? How long the time is! Ah, come, for thou procurest for us the greatest of all good, namely, the possession of God Himself. That is what I desire for you and for me. Amen.

SECOND SUNDAY AFTER PENTECOST

HOLY MASS

"And in every place there is sacrifice, and there is offered to my name a clean oblation."
—Malach. i. 11.

IT IS CERTAIN, dear brethren, that it behooves man as the creature to subject his entire being to God, the creator. As an offender, moreover, it is necessary for him to propitiate his creator by a sacrifice of propitiation; this was acknowledged in the Old Law by a number of sacrifices, offered up daily to God in the Temple. But those sacrifices could not make complete satisfaction to a God for the transgressions of his creatures, and it was necessary that there should be another sacrifice, holier, purer, which should continue to the end of the world, and which would be adequate to our indebtedness to God. This holy sacrifice is Jesus Christ Himself, who is God, like the Father, and man, as one of us. As then, upon Calvary, so now He offers Himself up every day upon our altars, and through this pure and spotless oblation He renders to God the honor due to Him, and pays the debt which man owes to his creator. He sacrifices Himself every day in recognition of the absolute dominion of God over His creatures, and the offenses which we offer to God by our sins are thus completely atoned for. Jesus Christ as mediator between God and men procures for us all the necessary graces in this holy sacrifice, because He is at the same time a sacrifice of thanksgiving. He gives God, for men, the most perfect thanksgiving, which we owe Him. But, dear brethren, in order to participate in all this good, we must do something on our part. That you may the better understand this I will teach you as well as it will be possible for me:

I. What a great good fortune it is for us to assist at Holy Mass
II. With what dispositions we should assist.

I.

Before showing you in what manner you ought to hear Mass, I must explain to you the meaning of the word holy sacrifice of the Mass. You know that the holy sacrifice of the Mass is the same as that which was once offered upon Calvary on Good Friday. The only difference consists in this: that the sacrifice which Jesus Christ offered upon Mount Calvary was visible; that it could be witnessed with human eyes; that there Jesus Christ was offered up to His heavenly Father at the hands of His persecutors, and that He visibly shed His blood. That is the meaning of the expression, "a bloody sacrifice." But in Holy Mass Jesus Christ offers Himself up to His heavenly Father in an invisible manner; we only see Him with the eyes of our faith, and not with the eyes in our head. This, then, dear brethren, is what is understood by the expression, "holy sacrifice of the Mass." But to give you an idea of the greatness of the merits of Holy Mass, it will be sufficient, my dear brethren, if I say to you, with St. John Chrysostom, that Holy Mass is a source of great joy for the entire court of heaven, that it consoles the poor souls in purgatory, and gives more glory to God than all the sufferings of the saintly martyrs combined, than all the works of penance of the anchorites. The reason is simply this: all those actions were performed by more or less guilty human beings, while in the holy sacrifice of the Mass the merits of the Passion and death of an Incarnate God, the equal to the Father, are offered up. You may see from this, my dear brethren, that Holy Mass is of infinite merit. We read, moreover, in the Gospel, that Jesus Christ converted many at the moment of His death; the good thief received the promise of paradise, a number of the Jews were converted, and the pagans struck their breasts, saying, "That was truly the Son of God," and the dead arose, the rocks were split open, and the earth trembled in its fastnesses. Yes, dear brethren, if we had the intention and grace to assist at Holy Mass in perfect realization of its nature, we should certainly be converted, even if we were as stubborn as the Jews, as blinded as the pagans, and harder than the rocks which were split asunder. "Surely," says St. John Chrysostom, "there is no more precious time in which to speak to God about our salvation than during Holy Mass, when Jesus Christ offers Himself to His Father to procure for us all the manifold blessings and graces. "When we are troubled," says this great saint, "we shall find abundant consolation there; if temptations beset us, let us only hear Mass and we shall find out how we can overcome the devil." Yes, dear brethren, if we had sufficient faith. Holy Mass would be the cure for all the evils which we meet with in this life, for is not Jesus Christ the true physician of our souls and bodies?

II.

I have said that Holy Mass is the sacrifice of the most adorable body and blood of Jesus Christ, which can only be offered up to God, not to the angels nor to the saints. You know that the holy sacrifice of the Mass was instituted on Maundy Thursday, when Jesus Christ took bread and transformed the same into His body, and then taking wine, changed it into His blood. At the same moment He gave authority to do the same to His Apostles and their successors; this latter fact constitutes the Sacrament of Holy Orders. The words of consecration are the principal part and essence of Holy Mass, and the priest officiates at this sacred function. The people, by uniting themselves with the priest, assist at Holy Mass, and, dear brethren, the best way to hear Holy Mass is to follow earnestly the priest in all that he says, in all his actions, as far as we possibly can follow him, and to endeavor to give ourselves up to the most lively sentiments of love and gratitude.

We may divide Holy Mass into three parts: the first part is from the beginning to the offertory, the second from the offertory to the consecration, the third from the consecration to the end. You must bear in mind that we are guilty of sin if we should voluntarily be distracted during any of these parts, a fact that should compel us to be very careful not to allow our mind to occupy itself with other things, with things that have no reference to the holy sacrifice of the Mass. From the commencement of the offertory we should consider ourselves as penitents, penetrated with the liveliest sorrow for our sins. From the offertory to the consecration let us contemplate how the priest offers up Jesus Christ to God the Father, and we should offer up through Him all that we are, our body, our soul, our possessions, and our life. After the consecration remember the great favor allowed to us, that we may partake of the most adorable body and precious blood of Jesus Christ, and consequently we should do all in our power to become worthy of this grace. So that you may understand this, dear brethren, I will give you three examples from Holy Writ which will show you how you should assist at Holy Mass, and how you should occupy yourself during the moments which are so fraught with happiness for those who fully comprehend them. The first example is that of the publican, which teaches us what we should do at the beginning of Mass. The second is that of the good thief, which instructs you how you should behave from the offertory to the consecration. The third is the centurion, who is your guide at Holy Communion. On entering the church you ought to reflect upon the happiness which is yours and make an act of faith and contrition for your sins, that render you unworthy to approach so holy, so great a God. Think at that moment of the behavior of the publican as he entered the temple to offer his prayers to God. St. Luke tells us that the publican standing at the entrance of the temple would not so much as lift his eyes toward heaven, but struck his breast, saying: "O God, be merciful to me, a sinner." See, dear brethren, he did not act as many Christians do who enter the church with a proud and overbearing deportment, "as if," to use the words of the prophet Isaias, "they wished to approach God like persons who had nothing upon their conscience for which they should humble themselves before God." Consider our publican: he thinks himself unworthy to enter the temple, and he chooses the most insignificant spot that he can find; he is so confused at the thought of his sins that he does not venture to lift his eyes to heaven. Oh how far removed is he from many so-called Christians who want the best seat and who hardly bow their heads at the consecration. O my God, how can we dare to assist at Holy Mass with such disposition! "Our publican on the contrary," says St. Augustine, "strikes his breast to show God the horror which he feels at having offended Him."

Ah, dear brethren, if Christians would hear Mass with the same dispositions as the publican, what graces would they obtain!

I say the good thief shows us how we should behave during the time from the offertory to the consecration, the time when we should offer ourselves up to God with Jesus Christ. Behold, dear brethren, how this happy penitent behaved when he was about to suffer the penalty of death; behold how the eyes of his soul were opened, that he might recognize his Redeemer! What wonderful progress, dear brethren, did he make during the three hours which he passed in the company of the dying Redeemer? He is bound to the cross, his heart and his tongue alone are free. Behold how readily he sacrifices both for Jesus Christ! He gives Him everything that he can give Him, he consecrates his heart to Him by faith and hope, he begs Him humbly for a little place in paradise; that is to say, in His eternal kingdom. He consecrates his tongue to Him by proclaiming the Redeemer as his Lord and God. He says, "We have deserved to suffer, but this one is innocent." Thus, while the other thief was reviling Jesus Christ by most terrible blasphemies, the good thief became the champion of the Lord, though even the disciples had forsaken Him. So great was his belief and love that he strove with all his might to convert the other thief. No, dear brethren, let us not be astonished to see such great virtuousness in the good thief, for nothing is more calculated to touch our hearts than the sight of our Saviour dying; there is no moment in which grace flows down upon us so abundantly, and yet we are daily witnesses of this. Ah, dear brethren, if at the offertory we offered ourselves, and if at the great moment of the consecration we were penetrated with a lively faith, a single Mass would suffice to free us from all the grave faults that are besetting us and to-make true penitents of us and perfect Christians.

I said that the centurion should serve us as an example at partaking of the Holy Table, really or in spirit. We may communicate spiritually by a fervent desire of being united to Jesus Christ. The example of the centurion is so worthy of admiration that the Church uses his very words at Holy Communion: "Lord," said this humble servant, "I am not worthy that thou shouldst enter under my roof, but say only the word, and my servant shall be made whole." Oh, if God could perceive the same humility in us, the same acknowledgment of our unworthiness, with what delight, with an abundance of grace, would He enter into our hearts! What strength, what courage He would grant us to conquer the enemy of our salvation.

Do we not want, dear brethren, after contemplating these great truths, to change our lives, to give up sin, and to return to God? Let us hear Mass with this intention, and if we do so with devotion we are sure that God will help us to overcome our sins. We must not be surprised that the devil puts so many evil and diverting thoughts into our heads during Holy Mass. Ah, he well knows what harm it will do us if we assist at Holy Mass with little reverence and devotion, or none at all.

The sacrifice of Mass being the remembrance of the Passion of Christ, let us not assist at it like such as the Pharisees, the bad thief, and Judas, assisted at the cross and reaped no benefit. No, no, but let us resolve to follow the examples referred to before, namely, the publican, the good thief, and the centurion, for then rest assured you will hear Mass in a proper way and partake of all graces obtained from God through this holy sacrifice. You will leave church justified, and as your crowning reward paradise will await you because your soul has found salvation in the Passion and death of our Lord. Amen.

THIRD SUNDAY AFTER PENTECOST

THE MERCY OF GOD

"Now the publicans and sinners drew near unto him, to hear him."
Luke xv. 1

BY HIS demeanor during His earthly life Jesus Christ indicated the abundance of His mercy toward sinners. We see how every one sought His society, and He not only not repulsed them, or at least kept them at a distance, but on the contrary. He took every possible opportunity of being among them, so as to win them for the Father. He seeks them by giving them remorse of conscience, leads them by means of His grace, and conquers them by His kindness. His kindness toward them is so great that He even becomes their advocate before the doctors and pharisees, who condemned them, and who would not suffer them to approach Jesus Christ. Furthermore, He justifies His behavior toward sinners by a parable which gives evidence of His great and beautiful love for sinners, when He says: "A good shepherd, who has a hundred sheep and loses one of them, leaves all the others behind and seeks the stray one, and when he has found it he takes it upon his shoulders to spare it the difficulties of the way, and when he has brought it back to his sheepfold he invites all his friends, that they may rejoice with him over the finding of the sheep which was thought to be lost." Again, the parable of the woman who had ten pennies, and having lost one, lighted a lamp so as to look for it in all the corners of the house, and after she had found it invited all her friends, that they might take part in her joy. "Even so," He adds, "does the whole court of heaven rejoice at the return of a sinner who is converted and does penance. I am not come to save the just, but sinners, those who are well need not the physician, but those who are sick." As you see, Jesus Christ applies both of these parables to Himself as illustrations of His compassion for the sinner. O what a happiness it is for us to know that God's mercy is infinite! Our heart should compel us to throw ourselves at the feet of God, who will be so glad to receive us. If we go to perdition, dear brethren, we shall have no excuse, for Jesus Christ Himself told us that His mercy was ever ready tB forgive us, no matter how deeply we had fallen. To impress these facts upon our hearts and minds I will show you today:

> I. The greatness of God's mercy toward sinners.
> II. What we must do on our part to merit it.

I.

Yes, dear brethren, the way in which God concerns Himself with us is consoling, but it imposes obligations upon us. Although we are guilty His patience waits for us, His love invites us to rise from our sins and to return to Him. His mercy protects us. "With patience," says the prophet Isaias, "the Lord waits for us, to show us His mercy. As soon as we commit sin, we deserve to be punished at once. Nothing is more deserving of punishment than sin." As soon as a man revolts against God all creation demands vengeance, saying: "Lord, wilt Thou that we destroy this sinner who has offended Thee? Wilt Thou, cries the sea to Him, that I should bury him in my depths? The earth says: Lord, wilt Thou that I open and bury him alive in hell? The air says: Lord, shall I suffocate him? The fire asks: O Lord, I pray Thee, let me consume him, and all creation cries for vengeance. But no, replies this good Jesus; leave him upon earth until the moment which my Father has ordained for him; perhaps I shall have the happiness of seeing his conversion.

Contemplate, for instance, the mercy of God toward the world before the deluge, when the vices of men covered the earth and it was steeped in the filthy waters of the most abominable vices. The Lord felt Himself obliged to punish it, but what warnings, what admonitions, what delays did He not give them before the chastisement! Long before He threatened them, so as to arouse them and bring them to their senses. When he saw that their crimes increased from day to day He sent Noe to them, whom He commanded to build an ark, which should take him a hundred years to build, and to all those who should ask him the reason of this construction he was to say that the Lord was about to destroy the whole world by a flood, but that, if they would be converted and do penance, He would alter His determination. Only when He saw that His admonitions were of no avail, that men mocked at His menaces, He found Himself obliged to step in with His chastisement. And even then we see how the Lord declared that He regretted having created them, thereby expressing the greatness of His mercy. He wished to say: "I would rather not have created you, now that I find myself obliged to punish you." Tell me, dear brethren, could God Almighty, as He is, have shown greater mercy?

From the beginning of the world, dear brethren, until the advent of the Messiah, we behold but mercy, grace, and kindness. And yet we may say that under the law of grace of the New Testament the benefits which He is lavishing upon the world are still more abundant and more precious. What commiseration on the part of the eternal Father, who had an only Son, and who consented that the only Son should give His life to redeem us all! Ah, dear brethren, if we remembered the Passion of Jesus Christ with, proper feelings of gratitude, how many tears would we shed? As you see, the mercy of God could go no farther, for He had one only Son, and He sacrificed Him to save us—this Son who was the dearest that He had. But what shall we say when we consider the love of the Son? He goes willingly, to suffer torments and even death to procure for us the blessedness of heaven. What did He not do for us during His life upon earth? He is not satisfied to call us by His grace, and to place all means of salvation at our disposal. Behold how He seeks after the strayed sheep! See how He traverses cities and villages in quest of them, to lead them to the abode of His mercy! Behold how He leaves His Apostles and waits for the Samaritan woman at Jacob's well, where He knew that He would meet her! He appeared before her and begins to speak to her, so that the gentleness of His speech, combined with His grace, should touch and console her. He asks her for a drink of water, that she herself may venture to implore Him for something far more precious, namely, for His grace. So pleased was He at the conversion of this soul that He declined, when His Apostles asked Him to partake of some food, as if to say: "I am not thinking of material food; I am so rejoiced at having gained a soul for my Father!"

Look in at the house of Simon the leper. He does not go there to eat, but because He knows that He will find there Mary Magdalen, a sinner. For this reason, dear brethren. He appears at this feast. Observe the joy revealed by His countenance as Mary Magdalen throws herself at His feet and washes them with her tears and dries them with her hair. But the Redeemer repays her abundantly by pouring out the fulness of His grace into her heart. Behold how He takes her part in opposition to those who are scandalized at her! His compassion is so great that He not only forgives her her sins, and drives out the devils who had taken possession of her heart, but He chooses her to be one of His companions. He desires that she should accompany Him during His entire life's journey, and that in the whole world, wherever the Gospel should be preached, it should be related what she did for love of Him. He will speak no more of her sins, which He has already washed away by the merits of His most adorable blood, which He is to shed.

Why do we find Him on the road to Capharnaum? Is it not to meet Matthew the tax collector and make him a zealous Apostle? Why on His way to Jericho? It is to convert the publican Zachaeus. Ask Him why He walks in the public square and He will tell you it is to defend the adulteress and to convert her. Reflect how He weeps when approaching the city of Jerusalem, which is an image of the sinner, for of it He said: "Ungrateful Jerusalem who hast murdered the prophets and put to death the servants of God. O that thou mayest accept today the graces which I bring thee!" See, my brethren, how God weeps over the loss of our souls when He sees that we will not be converted. How can we, after seeing all that Christ has done to save us, doubt of His mercy, when we are sure of His forgiveness if we give up sins and repent of them, no matter how numerous they may be? Yea, and even deeply though you may have fallen, so that in the eyes of God you are in a worse condition than was the prodigal son, who from a noble, rich youth was reduced to a servant to feed the swine and had not anything wherewith to satiate himself, not even the husks the swine left over. Yet how did the father anticipate his coming—even prepared a feast for again finding the lost son. Thus will your heavenly Father act toward you from the very moment that you form the resolution of being converted; at the first step which you take toward that happy end the divine heart is moved to compassion, to mercy. He receives you with endearment.

Jesus Christ, in speaking of these sinners through the mouth of His servant, says: "Let this Christian, who is converted, be clothed with the robe of baptismal grace which he had lost; let him be clothed with Jesus Christ, with His justice, His virtues, and His merits." See, dear brethren, how Jesus Christ treats us when we are so happy as to forsake our sins and to abandon ourselves to Him, O how great is God's mercy!

II.

What must we then do to obtain His mercy? We must earnestly pray for it. We read in history of a great prince who, when he was dying, was frightfully tempted to doubt the goodness and mercy of God. When the priest who was at his bedside saw that he was losing confidence he strove to restore the same by pointing out that God never refuses forgiveness to any one who asks Him for it. "No, no," replied the sick man, "there is no forgiveness for me. I have been too wicked." As nothing was of any avail, the priest took refuge in prayer. Thereupon God put into his memory these words, which King David prayed before His death: "Prince," he said, "listen to the words of a penitent king; you are a sinner as he was. Pray with him: 'God, Lord, have mercy upon me, for my iniquities are very great, and may the enormity of my sins be a motive to induce Thee to pardon me? "At these words the prince seemed to awaken as if from a stupor. He meditated for a moment, and then was overcome with joy, and prayed, "Ah, Lord, these words were indeed meant for me! Yes, my God, have pity upon me for that very reason, that I have sinned so grievously." He made his confession and received the last sacraments, while tears flowed down his cheeks; joyfully he died, as a sacrifice for his sins, and passed away peacefully with the crucifix in his hands. In very truth, dear brethren, what are our sins in comparison with God's mercy? A mustard seed as compared to a big mountain. Oh, how can we allow ourselves to go to perdition when it is so easy to be saved, and while Jesus Christ longs so ardently for our salvation? At the same time, if God is so good as to wait for us and to receive us, we must not misuse His patience; when He calls us, invites us to come to Him, we should go to meet Him; when He has received us, we should remain faithful to Him. Ah, dear brethren, for years, perhaps, God has been calling us; why, then, do we remain in our sins? He is always ready to offer us His grace; why do we not forsake our sins? We should not only renounce sin because God in His goodness forgives us, but gratitude should prompt us to lament the sins which we committed.

The leprous Samaritan serves us as an example. When he saw that he was cured he returned and threw himself at the feet of Jesus Christ to thank Him for the grace he had obtained.

According to the teaching of St. Augustine gratitude toward God consists chiefly in this, that a soul resigns itself and all its inclinations completely to Him. Listen to the Saviour, who, having cured ten lepers, and saw only one returning to thank Him, asked: "And where are the other nine; did I not heal them likewise?" As if He wished to say: Why do not the others come to thank me? St. Bernard says we ought to be grateful to God, for thereby we shall prevail upon Him to grant us many more graces. Have we not good reason to thank God for having created us, for having redeemed us by His Passion and death, for having given us the true faith when so many live and die outside the true fold. Now, dear brethren, as God's mercy and kindness are boundless, let us endeavor to profit by them. Then we shall have the happiness of pleasing Him and of preserving our souls in His grace, and this will procure for us the pleasure of enjoying everlasting bliss in His sacred presence and that of all His saints in heaven. This is what I wish you all. Amen.

FOURTH SUNDAY AFTER PENTECOST

HOPE

"Thou shalt love the Lord thy God."
Matt xxii. 37.

IF ST. AUGUSTINE says he would never cease to love God, even if there were no heaven to hope for nor hell to fear, because God is infinitely lovable and deserves to be loved, how much more reason for us to love God if He promises us an eternal reward to encourage us to put our faith in Him and to love Him above all things. If we perform this sacred duty worthily we are working for our sanctification and our glorification in heaven. As faith teaches us that God sees everything, and that He is a witness of all that we do and suffer, the divine virtue of hope for the crowning reward of heaven causes us to bear our sufferings with submission and resignation to the holy will of God. This beautiful virtue supported the martyrs in the tortures to which they were subjected, the anchorites in their severe penitential practices, and the weak and sick in their diseases. Yes, dear children, if Faith shows us the presence of God everywhere, Hope leads us on, by the joyful expectation of an eternal reward, to perform all our actions with the intention of pleasing God. As this virtue, dear brethren, sweetens all our sufferings, let us consider its benefits.

If we, dear children, acknowledge through Faith that there is a God, who is our Creator, our Redeemer, and the Supreme Good, that He created us so that we might know Him, love Him, serve Him, and possess Him, Hope teaches us that, although unworthy of this happiness, still we may hope for it through the merits of Jesus Christ. So that by our actions we may lay claim to this reward, three things are required of us: Faith, which makes God ever present to us; Hope, which causes us to perform our actions with the intention of pleasing God, and Charity, which unites us to Him as to our supreme good.

You will ask, what does "hope" mean? It means, dear brethren, to strive after something which will make us happy in the life to come; to have an ardent longing to be rid of all earthly evils, and to partake of that heavenly reward which is to satisfy us beyond all human conception. When Adam had sinned and was beset with many miseries, his greatest consolation consisted in the hope that his sufferings would not only procure pardon for his sins, but they would also gain merits for heaven. Oh, how good God is, dear brethren, who rewards the least of our actions if performed for His sake with such great bliss for all eternity. But that we may merit this great grace, it is the will of God that we should have as great confidence in Him as children have in their good father. To inspire us with a greater confidence, we know that many times in Holy Scripture He has caused Himself to be called "Father." He desires that in all the necessities of body and soul we should take refuge in Him. By giving Himself the name of "Father," He wishes to strengthen our confidence in Him. Behold how much He loves us. Through the prophet Isaias He tells us that He carries us all in His bosom. "A mother," says He, "who carries her child in her womb can not forget it, and if she should be so unnatural as to do so, still I never forget those who put their trust in me." He even complains that we place so little confidence in Him, and He exhorts us not to put our trust in kings and princes, because we then shall have our hopes disappointed. He even goes further, and He threatens us with His curse if we do not have great confidence in Him. Through the prophet Jeremias He says, "Cursed are those who do not trust in God!" and He continues, "Blessed are they who trust in the Lord!" I said that our temporal wants should move us to have a great confidence in God. He promises to care for us, to encourage us to take recourse to Him in all our needs, and He has worked miracles for those who placed their confidence in Him. We know from Holy Scripture that He fed His people in the desert for forty years with manna. During all the years which they passed in the desert their clothing did not wear out. He exhorts us in the Gospel not to be solicitous in regard to food and clothing: "Behold the fowls of the air: they sow not, neither do they reap, nor gather into barns: yet your heavenly Father feedeth them. Are not you of much more value than they, O ye of little faith? Be not solicitous, therefore, saying. What shall we eat, or wherewith shall we be clothed? Consider the lilies of the field, how they grow: they labor not, neither do they spin, and yet I say to you, that not even Solomon, in all his glory, was arrayed as one of these. Now, if God so clothe the grass of the field, which today is, and to-morrow is cast into the oven, how much more you, O ye of little faith? Seek ye, therefore, first the kingdom of God, and his justice, and all these things shall be added unto you." See how much He desires that we should put our trust in Him! When you pray He teaches us, "Do not say 'My God,' but say 'Our Father,'" for all know what unbounded confidence a child has in its father. When He appeared to Mary Magdalen after His Resurrection, He said to her: "Seek my brethren, and tell them, that I go to my Father, who is also their Father." Tell me, dear brethren, does it not appear to you, too, that our lack of confidence in God is the reason why we are so unhappy upon this earth?

The virtue of Hope consoles and supports us in the trials which God sends us. We have a beautiful example of this in holy Job stretched out on the dunghill, covered with sores from the sole of his foot to the crown of his head. He had lost all his children—they were killed in the ruins of his house; he himself driven from his bed on to a dunghill; forsaken by everybody; his own wife ridiculing and heaping abuse upon him, instead of consoling him; his dearest friends only causing him still greater sufferings by their remonstrances.

Meanwhile, although his condition was so pitiable, he never ceased to hope in God. "My God," he said, "I will never cease to hope in Thee, and to have confidence in Thy love toward all men. Why, O God, should I be discouraged and a prey to despair? I will confess my sins before Thee, which have been the cause of my sufferings, but I hope that Thou wilt be my Saviour. My hope is that Thou wilt one day reward me for the sufferings I have endured for Thy sake." See, dear brethren, we may call this true hope, because he did not cease to hope in God, although it seemed as if the fulness of God's wrath had descended upon him. Without seeking to know why so much suffering was his portion, he contented himself by saying that his sins alone were the cause of it. Behold, dear brethren, the great benefits which the virtue of Hope holds out to us. Lamented as unfortunate by his friends, forsaken by his own flesh and blood, despised by others, Job considers himself happy, because his confidence is placed in God. Ah, if we had such a great confidence in God in our sufferings, troubles, and sicknesses, what treasures should we not heap up for heaven! Oh, how blind we are! Instead of being inconsolable in our afflictions we had the firm hope that God sends them to us as so many means by which we can merit heaven, how gladly would we undergo them!

We must have a firm confidence in Jesus Christ, for we are sure that He will never forsake us in our necessities if we turn to Him as children to their Father; we ought to have, also, a great confidence in the Mother of God, who is so good and who so willingly assists us in all our spiritual and temporal wants by pleading for us with her divine Son. If, for instance, there is a sin upon our conscience that we are afraid to confess, let us throw ourselves at her feet, and we may rely that she will obtain for us the grace to make a good confession, and thus will procure for us the forgiveness of our sins. Yes, dear brethren, after God we ought to place the greatest confidence in the Blessed Virgin in all our spiritual and temporal needs.

The following wonderful example will serve as a proof of this. It is related in history that a certain young man for a long time led an excellent Christian life, which gave him firm confidence in gaining heaven, but the devil, eager to work his ruin, tempted him violently and so long, until at last the youth committed a mortal sin. Immediately after, he saw the enormity of his sin, and his first thought was to take refuge in the sacred tribunal of penance. But such a feeling of shame came over him at the thought of his sins that he could not make up his mind to go to confession. Tormented by remorse of conscience he foolishly resolved to drown himself, so as to put an end to his torments. When he reached the bank of the river he shuddered at the thought of the eternal damnation into which he was about to plunge himself, and, crying bitterly, he wended his way back and prayed that God might forgive him without confession. He attempted to gain peace of conscience by visiting churches, praying and practising penitential works, but in spite of all his prayers and penances remorse of conscience persecuted him persistently. God, in His great mercy, and at the intercession of His Blessed Mother, wanted to save the youth. One night, as the youth sat up, in great sadness, he felt a great desire to go to confession, and at dawn he arose and went to church, but just as he was about to go to confession he felt more than ever ashamed of his sin, and he had not the courage to do that which the grace of God had inspired him to do. The same thing happened to him repeatedly, shame held him back, and finally, in a moment of desperation, he again made up his mind to die rather than reveal his sin to the priest. All at once the thought struck him to recommend himself to the Blessed Virgin. He threw himself before Our Lady's Altar, confided to her his difficulties, and implored her, with tears in his eyes, not to abandon him. And behold how gracious the Mother of God was to him, how quickly she came to his assistance! Hardly had he knelt down before all his anxieties left him, his heart was completely changed, and he arose full of courage and confidence, sought out his confessor, and revealed all his sins to him. Ah, dear brethren, how miserable would have been the condition of this man had he neglected to take refuge with the Blessed Virgin! Eternal damnation would perhaps have been his fate.

To show us what great confidence we should have in Jesus Christ, and how we should never be afraid to ask Him for everything necessary for body and soul, our Saviour tells us in the Gospel how a man went to one of his friends in the night time to ask for three loaves, as some one had come to visit him and he had nothing to set before him, but the friend answered that he and his family were already in bed, and he did not wish to be disturbed. But the man continued to knock, and kept on saying that he had no bread for his visitor. Then the friend arose and gave him what he wanted, not because of friendship, but because of his urging. "Therefore," Jesus Christ concludes, "ask and it shall be given you: seek, and you shall find; knock, and it shall be opened to you." We may be certain, therefore, that whatever we ask the Father in the name of Jesus Christ He will give it to us.

In conclusion, I must yet say that our hope should be general, which means that whatever happens we must have recourse to God. If we are sick, let us put our trust in Him—He cured many sick persons during His earthly life—and if our health will contribute to the glory of God and the salvation of our soul we are sure that He will give it to us; if, on the other hand, sickness is more profitable for our salvation, He will give us the strength to bear it with patience and thereby merit eternal reward. If we find ourselves in any great danger, let us imitate the three youths whom they cast into the fiery furnace: their confidence in God was so great that the fire had no power over them, and only consumed the ropes with which they were bound, while they walked about the furnace praising God. In temptations, dear brethren, let us put our trust in Jesus Christ and we shall be certain not to fall. The loving Saviour merited our victory over our temptations by allowing Himself to be tempted. If, dear brethren, we have become entangled in any bad habit, and we are afraid that we shall not be able to get rid of it, let us put our trust in God; He merited for us countless graces, that we might be victorious over the devil. In this way we shall find consolation in our cares, which are inseparable from life.

It is pride which causes us to remain hardened in our sins and makes it so difficult for us to confess them. If we were humble we could not remain in our sins, nor should we be afraid to go to confession. Let us ask God, dear brethren, to grant us humility, so that we may fear sin and have recourse to the Sacrament of Penance if we have committed sin. We should often ask God for the beautiful virtue of Hope, which will show us how to perform all our actions with the intention of pleasing God alone.

Let us guard against giving way to despair in sickness and trouble. Let us remember that God sends us these so that we may fix our eyes and our hopes upon the eternal reward in heaven, which I wish you all. Amen.

FIFTH SUNDAY AFTER PENTECOST

THE SECOND COMMANDMENT

"Thou shalt not take the name of the Lord thy God in vain."

WE OUGHT TO BE WONDERING, dear brethren, that God found it necessary to forbid, by a special commandment, the misuse of His holy name. Is it conceivable, my dear people, that Christians make themselves tools of the devil by reviling so good and beneficent a God? Can we imagine that a tongue which has been consecrated to God in Holy Baptism, and has so often been honored with His most adorable flesh and blood, might be employed in reviling its Creator? Could we possibly do this if we really believed that God gave it to us, to magnify Him and to sing His praises? Surely this is a dreadful crime, which in a manner compels God to visit us with manifold miseries, and to abandon us to the devil, whom we serve with so much zeal? This crime must appear appalling to any one who has not entirely lost faith. And yet, in spite of the enormity, the horror, and the iniquity of this sin, there is hardly any sin more common than swearing, blaspheming, and cursing. Do we not often hear even little children swear who hardly know the "Our Father"? The second commandment, which forbids us to swear falsely, or unnecessarily, says: "Thou shalt not take the name of the Lord thy God in vain." In that commandment God tells us: "I order and command you to respect my name, because it is holy and worthy of the greatest reverence. I forbid you to profane it by using it in falsehood, an injustice, or without sufficient reason."

I will now try and show you, dear brethren, what is understood by:

I. Blasphemy and swearing.
II. Imprecations and curses.
III. Swearing falsely, or perjury.

Many persons do not seem to be able to distinguish these things and take one for the other, and for this reason they do not accuse themselves of their sins as they ought to.

I. Ignorant people frequently confound blasphemy with swearing. An unfortunate man may in a moment of anger or despair cry out: "God is not just, because He permits me to suffer this, or to lose that." He has blasphemed God, and not sworn, in using these words, and yet in confession he accuses himself: "Father, I accuse myself of having sworn." What he has really done was not swearing, but blaspheming. A person is falsely accused of something which he has not done. He says, to justify himself: "If I did this may I never see the face of God." This is not swearing, but a fearful imprecation. These are two sins which are just as grievous as false oaths. Another one calls his neighbor a thief, a rascal, and then accuses himself of having sworn at his neighbor. That is not swearing, but using injurious words. Still another uses foul, indecent words, and accuses himself of having used godless talk; he should accuse himself of having used obscene language. To swear, dear brethren, means to call God to witness our statements, and by perjury we understand a false oath; that is to say, if somebody takes an oath to confirm a falsehood.

The name of God is so holy, so great, and so adorable that, according to the testimony of St. John, the angels and saints in heaven cry out unceasingly: "Holy, holy, holy is the great God of the heavenly host; his name shall be praised from eternity to eternity!" When the Blessed Virgin visited her cousin Elizabeth, and that holy woman said to her, "Blessed art thou who has been chosen to be the Mother of God," the Blessed Virgin answered, "For he that is mighty hath done great things to me, and holy is his name." We also should have a great reverence for God's name, and never utter it without the greatest veneration, or take it in vain. St. Thomas says that it is a sin to take the name of God in vain; for instance, swearing is a sin unlike others, as in other sins insignificance of the circumstances diminishes the enormity of the sin. Stealing is, properly speaking, a mortal sin, but stealing something very trifling, only a couple of pennies, for instance, is still a sin, but only a venial sin. The same is true of anger and gluttony. But it is entirely different with swearing: the smaller the matter the greater the desecration. For the more insignificant the matter is the greater the contempt.

"The house of him," says the Holy Ghost, "who swears habitually fills itself with injustice, and the curse only departs therefrom when it is destroyed." Jesus Christ says in the Gospel that we should neither swear by heaven nor by the earth, because neither the one nor the other can hear us. If you wish to assert anything, say: "It is so, or, it is not so; yes or no; I did it, or, I did not do it"; everything that you say in addition to this is of evil. Besides this, a person who habitually swears is an irascible person, who is a slave to his own temper; he swears, whether lying or telling the truth. But you may say, if I do not swear to some things they will not be believed. There you are mistaken, for a person who is addicted to swearing is not believed, for it indicates a person without religion, and a person without religion is not considered truthworthy. If you desire, dear brethren, to be happy in this life, and that God should bless your houses, never swear, and you will see that everything will be well in your house. God tells us that His curse will descend upon the house where there is much swearing and destroy it. Why, my dear brethren, do you let yourselves be carried away and swear, although God has forbidden it by the penalty of misfortune in this life and perdition in the next?

II. There are many other more wicked desecrations of the name of God; for instance, when imprecations are added to swearing. An unfortunate man says: "If that is not the truth I do not want to go to heaven!" and so forth. Alas! O blasphemous sinner, the devil rejoices at thy vile and godless speech. Others, again, have the name of the devil on the tip of their tongue when the slightest thing vexes them. It is to be feared that a person who so frequently has the devil's name upon his lips must bear him also in his heart!

Another kind of swearing, or imprecations, are the curses made in our heart. Many believe that because they do not utter them with the lips they are therefore not sinning, but you are greatly mistaken, my friends. Some one has done you an injury, and you curse him in your heart and wish that evil may befall him and perhaps you carry these thoughts in your heart for a long time, and you believe that it does not matter because you did not utter them with your lips. My friends, that is a grievous sin, and you must accuse yourself of it distinctly or else you lose your soul. Ah, how few know the condition of their poor soul as it is in the sight of God!

There are persons who are still more culpable, for they swear to what is false. If you properly meditate over the contempt shown to God by perjury you would never dare to commit it. You behave toward God like a poor slave who would say to a king: "King, you must bear false witness for me. Does not the thought of perjury fill you with horror, dear brethren? God tells us in Holy Scripture: "Be holy, because I am holy." Do not lie and cheat your neighbor and do not commit perjury, because thereby you call the name of the Lord thy God to witness a lie, and do not profane the name of the Lord. St. John Chrysostom says: "If it is a fault to swear to the truth, how much greater a crime is it to swear falsely, or to a lie?" The Holy Ghost says that those who disseminate lies will perish. The prophet Zacharias assures us that the curse will fall upon the house of him who takes an oath to a lie, and that the curse will remain on the house until it is destroyed. St. Augustine says that perjury is a great crime, and like a wild beast that causes fearful havoc. This sin is still more grievous when imprecations are added to a false oath.

Many persons swear to a promise without having any intention of keeping the promise. Before we promise anything we should examine first whether we can fulfil our promise. And never promise anything under oath. If in a moment of anger we should vow to take revenge, it is quite certain that such promise must not be kept, but that, on the contrary, we should beg pardon of God. The Holy Ghost says that whosoever swears will be punished.

If you ask me how it is that nowadays we hear of so many false oaths, imprecations, horrible blasphemies, and curses, I can only reply that persons who commit such dreadful sins have neither faith, conscience, or virtue, but are forsaken by God. Oh, how much happier should we be if we only used our tongue, consecrated to God in Holy Baptism, to pray to so good and beneficent a God and to sing His praises! Since God has given us our tongue for this purpose, let us endeavor to dedicate it to Him, so that after this earthly life we may have the happiness of praising Him in heaven for all eternity, the blessing which I wish you all. Amen.

SIXTH SUNDAY AFTER PENTECOST

HOLY COMMUNION

"The bread which I will give, is my flesh for the life of the world."
John vi. 52.

WHO AMONG US, dear brethren, could think it possible that Jesus Christ, out of love for His creatures, would have gone so far as to nourish our souls with His adorable body and His precious blood unless He Himself had not assured us of this fact? A soul may receive its Creator, and as often as it desires! O abyss of goodness and love of God for His creatures! When the Redeemer clothed Himself in our flesh, says St. Paul, He hid His divinity and carried His abasement even unto an ignominious death. But in the adorable Sacrament of the Eucharist He, in His boundless love and mercy, hides His humanity also.

Behold, dear brethren, of what the love of a God for His creatures is capable! Of all the Sacraments there is not one that can be compared to the Holy Eucharist. It is true we receive in Baptism the adoption of God, and attain a title to the eternal kingdom of heaven; in the Sacrament of Penance the wounds of our soul are healed, and the friendship of God is restored to us; in the adorable Sacrament of the Eucharist, however, His most precious blood is not only applied us, but we are permitted to receive in reality the divine author of all grace.

But, alas, how few there are who know how to value the magnificence of God's grace! If we properly appreciated the great blessing of our privilege in receiving Jesus Christ we should unceasingly endeavor to deserve it. To give you an idea of the greatness of this blessing, let us consider:

I. The sublimity and importance of this Sacrament.
II. Its effects and blessings.

I.

I will not undertake, dear brethren, to describe to you the whole sublimity of this Sacrament, because that is not possible to mortal man;

one would be like God Himself to describe the magnitude of this miracle. We shall never cease wondering in the other life and through all eternity, that we miserable men have been allowed to receive so great a God. But in order to give you some idea of the great blessings of this great Sacrament, dear brethren, let us remember that Jesus Christ, during His earthly life, never went anywhere without distributing His richest blessings, and how great, therefore, and precious must be the gifts received in Holy Communion! In fact, the greatest good of man in this world consists in receiving Jesus Christ in Holy Communion, because Holy Communion is not only profitable and a food for our souls, but also, as we shall see, profitable for our bodies.

We read in the Gospel that Jesus Christ, at His entry into the house of Elizabeth, although He was still enclosed in His Mother's womb, filled Elizabeth and her child with the Holy Ghost; so that John was purified from original sin, and the mother cried out: "Whence is this to me, that the mother of my Lord should come to me." I will leave it to you, dear brethren, to consider how much greater is the good fortune of those who, in Holy Communion, entertain Jesus Christ, not only in their house, but in their hearts; who may retain Him not only for six months, as Elizabeth did, but for the whole time of their lives. If the holy and venerable Simeon, having for so many years ardently desired to behold the Redeemer, and at last, holding Jesus in his arms, was so carried away by joy, and so enraptured, that he cried out, in an ecstasy of love: "O Lord, what more can I wish for upon earth after having with my very eyes beheld the Redeemer of the world? I will now die in peace!" And again, dear brethren, what a difference between holding Him in arms for only a moment, and receiving Him into our hearts at Holy Communion? How little we appreciate our good fortune! When Zachaeus heard about Jesus Christ, he had a great desire to see Him, and the great crowd preventing him from seeing, he climbed a tree, and the Lord saw him, and said to him: "Zachaeus, come down, for today I will enter into thy house." He descended at once, and made the best preparation that he possibly could for the reception of the Redeemer. On entering into his house, the Lord said: "This day is salvation come to this house." Moved by the kindness of Jesus Christ, Zachaeus cried out: "Lord, the half of my goods I give to the poor, and if I have wronged any man of anything, I restore him fourfold." And thus the visit of Jesus Christ made a great saint of a great sinner. As Jesus, the Gospel informs us, entered into the house of St. Peter, the latter begged Him to cure his mother-in-law, who was suffering from a violent fever. Jesus Christ commanded the fever to leave her, and she was cured immediately and waited upon the guests at table. What was it that moved the Saviour to raise Lazarus out of death, after he had been dead for four days? It was because Lazarus had so often entertained Him in his house; therefore, our Lord showed such an attachment for him that He shed tears. On other occasions Jesus was implored by people to save their lives, other asked Him to heal their bodies, and no one went away without having obtained what he wanted. Is not this proof that He is always ready to grant all things which we ask of Him? What graces will He not shower upon us when He comes into our hearts, there to take up His abode? Who can understand the happiness of a Christian who, well prepared, receives Jesus Christ into his heart, which thereby becomes part of heaven?

But, you will ask, why is it that the greater number of Christians show so little appreciation for this happiness? How is it that many of them think little of it, and even mock those who often partake of it? These poor unfortunate people have simply never known nor enjoyed this great happiness. What happiness it is for a believing Christian to arise from the sacred banquet, and go forth with heaven in his heart! Fortunate is the house in which such Christians dwell! To possess in one's own house a tabernacle in which God is enthroned!

You will want to know, perhaps, if this happiness is so great, why the Church only commands us to receive Communion once a year? This command is not given for good Christians, but for the lax and indifferent Christians, for the good of their poor souls. In the early Church it was the greatest punishment for a Christian to be deprived of Holy Communion. The early Christians were allowed to receive every time they assisted at the Holy Sacrifice of the Mass. When the Church saw that many Christians neglected the salvation of their poor souls, she gave them the command to communicate three times a year, at Christmas, Easter, and Pentecost, hoping that the fear of sinning against this command would open their eyes. But when, in the course of time, Christians became even less zealous of the salvation of their souls, she made it their duty to receive Holy Communion at least once a year. How unhappy and blind is the Christian who must be compelled by law to partake of this great happiness! If, my dear brethren, you had no other sins upon your conscience but the neglect of your Easter duty, you would be eternally lost. Now tell me what inducement is there for your letting your soul fall into such a sad state? You say you are happy and contented. If I could only believe you! But where do you find your peace and contentment? Is it found in the thought that the soul awaits the moment of death only to be cast into hell? or, perhaps, because the devil is your master? How blind and unhappy is man when he has lost the faith!

II.

All the Fathers teach us that by the reception of Jesus Christ in Holy Communion we receive thousandfold blessings for time and eternity; in fact, this is such a fundamental truth that even a child, to the question, "Should we desire ardently to receive Holy Communion?" would answer, "Yes, indeed." "And why?" "On account of the excellent effects which it produces within us." "And what are these effects?" "Holy Communion unites us most intimately with Jesus Christ, weakens our inclinations to do evil, strengthens the life of grace within us, and is for us the foundation and the pledge of eternal life."

I said: 1. Holy Communion unites us most intimately with Jesus Christ. This union is so intimate, dear brethren, that Jesus Christ Himself says: "He that eateth my flesh, and drinketh my blood, abideth in me, and I in him, for my flesh is meat indeed; and my blood is drink indeed." Consequently, dear brethren, upon receiving Holy Communion, the adorable blood of Jesus Christ really flows in our veins, His flesh is really blended with ours; and for this reason St. Paul says: "It is not I who acts and thinks, but Jesus Christ acts and thinks in me. I do not live," he says, "but Christ liveth in me."

2. By receiving Jesus Christ in Holy Communion we receive an abundance of graces; by receiving Jesus Christ we receive the source of every blessing. Those who receive Jesus Christ feel their faith strengthened, and they are more thoroughly impregnated with the truths of their holy religion; they realize more clearly the enormity and the danger of sin; the thought of judgment frightens them more; the misfortune of the loss of God is more perceptible to them. In Holy Communion our courage is fortified; we are strong to combat, our actions are guided by purer motives, our charity increases more and more. The thought that we carry Jesus in our hearts, the rapture which we experience at that blissful moment, unites and binds us so much with God that our heart thinks of and desires but God alone. This, dear brethren, is one of the effects which Holy Communion produces in us, if we are so happy as to receive Jesus Christ worthily.

3. Holy Communion weakens our inclination to evil. It is very easy to perceive this. The most precious blood of Jesus which flows in our veins,

and His adorable body which is blended with ours, must necessarily destroy, or at least weaken greatly, our inclination to evil, produced in us by Adam's sin. It is certain, dear brethren, that after receiving Holy Communion we feel a new desire for heavenly and a fresh contempt for material things. How can pride enter into a heart which has just received a God who, by His entrance into this heart, has abased Himself unto self-privation? Would not a heart having received a God so pure, indeed holiness Himself, feel the greatest horror of the sin of impurity? Would a Christian having received Jesus Christ, who died for his enemies, wish harm to those who have offended him? Certainly not: it would give him pleasure to do good to them as much as lay in his power. Therefore, St. Bernard said to his monks: "My sons, when you feel less inclined to evil and more inclined to good, thank Jesus Christ who has granted you this grace in Holy Communion."

4. Holy Communion is a pledge to us of eternal life; that is to say. Holy Communion endows us with the expectation of heaven, with an assurance that heaven will one day be our abode. Moreover, Jesus Christ will cause our bodies at the resurrection to appear the more glorious the oftener we have received Him worthily.

Yes, dear brethren, if we really knew how to appreciate the greatness of this happiness, we should not care to live unless we were allowed to receive Jesus Christ as our daily food. We should consider all created things as not worth having; we should despise them, and give ourselves to God alone, and our aim would be to become daily more worthy to receive Him.

If such are the happiness and blessings, resulting from the worthy reception of this Sacrament, should we not strive to make ourselves worthy of receiving it frequently? The effects explained to you in this discourse we would all wish to have produced within us; therefore, I exhort you, venerate this great Sacrament and live so as to be able to receive your Lord and God, and to partake of His grace and blessing, so that at the end of time you shall, according to His own words, be raised from death to life everlasting, which I wish you all. Amen.

SEVENTH SUNDAY AFTER PENTECOST

ON FALSE AND TRUE VIRTUE

"By their fruits you shall know them."
Matt. vii, 16.

JESUS CHRIST could not have given us a plainer or surer mark whereby we might know the difference between good and bad Christians than by telling us we should know them, not by their words, but by their works. "A good tree," He says, "can not bear bad fruit, nor can a bad tree bear good fruit." Yes, dear brethren, those who possess only a false piety, a hypocritical or only a superficial virtue, will, in spite of all the precautions they may take, be unable to prevent the true condition of their heart from sometimes manifesting itself outwardly, either in words or deeds. Nothing, my dear brethren, is so prevalent as this pretended virtue, or, in other words, this hypocrisy.

So as to give you the right idea of the unhappy state of those poor souls who will, perhaps, be damned, although doing good, just because they do not good the right way, I will show you:

I. *A good Christian should not be contented to perform good works; he should know how to perform them properly.*

II. *It is not enough to be virtuous in the eyes of the world; we must be so in our hearts.*

I.

Now, if you ask me, dear brethren, how can we know whether a virtue is real, and whether it will lead us to heaven, the answer is: that in order to make an action pleasing to God, the following conditions must be fulfilled: First, the action should be sincere and perfect; second, it should be humble and without selfishness; third, it should be steadfast and enduring: If these conditions are found in everything you do, then you may be sure that you are working for heaven.

(1) We have said that an action must be sincere; it is not sufficient

that it shows itself only outwardly. It must come from our hearts, and love of God must be its prime cause and its beginning, for St. Gregory tells us that everything which God requires of us should be founded on the love which we owe Him. The action, therefore, should be nothing more than a sort of medium to express our intention. Words and actions that do not come from the sincerity of the heart are no more than hypocrisy in the eyes of God.

We say, further, our virtue should be perfect. That means, it is not sufficient for us to practise only those certain virtues to which we may be naturally inclined, but we should embrace them all; that is to say, all virtues the practise of which is possible for our state. St. Paul says that we should prepare a superabundant provision of all kinds of good works for our salvation.

(2) We said, also, that our virtue should be humble and free from selfishness. Jesus Christ tells us that we should never perform our actions in order that we may be praised by men. If we desire a heavenly reward, then we must hide the good which God works in us as much as possible, for fear that the devil of pride may rob us of the merit of those good works. But, perhaps, you will say, the good that we do, we do really for God, and the world has no benefit of it. My friend, I am not so sure about it. There are many who deceive themselves on this point. It might be easy to prove to you that your religion is largely on the outside only, and not founded in the soul. Tell me, would you not, rather than not, have people know that you observe all fast days? If you give money to the poor, or to the Church, would you not like to have this known by your neighbor? Does not that feeling make hypocrites of us?

The saints did exactly the contrary. And why did they? They knew their religion, and they sought to humble themselves to obtain the mercy of God. What poor Christians are those, whose religion is one of mood, of habit, and nothing else! You will, perhaps, think that these are rather strong words. Yes, without doubt, they are rather strong, but they are the strict truth. It must be my endeavor to produce in you a horror of the sin of hypocrisy. How many people, alas, although they do good works, will be lost because they do not know their religion thoroughly! Many people say a great many prayers, and even go frequently to the Sacraments; but they still keep their bad habits, and die in them, because they strive, at one and the same time, to be friends of God and friends of sin. Look at that man, who appears to be a good Christian. Just give him to understand, even if you have the right to do so, that he has wronged some one; point out his faults to him, or any wrong which he has been guilty of in his heart, and he will fly into a rage at once, and hate the sight of you. Hatred and ill-will spring up in his head. Look at another one. You can not have much of an opinion of his piety, for he answers you haughtily, and will not make up with those that have offended him.

The following example will show us how severely God punishes false virtue, which is so great a sin: We read in Holy Scripture that King Jeroboam sent his wife to meet the prophet Ahias, in order to ask advice about the sickness of his son, and he made her to disguise herself in the garb of a poor and pious person. He had recourse to this artifice because he feared that, if his people knew that he asked advice of the prophets of the true God, they would come to the conclusion that he had very little confidence in their idols. But he could not deceive God. When this woman entered the abode of the prophet, the latter cried out, before even having seen her: "Wife of Jeroboam, why dost thou seek to appear other than thou art? Approach, hypocrite. I have bad news to give you from the Lord our God. Bad news, indeed. Listen: The Lord hath commanded me to tell thee that he will send down all kinds of misfortune upon the house of Jeroboam; he will annihilate it, even unto the animals; those of his house that die in the fields will be devoured by dogs. Depart now, wife of Jeroboam. Go and acquaint thy husband with this. And at the moment when thou settest thy foot within the city, thy son shall die." Everything occurred just as the prophet had foretold; not one of Jeroboam's house escaped the vengeance of the Lord. You see, then, dear brethren, how God punishes this cursed sin of hypocrisy.

Moreover, I must tell you that it is not the size and greatness of deeds which give them merit, but the pure intention with which they are undertaken. The Gospel gives us a beautiful example of this. The Evangelist St. Mark relates that Jesus Christ, on entering the temple one day, beheld how the people cast money into the receptacle for offering, and He saw that many that were rich cast in much. Then He saw how a poor widow approached the receptacle humbly, and cast in two mites. Thereupon, Jesus Christ, calling His disciples, said to them: "Behold, many persons have cast considerable alms into the almsbox and see there also a poor widow who has only cast in two mites. What do you think of this difference? To judge by appearances, you think, perhaps, that the gifts of the rich have more merit; but I tell you that this widow has cast in more than all of them; for the rich cast in of their abundance, but she of her want hath cast in all she had. Most of the rich sought glory before men, and to be thought better than they were, while this widow hath given to please God alone." A beautiful example, dear brethren, which teaches us with what pure intentions and with what humility we should perform all our actions, if we desire to be rewarded for them. Certainly, God does not forbid us to perform our works before men, but He desires that they should be done for His sake alone, and not for the sake of the glory of the world.

(3) We have said, the third necessary condition for true virtue is perseverance. We must not be satisfied to do good for a certain length of time, such as to pray for a while, to mortify ourselves at times, to renounce our self-will, to bear with the weaknesses of others, to combat the temptations of the devil, to bear patiently contempt and calumnies, to watch over the movements of our hearts. No, dear brethren, we must persevere until death if we wish to be saved. St. Paul says that we must be firm and steadfast in the service of God, and that we should work at the salvation of our souls every day of our lives, knowing well that our labor will not be rewarded unless we persevere until the end. He says: "Neither riches nor poverty, neither health nor sickness, should induce us to neglect the salvation of our soul, and to separate ourselves from God: for we know that God will only crown that virtue which perseveres until death."

We see this in a remarkable manner in the Apocalypse in the person of a Bishop, who led such a holy life that God Himself lavished praises upon him: "I know thy works, and thy labor, and thy patience, and how thou canst not bear evil men; and thou hast tried them who say they are apostles and are not, and hast found them liars; and thou hast patience, and hast borne for my name, and hast not failed. But this I have against thee: that thou hast become negligent in the practise of these virtues. Be mindful, therefore, from whence thou art fallen, and do penance as thou didst before, or else I shall reject thee, and punish thee." Tell me, dear brethren, should not we be seized with fear when we hear how God menaced even a Bishop who had been negligent? Alas, what has become of us ever since our conversion! Instead of making progress daily, what tepidity, what indifference, is ours! No, God can not bear this perpetual inconstancy with which we turn from virtue to vice, and from vice to virtue again. Tell me, dear brethren, is this not your manner of living, too? Is your life anything else but an intermingling of sins and virtues? Do you not confess your sins, and the following day commit the same faults again? Or, maybe, even on the same day? How many there are who, for a certain length of time, seem to love God with all their strength, and then again forsake Him! What is it that you find so hard and difficult in the service of God that you are so soon discouraged, and return again to the world? And yet, at the moment when God allowed you to know your condition, you sighed, and you perceived how much you had deceived yourself! The reason of this misfortune is because Satan is angry at having lost you, and he works till he gets you back again, and hopes to hold you forever. How many faithless persons are there who have forsaken their religion, and yet they bear the name of Christians!

II.

Now, you will ask, how can we know if we have virtue in our hearts, that virtue which remains ever true to itself? Now, listen, dear brethren, and you will perceive whether you have that virtue on account of which God will receive you into heaven. A person who is truly virtuous does not waver in the least; he is like a rock beaten by the storm in the midst of the sea. Whether you are blamed, or calumniated, or mocked at, or regarded as a hypocrite, or treated as a prude, none of these things should be capable of robbing you of your peace of soul. You should be just as well disposed toward your enemies as if they had spoken well of you. You should not fail to show them kindness, although they have spoken badly of you. You should say your prayers, go to Confession and Holy Communion, and attend Holy Mass, with disregard of anything the world may say. Our virtue, also, to be true should be steadfast. That is to say, we must be just as resigned to the will of God and zealous under crosses and ill-fortune, as at the time when nothing disagreeable comes in our way. This is how the saints acted. Look at the great multitude of the martyrs who endured everything that the frenzy of a tyrant could think of, and who, far from neglecting God, were, on the contrary, drawn closer to Him. Neither torments nor persecutions inflicted upon them caused them to waver.

Let us, then, conclude, dear brethren, by remembering that our virtue must have its source in the heart, in order to be fruitful and pleasing to God. We must hide our good works. We should also be well on our guard so as to neglect nothing in the service of God; on the contrary, we should grow and increase in the knowledge and love of God. In this way the saints assured themselves of eternal bliss, the blessing which I wish you all. Amen.

EIGHTH SUNDAY AFTER PENTECOST

THE PARTICULAR JUDGMENT

"Give an account of thy stewardship."—Luke xvi. 2.

CAN WE, dear brethren, meditate upon the severity of the divine judgment without being penetrated with the liveliest fear? The days of our life are numbered, and, what is more, we know neither the hour nor the moment when we shall be called before the judgment seat of our eternal Judge. At the very moment when we least expect it, when we are least prepared, we may have to render this awful accounting! I assure you, dear brethren, if we ponder over this rightly, we should have good cause to despair, if our religion did not teach us that we may mitigate that moment by leading a life which will animate us with the hope that God will have compassion upon us. Let us be on our guard, dear brethren, that we may not be taken by surprise when that moment comes, like the steward of whom Christ tells us in the Gospel. I will now show you:

I. What we shall have to account for at the judgment.
II. How we should prepare ourselves for this judgment.

I.

We all know, dear brethren, that we shall have to undergo a twofold judgment: One at that great day of wrath, at the end of the world, in the presence of the whole world, when all our actions, the good and the bad, will be revealed before the eyes of all mankind. But before this awful, and for sinners so fatal day, we shall have already undergone another judgment, namely, at the moment of death, immediately after having breathed our last sigh. Man's vocation may be summed us in these words: To live, to die, and to be judged This is a sure and unalterable law for all men. We are born to die, and we die to be judged, and this judgment will decide for us eternal happiness or eternal misery. The general judgment at which we shall all have to appear, will only be the proclamation of the particular judgment underwent at the hour of our death. You all know, dear brethren, that God has numbered our years, and He has determined which of these years will be our last: the year, the day, the hour, will surely come, after which time will be for us no more. What will then become of the sinner, of the ungodly, who had fondly relied upon a longer life? Their calculations do not avail in that last hour. There will be no turning back, no hope, and no help.

At that moment, my brethren—mark this well, you who do not dread to pass your lives in sin—at that moment, when your soul leaves the body, you will be judged. But you will say, we know this well. Yes, but you do not realize it. If you realized it thoroughly, you could not remain in a state in which you might at any moment be cast into hell for all eternity. If you really appreciated this fact, you would not run the risk of so great a misfortune. Remember, the moment will come in which God will place the seal of immortality and eternity upon thy guilt as it will be found at that moment, and this seal will never be removed. O awful moment! so little contemplated, so brief and yet so long, which will pass away with such rapidity, and yet brings with it the awful consequences of an eternity. What will become of us, dear brethren, at that awful moment? We shall, each one of us, have to appear before the judgment seat of Christ, there to be judged, and to be asked for an exact account of all the good and the evil which we have done. God will demand an account of all the benefits which we have received, of all the gifts of nature, and of grace. We are held responsible for all these gifts. The gifts of nature concern body and soul. We shall have to give an account of the use we have made of our body. He will ask if you have employed its strength for the service of God, for your neighbor, in honest work, in the giving of alms, and in doing penance. Or if, on the contrary, you have employed your health and your body in the service of the devil. Then He will ask us whether we have misused the faculties of our mind for evil, to learn that which is wrong; whether we have read bad books, associated with ungodly persons, and taught evil to others. Whether we have employed our intellect to deceive others in business, to testify falsely, to revenge ourselves upon others, to revile religion. He will ask us whether we have not misused our gift of speech with words and songs against purity, with slander. He will ask us if we have used the powers of our reason to instruct ourselves in the truths of our Holy Religion, or whether we have made use of all these gifts to draw others into sin. God will ask us if we have made good use of our wealth, by reminding ourselves that we are only stewards of the same, and that everything which we shall have used for a bad purpose will be recorded against us as sins.

Now we come, dear brethren, to another item in this rendering of account which will be still more severe, namely, that concerning grace. God will point out to us the benefits which He has granted us, for instance, in permitting us to be born in the bosom of the Catholic Church, when there are so many others, alas, born outside the fold. He will show us how many years, months, weeks, and days of life He has granted us when we were in sin so that we might repent. We should have been plunged into hell if He had allowed us to die during that time. He will place before our eyes all the good thoughts, the good instincts, and the good desires that He has granted us during our life. So many graces despised! He will remind us of all the instructions which we have been allowed to receive, of all our Confessions and Communions, and the heavenly graces which we received in them. And we shall learn that so many Christians have not received the hundredth part of the graces that were given to us, and yet they sanctified themselves! Dear brethren, what has become of all our graces and blessings, what profit have we derived therefrom? What a sad moment that will be for a Christian who has despised them all, and derived no benefit from them! Is this your case? Listen to St. Gregory, who says: "My friend, consider this cross, and you will see what is cost God to merit life for us." St. Augustine, when reflecting upon the accounting which we would have to give for all graces received, exclaimed: "How unhappy am I, what will become of me, having received so many graces! I am more afraid on account of these graces than on account of sins committed, although they are very numerous!" What shall we say, dear brethren, when Christ reproaches us with our contempt and our misuse of the merits of His most precious blood? "Woe to you, ungrateful sinner!" He will say, "thou unfruitful vine, thou barren tree! What could I have done for thy salvation that I did not do? Did I not have reason to expect that thou wouldst bear good fruit for eternal life? Where are thy good works? Where are thy prayers, which would have rejoiced My heart? Where are thy Confessions—the Communions which should have caused Me to dwell in thy soul, and which would have compensated Me in a measure for the sufferings which I endured for thy salvation? Where are thy penitential works for the wiping out of past sins? Where are the good results of the many good inspirations accorded thee, good thoughts and desires, and the many opportunities prepared for thee?

Where are the Holy Masses through which thou couldst have made satisfaction for thy sins? Depart, wretched soul! thou hast only performed works of unrighteousness to renew My passion and death. Depart from Me! I curse thee for all eternity! Depart! On the day of general judgment I shall proclaim the good thou shouldst have accomplished, but hast not done, and all the graces which I granted thee, but thou hast not used." What terrible reproach! How awful will this account be!

This judgment will take place before three witnesses: before God, who will judge us; our guardian angel, who will present our good works; and Satan, who will reveal everything wicked which we have done during our lives! After they have spoken, God will judge us, and decide our everlasting destiny. How great will be the fear of a poor Christian who awaits his judgment, and whose fate will either be heaven or hell!

If it is so dreadful, then, to give an account of even the graces which God gave us, what will it be when we shall be asked and judged according to our sins? Perhaps you will say for your own consolation that you have not committed such monstrous sins. Perhaps not, in the eyes of the world; but how is it with your secret sins? Alas, how many unchaste thoughts and desires, how many thoughts of hatred, revenge, and envy, have soiled our mind and soul during a life of thirty, forty, or eighty years! How many thoughts of pride, of jealousy, how many desires to injure our neighbor, or to deceive him! And when it comes to sinful acts! When God asks us about certain unchaste actions, and certain shameful deeds, about unworthy Confessions and Communions, about our deceitfulness by which we have injured others!

II.

This judgment will take place in the very moment of death—we might say, upon the deathbed—for the Apostle clearly states: "It is appointed unto men once to die, and after this the judgment." (Heb. ix. 27.) No intermission, therefore, between death and judgment: one follows the other one immediately.

Is not this thought sufficient to fill us with fright? And who does not tremble at the thought that God will let nothing pass unexamined, not even the good works, so as to find out if they were really meritorious! Because so many good deeds are performed solely for the sake of the world and out of a desire to be observed and be considered virtuous, therefore so many good actions have no merit in the eyes of God! If even the saints dreaded this moment, and practised long and severe penances, how may we hope that God will have compassion upon us? Cast us not into hell, O Lord! Rather let us suffer any evils that Thou willst send us in this life! Yes, we should have a great sorrow for our sins, and weep over them, like King David, who wept over his sins until his death. We should humble ourselves profoundly before God, by accepting any suffering that God may send us in this life, not only with devout submission, but even with joy, for there is no alternative. We must suffer either in this life or the one to come, where our tears will be useless and our penance without merit. We must never forget that we do not know the day of our death, and that if, unfortunately, we should be overtaken in the state of sin, we should be eternally lost. What, then, shall we do, dear brethren? We must be completely blind if, having pondered on these truths, we do not acknowledge that no man may justly say he is ready to appear before Christ. In view of this certainty, let us take steps to draw nearer to God, let us lead a good and God-fearing life, so as to assure ourselves of a favorable sentence if we should suddenly be called to judgment. How blinded is the sinner! How lamentable is his lot! No, dear brethren, let us no longer continue in our folly. Christ may knock at our door at the moment when we least expect Him. Happy they who have not waited till this moment to make their preparations! This is what I wish you all. Amen.

NINTH SUNDAY AFTER PENTECOST

THE SOUL

"And when He drew near, seeing the city, He wept over it."
Luke xix, 41.

WHEN JESUS was about to enter the city of Jerusalem, He wept over it, saying: "If thou wouldst at least have understood the grace I bring thee, and wouldst have derived benefit therefrom, then thou wouldst have still obtained forgiveness; but no, thy blindness has gone so far that all these graces have served only to harden thee, and to increase thy misfortune; thou didst kill the prophets and the children of God, and now thou wilt reach the pinnacle of thy crimes by putting to death the Son of God Himself." This it was, my dear friends, that caused Jesus to shed copious tears when He was about to enter the city. In the calamity thus foretold, He foresaw and deplored the loss of so many souls, far more guilty, because favored with so many more graces, than the Jews. What moved Him so deeply was that, notwithstanding His merits and His bitter passion, which would have been sufficient to redeem more than a thousand worlds, the greater part of humanity would be lost. Indeed, even among ourselves, He perceived those who despise His graces and employ them only for their own destruction. Who would not tremble, when seriously thinking of saving his soul? Has not Christ warned us under His tears: "If my death and my blood do not serve for thy salvation, they will arouse the everlasting wrath of my Father."

Is it conceivable, my friends, that in spite of all Jesus has done for the salvation of our soul, we could be indifferent? For the purpose of expelling this indifference from among us, let me endeavor to show you:

    I. What a soul really is.
    II. Our obligation toward our soul.

I.

My dear friends, if we would really appreciate the value of our souls, with what care and zeal would we not try to save it! But we never really comprehend its value. To show the great value of a soul is impossible to mortal man. God alone knows the beauties and perfections with which He has adorned a soul. Let me point out to you that God has created heaven and earth, and all they contain, and all these wonders have been created for its benefit. Our catechism gives us an indication of the magnificence of the soul. If you ask a child, "What is understood by saying that man is a creature whose soul is made to the image and likeness of God?" the child will answer, "That the soul, like God, possesses the faculties to reason, to love, and to act on its own free will." This, my friends, is the highest testimonial to the qualities with which God has adorned the soul, that it was created by the three persons of the Most Holy Trinity after their own likeness. A spirit like unto God, capable for all eternity of recognizing the sublimities and perfections of God; a soul which is the object of love of the three divine persons, a soul capable of adoring God in all His works; a soul whose whole destiny will be to sing the praises of the Almighty; a soul which has freedom in its actions, so that it may give its affection and its love wheresoever it pleases. It is free to love God or not love Him, but when fortunate enough to turn to God in love, then God Himself seems to be the will of such a soul, and dwells therein in happiness. We may positively state that, since the creation of the world there has never been anything refused to a soul if it was given over entirely to His love. God has instilled our souls with desires which find their gratification not in this world. Give a soul all the joys and treasures of this world, and it will not be satisfied, for the simple reason that God has created the soul for Himself. He alone is capable of satisfying its longings.

Yes, my friends, our soul is capable of loving God, and the love of God alone forms its happiness. If we love Him, all the good and the pleasures which we could ever hope for on earth or in heaven, are ours. We are furthermore enabled to serve God, that is, to glorify Him in our works and actions. There is nothing, down to the most insignificant action, by which it would not be possible for us to glorify the Lord, provided we perform this action out of love for Him. Our occupations upon earth are different from the occupation of the angels in heaven only inasmuch as we can not as yet behold the Lord with our human eyes, but only with the eyes of faith.

Our soul is so noble, adorned with such beautiful qualities that God entrusted every soul to the care of a prince of His heavenly household, to a guardian angel. Our soul is so precious in the eyes of God, that in His wisdom He could find no worthier food for it than His own divine body, of which the soul may partake as its daily bread, if it so desires. St. Ambrose says, that God esteems our soul so much, that if there had been only one soul in the world, He would not have considered it too great a sacrifice to die for this one soul. He said to St. Teresa: "Thou art so agreeable to me, that, if there had not been a heaven, I would have created one for thee alone."

"O body, how happy thou art!" exclaims St. Bernard, "to harbor a soul which is adorned with such beautiful graces!" Our soul is something so great, so precious, that nothing but God alone surpasses it. God once showed a soul to St. Catherine. She found it so beautiful that she exclaimed: "Oh, my Lord, if my faith did not teach me that there is only one God, I should believe this soul is another God. I can now understand that Thou hast died for so beautiful a soul!"

Our soul, my dear friends, will be as immortal as God Himself. Can we be surprised, therefore, that God, knowing the value of the soul so well, weeps such bitter tears at the loss of such a soul?

II.

Now, let us consider how much care we must employ to preserve in our soul its great beauties. Oh, my friends, God is so sad over the loss of a soul, that He even wept over it. Already in His prophets, He weeps and bewails the loss of souls. We can see this clearly in the person of the prophet Amos. The prophet says: "When I had retired into solitude and meditated upon the terrible number of crimes which God's own people committed every day, and when I saw that God's wrath was ready to descend upon them, and that the abyss of hell was about to open and devour them, then I gathered them together, and said to them, with bitter tears: Oh, my children do you know what my occupation is by day and by night? It is to recall to my mind, in the bitterness of my heart, all your sins. If I fall asleep from exhaustion, I rouse myself immediately, and cry out, my eyes bathed in tears and my heart torn with pain: Oh, my God, my God! is there a soul left in Israel which does not offend Thee? And then, my mind filled with this sad and deplorable state of things, I speak to the Lord and, sighing bitterly in His presence I say: Oh, my God, what must I do to obtain pardon for them? And now listen what the Lord has told me: Prophet, if thou wouldst obtain pardon for these ungrateful people, go into their streets and public places, and let them resound with your lamentations; go into the stores of the merchants, and into the workshops; go into the courts of law; go to the houses of the rich, and the huts of the poor, say to them all, where thou findest them within or without the gates of the city: Woe, woe, unto you, who have sinned against the Lord."

The prophet Jeremias, dear brethren, goes further still. To show us how grievous the loss of a soul is to God, he exclaims at a moment when he was inspired by the spirit of God: "Ah, my God, what will become of me? Thou hast confided to my care a rebellious people, an ungrateful nation, who will neither listen to Thee nor be subject to Thy guidance. Alas! what shall I do? What resolution shall I take? And the Lord answered me: So as to show them how sorrowfully I am touched at the loss of their souls, take thy hair, tear it from thy head, and throw it far from thee: for the sins of this people has obliged me to forsake them, and my anger is enkindled in the interior of their souls." When the anger of God is enkindled on account of sin, that is the greatest sickness of the heart. "But, O Lord," said the prophet, "what shall I do to induce Thee to turn away Thy angry regard from Thy people? Take a sack as raiment, said the Lord to me, strew ashes upon thy head, and weep without ceasing and in such abundance that thy tears will cover thy face, and weep so bitterly that your sins will be drowned in your tears."

Do you realize, dear brethren, how grievous the loss your souls is to God? You see how miserable we are when we destroy a soul which God has so loved that He, when He had not yet eyes to weep with, borrowed the eyes of the prophet to shed bitter tears at their loss. The Lord says by His prophet Joel: "Weep over the loss of souls, as a young wife who has just lost her husband, who was her only consolation, and who is exposed to all kinds of misfortune."

If we then consider what it had cost Christ to save our souls; if we consider His whole life, beginning with His lowly birth to His last breath on Calvary, all this suffering of a Godman, infinite in value, will tell us the value of our soul, because all He did was to redeem that soul, was the price paid for our souls.

If, on the other hand, we see what the devil is doing in order to destroy your soul, indeed your soul must be very valuable if he uses all his forces to destroy it. We will, however, not look into this sad picture. Enough to know that he is our greatest enemy, and that we must fight him, and that, with Christ's grace, we can overcome him.

How true are, therefore, the words of Scripture: What does it profit man to gain the whole world if he lose his soul? O beloved brethren, the knowledge of the value of your soul should move you to guard it as your greatest treasure. Do not allow sin to blemish or to destroy it. As you know that sin will cause the loss of your beautiful soul, guard it, and let this be your resolution on this morning not only to avoid all mortal sin, but even every wilful venial sin, so as to save your soul for heaven, and allow it to reach its destiny, it home, and its reward, the eternal sight of the great glory of God. Amen.

TENTH SUNDAY AFTER PENTECOST

RASH JUDGMENT

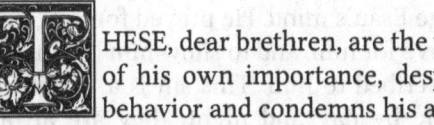

"O God, I give thee thanks that I am not as the rest of men, extortioners, unjust, adulterers, nor such as this publican."
Luke xviii. 11.

THESE, dear brethren, are the words of the proud man who, full of his own importance, despises his neighbor, criticises his behavior and condemns his actions though they be influenced by the most innocent and purest motives. He finds no good in anything but that what he says or does himself. You may see him constantly watching the words and actions of his neighbor and upon the least pretext, he blames, judges and condemns without mercy or inquiry. O accursed sin, thou art the cause of enmities, hatred, dissensions, and of eternal damnation of souls! Yes, dear brethren, we see that the person addicted to this sin, is scandalized at everything. Our Lord must regard this sin as a very great one and the devastation which it occasions in the world must be awful, because, so as to inspire us with a horror of it, He has so clearly and unmistakably characterized it for us in the Pharisee. How stupendous and how frightful is the evil which this execrable sin brings in its wake! And how difficult it is for those addicted to it, to give it up! To induce you, dear brethren, never to allow this dreadful fault to dominate you, I will describe it to you as well as I can.

I say in the first place, rash judgment is a pre-judicial thought or word directed against our neighbor's honor without sufficient cause. It can only proceed from a bad heart, filled with pride and envy; for a good Christian, who is penetrated with the thought of his own faults, does not think or judge bad of others; at least never without good reason, and only when he is obliged by duty to watch over them. We say, dear brethren, that rash judgment arises from a proud and envious heart, and this is easily understood. The proud and envious have a good opinion only of themselves and they attribute everything that their neighbor does to bad motives: the good which they perceive in their neighbor, angers and vexes them. Holy Scripture gives us a true example of this in Cain, who interpreted all his brother's actions as bad. When he saw that the latter was agreeable to God, he determined to kill him. It was the same with Esau who wanted to kill his brother Jacob. He spent his time finding out what the other did, and he was suspicious, and found nothing right that his brother did. His brother Jacob, who possessed a good, humble heart, thought no evil of his brother; he loved him with all his heart, always thought well of him, excused his actions, although they were bad, and although Esau even thought of taking his brother's life. Jacob did everything in his power to change Esau's mind. He prayed for him, even gave him presents, to prove his love for him, and to show him that he had not those motives which Esau ascribed to him. This sin is a worm that gnaws, it consumes these people by day and night: they are always gloomy and dejected without being willing to say what troubles them, as their pride would thereby be hurt. This sin kills by a slow fire. O what a sad life! But all the happier is the life of those who do not criticise their neighbors, and who take everything for the best! Their soul is at peace, they think badly only of themselves, and in consequence humble themselves before God and implore His mercy. Listen to a beautiful example.

We read in history of the fathers of the desert, that a religious who had led a pure and chaste life, was attacked by a sickness which eventually caused his death. When near death, and all the brethren surrounding his bed, the superior begged him to tell them in what virtue he considered himself most agreeable to God. "My father," replied the good religious, "it is difficult for me to tell you this, but under obedience, I will do so. Since my childhood I was exposed to the most terrible temptations of the devil; but the more he tormented me, the more did God console me and the Blessed Virgin, who one day, when I was greatly tormented by a devil, appeared, and drove away the devil, and exhorted me to virtue. To give you, she said to me, the best means to virtue, I will reveal to you something from the infinite treasury of my son; I will teach you three things, which, if you practice them rightly, will make you agreeable in the eyes of God, and which will put you in condition to easily overcome Satan, who desires your eternal ruin. You must humble yourself; never seek at meals for that which tastes good to you; in dress observe simplicity; in all your actions never seek that which will exalt you in the eyes of the world, but that which would humble you; never judge your neighbor harshly, no matter what you may perceive in his actions or words, for the thoughts of the heart do not always agree with the outward actions. Think well of everybody; this is pleasing to God. With these words the Blessed Virgin vanished. I have faithfully followed the path pointed out to me and hope that it has made me deserving of heaven."

Thence, dear Christians, we see that only a bad heart judges its neighbor rashly. How often, in fact almost always, do we not have to repent having judged or spoken harshly of others, when in the course of time, and upon thorough inquiry we find that what has been said about our neighbor, is false. In judging rashly we act like the judges of the chaste Susanne, who would, upon the accusation of the two false witnesses, not give her time to defend herself. Others imitate the presumption and malice of the Jews who spread abroad that Christ was a blasphemer, and possessed of the devil; others again behave like that Pharisee, who looked upon St. Mary Magdalen only as the notorious sinner without inquiring whether she had renounced her sins or not, although he saw her weep, confess her sins, and prostrate herself at the Saviour's feet.

The Pharisee in today's gospel, dear brethren, whom the Saviour presents to us a notorious type of all those who think and judge rashly of their neighbor, fell probably into three sins. By judging the poor publican, he thinks bad of him, judges him rashly and condemns him, without even knowing the disposition of his heart. His opinion is founded only upon conjecture. This is the first characteristic of rash judgment. He compares the publican to himself in consequence of his pride and his malice: this is the second characteristic. Finally he judges and condemns him, without knowing whether what he says of him is true or false, whilst this publican retires into a corner of the temple, strikes his breast, and implores forgiveness of God.

The reason why some people like to indulge in rash judgment is because they consider it a small matter, whereas it frequently becomes a grievous sin, especially if the occasion is important. But you will say, this only takes place in my heart. It is just this which makes the sin so great, because our heart is created only for the love of God and our neighbor, and therefore this is treachery. For often we tell people by words that we like them and have a good opinion of them, whilst in reality we hate them. Still there are persons who believe that a thought is not a sin, if it is not expressed in words. Though this sin, committed only in the heart, is smaller than if revealed outwardly, it is nevertheless a great injustice. If this sin is so great if perpetrated only in our hearts, I will leave it to your consideration how great it must be in sight of God when expressed in words. Before speaking about anything we must investigate the case thoroughly, before we pass sentence upon it; for appearances often deceive, as we know from our own experience. Look at a judge when sitting at court over some offender; he lets the witnesses come one after another and questions them. He takes all possible pains to obtain a confession from the accused one. You know that if there is the slightest doubt, he does not pronounce sentence; and when he finds himself obliged to pronounce sentence, he does so reluctantly, for he is always in fear that he may have condemned an innocent person. Ah, dear brethren, how few rash judgments would there be if such precautions were taken before we judge of the conduct and actions of others. There would be fewer souls in hell!

God gives us in our ancestor Adam, a beautiful example of the way in which we should judge our neighbor. The Lord had seen and heard what Adam had done and said; He could have condemned him without further inquiry; but no; to show us that we should not be hasty in condemning our neighbor's actions. He questioned our first parents, one after the other, so that they themselves might acknowledge the evil that they had done.

Whence come so many hasty judgments of our neighbor? From the great pride which blinds us, so that our own countless, and often much greater faults are overlooked by us.

I have seen persons who pronounced an entirely false judgment; but although they were shown their mistake they would not desist from it. Alas, poor blind souls, God awaits you, and you will be compelled to acknowledge that your pride caused you to think bad of your neighbor. Furthermore, in order to be able to judge unerringly of our neighbor's words and deeds, we should have to know the state of his heart, and his real intentions. We do not take the proper precautions to investigate, dear brethren, and this is the reason why we make mistakes in judging our neighbor's conduct. We act just like condemning a person to death upon the testimony of untrustworthy persons without giving him time to defend himself.

But you will say, we only judge of what we see, what we hear and what we are witnesses of: "I saw what I am asserting; I heard with my own ears what he said: therefore I can not be mistaken." Very well! If you are anxious to judge, begin by judging your own heart, scorched with pride and arrogance: you will find that you are infinitely more culpable than your neighbor whom you would judge so rashly. You may then find reason to fear that one day you see that very neighbor of yours entering heaven, while you are dragged by the devil away to hell. Alas, miserable pride," says St. Augustine, "you dare to judge your brother on the slightest pretext, and you do not know whether he has not already repented of his fault, and belongs again to the number of God's friends. Take care that he does not take your place, which you are greatly in danger of losing by your pride." Yes, dear brethren, all these rash judgments and misrepresentations, and misconstructions, come only from those who have a secret pride, who do not know themselves, and who think they know their neighbor's mind, which is known to God alone. If we could only succeed in eradicating this greatest of the capital sins from our hearts, then we would never suppose that any of our fellow men were doing wrong; we should never take pleasure in watching their conduct; we should be satisfied to lament our own sins and strive as much as possible to improve ourselves. Nothing else would trouble us. No, dear, brethren, I do not believe that there is another sin more to be feared and more difficult to renounce than the sin of rash judgment, even by some persons who appear to perform their religious duties faithfully.

Now tell me, dear brethren, what foundation have we for all this judging and criticising? Only appearances, and more often than not, just a "They say". Or perhaps you saw and heard it yourself? Still you can be mistaken even in seeing and hearing. For we do not know the interior state of a person and the motive for his actions. If you had seen how the beautiful Judith took off her mourning garments, and surrounded herself with everything that nature and art offered to increase her extraordinary beauty, you would have exclaimed on seeing her enter the apartment of the enemy and to all appearances endeavored to find favor in his eyes, "What a bad woman!" Instead of which she was a pious widow; chaste and pleasing to God, who thus imperilled her life to save her people. Tell me, dear brethren, what would have become of your rash judgments, and your habit of thinking evil of your neighbor, if you had seen the chaste Joseph leaving the room of Potiphar's wife, and if you had heard that woman screaming, and seen her holding in her hands a piece of Joseph's mantle, and pursuing him as one who wanted to dishonor her? At once, without further inquiry, you would have thought and said that this young man was bad and depraved, that he had even laid a snare for the wife of his master, from whom he had received many kindnesses. And he was really condemned by his master Potiphar, and every one looked upon him as guilty, and despised him; but God, who knew the heart and innocence of

Joseph, rejoiced at his action, because Joseph feared the loss of his good name and his life less, than the loss of his innocence and the perpetration of a grievous sin.

Do you understand now, dear brethren, in what danger we are of judging our neighbor's actions wrongly, in spite of all that we may see and hear? This should warn us not to judge the actions of others and if obliged, as parents or teachers, to watch their conduct, only upon careful observation and investigation. In regard to our neighbors uncalled for judgment is nearly always wrong. Yes, dear brethren, I have known persons who judged harshly of their fellow men's intentions, when I knew positively that they were good. I tried to teach them differently, but without avail.

Tell me, dear brethren, have we any better foundation for judging our neighbor's actions than those persons had who saw the beautiful Judith adorn herself magnificently and visit Holofernes? No, dear brethren, we are no surer of what we see and hear, than were those who saw Potiphar's wife with a piece of Joseph's mantle in her hands, and heard her claim that he had attempted to assault her. Here you have two examples which the Holy Ghost gives us, to show us how deceitful appearances are, and how greatly we sin by forming rash judgments. Happy, therefore, are they, who do not concern themselves about their neighbor's conduct, for which they are not answerable, who think only of themselves, who acknowledge their own faults, and try and amend them with all their strength! Happy are they, whose hearts and minds are occupied solely with the fear of God, and use their tongues only to beseech pardon of God, and their eyes to weep over their own sins. Amen.

ELEVENTH SUNDAY AFTER PENTECOST

DETRACTION

"And the sting of his tongue was loosed; and he spoke right."
Mark vii. 35.

IT IS GREATLY to be desired that it might be said of each of us what the Gospel says of this deaf mute, whom Christ healed, "He spoke right." Alas, on the contrary, can we not be reproached for very frequently speaking wrong, when we speak of our neighbor? In fact, what is in that respect the behavior of the greater part of the Christians of today? They criticise, censure and generally denounce the actions of their neighbor: this is of all evil habits the most common, the most widespread, and perhaps the most vicious and the most harmful. It is a vice which we can never sufficiently detest; a vice, which brings in its train the saddest consequences, and spreads harm, and affliction everywhere. Ah, that God would give me the coal with which the angel cleansed the lips of the prophet Isaias, so that I might purify the tongues of all men. How much misery would be banished from the face of the earth, if we could exterminate backbiting, slander, defamation of character! If, my dear brethren, I could inspire you with great horror of these great wrongs, you might be delivered from them forevermore, and I will therefore attempt to show you:

What detraction is; in what different ways we may become guilty of it, and what other sins are very often caused by it.

I will not attempt to show you the enormity and heinousness of this vice of detraction, which causes so much misery, and which is the origin of so many other sins, of so much hatred, even of murders, and lifelong enmities. This vice spares neither good nor bad; it is enough for me to tell you, that this vice is one of those that are responsible for most of the souls that go to hell. It is necessary to know the many various ways in which we may become guilty of this sin, so that knowing this evil, we may the more easily avoid it, and avoid the harm which it causes in the lives of others. If you ask: What is detraction, I have to answer: It consists of making known a defect or fault of our neighbor unnecessarily, and in such way as to cause him injury, to his good name or otherwise. This may happen in various ways.

When we impute something bad to our neighbor which he has not committed a defect which he does not possess, we commit calumny; a most detestable act, which unfortunately, and in spite of its great wrong, is very common. This is not detraction, it is more sinful, but from detraction to calumny is only a small step. If we are honest, we must admit that we invariably add something to, or magnify the bad which we know of our neighbor. A slanderous story that has passed from tongue to tongue, no longer resembles that which was said at first, it has been so much engrossed and aggravated; from which fact we must conclude that a detractor is almost invariably also a calumniator, and a calumniator is a very wicked person.

We exaggerate as a rule the bad that our neighbor does. When you notice any one commit a fault what do you do? Instead of covering it with the mantle of charity, or at least trying to excuse it, you like to exaggerate it.

St. Francis of Sales says: "Do not say this or that one is a drunkard, and a thief, because he once stole or was intoxicated; Noah and Loth were intoxicated once, and yet neither the one nor the other were drunkards." St. Peter was not a blasphemer because he blasphemed once. A person is not vicious, because he once fell into sin, even not if this happened several times; therefore, we run danger of being guilty of detraction if we accuse them. When Simon saw Magdalen weeping at our Saviour's feet, he said: "This man, if he were a prophet would know surely that this woman at his feet is a sinner." He was greatly mistaken: Magdalen was no longer a sinner, but a holy penitent, because all her sins had been forgiven her. Consider the proud Pharisee, who in the Temple praised his own good works, and thanked God that he was not like others, adulterers, extortioners, and thieves, or like the publican. He denounced the publican as a sinner, when at that very moment this publican was justified. "My dear children," exclaimed St. Francis de Sales, "since God's mercy is so great that one moment suffices for Him to pardon the greatest crimes, how dare we say, that a man who yesterday was a great sinner, is the same today!" We invariably deceive ourselves if we think bad of our neighbor, no matter what reasons we have for our opinion. We are also

ELEVENTH SUNDAY AFTER PENTECOST

guilty of detraction when without sufficient reason we disclose secret faults or bad actions of our neighbor. There are persons who think that if they know anything bad about their neighbor, they may tell it to others, and make it a subject of conversation. This is a grave error. Our faith enjoins upon us nothing so much as love of our neighbor. Reason itself tells us that we should not do to others, what we do not wish done to ourselves. Let us look at this subject more closely: Would we like it if someone saw us commit a fault, and then went and made it known to everybody? Certainly not; on the contrary, were he charitable enough to hide it, we should feel very grateful to him. Consider how annoyed you feel when anyone says anything derogatory of you or your family. Justice and charity are opposed to this carrying of tales. As long as our neighbor's faults are concealed he preserves his good name; but as soon as you make them known his reputation is injured and you thereby cause him a greater injustice than if you robbed him of his belongings, for the Holy Ghost tells us that a good name is above riches.

We commit the sin of detraction when we put a disparaging interpretation on our neighbor's good actions. Such persons impute motives to you, which you never had; they slight all your doings and sayings: If you are pious and perform your religious duties faithfully, you are in their eyes, a hypocrite. They say sneeringly, that you are a saint in church, but a devil at home. If you do good works, they claim that you do them from pride, to show yourself. If you avoid association with evil doers, they call you an idiot. If you look carefully after your affairs they say you are miserly. Yes, dear brethren, we may say with truth, that the tongue of the detractor is like a worm which gnaws all good fruits: that is to say, the best actions of man, and seeks to make them look bad.

We may commit the sin of detraction even by significant silence; when some one is praised in your presence, you remain silent; but the expression of your face, your scornful, significant smile causes suspicions of the one who is being praised. Others clothe their evil work in the dress of pretended pity. "You know So-and-so," they will say. "Have you heard what happened to him? Ah, it is too bad that he was so careless! You would hardly have believed that he would do such things!" St. Francis says that such detraction is like a poisoned arrow that is dipped into oil, so that it may penetrate deeper. But the most atrocious detraction and the most lamentable in its consequences is that, when we carry back to others what has been said of them. Such informants produce the most frightful evils, arouse hatred, even bloodshed.

To understand how culpable such persons are, the Holy Ghost says: "God hates six things; but the seventh he abhors, and that is 'talebearing'."

Here we have briefly the various ways in which we can commit the sin of detraction. Examine your heart and see whether you have not been guilty in one of these ways.

We must not be anxious to believe all the bad that we hear about others; even if appearances are against the accused, we should not readily believe. Remember that St. Francis de Sales was once accused of having killed a man, so that he might live with his wife. The Saint left it all in God's hands, and had no fear for his good name. To those who advised him to defend himself he made answer, that he would leave the task of making reparation to the care of the one of whose permission his good name had been smirched. That calumny is one of the greatest afflictions for man is proved by the fact that God permitted the Saints, to whom He sent the greatest trials, to be calumniated. If detraction or calumny is our share, the best thing that we can do, is to keep silent, beseech God that we may bear it for love of Him, and pray for our calumniators. Console yourselves with the thought that God permits it to befall those whom He regards with a merciful eye. When anyone is calumniated God has decided to lead that one to a high state of perfection. We ought to commiserate those who slander us; but for ourselves personally we should rejoice; for these are trials which will count for us in heaven.

Let us return to our subject, because our chief object is to learn how the detractor injures himself. Detraction may easily become a mortal sin, and certainly is a mortal sin in important matters, where grave results are the consequence. St. Paul numbers it amongst those sins which close heaven against us. The Holy Ghost says that the detractor is cursed by God, that he is an abomination before God and men. Detraction is great or small according to circumstances, or to the dignity of the person spoken of. It is a greater sin to make known the defects and faults of our superiors, our parents, of husband or wife, brothers, sisters, or relations, than those of strangers, because we should have more charity for our friends than for others. To speak badly of persons consecrated to God, of the servants of the church, is a much greater sin on account of the lamentable results to religion and of the detriment to their position. The Holy Ghost speaking by the mouth of the prophet says: "To abuse and revile His (the Holy Ghost's) servants is to touch the apple of His eye"; that means, nothing can offend Him more. This sin consequently is a crime, the enormity of which surpasses all comprehension. Christ also said: "Whosoever despises you, despises me."

After all this, dear brethren, you will readily admit, that for a good confession it is not sufficient to say that you have slandered your neighbor; you must also say whether it happened from levity, hatred or revenge, or whether we sought to injure our neighbor's reputation. We must mention of what persons we spoke; whether it was about superiors, parents, or persons consecrated to God, and whether we spoke this to one or many persons: all this is required for a good confession.

Some people when asked whether their detraction injured their neighbor, answer no. You are in error, my friends! Every time that you reveal an unknown fault of your neighbor's, you injure him; for in every case you lessen the respect which those who are listening to you, had for him. Hence we may conclude that we can hardly ever say anything bad of our neighbor without in one way or another injuring his good name. But you will say, when it is already known, then there is no more harm. My friends, if the whole body of some unfortunate person was covered with leprosy, except a small part, and if you said: Because nearly the whole body is covered with leprosy this place ought to be covered too, would this be charitable and just? You must, on the contrary, have compassion upon the unfortunate person, conceal and excuse his faults as much as possible. Consider, whether it would be right, if, seeing a sick man on the brink of an abyss, we would take advantage of his feebleness and of his perilous position to push him down? Now we do the same thing when we dwelt upon the know defects of others. But you will say, may we not tell them to a friend under the seal of secrecy? There again you are in error, for why should you expect others to keep a secret when you cannot yourself do so? It is like saying to a person: "My friend, I want to tell you something, but be wiser and more reliable than I; do not break the secret which I am about to break." The best thing is to be silent in matters that do not concern us, no matter what is said or done do not meddle with anything, except to work for your own salvation. The Holy Ghost says: "Those who speak too much, do not always speak well."

I hope to God, that my words have made a lasting impression upon your minds and hearts, and that you have realized the great wrong of evil speaking. I may safely say that a majority of us have suffered one way or the other by detraction, slander or calumny, and the bitter woe and heartache caused by these sins are perhaps not unknown to you. Be careful then, not to do to others that which you do not wish done to you.

Sometimes, when desiring to pay a high tribute to the good qualities of a friend, we say: He never speaks ill of others. This proves that we are conscious of the wickedness of evil speaking. Let us then try and earn this high tribute for ourselves, and let us show to our neighbor the mercy which on our last day we shall expect of God. Amen.

TWELFTH SUNDAY AFTER PENTECOST

THE FIRST COMMANDMENT

"Thou shalt love the Lord thy God with thy whole heart, and with thy whole soul, and with thy whole strength."
Deut. vi, 5.

THE LORD gives us the commandment that we should love Him as He loves us, with our whole heart, undivided; with our whole soul and with our whole strength; and He promises us eternal reward if we keep the commandment faithfully, and threatens eternal punishment if we do not keep it. If we are beset by so many troubles in this world, it is because we neglect the commandments of God; for He Himself has said: If you keep my commandments faithfully, I will bless you in many ways; if, however, you transgress them, you will be cursed in everything that you do. If then, dear brethren, we wish to be happy in this world, as far as that is possible, we have no other means thereto but that of keeping faithfully the commandments of God, and we shall see, that as we turn aside from the path pointed out to us by the commandments of God, soul and body will be unhappy in this as well as in the next world. Our eternal blessedness depends upon our faithful observance of the commandments which the good God has given us, but God rewards already in this life those that are faithful to Him, and I will show you today.

The Happiness of those who obey the commandments of God and the Unhappiness of those who do not.

If, dear brethren, we open the Scriptures, we shall find there, that all those who made it their duty to observe rightly the commandments of God, were always happy, because God never abandons those who make it their duty to do that which He commands them to do. Already Adam is a good example of this. As long as he observed the commandments of the Lord faithfully, he was in a blissful state in every respect; his body, his soul, his mind and all his senses were directed to God alone; even the angels descended from heaven to bear him company. The bliss of our first parents would have remained the same forever, had they continued faithful to their duties; but this happy state did not last long. The evil spirit, envious at such bliss, plunged them into ruin, and robbed them of all their possessions, which they should have enjoyed for all eternity. As soon as they had the misfortune to transgress the Lord's commandments, everything went wrong with them; troubles and cares, sickness, fear of death and judgment and of punishment in another life took the place of their former bliss; their life now was nothing but a state of tears and sufferings.

The Lord said to Moses: "Tell my people that if they faithfully observe my commandments, I will fill them with all kinds of blessings; but if they dare to transgress them, I shall punish them with all kinds of sufferings." God said to Abraham: "Because thou hast faithfully kept my commandments, I will bless thee in everything. I will bless all those who bless thee; I shall curse all those who curse thee; out of thy race the Redeemer of the world shall be born." He made know to Abraham's people, when the time had arrived for them to enter into the promised land: "The people who dwelt in this land committed great sins; for this reason I shall drive them out, and put you in their place. But take care not to transgress my commandments. If you keep them faithfully, I shall bless you in and above everything. When you are in the fields or in your houses, I shall bless your children, who will then love you, respect and obey you, and give you all kinds of consolation. I will command the heavens to give you rain at the proper times, as much as will be necessary to water your fields and your meadows; everything will prosper with you." In another place in the Scriptures, God says: "If you keep my commandments faithfully I shall watch unceasingly over your preservation; you can be without fear in your houses; I will prevent the wild beasts from harming you; you will be able to sleep in peace; nothing shall disturb you. I will always be with you. I shall walk with you. I am your God, and you will be my people." Again He says to Moses: "Say unto my people, that if they keep my commandments, I will deliver them from all evils that oppress them." And the Holy Ghost says that "he who keeps the commandments of the Lord, is happier than if he possessed all the wealth of the earth."

Now, have you ever considered, that God lays such stress upon the keeping of His commandments, and that He promises such great benefits in return for their faithful observance? You will then agree with me, that our whole happiness consists in keeping faithfully the commandments. To prove to you, dear brethren, that as soon as we transgress the commandments, we can only be unhappy, let David serve us as an example. As long as he trod the path which the commandments prescribed to him, everything prospered with him: he was beloved, esteemed and obeyed by his neighbors. But the very moment that he no longer observed the commandments, his happiness came to an end, and all kinds of trouble beset him. Anxiety and remorse of conscience took the place of that peace and contentedness which he had hitherto enjoyed. Tears and sufferings were his daily bread. As he was one day bemoaning his sins, he was informed that his son Amon had been pierced with a sword by his brother Absalom in a fit of drunkenness. Absalom tried to depose his father, even to kill him, that he might reign in his stead; David was obliged to hide in the woods to escape death. Moreover, the plague slew a large number of David's subjects.

Solomon affords us another example: As long as he kept faithfully the commandments, he had the admiration of the world; his renown reached to the furthermost parts of the earth; the queen of Saba even came from afar to witness the wonders which the Lord had worked in him; but as soon as he had the misfortune no longer to observe the commandments, everything went wrong with him. Upon hearing these examples, even from the Old Testament only, you will agree with me, dear brethren, that all our troubles arise from the fact that we do not observe the commandments of God faithfully, and that if we expect happiness and peace, as far as we may expect to possess such in this world, in this vale of suffering and sorrow, then, I say, the only means of securing these benefits is, to do everything in our power to please God—everything, therefore, that He bids us to do in His commandments.

But if we pass to the New Testament, we find that Christ Our Lord exhorts us constantly to observe the commandments, and promises great reward. Jesus Christ promises us heaven, because nothing of this earth is capable of gratifying the heart of man, who is created for God only, who cannot find happiness but in God. Jesus Christ exhorts us urgently to care little for the things of this world, and to look for the blessings of heaven, which can never come to an end. We read in the Gospel, that Jesus Christ, being on one occasion amongst certain people who appeared to think only of their corporal necessities, said to them: "Be not so solicitous as to what you shall eat, and wherewith you shall be clothed. And, desiring to make them understand that everything concerning the body was of little consequence, He said to them: "Consider the lilies of the field, they toil not, neither do they spin; and behold your heavenly Father clotheth them; for I say unto you that not even Solomon in all his glory was arrayed as one of these. Observe the birds of the air, they neither sow nor reap, nor do they gather into barns, yet behold how your heavenly Father cares for them. O, ye of little faith, are you not of more account than they? Seek first the kingdom of heaven; that is to say, keep My commandments faithfully, and all things else shall be added unto you over and above."

Now what are we to infer from these words, dear brethren? Only this, that a Christian who seeks in the first place to please God and to save his soul, will never want for his corporal necessities.

But, you will say, perhaps, if we have nothing, no one will give us anything! I will answer that everything we have comes from the beneficence of God and not from ourselves. If you wish, dear brethren, to experience the magnitude of the goodness of God, then make it your duty to observe exactly what the commandments order you, and you will see with amazement how God cares for those who strive to please Him. If you wish to see a proof of this, turn to the pages of Holy Scripture, and there you will find full confirmation of this. We read for instance in Holy Writ that the prophet Elias hid himself in the woods in order to escape the persecutions of Queen Jezabel. There, deprived of all human aid, do you think that the Lord allowed him to die of hunger? No, dear friends, certainly not. The Lord did not lose sight of His faithful servant. He sent at once an angel from heaven, to console him, and to bring him everything that was necessary for his maintenance. Behold too, how the Lord cared for the widow of Sarepta. He said to His prophets: "Seek this good widow who serves me so faithfully and keeps My commandments; increase her store of meal, that she may not suffer hunger." Another instance is His command to one of the prophets, Habacuc, to take food to Daniel in the lions' den at Babylon. All these examples are taken from the Old Testament, but in the New Testament the miracles which God works in favor of those who observe His commandments are not less great or numerous. Behold how God, with five small loaves and two fishes fed the thousands of people, who, following Jesus Christ, sought the kingdom of Heaven, and the sanctification of their souls. See, how for forty years He provided for the sustenance of the holy hermit Paul by means of a raven; an unmistakable proof that God never loses sight of those who love Him, and that He supplies them with everything that is necessary. O my God, how great is Thy love for those who love Thee! What care dost Thou take that they may not want! Tell me, dear brethren, who let every day provisions be carried by a dog to St. Roch in the desert? Was it not God, dear brethren? And why did God take so much care for the maintenance of all the Saints, unless it was because they faithfully observed the commandments which He had given?

Yes, dear brethren, we may safely say that the Saints found all their happiness in keeping the commandments, and that they would sooner have endured martyrdom than to transgress them: and did not the martyrs suffer tortures and death, just because they would not transgress the commandments of God?

What shame for us then, dear brethren, when at the judgment day we will face these martyrs; we who so often are prompted in our actions by even the mere thought of "What will the world say?"

Yes, dear brethren, if we wish to gain true happiness, God's own words and history, both of the old and new law, teach that the exact observance of the commandments is required. And since God in His mercy assists us with His Grace in observing them, why should we start back and be so fearful?

Let our firm resolution this morning be, to obey faithfully the commandments of God, and not to let any consideration of earthly gain or loss, of fear or favor, induce us to transgress them, so that at the end of our days we may have the great good fortune of looking back upon a God-fearing and faithful life, which will open for us the gates of an eternal reward, which I wish you all. Amen.

THIRTEENTH SUNDAY AFTER PENTECOST

ABSOLUTION

"Whose sins you shall forgive, they are forgiven them; and whose sins you shall retain, they are retained."
John xx. 23

DEAR BRETHREN, our divine Redeemer, dearly paid with His own life the price to make these words efficacious: "Whose sins you shall forgive, they are forgiven them: and whose sins you shall retain, they are retained." What tortures, what suffering, and what an agonizing death! We are so superficial, so careless, so worldly, that many of us think it depends upon the priest to give or to withhold absolution, as he thinks best. No, dear friends, in this you are very much mistaken. The minister of God is but the dispenser of the graces and merits of Jesus Christ; he can only dispense them according to prescribed laws. An awful responsibility it is for a priest to exercise this sublime office, in which he runs the risk of being himself condemned while saving others. An exact account will be demanded from the priest on the day of judgment, when all the absolutions that he has pronounced will be examined by God Himself, as to whether he has been too lavish with the graces of heaven or too strict. How difficult it is sometimes, to be correct in judgment, to be always accurate! How many priests at the last day will wish that they had never taken Holy Orders, but had remained laymen!

The priest has the power to remit sins, and he also has the power of retaining them, and St. Gregory the Great says, that a priest should thoroughly investigate the disposition of a penitent before he gives him absolution. He should see whether his heart is changed, and if all those resolutions have been made which a converted sinner owes to God.

It is therefore clear that the dispenser of grace must postpone or withhold absolution from certain sinners, if he does not want to be lost together with this sinner. I will try and show you therefore:

I. *What absolution is; and to whom it should be given or withheld.*
II. *One of the principal reasons why it must be withheld.*

Listen well, because this is a very important subject, it is a question of your salvation or damnation.

I.

How fortunate is man, dear brethren, and yet how culpable! I say fortunate, for, having lost his God, heaven, and his soul, he has at his disposal such an easy means to recover what he lost. A wealthy man, who loses his fortune, is often unable to recover it; the Christian, however, having lost his eternal fortune, can regain it with but little sincere effort. O my God, how great is Thy love for the sinner, for Thou dost offer him this means of regaining heaven! But I said also culpable, for we could obtain so many benefits and yet we despise them! You have forfeited heaven, my friend, and yet you live on in this wretchedness? You, sinful man, can escape perdition and regain salvation! And yet, you hesitate!

In order to explain to you what absolution is, I will say it is a verdict which the priest, authorized by Jesus Christ, pronounces in His name, whereby our sins are remitted, are wiped out as completely as if we had never committed them, provided the penitent receives absolution with the proper dispositions demanded by this Sacrament. Who can help but admire this merciful verdict? O happy moment for the contrite sinner! Our poor soul, delivered from the tyranny of the evil spirit, restored to the friendship and grace of God, recovers peace, that precious peace which constitutes man's whole happiness in this world and the next His innocence is restored to him with all its claims upon the kingdom of God, of which sin had deprived him. But, remember, this grace is only given to those who deserve it; that is to say, to those who, although sinners, are converted sinners; those who are sorrowfully repentant for their past lives, not only because they had lost heaven, but because they had offended grievously Him who deserved to be loved infinitely.

There are sometimes reasons which may induce the priest to postpone absolution. The church herself has given laws, which the priest is unable to set aside. The priest's duty is to apply these laws in the right way, and it is your duty, not to murmur or complain if he finds it necessary to refuse or postpone absolution. If a priest refuses it to you, it is because he has your real interest at heart, and an ardent desire to save your soul, and you will comprehend this rightly at the day of judgment: You will then perceive that it was his most fervent wish to lead you to heaven, which induced him to postpone the absolution. Had he given it to you as you wished, he would have been damned. You ought therefore, dear brethren, never to murmur when a priest does not give you absolution; on the contrary, you ought to thank God, and do everything in your power to deserve this grace.

II.

Among the reasons which oblige the priest sometimes to refuse or postpone absolution are, for instance, insufficient preparation, absence of true contrition, refusal to make restitution, etc. But there is another reason which I will make the chief object of our meditation today, and that is a neglect of the Christian to inform himself of the essential truths of his Holy Religion.

St. Charles Borromeo tells us explicitly that "absolution cannot be given to persons who do not know the principal facts of the Christtian Religion, and the duties of their state of life; particularly when their ignorance arises from their indifference concerning their salvation." The laws of the Church in this connection also forbid absolution to be given to fathers or mothers who do not teach their children, or have them taught, in everything that is necessary for their salvation.

What, then, are the essentials of our holy Religion? Listen and I will tell you what every Catholic must necessarily know.

A Christian should know the Our Father, the Hail Mary, the Creed, the *Confiteor*, the three acts of Faith, Hope and Charity, the commandments of God and the Church and an act of contrition. By this, I do not mean that you must know the words only, but you must be able to give an explanation of each article in particular and say what they mean. This is what is expected of you and not simply to know the words. You must know that the Our Father was composed by God Himself; that the Hail Mary was composed partly by the angel who came to announce the Mystery of the Incarnation to the Blessed Virgin, and partly by the Church; you must know that the creed was composed by the apostles after the descent of the Holy Ghost, before they went out into the world; so that since the first beginning, the same Religion and the same Mysteries are taught in all parts of the world. The creed contains the sum and substance of our entire Holy Religion, the mystery of the Most Holy Trinity, which is one God in three Persons, namely, God the Father, who created us, God the Son who redeemed us by His death and passion, and God the Holy

Ghost, who sanctified us in Baptism. When you say: I believe in God the Father Almighty, Creator, etc., you must mean, I believe, that the eternal Father created everything, our bodies and our souls, that the world was not always in existence, that it will not always be, that it will one day be destroyed. I believe in Jesus Christ, means: I believe that Jesus Christ, the second Person of the

Blessed Trinity, became man, that He suffered and died to redeem us, to merit heaven for us, of which we were deprived by the sin of Adam. I believe in the Holy Ghost, the Holy Catholic Church, means: I believe that there is one Church, which is the one that Jesus Christ Himself founded, that in her He has deposited all His graces, and that this Church will endure until the end of the world. When you say: I believe in the Communion of Saints, you must mean: I believe that all Christians take part in one another's prayers and good works, I believe that the Saints, who are in heaven, pray to God for us, and that we can pray for those who are in purgatory. When you say: I believe in the forgiveness, you mean, I believe that in the Church of Jesus Christ there are Sacraments which remit all sin, and that there are no sins which the Church of Jesus Christ cannot remit. If we say: The resurrection of the body, that means that the very same bodies which we now have, will one day rise again, that our souls will return to them to accompany them to heaven, or to hell, as we shall have deserved. When we say, I believe in the life everlasting, that means: I believe that the next life will have no end, that our souls will last as long as God Himself, who is without end. When you say, from whence He shall come to judge both the living and the dead, means, I believe, that Jesus Christ is in heaven, body and soul, and that He Himself will come to judge us, and to reward those who have been good, and to punish those who have been bad.

We must know, furthermore, that the Commandments of God were given to Adam at his creation; that is to say, that God wrote them in his heart, and that afterwards, God gave them to Moses written upon tablets of stone, upon Mount Sinai. They are the same which our Lord renewed when He came down upon earth to save us. I say that you must know the acts of Faith, Hope and Charity. I repeat, not the words only, but the meaning of them. Faith enables us to believe all that the Church teaches. Although we may not be able to comprehend some of the mysteries, it teaches us to believe that God sees us, and that He watches over us; that He will either reward or punish us according to our acts of good or evil; that there is a heaven for the good, and a hell for the wicked; that our Lord

THIRTEENTH SUNDAY AFTER PENTECOST

suffered and died for us. Hope teaches us to do all our actions with the intention of pleasing God, and that they will be rewarded through all eternity. In this world the Love of God consists in our loving God above all created things, and preferring Him above all things, even our own life.

This, my dear brethren, is what is meant when we say that you must know the Our Father, the Hail Mary, the Creed, the Confiteor, the one only God, and your three acts. If you do not know this, then you know nothing that is necessary for you to be saved; you should be able when you are asked about these things to explain them: But this is not all: you should also know what the mystery of the Incarnation is, and what the word Incarnation means. You must know that this Mystery means, that the second Person of the Blessed Trinity took upon Himself a body like ours, in the womb of the Blessed Virgin Mary, by the operation of the Holy Ghost. We celebrate this mystery upon the 25th of March, the feast of the Annunciation; for on this day the Son of God united His divinity with our humanity; He took a body like ours, but without sin, and He took all our sins upon Himself, to satisfy His Father's justice. You must know that Jesus Christ died, that He died as man, and not as God, because as God He could not die;—that He rose again upon Easter day, when He united His soul again to His body, and that after remaining upon earth for forty days, He ascended into Heaven upon Ascension day. That the Holy Ghost descended upon the Apostles on the day of Pentecost. You should be able to tell the Sacraments. If you are asked by whom they were instituted you must answer that they could only be instituted by Jesus Christ, not by the Blessed Virgin or the Apostles. You should know what are the effects of each Sacrament, and what is the disposition which we must have to receive them properly; you should know that Baptism wipes out original sin, which was the sin of Adam, and Which we all have when we come into the world; that the Sacrament of Confirmation is conferred upon us by the Bishop, and that by it we receive the Holy Ghost with the abundance of His graces; that we partake of the Sacrament of Penance when we confess our sins to the priest, and that if we confess them properly, all our sins are effaced by the absolution of the priest. In the Holy Eucharist we believe that there is really and truly present the adorable body and the most precious blood of Jesus Christ. The Sacrament of Extreme Unction helps us to die well, and it was instituted to cleanse us from the sins which we have committed by all the different senses. Holy Orders confer upon man the power which Jesus Christ gave to His Apostles. The Sacrament of Matrimony sanctifies the union of husband

and wife if they are united according to the laws of the Church.

Now, my dear brethren, if I had asked you about these things, would you have been able to answer all these questions rightly? Yet, they must be known to every Christian, at least in general. Now, if a priest postpone absolution, because you do not know the principal truths of Holy Religion, is he to be blamed or you? From this you may conclude how necessary it is to be instructed in Holy Religion, what care you should take to learn so as to be enabled to participate in its benefits.

And one of these great benefits, indeed, one of the greatest, is the Absolution, given by the priest to the penitent, by the power of Our Lord Himself. I will not conclude my words without an earnest warning to parents not to neglect the instruction of their children in our Holy Religion, so that on judgment day the parents may not be called to task, if the children have been refused absolution because they did not know their Religion. Amen.

FOURTEENTH SUNDAY AFTER PENTECOST

THE LOVE OF GOD

"Thou shalt love the Lord thy God."
Luke x. 27.

WE READ in the Gospel, my dear brethren, that a young man approached Jesus Christ, and said to Him: "Master, what must I do to possess eternal life?" Jesus Christ answered him: "What is written in the law?" "Thou shalt love the Lord thy God," the young man answered, "with thy whole heart, and with thy whole soul, and with all thy strength, and with all thy mind, and thy neighbor as thyself. I do all these things." "Well, then," Jesus Christ answered him, "sell all that thou hast, and give it to the poor, and thou shalt have a treasure in heaven." Jesus Christ wished to demonstrate that it is by deeds and not by words that we show whether we really love God. "If," says St. Gregory, "to love Him it sufficed to say that we loved Him, this love would not be so uncommon; for there is certainly no one who, if they were asked whether they loved God, would not immediately answer that they loved Him with their whole heart. The just would say so, and so would the sinner. The just, however, would say so, trembling, like St. Peter, while the sinner probably would say so in a confident manner to make the impression of sincerity; only he deceives himself, for the love of God does not count in words but in deeds."

Yes, my dear friends, to love God is something so fair, so reasonable, and so natural that those among us whose mode of life is inconsistent with it, still imagine and are convinced that they love Him. And this, dear brethren, is because we all seek happiness, and the love of God alone can procure it for us. And this is the reason why even the sinner endeavors to convince himself that he loves God. At the same time nothing is really so rare as the true love of God. Let us see in what this love consists, and how we may know whether we love God. To understand this better, let us consider:

I.—What God has done for love of us, and
II.—What we ought to do for love of Him.

I.

It is a fact, dear brethren, that God has created us for the sole purpose to love Him and to serve Him. Why, dear brethren, did God plant into our hearts a craving for something so great and so magnificent that nothing created can satisfy it? So that we might thereby be induced to cling firmly to Him, and to love Him, because He alone can satisfy us. If man possessed the whole world, he would still not be contented; there would always be something wanting for our complete happiness, and yet we are so convinced that we are created to be happy, that we never in our life cease to seek happiness, and to do everything that we possibly can to attain it. What is the reason, then, that regardless of all our endeavors, our pains, and our labors, we can never feel contented? It is because we do not direct our attention and our mind toward that object which alone is capable of fulfilling our desires, toward God. Believe me, dear friends, seek the friendship of God, and then you will have found happiness. And in order that you may feel urgently impelled to love so good a God, who is so worthy of being loved, and so able to satisfy perfectly all the desires of our hearts, let us briefly consider what our God has done for us, let us follow the course of His life until His death.

Consider Him, dear brethren, from the moment of His Incarnation until His thirtieth year. Are there not the greatest proofs of His love for us? At His Incarnation He became man like us and for us. By His birth He has exalted us to the highest dignity to which a mere creature can be raised. He made us His brothers! O what love of us! Have we ever rightly understood it? At His presentation in the Temple He offered Himself up to His Father to redeem us all. Later, in the home of St. Joseph, He became a model of the love and respect which we should have for our parents and superiors. In His active life, everything that He did was done for us: His prayers, His tears, His nightly vigils, His fasts, His sermons, His journeys, His conversations, His miracles—He did all these things for our salvation. Observe, dear brethren, with what zeal He sought us in the person of the Samaritan woman; behold, with what fervent love He receives sinners in the person of the prodigal son; see with what meekness He condones the justice of His Father who would punish us in the person of the adulteress. In His life of suffering, what abuses, what torments did He endure? He is

FOURTEENTH SUNDAY AFTER PENTECOST 267

bound, and struck in the face with clenched fists, accused, condemned, and finally crucified for us. And did He not die for us, under the most cruel and most indescribable sufferings?

Ah, my dear brethren, who can understand what He has done for us? Jesus Christ could have made satisfaction for our sins to the justice of the Father by one drop of His blood, by one tear, but that which could satisfy justice could not satisfy the fervent love of His heart for us. It is His love of us again which caused Him to anticipate the sufferings which He was to undergo upon the cross. O abyss of tenderness, of a God-love for His creatures!

Let us go still further, dear friends. This divine Redeemer wishes to shed the last drop of His precious blood for us, to cleanse us from all our misdeeds. After atoning for our pride by His crowning with thorns, for our countless sins of the tongue by the gall and vinegar, the sins of impurity by the cruel and painful scourging, all our wicked actions by the wounds of His hands and His feet, He wished to expiate all our evil desires by the wound of His divine Heart, because it is in the heart that all our sins have their source. O miracle of the love of a God for His creatures!

But His love goes still further. When He saw that He would soon be separated from us by death, He worked a great miracle so as to remain always with us: He instituted the great Sacrament of love, wherein He left us His most adorable flesh and His most precious blood, so as never more to forsake us until the end of the world. What love for us, my dear brethren! A God wishes to feed our soul with His own Being! In this great and adorable Sacrament He offers Himself daily to the justice of God, makes satisfaction again for our sins, and obtains all kinds of graces for us.

No, dear brethren, you have never reflected upon it, how much God loves us. Would it be possible for us to sin and offend Him when we can only be happy by loving Him? If I were to ask you if you loved God, you would say without doubt, yes, we love Him; but that is not sufficient, you must give proof of this. But where, dear brethren, are the proofs which reveal the sincerity of our love of God? What sacrifices do we make for Him? Where are our works of penance? The little good which we do is done often without a right intention. Other considerations than the love of God often prompt us to do good works, and the good deeds done purely for the love of God are, alas, but few.

II.

If, my dear brethren, you wish to know now, how we can tell whether we really love God, listen to what I am going to say to you, and then judge for yourselves whether you have that true love. Observe that Jesus Christ Himself has said to us: "Whosoever loves me, keeps my commandments, but he who does not love me, does not keep them." It is, therefore, very easy for you to know whether or not you love God. The commandments, my friends, and the will of God, are one and the same thing. He commands and He wills that you should fulfil the duties of your state of life, conscientiously and sincerely. He commands us to believe in Him, and to be faithful to Him. The Saints, and particularly the Martyrs, proved their love of God by suffering persecution and death rather than be unfaithful to God.

God's will is that we be subject and respectful to our parents, our superiors, and all those whom God has placed over us to guide us. It is the will of God that superiors should treat those under them without overbearing or harshness, with love and kindness, as they should wish to be treated themselves. It is the will of God that we should be kind and charitable toward every one, and that we should feel contempt for the praise or the censure of men.

St. Ambrose tells us: "If any one despises us, we ought not be troubled, but think, on the contrary, that if they really knew us as we are, they would say much worse about us." Or as St. John says: "When any one reviles us, it is the will of God that we should be ready to forgive them, and to embrace every opportunity of doing them a service." His will says, that we should never give way to gluttony; that in our conversations we should conceal and excuse our neighbor's faults. It is the will of God that in all our sufferings we should not murmur, but bear them patiently and with resignation to His will. God wills that we acknowledge that all things come from Him, and that they will serve for our good if we only make the right use of them.

This, dear brethren, is what the commandments demand of us. If you love God, as you say you do, you will do all these things. You will conduct yourself in this way. If not, then no matter how often you may repeat that you love Him, St. John tells you that you are liars, and that the truth is not in you. Let us examine, my friends, our conduct and our way of living, and then let us consider closely our actions.

Night and morning, you fold your hands and say in your prayers: "My God, I love Thee with my whole heart, and above all things." And when so praying you believe that you are speaking the truth; and yet a few hours later your hands may be busy injuring your neighbor, or used to

FOURTEENTH SUNDAY AFTER PENTECOST 269

indulge in drunkenness and gluttony, and your mouth, which has expressed your love of God will, perhaps, be soiled with oaths, tale-bearing, calumnies, and all sorts of slander, thus dishonoring and abusing that same God to whom you have just said that you love Him with your whole heart. Do your actions prove your words? Suppose, for example, you would go to a good friend of yours, take him by the hand, and assure him of your great love and faithfulness, and then go about, abuse his good name, work against his best interests, and do everything possible to offend him. What would you think of such action? Wouldn't it be just the most shameful way to act? And yet, do you not treat in such manner your best friend, your creator, your God?

Alas, our miserable body induces us unceasingly to do evil, while our conscience and the inspirations of grace encourage us to do good. Dear brethren, to love God means to struggle; it means to resist courageously all temptations. In this way we shall give proofs of the love which we have for God; it will enable us to rather sacrifice all than sin against so good a God.

St. Justin tells us that love has generally three effects: Those whom we love we delight in thinking of, in giving them anything, and in suffering for them gladly. This is what we should do for God, my dear brethren, if we really love Him. I say (I) that we should often think of God. Nothing is more natural than to think of those whom we love. Look at a miser. Is he not completely taken up with his possessions, and the means to increase them? Whether he be alone or with other people, nothing is capable of diverting him from these thoughts. Look at the worldling. The object of his love will occupy his mind till he ceases to breathe. O if we would really love Jesus Christ only even as much as the miser does his money and treasures, as the drunkard his drink, as the sensual man the object of his passion, should we not be continually occupied with the love and the glory of Jesus Christ? Alas, my dear friends, we busy ourselves with a thousand worthless things, but we spend hours and days without thinking of God. And yet, have we, dear brethren, among our friends, one more generous, or more beneficent?

I say, (II) if we really love God, we shall give Him everything which we possibly can give Him with the greatest pleasure. If we have wealth, let us share it with the poor, and it will be the same as if it were given to Jesus Christ Himself. "Whatsoever you do to the least of these my brethren, you give it unto me." What an honor, my friends, for a creature to be able to be generous toward his Creator, his God, and his Redeemer!

It is not only the rich who can give, but all Christians, even the poorest. We are not all wealthy so as to be able to give to Jesus Christ in the persons of His poor, but we all have a heart, and it is just this gift which He prizes so highly. He urgently desires it. I ask you, dear brethren, can we refuse Him that, which He so earnestly desires, He, who has only created us for Himself? Ah, if we considered this rightly, should we not say to the divine Redeemer: "Lord, I am only a sinner, have mercy upon me. Behold, I am Thine only"? How happy should we be if we could make this sacrifice for God! How great would be our reward!

The best proof of love, however, which we can give to God, is when we suffer for His sake, for if we would consider properly what He has suffered for us, we could not help but bear patiently all the wants of life, the persecutions, the sicknesses, the weaknesses.

We must conclude from all this, my friends, that our whole and our only happiness upon earth depends upon our fidelity to God. In all our actions, God alone must be our aim, for we all know from our own experience, that nothing in this world can make us happy; the whole world, with all its possessions and its pleasure, can not satisfy our hearts. Never lose sight of the fact, dear brethren, that everything created will forsake us. There will come a time when everything earthly that we possess will pass into other hands. But if we have the great happiness of possessing the love of God we shall reign in heaven in a bliss that will last for all eternity. Love God, and prove your love by serving Him faithfully, and ardently strive to possess Him, and the love of God will be your salvation at the hour of death. Amen.

FIFTEENTH SUNDAY AFTER PENTECOST

THE NATIVITY OF THE BLESSED VIRGIN

"Of whom was born Jesus."
Matt. i. 16.

HERE, my dear brethren, expressed in a few words, is the most complete praise which could be given to Mary, by saying that of her was born Jesus, the Son of God. Yes, Mary is the most beautiful creature that ever came forth from the hands of the Creator. God Himself elected her to be the star from which His most precious and richest blessings should shine upon all those who place their confidence in her. God presents her to us as a beautiful mirror, in which He is reflected, a perfect model of all virtues. Consequently the Church looks upon her as her Mother, her protectress, and her powerful helper against her enemies, and she celebrates today the happy day on which this lovely star first illumined the earth. Let us, my dear friends, abandon ourselves to a holy joy with the whole Church, and contemplate why we admire in this holy Virgin:

 I.—The model of perfect virtue, and
 II.—The mediator between God and mankind.
 III.—The Blessed Virgin, dispenser of graces.

Give me your earnest attention, for to speak of Mary must touch your hearts, because we are talking of the object of your confidence and love.

I.

My beloved brethren, if it were necessary, so as to inspire you with a loving devotion to Mary, to show you how great is the happiness of those who confide in her, how powerful is her aid, and how numerous the graces and the favors which she can obtain for us—if it were necessary, I say, to prove to you the blindness, and the misery of those who are indifferent, and disregard so good, so tender, so powerful a Mother, I need only refer to the Prophets and the Patriarchs, and all the great things, which the Holy Ghost inspired them to say of her, should be a source of reproach for the little esteem in which we often hold this good Mother. Furthermore, if I were to relate to you how her example was followed by the Saints, we should be moved to lament our blindness, and to revive our confidence in her. In the first place nothing is more capable of inspiring in us a tender devotion to the Blessed Virgin as the first passage which we read of her in Holy Scripture, where we behold God Himself the first One to announce Mary's coming.

When our first parents had the great misfortune of falling into sin, God, moved by their condition, promised that a day would come when a Virgin should be born, and she would bear a Son, by whom the misery caused by their sin would be redressed. In consequence of this, the Prophets have never ceased, time and again, to proclaim for the consolation of the human race, sighing under the tyranny of the evil spirit, that a Virgin would bear a Son, who would be the Son of the Most High, and be sent by His Father to redeem the world, lost by Adam's sin. All the Prophets foretold that she would be the most beautiful creature that had ever appeared upon earth. They called her the Morning Star, which would eclipse all others by its radiancy and beauty, and would guide the traveler upon the sea— a perfect model of every virtue. With justice, therefore, the Church in holy joy, says to the Blessed Virgin: "Thy birth, O Blessed Virgin Mary fills the whole world with a sweet consolation and a holy joy, because of thee was born this sun of justice, our Jesus, our God, who has taken away from us the curse in which we were plunged by the sin of our first parents, and filled us with all kinds of blessings." In fact, although the Blessed Virgin wandered in the common path of life, yet the Holy Ghost willed that her soul should be the most beautiful, and the richest in grace. He willed, also, that her body should be the most beautiful body which had ever appeared upon earth. Scripture compares her to the dawn of morning, to the moon at its full, to the sun at midday. From the time of Adam's fall, the world was covered with a terrible darkness. Mary appeared, and, as a beautiful sun, dispersed the darkness, and revived hope. Must not God, dear brethren, have said to Mary, as He did to Moses: "Deliver my people who are groaning under the tyranny of Pharao; announce to them that their deliverance is at hand, and that I have heard their prayers, their sighs, and their tears."

O what treasures Mary's birth brings for heaven and earth! The evil spirit trembles with fury and despair, because he beholds in Mary she who is to crush his head. Whereas the angels and the blessed make the vault of heaven ring with songs of joy at the birth of a queen who will add new glory to their splendor.

But because God wished to show us that heaven can only be gained by humility, self-denial, poverty, and suffering, He decreed that the birth of Mary should be accompanied by ordinary circumstances. She was born in a state of weakness, her cradle was moistened with tears like that of other children who, when they are born, seem to foresee the misery to which they will be subjected through life. As the Holy Ghost tells us through the mouth of the prophets: "The day of death is preferable to that of birth." Mary was born in a state of obscurity. Although she was of the race of David, and numbered among her ancestors Patriarchs, Prophets, and Kings—all these honorable ancestors, so much sought after by the people of the world, had passed into oblivion, she had nothing more splendid than virtue, which, in the eyes of men, does not call for much esteem.

God had permitted this, so that this birth might be in accordance with that of His divine Son, of whom the Prophets declared that He would have no place of rest to lay His head. If, however, she came into this world so poor of earthly riches, still she is rich in the gifts of Him whose Mother she was predestined to be from all eternity. Do we, said one of her great servants, a saintly Bishop of Geneva, wish to know who this crowned Virgin in the cradle is? Let us ask the angels. They will tell us that Mary infinitely surpasses them in grace, merits, and dignity, and in all other perfections. St. Basil tells us that the eternal Father, from the creation of the world until Mary's arrival, had not found a creature who was pure and holy enough to be the Mother of His Son. How often have not the Patriarchs and the Prophets cried out, amid sighs and tears: "When will the happy moment arrive, when the Blessed Virgin shall appear in the world? Blessed the eyes that shall behold this creature who is to be the Mother of the Redeemer of the world!"

II.

It would be impossible, my dear brethren, not to love Mary, if we reflected for a moment upon her affection for us, and the benefits which she never ceases to lavish upon us. "Alas," exclaims St. Bernard, that great servant of Mary, "how blind and miserable are we that we do not love so kind and good a Mother! The world, without Mary's prayers, would long ago have ceased to be, and on account of our sins, have fallen back into chaos." The same Saint tells us that all the graces which we obtain from heaven, pass through Mary's hands. Another Father of the Church tells us: "Mary is like a good parent who is not content with caring for her children in general, but watches over each one of them in particular." If God had treated us as we deserved after many of our sins, we should long ago have been burning in hell. O how many are in those flames who would not be there if they had had recourse to Mary! She would have implored her Son to prolong their lives, to give them time to do penance.

If this misfortune has not happened to us, dear brethren, we may thank Mary for it; it is she to whom we really owe it. She throws herself at the feet of her divine Son, and says to Him: "My Son, a little more time for this sinner; perhaps he will amend, perhaps he will act differently than he formerly did." What does she do to avert the wrath of the Father? She points out to Him all that His Son did and suffered, to repair the honor of which He has been deprived by sin. She hastens to remind her Son of everything that she suffered during her life for His sake. "My Son," she says to Him every moment, "just a few days longer, perhaps he will amend." O how great is the affection of a mother! And yet there are some who despise her; others not only despise her, they despise by their mockeries all those who have confidence in her! Now, dear brethren, although they have only shown contempt for her, she has, nevertheless, not forsaken them, for were this the case, these mockers would already be in hell.

When we love some one, we are happy to possess his or her picture. It is the same if we love the Blessed Virgin, my dear friends. We consider it an honor and a duty to have her picture in our house, to remind us frequently of this good Mother. Furthermore, those parents who are truly Christians should never omit to inspire their children with a tender devotion to the Blessed Virgin. This is the best means to call down the blessings of heaven, and the protection of Mary upon your families.

III.

The Blessed Virgin is not only a dispenser of graces, but also a rampart against the assaults of the evil spirit! Once, when St. Dominic, her great servant, was about to drive the evil spirit out of one possessed, the evil spirit declared, with loud voice, that the Blessed Virgin was his bitterest enemy, for she brought all his intentions to naught; that without her the world would be without religion, as he would have been able to destroy the Church by schism and heresy. Thus you see, dear brethren, what valuable help Mary is to all who call upon her in their battle with the archfiend.

It is safe to say that all Christians have a great devotion to Mary, with the exception of those hardened sinners who have long lost their faith, and who wallow in the mire of their passions. The evil spirit strives to hold them in blindness until the moment of death opens their eyes. Ah, if they had taken refuge in Mary, they would not have fallen into hell as they did!

But, again, my dear friends, it is not enough to honor Mary only with our lips in order to deserve her protection. We must also endeavor to acquire those virtues of which she was such a shining example. We must strive to acquire her great humility. Although she well knew that God had exalted her to the highest of all dignities, to be the Mother of God, Queen of heaven and earth, she despised no one. She looked upon herself as the least of creatures.

We must also aspire to her extraordinary purity, which made her so pleasing to God. Her modesty was so great that God regarded her with delight. We must, my dear friends, detach ourselves from the things of this world, and think only of heaven, our true country. After the ascension of her divine Son, she only languished upon earth. She endured life, indeed, with patience, but she ardently awaited death, which would reunite her with her divine Son, the sole object of her love.

How often did she not cry out with the Prophet: "My God, how much longer wilt thou permit my banishment to last? O when will that happy moment come when I shall be united to Thee forevermore? O if you see my beloved, tell Him that I languish with love!" God took her out of this world where she had suffered so much during her long pilgrimage. She died, but it was neither old age nor the feebleness of nature that caused her death, but it was her love for her divine Son. Her first breath had been an aspiration of love; it was proper that her last should be a sigh of love.

She knew no fear, because she had never offended God by sin; she had no sorrow, because she was never attached to the things of the world; she sighed only for Jesus, and death procured this happiness for her. She beheld Him coming to meet her, with the whole court of heaven, to honor her triumphant entry into heaven. Thus did this holy Virgin fall asleep in the embrace of the Lord; thus did this beautiful star vanish, which had illumined the world for seventy-two years. Thus triumphed over death she who gave birth to the author of all life!

What should we conclude from all this, dear brethren? This, that like Mary we are striving for the same happiness, and that it should be our sole purpose so to strive that we may merit it. This is what wish you all! Amen.

SIXTEENTH SUNDAY AFTER PENTECOST

HUMILITY

"Every one that exalteth himself shall be humbled; and he that humbleth himself shall be exalted."
Luke xviii. 14.

COULD OUR REDEEMER, my dear brethren, have pointed out to us more clearly or distinctly than in these words the necessity of humbling ourselves, of holding ourselves in disesteem in our thoughts as well as in our words and actions, so that we might be exalted to sing the praises of God for all eternity? When Jesus once was in the company of Pharisees, and beheld that many of them boasted of their good deeds, and how they despised others, He gave them this parable: "Two men," He said to them, "went up into the Temple to pray. The one was a Pharisee, the other a Publican. The Pharisee stood proudly erect, and prayed by himself thus: O God, I thank thee that I am not as the rest of men, extortioners, unjust, adulterers, or even as this Publican. I fast twice in the week, and give a tithe of all I possess." This is his prayer, St. Augustine tells us. You can very well perceive that this prayer is only an affectation of vanity and pride. He does not come to ask God to grant him grace, but to extol himself, and to treat with contempt those who really do pray. The Publican, on the other hand, stood afar off from the altar, and did not even venture to raise his eyes up to heaven. He struck his breast, and said: "My God, have mercy upon me a sinner." "I say to you," Jesus Christ added, "that this one went home justified, rather than the other." The Publican's sins are forgiven him, but the Pharisee, with all his good deeds, returns to his home more culpable than when he left it. If you wish to know the reason, it is this: The humility of the Publican, although a sinner, was more pleasing to God than all the superficial good works of the proud Pharisee. And Jesus Christ in this example, demonstrates that every one who exalteth himself shall be humbled, and he who humbleth himself shall be exalted. Yes, dear brethren, the only way which leads to exaltation in the next life is humility. Without humility, that lovely and rare virtue, you will be as unlikely to reach heaven as without Baptism. Let us, therefore, today, dear brethren, understand the duty of humbling ourselves, and the motives which should encourage us to do so. I will show you:

I.—*That humility is a virtue which is absolutely necessary for us if we wish to please God by our actions, and to be rewarded in the next life.*

II.—*That we have every reason to practise it, toward God, as well as toward ourselves.*

I.

Before making you comprehend how greatly we stand in need of this beautiful virtue, which is as necessary as Baptism, as necessary as the Sacrament of Penance after mortal sin, I must tell you in what consists this amiable virtue, which gives to all our actions such great merit, and adorns all our good works so abundantly. St. Bernard, the great Saint who practised it in such an extraordinary manner, forsook fortune, friends, parents, and relations to pass his life in the desert with wild beasts, and there to lament his sins, tells us that humility is a virtue by which we learn to know ourselves; and it is just this which impels us to think little of ourselves, and above all things not to take pleasure when we are praised. I say (1) this virtue is absolutely necessary for us if we wish to see our actions rewarded in heaven, for Jesus Christ Himself has told us that we can as little expect to gain heaven without humility, as without Baptism. St. Augustine tells us: "If you ask me which is the first virtue for a Christian, I tell you that it is humility. If you ask me which is the second, I say to you it is humility. If you again ask me which is the third, I still say that it is humility, and as often as you ask me this question I shall always give you the same answer."

If pride produces every sin, we can just as well say that humility produces every virtue. With humility you have everything which you ought to have to please God and to save your soul, and without humility all the other virtues will be of no avail. We read in the Gospel that some mothers presented their children to Jesus Christ that He might bless them. The Apostles wanted to turn them away, but our Lord would not permit this, and He said to them: "Suffer the little children to come unto me: for of such is the kingdom of heaven." He embraced them, and gave them His blessing. Why did the divine Redeemer receive them so lovingly? For the reason that children are simple, humble, and without guile. If, therefore, my dear brethren, we desire to be received kindly by Jesus Christ, we too, must be simple, and humble in everything that we do. "This," St. Bernard tells us, "was the beautiful virtue on account of which the eternal Father regarded the Blessed Virgin with delight, and if this virtue," he says, "drew down upon her God's regard, it was also by her humility that she conceived the Son of God. If the Blessed Virgin is the Queen of angels, she is also the Queen of the humble." St. Teresa once asked our Lord why the Holy Ghost imparted and revealed Himself in the Old Testament, to the Patriarchs and Prophets, but does so no longer? Our Lord answered her that this happened because they were more simple and humble; but now men have a false heart, and are full of pride and vanity. God does not impart anything to them. He does not love them as He did the good Patriarchs and Prophets who were simple and humble. St. Augustine tells us: "If you were profoundly humble, and acknowledged that you were nothing, deserved nothing, then God would grant you abundant graces. But when you exalt yourselves, and think so much of yourselves, then He will withdraw Himself from you, and abandon you to your misery."

In order to show that humility is the most beautiful, as well as the most precious of all virtues, our Lord begins His beatitudes with humility, by saying: "Blessed are the poor in spirit, for to them belongs the kingdom of heaven." St. Augustine tells us that the poor in spirit are those who have humility for their portion. The prophet Isaias said to God: "Lord, upon whom does Thy holy spirit descend? Is it perhaps upon those who bear a great name in this world, and upon the proud?" "No," said the Lord, "but upon those that are humble of heart."

This virtue renders us not only pleasing to God, but also to man. Everybody likes an humble person; they are glad to be in his or her company. Otherwise, what is the reason that children are so generally loved unless it is because they are simple and humble? A person who is humble yields in all things, never contradicts any one, or grieves them; is always contented, and strives to hide from the eyes of the world. Just as much as proud persons are disliked, are humble persons liked, because they make no pretensions; every one respects and loves them. This is the reason why the society of those who possess this beautiful quality is so much desired.

(2) I say humility is the foundation of all other virtues. Whoever earnestly desires to serve God well, and to save his soul, should begin to practise this virtue in its entirety. Without this our piety will resemble

straws, which we have planted, and which the first storm of wind will blow down. Yes, dear brethren, the evil spirit is not much afraid of piety which has not humility for its foundation, because he well knows that he can destroy it if he wants to.

It is related in the life of St. Anthony that God showed to him the world full of snares, which the evil one had set to entrap men into sin. He was much surprised and frightened, and he said to God: "O Lord, who is able to avoid so many snares? "Then he heard a voice which said to him: "Anthony, those that are humble are so because God grants His grace to the humble, so that they may resist temptation, while He permits the evil one to deride the proud, who, as the opportunity presents itself, fall into sin. Persons, on the contrary, who are humble, he does not dare to assail.'"

When we are tempted, dear brethren, let us remain protected under the cover of humility; then we shall find that the evil spirit has very little power over us.

In what does humility consist? Listen, I will tell you in the first place that there are two kinds of humility: exterior and interior humility. The exterior humility consists (1) in that we do not praise ourselves, that we do not talk of our ability and cleverness. (2) That we hide the good which we may have done. For instance: alms-giving, prayers, our works of penance, the services which we have rendered to our neighbor, the interior graces which God has granted us. (3) That we take no pleasure in being praised; that we divert the conversation from the success we have had, by ascribing it to God, or by showing that it is distasteful to us. (4) That we never dispute with others. We should yield to them in everything that is not contrary to our conscience. We ought not to think that we are always right. If we think we are right, we ought also to think that we are easily mistaken, and we must never want to have the last word, which is a proof of a very proud spirit. (5) We should never be sad when people appear to despise us, nor complain of this to others. That would be a proof that we have no humility, for if we had we should think they could never treat us as bad as we deserve on account of our sins. We should, on the contrary, thank God, as King David did, who returned good for evil, because he thought how little he himself had appreciated God by his sins. (6) We should never excuse our faults, when we have done anything to draw down censure upon ourselves. Even when we are wrong- fully accused, unless the honor of God is at stake, we should rather suffer in silence.

You see here, dear brethren, in what exterior humility consists. Now, in what does the interior consist? It consists (1) therein, that we have a poor opinion of ourselves; that we never approve of ourselves at heart when we have done anything well, but that we look upon ourselves as unworthy and incapable of bringing a good deed to a successful termination without the help of God. (2) That we do not mind other people knowing our faults, that thereby we may have occasion to improve our lives. (3) That we should be quite contented that others should surpass us in wealth, in intelligence, in virtue, and in other things. That we should subject ourselves to the will and opinion of others, when this is not in opposition to our conscience.

This, my dear brethren, is called possessing Christian humility, which renders us so pleasing to God, and so amiable to man. Look well now whether you have it or not. And if you have it not, then spare no pains, if you would be saved, to implore it of God, until you obtain it, because without it we can not enter heaven.

II.

And why should we practise humility? Dear brethren, a Christian who knows himself thoroughly should feel urged to humble himself for more than one reason. I will name three: the consideration of God's glory, the example of Jesus Christ, and our own wretchedness. (1) Who can contemplate the immensity of a God, without humbling himself into the dust at the thought that God created heaven and earth out of nothing, and that with one word He could turn heaven and earth into nothing again? A God who is so great, and whose power is boundless; a God filled with every perfection; a God with His never-ending eternity, His great justice, His providence, who rules everything so wisely, and looks after everything with such care, and we a mere nothing!

(2) I say: The example of Jesus Christ should make us humble. "When I," says St. Augustine, "contemplate a God who from His Incarnation unto the cross, led only a life filled with abasement and ignominy, Ought I to be afraid of humbling myself? A God seeks abasement. I, a worm, should exalt myself? My God, destroy this pride, which separates us so much from Thee!"

(3) The third motive, dear brethren, which ought to humble us, is our own wretchedness. We need only consider it more closely, and we shall find innumerable reasons to humble ourselves. "Ah," the holy Job tells us, "what are we? Dust before our birth, miserable when we come into the world, waste when we leave it. We are born of woman," he tells us; "we

live only a short time. During our life we weep a great deal, though it is but short, and how soon are we snatched away by death! "Judge, then, if we have the slightest occasion to exalt ourselves! Whoever, therefore, has the presumption to think that he is of some account is a fool who has never known himself, because when we know ourselves we can only despise ourselves."

We have no less reason to humble ourselves as regards grace. The few gifts and talents which we have, all come from the generous hand of the Lord, who bestows them when He likes, and we can not, therefore, boast of them.

Finally, I say: We ought to humble ourselves at the sight of the glory and blessedness which await us in the next life; for of ourselves we do not deserve anything. O how loving is God who gives us the hope of such benefits, we who have nothing, and deserve nothing!

What, then, should we conclude from this, dear brethren? We should daily ask God with our whole hearts for humility, for the grace to know that we are nothing of ourselves, and that our corporal as well as our spiritual welfare proceeds from Him alone. Let us, therefore, practise humility as much as we are able. There is no virtue more pleasing to God than that of humility, and in possessing it we shall possess all the other virtues. Even if we are great sinners, we still have the certainty that if we are humble, God will forgive us. Yes, dear brethren, let us hold fast to this beautiful virtue. It is that which will unite us to God, which will let us live at peace with our neighbors, which will make our crosses less heavy, which will give us the blessed hope of one day seeing God. He, Himself, tells us this: "Blessed are the poor in spirit, for they shall see God!" This it is that I wish you all. Amen.

SEVENTEENTH SUNDAY AFTER PENTECOST

CHARITY

"Thou shalt love the Lord thy God with thy whole heart."
Matt. xxii. 27

TO SERVE GOD PERFECTLY, it is not sufficient only to believe in Him. Of course, we must believe all the truths which the Church teaches us, and without faith all our works are without merit in the sight of God. Faith is absolutely necessary for us that we may be saved. At the same time this precious faith, which reveals to us beforehand the beauties of heaven, will one day leave us, and be transformed into knowledge, because in the next life there will be no more mysteries.

Hope, which is a gift of heaven, is necessary for us to have upright and pure motives, to please God in all our actions, to gain heaven and avoid hell. But Charity urges us on to love God because He is infinitely good, infinitely amiable, and deserves to be loved.

But, you will ask, how can we perceive whether we have this beautiful virtue so agreeable to God, which urges us to love God, not from fear of the punishments of hell, or the hope of heaven, but solely on account of His infinite perfections? It is Charity which will form our whole happiness, for the bliss of the blessed consists in love. Let us, therefore, see, my dear friends, whether we have this beautiful virtue, which is capable of rendering us so happy, and if we should be so unfortunate as not to possess it, let us seek to acquire it with all our strength.

I.

If I should ask, what is Charity? the answer is, it is a virtue that comes to us from heaven, by which we love God with our whole heart, and our neighbor as ourselves, for the love of God. But now you will ask, what does it mean to love God above all things and more than ourselves. I tell you that it means to prefer Him to all created things. It means to rather lose fortune, good name, parents, friends, children, husband, or wife, and even our own life, than to lose God by committing a mortal sin. St. Augustine tells us, that to love God perfectly means to love Him without measure, even if there were no heaven to hope for, or hell to fear. It means to love Him with the whole capacity of our heart. If you ask for the reason, it is, because God is infinitely amiable, and worthy of being loved. When we really love him, then neither sufferings, nor persecutions, nor contempt, nor life, nor death are capable of taking this love away from us, which we owe to God.

We must feel ourselves, dear brethren, that if we do not love God we shall be unhappy, very unhappy. If man was created to love God, he can only find his happiness in God alone. If you wish to be firmly convinced of this, look at the people, and ask those who live without loving God. Observe those persons who neglect prayer and the Sacraments. See in what a state of trouble and loss they are. They curse themselves, sometimes kill themselves, or die of worry. An avaricious man is never satisfied, whether he have much or little. Is the drunkard happy? The proud man is never at rest; he is always afraid of losing his wealth or position. The revengeful man, thirsting for revenge, can not sleep by night or day. Look at the shameful unchaste man, who seeks his happiness in the sins of the flesh. He goes so far that he not only loses his good name, but his fortune, health, and soul, without finding anything to satisfy him. And why can not we be happy in these things which appear to satisfy us? It is because, as we were only created for God, He alone is capable of satisfying us, of making us truly happy. Blind as we are, we cling to life, to the world with its goods and pleasures. Yes, we may as well say that we cling to everything which is calculated to make us unhappy. The Saints were wiser than we are. They despised all things, to seek God only. How insignificant is everything upon this earth to those who really love God! How many great ones of the world, how many princes even, and kings and emperors were there not, who forsook all things that they might be more at liberty to serve God in the desert or in the cloister! How many others, to give proof of their love of God, have mounted the scaffold? O my dear friends, how happy are they who have the privilege of detaching themselves from the things of this world, that they may remain united to God alone! Alas, how many are there not among you, who are twenty, thirty, or more years of age, and have not yet asked God for that Charity which the catechism tells us is a gift of heaven? We ought not, then, be astonished that we are so worldly, and so little spiritual. This way of conducting ourselves can only lead us to a miserable goal, to an eternal separation from God! Is it possible, my friends, that we are not striving for our real blessedness, which is God alone?

If I, then, were to ask, What is it to love our neighbor? the answer would be. The love of God causes us to love Him more than our wealth, our health, our good name, and even our life, and the love which we should have for our neighbor should enable us to love him as ourselves, so that all the good that we should wish for ourselves, we should wish for him. We must have this charity without which there is no heaven to hope for, and no friendship with God. Now, what do we understand by the word, our neighbor? Nothing is easier of comprehension. Every one of our brother men, even those who have wronged us, who have injured our good name, and calumniated us, or who have even sought to take our life. We ought to love them as we love ourselves, and wish them all the good that we wish ourselves. It is not only forbidden for us to wish them ill, but we must also render them service if they require it of us, and we are able to do so. We ought to rejoice when our enemies are successful in business, and we should feel sorry when they meet with reverses or losses, and we must take their part when others speak bad of them. We should tell others the good we know of them, and not avoid their society. Behold, my dear friends, this is how God wills that we should love our neighbor. If we do not believe this, then we must admit that we neither love our neighbor nor do we love God. We are bad Christians, and we shall be lost!

Now, you will ask me, how may we know whether we have this beautiful and precious virtue, without which our religion is only a pretension? A person, dear brethren, who has brotherly love, in the first place, is not proud; he does not care to rule others. You will never hear him censure other people's behavior, and he does not care to speak of what he does. A person who has brotherly love does not inquire into the motive of other persons' actions. He never thinks that he behaves better than they do. He does not exalt himself above his neighbor. On the contrary, he thinks that every one else is better than he. He is not cast down when people have a poor opinion of him. He is even contented, because he thinks that he deserves to be still more disesteemed.

A person who is charitable, avoids as much as possible hurting the feelings of others, because Charity is a mantle used to conceal our brother's faults. Those who have charity accept with patience and resignation to the will of God everything that happens to them, sickness and adversity, because they believe that all these things remind them that they are sinners, and that their life here below is not the eternal one.

Those, also, have charity who are not avaricious, and think not of accumulating the goods of this world. They work because it is the will of God, but they do not rely only upon their labor, and are without eagerness to accumulate treasures. They put their trust in Providence, which never abandons those who love it. As charity reigns in their heart, all the things of earth are as nothing to them. They observe that all those who run after this world's goods are the most unhappy. They employ their means, as far as they possibly can, in good works, to atone for their sins, and to gain heaven. They are kind toward everybody. All the good that they do is done in God's name. They assist the poor, whether they be friend or foe. The charitable man does as St. Francis de Sales did, who, when he gave an alms, rather bestowed it upon those who had in some way injured him, than upon those who had done him good. The reason why he did this was because such conduct is more agreeable to God. If you are charitable, you must never inquire whether those to whom you give have done wrong, or whether they have seriously offended any one, or whether they are good or not. They ask you in God's name, then give it to them thus. This is all you have to do that your alms may be deserving of reward.

It is unnecessary to point out to you that a person who has love for his neighbor is free from the shameful vice of impurity, because a person who is so fortunate as to have this precious virtue in the soul is so united to God, and performs all his actions according to the divine will, that the evil spirit of impurity can not find room in his heart. The fire of divine charity so inflames his heart, his soul, and all his senses that he is invulnerable against the assaults of the evil one. Yes, dear friends, we may say that Christian charity purifies our senses.

Charity is not envious. It is not sad when others have spiritual or temporal advantages. You will never see persons who have charity angry because another is more fortunate than they are, or because another is more praised, or more thought of. Far from this being the case, they thank God for it.

He who has charity is not subject to anger, for St. Paul tells us that charity is patient, blind, and meek toward every one. How often do we not get angry at trifles. We complain, we get excited, we speak haughtily, and for several days we remain in this condition. But you will say, I am accustomed to speak thus, and then my anger is soon over. You ought rather to say that you have not charity, which is patient and meek, and that you do not behave yourself as beseems a good Christian. Tell me, if you had charity, would you not bear patiently, and even cheerfully, a word that was said against you, an insult, or some trifling wrong? But he attacked my good name. Ah, my friend, what good opinion do you want people to have of you—you, who ought to know your faults better than they?

Charity is the noblest and most active of all the virtues. It moves men to disesteem everything which is base and contemptible, and of short duration, that they may be united to God and those goods which will never pass away. Charity may be compared to gold, the most precious of all metals, which adorns and beautifies everything that is richest upon earth. Charity is the ornament and adornment of all other virtues. The least little action accompanied with meekness and humility and charity of heart, is of more value and far surpasses anything that we can imagine.

Yes, dear friends, charity supports and animates faith. Without charity, faith is dead. Hope, the same as faith, can not exist without charity.

II.

Let us recognize, then, the value of this virtue, and the necessity of possessing it that we may be saved. Let us, at least, determine to pray to God for it every day, for without it we can not work out our salvation. We can say that when charity enters our heart it brings all the other virtues with it. Charity purifies and sanctifies all our actions. Charity perfects the soul. Charity renders all our actions worthy of heaven. St. Augustine tells us that charity contains all the other virtues, and that charity is found in all the other virtues. Charity, he tells us, leads all our actions to their final aim, and gives them admission to God. St. Paul tells us it surpasses the gifts of heaven. In his Epistle to the Corinthians, he exclaims: "If I had the tongues of angels, but had not charity, I should resemble a cymbal which vibrates and only produces one sound. If I had the gift of prophecy, and such great faith that I could remove a mountain from one place to another, but had not charity, I should be nothing. If I gave all my fortune to the poor, and my body to be tortured, it would all avail me nothing if I had not charity in my heart, and did not love my neighbor as myself." You see here, dear brethren, the necessity for us of praying to God with our whole heart for this incomparable virtue, for without it all the other virtues are of no avail.

Let us take Jesus Christ as our model. Let us consider what He did for all men, even for His executioners. Behold how He prayed for mercy and forgiveness for them. He loves them. He offers up the merits and the sufferings of His death for them. He promises them pardon. If we have not this charity, then we have nothing. We are only mock Christians. We must love everybody, even our greatest enemies, or we shall be lost. As this beautiful virtue, my dear friends, comes from heaven, we must, then, direct our prayers to heaven to obtain it, and we are certain of being heard. If we possess charity, then God will be pleased at everything that we do, and we shall thereby be sure of Paradise. This is the happiness which I wish you all. Amen.

EIGHTEENTH SUNDAY AFTER PENTECOST

LUKEWARMNESS

"But because thou art lukewarm, and neither cold nor hot; I will begin to vomit thee out of my mouth."
Apocalypse iii. 16.

CAN WE, my dear friends, listen without fear to this expression from the mouth of God Himself against a bishop who seemed to be fulfilling all the duties of a worthy servant of the Church? This man led a well regulated life, and his fortune was not spent in the ways of the unjust. Far from approving vice, he opposed it vigorously. He gave no bad example, and his life seemed really worthy of being imitated by others. And yet, notwithstanding all this, we learn that the Lord let St. John say to him, that if he should continue in his way of living, He would cast him out, i. e. punish him, and not admit him to salvation. Yes, my friends, this example must fill us with all the more horror because there are so many who tread in the same path, live in the same manner, and consider their salvation perfectly assured. Oh, how really small is the number of those who, in the eyes of the world, are positively lost or positively saved! Which path do we follow? Are we on the right path? We should tremble at the thought that we do not know. Let us try, then, to discover whether we are so unfortunate as to belong to the lukewarm. I will tell you:

I.—How you can tell whether you belong to the lukewarm, and
II.—The means by which you may avoid that misfortune.

I.

If, my dear friends, I speak to you today of the terrible condition of a lukewarm soul, I do not mean those who never go to Confession and Communion. Such people are not lukewarm. They are cold, and their souls are lost, even if they still come to Church and perform some good works.

Let us leave them to their perdition, because they wish for no better. But you may ask, will not all those who receive the Sacrament at least at Easter time, be saved? Surely, my friends, not all of those will be saved, because if all those who make frequent use of the Sacraments would be saved, the number of the elect would not be as small as in reality it is. But let us acknowledge at the same time that all those who will have the great happiness of going to heaven, will be chosen from those who make frequent use of the Sacraments, and not from those who do not go to Communion and Confession at least at Easter-time. You will think that, if all those who do not perform their Easter duty will be damned, the number of the condemned will be very great. No doubt it is very great. Whatever may be said to the contrary, there is no doubt that all those who lead a sinful life must share that fate. Is not your heart troubled at this thought?

Again, my dear friends, I do not classify as lukewarm those who are striving to belong to the world without ceasing to belong to God. One moment you will see them throw themselves down upon their knees before God, and the next you will see them perform the same act before the idols of this world. The poor blind man! He stretches forth one hand to the Almighty and the other to the world, calling to both for help, and promising his heart to both. He loves God— at least he would like to love Him—but at the same time he wants to please he world. But, soon tiring of his efforts to give himself to both, he finally gives himself entirely to the world.

Now, let me tell you, my friends of the condition of a lukewarm soul. A lukewarm soul is not yet quite dead in the eyes of the Lord, because faith, hope, and charity, which are its spiritual life are not entirely extinguished in it. But it is a faith without zeal, hope without firmness, love without ardor. Let me describe to you a zealous Christian, i. e., a Christian who really and ardently longs to save his soul, and then a person who leads a lukewarm life in the service of God. Then we will compare the two, and you will see to which class you belong. A good Christian is not satisfied to simply believe in the truths of our holy religion. He loves them, he ponders over them, he tries in every possible way to acquire a knowledge of them; he loves to hear the word of God, and the more he hears it, the more he longs for it. He believes not only that God sees him in all his actions, and judges them all at the hour of death, but he trembles at the thought that he will have to render an account of his whole life to God. He not only thinks of this, and trembles over it, but he strives earnestly to improve himself daily. He never ceases in his endeavors to find new ways in which to do penance.

How different from this is the Christian who lives a lukewarm life! He still believes in all the truths which the Church believes and teaches, but his faith is so weak that his heart has not part in it at all. He does not doubt that the good Lord sees him, and that he is ever in His holy presence. But while believing this, he does not amend, nor sin the less. He falls into sin as easily as if he did not believe in anything. He is fully convinced that so long as he remains in this condition, he is an enemy of God, and yet he makes no effort to extricate himself from it. He knows that Jesus Christ has given to the Sacrament of Penance the power to remit our sins, and help us in the acquisition of virtue. He knows that this Sacrament gives us graces in accordance with the state of mind in which we receive it. But all this has no effect. He remains throughout his life just as indifferent, just as lukewarm. His Confessions and Communions are few and far between. He generally waits for a great feast-day, or a jubilee, or a mission, or he goes because others do so, and not because his poor soul needs it. He not only does nothing to merit this happiness, but he does not even envy those who partake of it frequently. If you talk to him of heavenly affairs, he is uninterested. Nothing touches him. He hears the word of God, but it wearies him. He listens to it from habit. Long prayers he dislikes. His mind is full of what he has done, or is going to do. His poor soul is fighting the battle of death. It is still living, but it is unable to do anything for heaven.

The hope of a good Christian is firm; his trust in God is unshaken. He never loses sight of the next life. The remembrance of the sufferings of Jesus Christ is ever present to his mind, is always in his heart. At times he directs his thoughts to hell, so as to picture to himself how great is the punishment for sin, and how boundless the misery of those who commit it. At times he raises his thoughts to heaven, to arouse his love of God, and that he may be sensible of the happiness of those who prefer God above all things. He represents to himself how great the reward is of those who forsake all things to do the holy will of God. Then he longs for God alone, and desires Him only. The goods of this world are as nothing to him. The pleasures of this world fill him with aversion. He does not fear death in the least, because he well knows that it will merely deliver him from the miseries of this life, and unite him with God forever.

But a lukewarm soul is very far from thinking thus. The next life is no serious consideration for him. If he does think of heaven, it is without a real desire to enter there. He knows that sin closes the doors of heaven against him. At the same time he does not strive to amend, at least, not in an earnest manner. Consequently, he finds himself always in the same condition. The evil spirit deceives him by inducing him to make numerous good resolutions to do better, to be more cautious in his words, more patient in his trials, kinder to his neighbor. But all this does not make the slightest change in his way of living. For twenty or more years he has made these good resolutions without, however, losing any of his bad habits. And if he could pass his life without crosses and trials, he would never want to leave this world. If you hear him say that this life is very long and miserable, it is only when everything does not go as he wishes. When God sends him crosses or want, to compel him, as it were, to detach himself from this life, behold! he is filled with bitterness, gives way to complaints and murmuring, and very often to a sort of despair. He appears not to understand that it is God who sends him these trials for his own good, to detach him from this life and to draw him to Himself. What has he done to deserve this, he thinks to himself, as there are so many others more culpable than he, who are not subjected to such visitations?

A good Christian, my friends, is seldom occupied with the things of earth. If you speak to him about them, he is as indifferent as the people of the world when you speak to them of the things of eternity. Finally, he lets his happiness consist in crosses, tribulations, prayer, fasting, and the thought of God. Now, the lukewarm Christian loses his trust in God, though, perhaps, not entirely; but he does not distrust himself sufficiently. Although he very often is exposed to the occasion of sin, he still believes that he will not fall. If he does fall, he ascribes it to his neighbor, and assures himself that another time he will be more firm.

He who really loves God, and is anxious to save his soul, will employ every possible precaution to avoid the occasions of sin. He will not only avoid the grievous faults, but he will also be very careful to avoid the very least of them. He considers everything that can displease God as a great evil, or rather, everything that displeases God, displeases him, too. He considers that he is standing at the foot of a ladder which he must ascend. He perceives that to reach the topmost rung he has no time to lose, so that every day he advances from virtue to virtue, until the day of eternity. He is an eagle which cleaves the air, or rather as the lightning which, from the moment that it appears until it vanishes, loses none of its velocity. Yes, dear friends, this is what a soul does who works for God, and who ardently desires to behold Him.

EIGHTEENTH SUNDAY AFTER PENTECOST

This sort of love for God is not to be found in the lukewarm soul. You do not perceive that ardent desire, and the burning flame which overcome all obstacles to salvation. If you want to picture to yourselves, my dear brethren, the condition of a lukewarm soul, I can only tell you that it resembles a turtle, or a snail. They move about in such a slow way that you can hardly tell whether they have changed their position or not. The love which lukewarm Christians feel for God in their hearts, is like a tiny flame which is buried under a heap of ashes. This love is so surrounded with earthly thoughts and desires that if it is not choked, it is prevented from progressing, and is gradually extinguished. The lukewarm soul goes so far that he is indifferent about his ruin.

A Christian who leads a lukewarm life still fulfils his duties, at least, as far as appearances are concerned. He may say his prayers every morning upon his knees, he may go to the Sacrament once a year and even more frequently, only in all this he shows so much reluctance, so much aversion, so much indifference, so little preparation, so little change of life, that you can see plainly that he does his duty from habit and negligently, because he is compelled to do it. His Confessions and Communions may not be sacrileges, but they are Confessions and Communions without result. Instead of making him more perfect and more acceptable to God, they render him still more culpable. A lukewarm person thinks very little about the state of his soul, and he seldom reflects upon the past. If he does think of his soul, he believes he ought to be perfectly satisfied because he has confessed his sins. He thinks of the needs of his soul, but in a feeble way only. He appears in God's presence without knowing what he is going to ask for.

II.

Now, my dear friends, examine yourselves, and find out upon which side you stand: On the side of the sinner who has given up everything; who thinks no more about the salvation of his soul; who plunges into sin without any remorse of conscience? On the side of those just souls who behold God alone, and seek after Him? Or do you belong to those poor souls, to those lukewarm, indifferent Christians, that I have just described to you? On which path are you walking? Who can say that he is not a sinner, nor lukewarm, but one of the elect! Alas, my friends, there are many who, in the eyes of the world, appear to be good Christians, but in the sight of God, who knows our intentions, are but lukewarm.

But you will say to me, what means shall we employ that we may get out of this miserable state? Let me first tell you that those who live in lukewarmness are, in a certain sense, in greater danger than those who live in mortal sin. A sinner laments his condition when his conscience awakens. He even longs to leave his sinful life, and he will leave it some day. But a soul which lives in lukewarmness never thinks of quitting that state, because he even thinks that he stands well with God. What shall we conclude from all this? This, dear brethren, that the lukewarm soul is in the sight of God more offensive, so that He will spit it out, that is, will leave it to perdition. O how many souls are ruined by this state!

If you desire to shake off this lukewarmness, dear brethren, you should betake yourselves from time to time to the portals of the abyss, whence you can hear the shrieks and howls of the lost, then you would have an idea of the tortures which they have to undergo, because, during their life they neglected the affair of their salvation. Raise up your thoughts to heaven, and behold the glory of the Saints, which is theirs because, while they were upon earth they fought and did violence to themselves. See with what zeal and earnestness those religious shut themselves up in the cloister, seeking to become worthy to receive the Sacraments frequently. See how willingly they forgave, and did good to those that persecuted them, or spoke badly of them. Look at their humility! How they despised themselves, and how much they dreaded the praise and good opinion of the world. See how carefully they avoided the least occasion of sin, and what copious tears they shed over their past sins. See how pure their intention was in all their good works. They thought only of God, and sought to please Him only. Let us conclude, dear brethren, by saying that there is no state so much to be feared for a person as that of lukewarmness, because a great sinner is more easily converted than a lukewarm soul. Let us pray to God with our whole hearts, if we find ourselves in this state, that He may grant us the grace to leave it, and to take that path which all the Saints have taken, that we may attain to the bliss which they enjoy. This is what I wish you all. Amen.

NINETEENTH SUNDAY AFTER PENTECOST

INTEMPERANCE

"Be not drunk with wine, wherein is debauchery"
Eph. v. 18.

ST. PAUL assures us that the drunkard will not enter into the kingdom of heaven; drunkenness must, therefore, my dear brethren, be a very great sin. This is easily understood, for no matter how we look at it, this sin is even a disgrace among men, even in the eyes of the heathen, and Christians should be more afraid of this vice than of death. The Holy Ghost speaks of it in an awe-inspiring manner. He tells us: "Woe unto you who drink wine in moderately, and who become drunk, woe to those who arise in the morning with the thought of giving themselves up to drunkenness." Alas, dear friends, very few of those once addicted to this terrible vice, ever break themselves of it. There are persons who see no wrong in getting drunk upon every occasion; others imagine that so long as they do not get so drunk as to lose their reason, they do not commit a great sin; others again excuse themselves, saying they are led into it by their companions. To undeceive all those who hold these views I will show them:

I. *The enormity of this vice.*
II. *The folly to excuse the same.*

I.

To show you properly, my dear brethren, the enormity of the sin of drunkenness, I should have to show you the full extent of evil which this vice entails for time and eternity, and this is beyond mortal man to do, because it is known to God alone. Everything that I might say to you upon the subject will be insignificant in comparison to what the evil really is. In the first place you will agree with me that any one having a little common sense and religion, cannot be indifferent and insensible at the loss of their good name, their health, and their salvation. It is a plain fact that the drunkard, by his excesses, ruins his health, and draws down upon himself the loathing of men and the curse of God. I should think, dear friends, that this alone should be sufficient to inspire you with sufficient horror of it. What a disgrace for a person, especially a Christian, to let himself sink to the level of the vulgar and beastly sot. The Holy Ghost tells us in Holy Writ that the drunkard should be joined to the unreasoning cattle, that he may learn moderation in drinking from them. When we want to persuade a sinner to renounce his sins, we hold up to him the example of Jesus Christ and of the saints; but the drunkard is so low that the example of the beasts is held up to him, and we need not hesitate to select the uncleanest of them all. What a terrible blow is this to the dignity of human nature. St. Paul tells us that drunkards should not be tolerated amongst men, but that they should be driven forth into banishment amongst the animals of the wilderness. This vice is odious even in the eyes of the heathen. It is recorded in history that in the ancient city of Sparta, whose inhabitants were very abstemious, upon a certain day every year a slave was made drunk and brought upon the public square so as to show the young people how unworthy this vice was of reasonable creatures. When the young people beheld this man they were sufficiently disgusted to abstain entirely from intoxicating drink. You see, my friends, that although pagans they would not give way to a passion which reduced man to such disgraceful condition.

This sin is not one which is renounced with advancing age, and an habitual drunkard is seldom converted. The reason is this: intemperate people have no faith, no piety, no respect for anything sacred; nothing is capable of opening their eyes to their unhappy state. If you remind them of death, judgment, or hell, if you speak to them of the bliss which God has prepared for those who live a good life, the answer they give you is a scornful smile, which means: "Perhaps you think you can frighten me as you would little children; but I do not belong to those who believe everything that is said to them." And this is all you can obtain from them. They imagine with death everything is at an end. Their God is wine, and they cling to it. Beware, godless man, the Holy Ghost says to such as you, "the wine which thou drinkest immoderately, is a viper, which will cause thy death."

Behold, my friends, with what horror the Holy Ghost inspires us for this sin, for He tells us not to look upon the wine when it is red. If you drink immoderately, he says further, it will sting you like a snake, and poison you like a basilisk. Do you wish to know, St. Basil asks us, what a drunkard is? Well, he is a receptacle for the refuse of the saloon. The drunkard usually is sickly; he is incapable of doing anything else but to ruin his health. This passion must be a very ignoble one, for even the world, bad as it is, holds the drunkard in contempt, and looks upon him as a public nuisance. Is he not detested when, through his neglect, his business is ruined, and his family reduced to poverty? Is he not abhorred for the scandal that he gives by his shameful life? Where will you find a father who would give his daughter in marriage to a drunkard, if he knows him to be one? Where would you find a young girl to accept for a husband a young man given to drink? Where would you find a decent and respectable man who would let himself be seen in the company of a drunkard? St. Basil tells us that even the animals, if capable of understanding the real condition of a drunkard, would not suffer him in their company—they would consider themselves disgraced thereby. I think you can now, my dear brethren, form an idea of the enormity of the sin of intemperance. We find it very dreadful, and yet only have a very limited knowledge of the malice worked by this sin.

The council of Mayence proclaims that the drunkard transgresses all the ten commandments. If you desire to be convinced of this, examine them one after the other, and you will see that a drunkard is liable of doing everything forbidden by the ten commandments. St. John Chrysostom says in addressing the people of the city of Antioch: "Take care, my children, not to give way to drunkenness, because this sin so disgraces mankind, that it lowers them beneath the unreasoning animal. Alas, dear brethren, must not this sin be terrible in the sight of God?

II.

We shall see, my dear brethren, that drunkards have no excuses to justify their excesses. St. Augustine says that, although the drunkard is condemned by everybody, he believes that he has sufficient excuse for his misconduct. The one will say his friends are the cause of his intemperance. St. Augustine tells us: "What, miserable man, you have been drinking and making yourself the friend of drunkards, of ungodly men, whilst at the same time you became the enemy of God!" But it is not your friends, it is your own evil desire that makes you drink. There are others who claim that they can drink a great deal without feeling the effects of it, but, my friend, do not let this deceive you. Although you may not lose your senses, you are not less culpable if you drink to excess. There are those who say:

"We do it for business, to transact money matters, etc." Alas, my friend, do you really believe you can properly attend to business matters, when under the influence of strong drink? Have you not heard of many men, who, dazed by drink, were lured into business transactions by which they lost their all— business, property, home, and honor? What conclusion should we draw from all this, my friends? Just this. That those addicted to intemperance should enter seriously into themselves and remember what the Lord has said through the mouth of the prophet Joel: "Arise, drunkard, because all kinds of evils await thee. Weep and lament at the sight of the punishments which the just wrath of God prepares for you in hell on account of your drunkenness." Arise, miserable man, at the cry of that wife of yours, whom you have ill treated in your cups. Wake up, drunkard, at the cry of your poor children, whom you drive to the poor-house, and, probably, to death by privation. Listen, shameless drunkard, to this neighbor, who demands the money that you owe him, and which you squander in debauchery and in the saloon. He needs it for the support of his wife and children, who are suffering from want on account of your iniquity. Alas, miserable man, what did you promise so often to God in the Sacrament of Penance? You promised not to fall again into your disorderly ways. How have you kept this solemn promise? And what have you deserved? Nothing better than hell, there to burn for all eternity. You have deserved to be seated at the table of the evil spirits, there to be nourished and entertained with the rage which they have towards Jesus Christ Himself. You will be the victim upon which the just anger of God will fall heavily for all eternity!

You perhaps never have pictured to yourselves the gravity of the sin of drunkenness, of the state to which it reduces those who are its slave, of the evils which it causes them in this life, and of the punishments which it prepares for them for the other life. Do penance, you drunkard, for your disorderly life, for the bad examples that you have given. Cry to heaven for mercy, that you may obtain pardon of the Lord. Let us ask God to preserve us from this awful sin, which makes it so difficult, in fact, almost impossible, for those addicted to it to save their souls. Lead temperate, good lives, so that you may be an ornament to your faith, your community, and to your family. Follow the path that guides to eternal happiness. Amen.

TWENTIETH SUNDAY AFTER PENTECOST

EXTREME UNCTION

"And prayed him to come down and heal his son."
St John iv. 47.

MY DEAR CHRISTIANS: St. Luke, the Evangelist, tells us of the Saviour, that as He walked about, every one of His footsteps was marked by an act of benefaction. Not a sick person came to Him, but was healed, not one in trouble, but received consolation, not one in need, but was assisted, not a sinner to whom He did not say the consoling words, "Thy sins are forgiven thee." The Gospel of today speaks of such an act of healing, which He practiced on the son of a certain ruler. The troubled father said with great faith: "Lord, come down before that my son die." And Jesus said to him: "Go thy way, thy son liveth." And the man believed in the word of Jesus, and the son recovered at the same moment that Jesus had said: "Thy son liveth."

What the Saviour was to the sick and needy while He was on this earth, He is still to them today, for, as the Apostle says, Jesus Christ is always the same, yesterday and today, and for all eternity. Though he no longer wanders in our midst, yet He still manifests Himself to all those who approach Him with a believing heart and steadfast confidence; He is our consoler, helper, Saviour and dispenser of grace in good as well as in evil days. As He once with His own hands healed the sick, so does He now allow them to partake of His grace and His aid, in a Sacrament, which He has specially instituted for the consolation of the sick, the Sacrament of Extreme Unction.

It is of this Sacrament that I wish to speak to you today to show you:

I. That it is really a Sacrament of the church of Jesus Christ, and
II. What its effects are upon the sick.

I.

My dear Christians: There is no time in our life when we are more in need of consolation, assistance and ease of mind than in the days of sickness. When the body, tortured by pain, lies upon the bed of sickness and the increasing affliction reminds us of the nearness of death, then the deceptions of this life vanish, the awe-inspiring thought of eternity fills our heart, our sins and transgressions burden our conscience with their full weight and fill our mind with disquietude and anxiety. Soon the thought about the coming judgment arises, and the patient, in the anguish of his heart, seeks for a consoler and helper to give rest to his suffering soul. Where should he seek it and find it? Where, indeed, but with our Saviour, who has said: "Come to me, all ye that are heavily laden and weary and I will refresh you." Jesus Christ who cares for all would not in His unbounded charity leave His faithful without help and consolation in that most momentous and critical hour of their lives, and has, therefore, instituted a special Sacrament for the sick and dying. Through this Sacrament they are to receive consolation and material and spiritual help. St. James assures us of the institution of this Sacrament when he writes: "Is any man sick among you? Let him bring in the priests of the church, and let them pray over him, anointing him with oil, in the name of the Lord. And the prayer of faith shall save the sick man, and the Lord shall raise him up, and if he be in sins, they shall be forgiven him." These are the words which Holy Writ contains in regard to the Sacrament of Extreme Unction. Would St. James have instructed the faithful to turn to the priests of the church so that they might partake of divine grace through this Sacrament, if it had not been so ordained by Jesus Christ? And would the holy Apostles and the priests of the church have made use of the anointing of the sick for the purpose of gaining for them forgiveness of sin if Christ had not commanded and empowered them to do so? It is, therefore, certain that Christ has instituted Extreme Unction as a special Sacrament; otherwise the Apostles would not have practised it, nor would they have admonished the faithful to make use of this Sacrament; nor could the Apostles and their successors have remitted sins through anointing. The remission of sins is one of the chief effects of anointing according to the words of St. James. No man could order or establish a means, wherewith to remit sins, not even the Apostles could do that. Christ alone, the Son of God, to whom all power was given in heaven and earth, could do this. And he has ordered for his faithful, who were stricken with sickness, a remedy, whereby the still remaining sins could be remitted, and grace, consolation and relief could be given them in their sickness, and this remedy is the Sacrament of Extreme Unction. According to tradition in the church, Extreme Unction has always been considered a Sacrament or means of grace, and was as such received by the faithful. For fifteen centuries this Sacrament had not met with any opposition, until the time of the so-called Reformation. It would lead me too far, if I were to mention all the places where the fathers of the early church, who received the doctrines of the faith direct from the Apostles, speak of Extreme Unction. We believe in the judgment of the infallible Church of Jesus Christ; and she has declared as follows in the Council of Trent: "If any one asserts that Holy Anointing is not truly and really a Sacrament, instituted by Christ our Lord and as proclaimed by St. James, but merely a practice adopted by the fathers, or human invention, let him be excommunicated."

This Sacrament is administered by the anointment of the organs of the five senses with a holy oil that is blessed for this purpose by the Bishop on Holy Thursday. While the Priest anoints the eyes, ears, mouth, nose, hands and feet he says the words: "Through this holy unction and through His most tender mercy, may the Lord pardon thee, whatever sins thou hast committed by taste, speech, hearing," and so forth. What then is the effect of this Sacrament?

II.

St. James demonstrates in the above-mentioned words that the first effect of holy unction is to increase the sanctifying grace in such manner that the sick person, after having already been cleansed in the eyes of the Lord through the Sacrament of Penance, is drawn now closer to God. According to the words of the Apostle the patient obtains, besides this, relief from his sins and alleviation of his suffering.

One effect of holy Unction, therefore, consists in the fact that it will assist the patient in regaining health. Though sicknesses are visitations from God, it is the will of God that we should use the ordinary means which He has created for healing the ills of human flesh. Holy Scripture says: "Honor the physician and obey him, for he is sent by God." When people in sickness, as is so often the case, say: "What is the use of sending for the doctor? If I am to die, I shall die anyway," they act as one who having fallen into the water would not make the least effort to save himself, saying to himself, "What is the good of it? If it is not to be I shall not drown." The patient must do everything necessary to bring about his recovery, one of the means of which is, besides the ordinary remedies prescribed by the physician, the Sacrament of Extreme Unction, which, as St. James says, will aid a sick person. As sure as Christ is the Son of God, so surely will He help a sick person in this Sacrament, if it is received in true faith, with a lively confidence and a contrite heart. Of course there are many who have received Extreme Unction and have not recovered, but that is not the fault of the Sacrament. They have either not received it in the proper spirit, or, it was not best for the salvation of their souls that they should be restored to health. Many, who in the days of their youth never thought of God and who led a vicious life, are thrown upon a bed of sickness, so that they should reform and return to God. And they generally do it, too; they arrive at a knowledge of their sins and do penance; but God does not return to them their health, for He may know that, recovered, they will fall back into their old sins and forfeit their salvation. Therefore even if holy Unction does not always restore health that fact has nothing to do with the power of that Sacrament; it is a well known fact, even among physicians, that many people are restored to health by this great Sacrament.

This Sacrament causes—as one of its principal effects—an improvement in the patient's condition. St. James says: "The Lord will help the sick;" that is, through His grace He will give them consolation and courage to bear sickness in patience and overcome all temptations. Every one, who has been sick himself, or has had much to do with sick people, knows that what we need most in days of sickness is consolation and relief. How terrible sickness often is. Tortured with pains, the patient throws himself about on his bed, his whole body burning with fever; he finds no rest day or night; he has a disgust for everything and in despair he longs for death. But to these tortures there is often added the suffering of the soul. The thought of separation from his possessions, from his friends and pleasures, from his loved ones, whom he may have to leave without anybody to care for them, fills his heart with great sorrow. And then there appear to his mind's eye the days of his former life; the sins and iniquities of which he has been guilty worry him; the thought of death and of judgment fill him with terror and anguish. Who then is there to ease his pains, give consolation to his anguished heart, forgive his sins and take the terror away from death and judgment? Who else, but Jesus Christ, who has said: "Come to me, all ye who are heavily laden and weary, and I will refresh you." Every one who receives the Sacrament of Extreme Unction with a living faith, full confidence and a contrite heart, to him will be imparted consolation and relief in those dark hours, alleviation of pain, strength against despair, peace of mind about his former life and fortification in the agonies of death.

Another principal effect of this Sacrament is a pardon of sins. If the sick person is in sins they will be forgiven him. Of course there is another Sacrament instituted for the forgiveness of sin, the Sacrament of Penance, but also holy Unction has its sin- remitting power. A sick person who is incapable of confessing, or unconscious of his sins, but who has true repentance in his heart, will be forgiven his sins, even the most grievous, by this Sacrament of Extreme Unction. Does not St. James say, that if the sick man be in sins, they shall be forgiven him? And though we may have purified our soul in the Sacrament of Penance, yet there are still a great many lesser sins, weaknesses and imperfections remaining. See then how Christ in His love for us has seen to it that we can be freed from these faults, defects and imperfections and become worthy of being received into heaven, into which there shall enter nothing impure. He lets His holy Church administer to us this Sacrament of Extreme Unction, so that we may obtain thereby the necessary purification and be prepared for our journey into eternity. "If the sick man be in sins they shall be forgiven him." We have learned then, my dear Christians, that holy Unction is a Sacrament instituted by Christ for His faithful in sickness and that it brings us aid, consolation and relief, forgiveness of sin, supernatural strength in the agonies of death, and eternal life. How thankful we ought to be for this to our Redeemer! Let us join in the song of the Psalmist: "Blessed is the Lord, and His mercy is above all His works." How much, how infinitely much of an advantage have we over those who, not belonging to our faith, reject the Sacrament of Extreme Unction! They have nothing to aid them, console them and strengthen them in that awful moment, when they are mostly in need of consolation and relief. No priest, endowed with a high authority and power, approaches their bed of sickness and administers to them in the name of Jesus Christ forgiveness of sin in the Sacrament of Penance, the pledge of eternal life in the Sacrament of the Altar, and purification from the last imperfections, heavenly consolation, and material relief in the Sacrament of Extreme Unction. They have to rely upon themselves and upon the consolation which they may find in their past lives—a poor consolation— which offers little confidence at the approach of death.

Let us thank the Lord, then, that He has instituted this holy Sacrament for our relief in the days of sickness. Sooner or later we shall all be thrown upon the bed of sickness and be hurried on towards death. Let us then call in good time for a priest, so that he may, with the other Sacraments, also give us the Sacrament of Extreme Unction. Let us receive them with a firm faith in Jesus Christ, the Son of God and Redeemer of the world, with a living confidence in the mercy of God and the merits of Jesus Christ, with a heart free of sin, with repentance for our faults and shortcomings, with humility and piety, and the Lord will let us partake of all His graces and mercies, which He has connected with a worthy reception of this Sacrament, will give us aid and consolation, relief and ease of mind, purification from sin and courage to combat victoriously the terrors of death. Amen.

TWENTY-FIRST SUNDAY AFTER PENTECOST

ANGER

"And laying hold of him, he throttled him, saying: Pay what thou owest."
St Matt, xviii. 28.

HOW VERY differently from God do men reason and act! This wicked man, who had just obtained remission of all his debts was so little thankful and so little inclined to be lenient toward his fellow men, that no sooner did he catch sight of a man who was in debt to him, he flew into a passion, attacked and almost throttled him, and although this man threw himself at his feet and begged for mercy he did not restrain his anger, but would not rest until he had the poor man in prison. Thus, my dear friends, do men act. The master represents God. If He is willing to remit all we owe to His justice, if He treats us with kindness and leniency, He does it so that we should act in the same manner towards our brethren. An ungrateful and irascible man soon forgets what his God has done for him. For the least reason he flies into a passion and abandons himself to it, making himself unworthy of the very name of a Christian and greatly offending thereby God, who is so forgiving and kind.

In order that you may appreciate the great offence offered to God by Anger, I will try and show—

I. Why Anger offends God.
II. How Anger leads to other sins.

I.

I will not speak of the trivial expressions of impatience and of irritability which we hear so frequently. Even if not grievous sins, yet you should not omit to accuse yourselves of them, as they easily lead to more serious things. Anger is a violent and vehement commotion of the soul, which resents and rejects with all its power something displeasing to it.

There is also a holy anger, which arises from the holy zeal with which we may defend the affairs of our God and our Religion. St. Thomas says, that man may become angry sometimes without offending God, according to the words of the royal prophet: "Be angry, but sin not." There is, therefore, a just and reasonable anger, which may be better called zeal, which fills our soul when we stand up for the affairs of God. Holy Writ records many such examples.

Moses acted in holy zeal when enraged at the fact that the Israelites were worshipping a golden calf and despising the true God. He had many of them killed to avenge the Lord, who, in fact, had commanded him to do this. Jesus Christ Himself acted in holy zeal when He went into the temple to drive out all who were buying and selling therein, saying to them: "It is written: My house shall be called the house of prayer, but you have made it a den of thieves." Of this kind is the anger of a pastor whose heart is filled with zeal for the salvation of his flock and for the honor of his God. Woe to the priest who remains silent, when he sees his God dishonored, and souls erring from the right path! If he does not want to be himself damned, he must, if disorder gets the upper hand in his parish, disregard all fear and combat it with holy zeal, though he be persecuted, even killed for it.

I say, therefore, that this is a holy anger, approved and praised by God. If your anger would always be of this kind, then you would gain but praise for it. But the sinful anger we behold in the quarrels and enmities between neighbors, between brothers and sisters; there we must recognize what a dangerous, mad, sinful and cruel passion anger is. The pernicious effect of this passion is no doubt known to you from experience. The Holy Ghost says: "He that flies into a passion loses not only his soul and his God, but he also shortens the days of his life."

The Prophet Isaias tells us that a man who is in anger is like water stirred up by a storm. A beautiful picture, my friends. Indeed, nothing represents heaven better than a calm sea; it is then like a great mirror, in which the stars reflect their heavenly lustre, but as soon as a storm disturbs the water all these heavenly reflections disappear. Even so it is with the man who has the good fortune of possessing patience and gentleness; he is truly an image of the Lord. But when anger and impatience disturb this repose, the image of God disappears. He then ceases to be the image of God and becomes the image of the evil spirit. What are the sentiments of the evil spirit? the sentiments of hatred, of revenge, of discord, and even so are the notions of a man in anger. What are the utterings of the evil spirit? They are imprecations and curses. And what comes forth from the mouth of the person in a passion but imprecations and curses? Oh, my God, what terrible company is a person who is subject to fits of passion! Look at that poor wife, who has a husband of that kind. If the fear of God is in her heart and if she wishes to prevent him from committing other sins, she has to remain silent, however much she may wish to resent his insults. She has to be contented to sigh and weep in silence, so as not to make their married life insufferable and to avoid giving scandal. The irascible man will say for his excuse: "Why do you contradict me, knowing that I am a man of rash temper?" Well, my friend, if you allow your temper to be rash, what right does that give you over others? Are not others as good as you? Why don't you tell the truth and say that you are short of religion? What right have you, if you have the fear of God in your heart, to allow yourself to be governed by your passions, instead of making yourself their master?

But if there are unfortunate wives with ill-tempered husbands, there are, on the other hand, husbands so unfortunate as to have wives who will never speak a kind word to them, and who become excited and violent on the smallest provocation. How unfortunate is the household where neither one nor the other will give in and where there is continuous quarrelling, anger and dispute. Oh, dear Lord, is this not like the hell upon earth? And what school are the poor children passing through in such a household? What lessons of charity, patience and gentleness may they learn? How many poor children are crippled for life by the punishments they receive from parents in fits of anger. And anger never appears alone. It is always accompanied by other sins, as we shall soon see.

II.

Anger is the cause of swearing and cursing, of blasphemy and malediction. The Holy Ghost assures us that the house of a man who is addicted to swearing is full of injustice and that it will be visited by the punishments of God until destroyed. Can any one listen without shuddering to these unfortunate people who dare go so far in their anger as to swear by the holy name of God, that adorable name, which the angels repeat incessantly with so much joy: Holy, holy, holy is the Lord God of armies. Thy name be praised for all eternity!

Never forget, my good friends, that the tongue has been given to you to praise God; that it has been consecrated to Him in holy Baptism and holy Communion.

What makes the sin of cursing and swearing all the worse is this: If parents are in the habit of committing this sin the children will acquire the same habit and the vice will become hereditary in the family. If there are so many houses which harbor unhappiness and are the lurking place of the evil spirit and a picture of hell, you will find the explanation in the blasphemies and curses which have descended in these families from generation to generation.

And how great is the sin of those, who, in their passion, even curse themselves! This is a terrible crime, a crime against nature and against grace, for nature and grace fill us with love to ourselves. A man who curses himself is like a maniac who kills himself with his own hand. If they would take the trouble of thinking over what they are saying in their anger and passion they would never have the courage of uttering these maledictions against themselves, maledictions which almost force the Lord to condemn them. Oh, how unfortunate is a man who is subject to anger and passion. He forces the Lord to punish him, the same Lord who wishes nothing but his weal and welfare. But you will say: "What should we do to avoid the sin of anger, which is so terrible, and fraught with such evil consequences?" All sufferings in this world should remind us that it is only just that, as we have revolted against God, others should revolt against us. We should never give others reason to curse and to swear. Children should be particularly careful not to cause their parents to become angry. Parents should remember that they have nothing more precious in this world than their children, and that instead of cursing them in anger they should bless them. If anything happens contrary to your wishes, do not fly into a passion, but rather say, "God bless you." Act like holy Job, who through all his sufferings praised the name of the Lord. Look at his great submission to the will of God. If you do the same, the evil spirit will flee from you, all your goods will be blessed and all that has been taken from you will be restored to you twofold. If in an unguarded moment you should be taken with anger, and one of those bad curse words should escape from your lips, make immediately an act of contrition, ask forgiveness and promise to avoid committing this sin again. St. Teresa said that the whole of heaven rejoices when we pronounce reverently the name of God, while there is joy in hell when we use bad language. A Christian should never lose sight of the fact that the tongue has been given to him to praise the Lord in this world and to thank Him for all the good with which He has blessed him in this life, so that through all eternity we will praise Him with the angels and the saints. This will be the lot of those who have followed the example, not of the evil spirit, but of the angels and saints, yea, even of our Lord Himself, who was the true model of meekness and gentleness, and who may at the end of our days take us all into His kingdom. Amen.

TWENTY-SECOND SUNDAY AFTER PENTECOST

THE SOUL OF MAN THE IMAGE OF GOD

"Whose image and inscription is this?"
Matt. xxii. 20.

IN ORDER to make the meaning of today's Gospel easier of comprehension, it will be useful to mention some particulars referring to the customs of those times. The time of prophecy (Gen. xlix. 10) had been fulfilled, the sceptre was taken away from Judea, the Romans ruled over Judea and Herod had been placed there as a representative of the Roman government. For this reason the followers of the Romans were called Herodians, from whom the Pharisees, as their political opponents, were scheming to wrest the government of the Jews. As parties they hated one another. But as we read in the history of the passion of Jesus that Pilate and Herod were friends, so in today's Gospel are the Herodians and Pharisees acting in harmony. The reason is that Christ was obnoxious and a continuous reproach to both of them; to the Pharisees because He put their pride and hypocrisy to shame, and to the Herodians because He fearlessly censured their immorality.

Therefore, they put to Jesus the cunning question, whether the Jews, the chosen people of God, ought to pay tribute to the heathen. The enemies of Jesus thought thus: if He says yes, He will affront the Jews: if He says no, the Romans will get him into trouble. Jesus, the Eternal Wisdom, asked for the coin, and, pointing to the image of the emperor. He said: "Give unto Caesar, that which is Caesar's, and to God, that which is God's."

May these words be taken to heart, particularly by those in our days, who hold public office. Our people are likely to forget the first part of this sentence, and those in public positions the second; hence so much misery in the world. But let us today apply the question of our Lord: "Whose image and inscription is this?" to our souls; for the soul of man is the image of God, and more particularly:

I. The image in nature by reason and will.
II. The supernatural image by sanctifying grace.

I.

"Let us make man to our own image and likeness!" (Gen. i, 26.) Man is not a God, he is a creature, but a creature after God's likeness. The animal is a creature, too, but not an image of God. An animal has instinct, even some powers of memory, but no reason; it makes no resolutions, it does not reflect, it cannot invent anything, it only follows its impulses, called instinct, it always remains on the same intellectual level. Such is the difference between man and animal in reason. The difference is even more marked in the will. The animal obeys its impulses, and cannot otherwise, but man is guided in his actions by his own free will, and no one can check him. Therefore man, gifted with reason and a free will, is in his nature the image of God. Endowed with reason we must perceive the truth, investigate and distinguish lies from truth. And endowed with will power, we must choose, love and perform the good. This natural likeness to God is unfortunately often disfigured or even destroyed by man. Reason, created to seek truth, is misused; for instance, if we do not employ it for the knowledge of the truths of faith; if it is immaterial to man whether he lives in error or not; if we lie; conceal the truth from others. Why is truth hated by so many? Because truth is severe and demands of men that they conquer themselves and curb their passions. Therefore Jesus says: "For everyone that doeth evil, hateth the light, and cometh not to the light, that his works may not be reproved." (John iii, 20.) Furthermore, we sin against reason which makes us the image of God, if we do not endeavor to attain that knowledge which is necessary for every Christian in his calling. For this reason those parents sin who deprive their children of instruction, and young people sin, who do not attend school properly. A Christian also sins against reason who destroys it, and limits its activity. To these belong in the first place drunkards, who in their cups no longer know what they are doing. It is the same with those living impure lives, because one of the consequences of impurity is dulness of reason, of which the Apostle warns us with the words: "The sensual man perceiveth not the things that are of the spirit of God. (1 Cor. ii, 14.)

The powers of the will, the second feature of our likeness to God, are also misused and destroyed by sin. No one can compel -us to do anything against our will, not all the kings of the earth, nor the devils in hell. But this will power is weakened if we give way to our passions. With every fresh sin the power of evil inclinations increases, and so does increase the weakness of the will. Sin gains command over man little by little, until he is its slave, and then the unfortunate man excuses himself with the words: "I cannot help it, it is my nature," but this excuse is not true. Man can do all things he wills with the help of God—with God's assistance, I say, and this is obtained through prayer. And because such sinful men do not pray, they therefore have no determination of will, and live on in their sins. Their hearts are hardened and in such men a hatred forms itself against everything good and godly. They carry on by word and writing an unremitting war against the truth. No weapon is too sharp for them, but their principal weapons are lies and calumny, with which they besmear everything good and pious.

If you wish to see such distorted images of God, you can find them in all ranks of life; among the world's authorities, many of which are opposed to the Church, the proclaimer of the truth; in commercial and laboring classes, where they, like Judas, sell their faith and their conscience for some pieces of silver; among those who are too lazy to employ their reason and will and who find begging easier than working to earn their own living; among the rich, to whom their money is their god and who think of nothing but business and amusement. You see, my dear friends, in all such people the will is diseased and corrupted; they crave for sin; they love sin and they die in sin. As a consequence of this perversity of reason and will:

II.

The *supernatural* image of God in man, the sanctifying grace, becomes also destroyed. What does it matter to such people, whether they retain the grace of God or not? They have lost their innocence. Whether they live in mortal sin or not they do not care; they live in this terrible state year after year, heap sin upon sin, never think of confession, or, if they do, make it in a superficial manner, so that they are an illustration of the words of Jesus: "Then he goeth and taketh with him seven other spirits more wicked than himself; and they enter in and dwell there: and the last state of that man is made worse than the first." (St. Matt, xii, 45.) Such people avoid scrupulously the word of God, so as not to be disturbed in their life of sin. They appease their conscience with the words: there are others no better than we are. They never pray, or, when they do, it is easy to see that they pray with their lips and not with their hearts. How can such a soul be the image of God? No, it is the image of another one, and, shall I tell you of whom? ieYou are of your father the devil, and the desires of your father you will do." (St. John viii, 44.) And as Christ calls him: "Your adversary the devil, as a roaring lion, goeth about, seeking whom he may devour." (1 St. Peter v, 8.) Thus we find in our days a great part of mankind filled with hatred towards God, Christ and the Church; and the consequences of this hatred are rebellion against lawful authority; they are lawlessness and disorder. All that is right is despised and stamped under foot, while might gains the upper hand over right. And not satisfied with their own estrangement from God, they in their devilish wickedness try to ruin many others and destroy their happiness for time and eternity.

You see, my dear friends, this is the distorted image of God. There is salvation only in one thing: that is, "Give to God the things that are God's." (St. Matt. 22, 21.) Man is God's creation and property. Give then to God your reason, your heart and your will. Use them only for God and you will be saved; you will be for all eternity God's property, as children of His grace and charity. Amen.

SERMONS FOR THE FEAST DAYS OF THE YEAR

FEAST OF ALL SAINTS

" I beseech thee, my son, look upon heaven."
II. Mach. vii. 28.

TODAY, my dear Christians, is a day on which, more than on any other, the faithful look up to heaven and reflect, how supremely happy the saints are who enjoy the bliss of heaven at the throne of God; a day on which, by meditating on the never-ending happiness of the saints, an ardent longing is stirred in our hearts that we may one day take part in this happiness. But to reach this happiness we must not be satisfied with meditation alone. We must consider the way of living of the saints upon earth, and ask the question, How did they obtain their blissful state in heaven? We will consider in turn—

I. *The state of the saints on earth,* and
II. *The state of the saints in heaven.*
May the Lord bless our meditation.

I. The state of the saints on. earth, my dear Christians, was neither pleasant, nor easy, nor sweet, as the children of this world desire it or try to make it. No. Theirs was a lot both hard and difficult! They trod the paths which their Saviour himself had pointed out to them in the words: "So likewise every one of you that doth not renounce all that he possesseth cannot be my disciple" (Luke xiv. 33). They followed the path on which Jesus Christ had promised them crosses and tribulations with these words: "If any man will come after me, let him deny himself and take up his cross and follow me" (Matt. xvi. 24). They followed the path which Jesus calls a "narrow" way with the words: "How narrow is the gate, and strait the way that leadeth to life" (Matt, vii. 14). They followed in the service of God a threefold hard path—namely, the path of renunciation. They renounced all worldly treasures and goods; they often gave all that they possessed to the poor, and then they themselves led a life of poverty. They wanted to be the disciples of Jesus, who in this world "had nowhere to lay his head" (Matt. viii. 20). They renounced all honors, all the dignities of man. Many of them who came of princely and royal families renounced their title to the princely or royal throne which would have given them in the eyes of the world the highest honors, and they lived, unnoticed by the world, a life of the greatest humility and retirement, bearing in mind the words of Jesus: "He that humbleth himself shall be exalted" (Luke xviii. 14). They renounced all the pleasures and delights of the world, for they knew that they draw the heart from God and defile the soul with sin, and they sought only their joy in God by leading a holy life in His service, through which they said in the words of the prophet Isaias: "I will greatly rejoice in the Lord, and my soul shall be joyful in my God" (Isaias lxi. 10). And by all this renunciation they felt in their souls the highest possible happiness; in them was the word of the Psalmist fulfilled: "Blessed is the man who hath not had regard to vanities" (Ps. xxxix. 5).

Dear Christians! We all have today the desire—yes, even the ardent longing—to enjoy one day with the saints in heaven their glory and their happiness. But let us consider well that the Christian whose thoughts and actions are only directed toward transitory treasures, honors, and pleasures is not on the path where the joys of heaven are found. Christians must not desire what is earthly, but what is heavenly; not what is false, but what is true; not what is temporary and fleeting, but what is eternal and never-ending. Therefore our hearts must not be set upon the treasures, honors, and pleasures of this world, so that we may not miss the end for which we were created—heaven. "For what doth it profit a man if he gain the whole world and suffer the loss of his own soul?" (Matt. xvi. 26). Our Saviour calls to us Christians and exhorts us to strive after the happiness of heaven with these words: "Seek first the kingdom of God" (Matt. vi. 33). "The fool," says St. Ambrose, "holds with them who are of the world; the wise man prefers the eternal glory of heaven" (Serm. 37).

The saints of heaven, I will say further, chose to reach heaven by the way of mortification. The saints got to heaven by their virtues. Virtue and sin cannot dwell together in the soul. So that virtue might grow and strengthen, the saints uprooted the wicked propensity to sin in their flesh by practicing mortification. They considered it the object of their lives daily to mortify the desires of the flesh through the spirit, to overcome them, to struggle against them, and to uproot them entirely. "That was," as one of the saints said, "their work and their struggle." For that reason they fasted strictly; only tasted the poorest kind of food so as to give to their bodies only strength absolutely necessary. St. Makarius, to mortify himself, for seven long years only ate raw herbs and vegetables moistened in water. We know that many of the holy hermits lived on herbs and roots. Besides this strict fasting, they practiced mortification by chastising and scourging their bodies. They wore hair shirts and coarse garments of penance next to the skin, scourged their bodies with heavy cords and whipped themselves till the blood came. At night they did not lie on a soft bed, but most often on the hard ground, and only for a few hours to rest from their labors. We read in the life of St. Casimir, a Polish prince, that he wore a hair shirt in the midst of the gay pleasures and frivolities of the court; of Louis, King of France, that he never left off his hair shirt; of the pious Philip II of Spain, that on his dying bed he gave his own son Philip a scourge covered with blood, with these words: "Keep this scourge which has so often been stained with my blood."

You see, dear Christians, this is how the saints mortified themselves. They crucified their bodies inclined to sin, rooted out the cause of sin, so as to overcome all the temptations of the wicked one. What would some of the delicate children of the world say to this, those who never do the least harm to their worldliness, nor fast, nor deny their bodies anything, and therefore in time of temptation they are exposed to sin? Do they not think that what the saints did was a great deal too hard? That they did unnecessary things which God did not require of them? If God does not require such a harsh life of penance, still our Saviour's words are there when He says: "The kingdom of heaven suffereth violence, and the violent bear it away" (Matt. xi. 12).

Lastly, the saints in heaven chose, so as to reach heaven, the way of the cross and suffering. They understood those words of Jesus: "If any man will come after me, let him deny himself, and take up his cross and follow Me" (Matt. xvi. 24). For this reason they endured patiently the dungeon and fetters, the agonies of the stake and the scaffold; allowed themselves to be torn asunder by wild beasts and, like their Lord and Master, be bound to the cross, remembering the words of St. Paul: "If we suffer with Him, that we may be also glorified with Him" (Rom. viii. 17). That is why they bore all sufferings, not only with the greatest patience, but also gladly and with joy. As St. Paul said of himself: "I am filled with comfort; I exceedingly abound with joy in all our tribulation" (II. Cor. vii. 4). So could these saints say. "Never in my life," cried out St. Dorothy, in the midst of her martyrdom, "have I experienced such joy," and St. Andrew saluted the cross on which he was nailed with these words: "O, thou cherished and ardently longed-for cross! Thou bringest me happiness; therefore I approach thee with joy!" The saints, besides bearing with the greatest joy every pain which God sent them, even prayed to God when they were free from suffering that He would not send them pleasures, but sufferings. St. Teresa's lifelong desire was "to suffer or to die." St. Francis Xavier had such a great desire to suffer for Christ that once, when he was filled with consolation and happiness, he cried out, "It is enough, O Lord, it is enough!" while, on the other hand, when tribulation and suffering beset him, he cried: "Still more, O Lord, still more!" He was often heard to say these words: "O Lord, take not this cross away from me, or if so, then give me in its place a heavier one."

My dear Christians, are we not astonished at what the saints have suffered, at the patience which they exhibited in all this suffering, at the longing which they showed for crosses and sufferings? And we—we complain when we have to suffer a little! We bear with impatience the slightest adversity sent to us from God. Let us remember that "through many tribulations we must enter into the kingdom of God," and let us bear the little suffering which God sends us with patience and submission, so that we may by this, like the saints, obtain the everlasting joys of heaven.

So as to encourage us, let us consider what reward the saints have obtained in heaven for their hard and difficult lot while on this earth.

My dear Christians, the saints of God have undertaken and borne great things while on earth, and great things will God give them for all eternity, namely, heaven. They renounced everything in this world; they can, therefore, according to God's own promises, expect great things in the other world. They mortified themselves on earth, and therefore they can enjoy themselves for all eternity. And what are the joys which they have received from the Giver of all good gifts? I answer:

Joy without pain. Whenever man has any happiness the pain is not far off. If we enjoy a day of festivity, it is soon followed by a day of suffering. If we enjoy good health it is soon followed by indisposition or probably sickness. Here below our happiness is never perfect; it never lasts long; it is never enduring. But what is the joy of the saints in heaven? Unchangeable and undisturbed. "Joy and gladness," says the Holy Ghost through the prophet Isaias (li. 11), "they shall obtain; sorrow and mourning shall flee away". "And God shall wipe away all tears from their

ALL SAINTS

eyes," so we read in the Apocalypse of St. John (xxi. 4): "and death shall be no more; nor mourning, nor crying, nor sorrow shall be any more." Oh, true life! Oh, eternal life! Oh, life of never- ending happiness! There is joy without pain; rest without work, honor without shame, riches without loss, health without sickness, abundance without want, life without death, happiness without suffering. St. Augustine says: "It is easier to say what is not in heaven than what is in heaven." There is found no death, no mourning, no weariness, no weakness, no hunger, no thirst, no heat, no sickness, no infirmity, no sadness, no melancholy. Now these things are not there. Do you wish to know what is there? There is an everlasting home where youth never grows old, where love never grows cold, where beauty never fades, where pleasure never ceases. For this reason the angels are portrayed as beautiful, youthful figures, although they have been created for over six thousand years; there nothing decays; nothing loses its strength and beauty.

These joys without suffering are then unspeakable, great joys. "Oh, how great," says the Psalmist David, "is the multitude of Thy sweetness, O Lord, which Thou hast hidden for them that fear Thee!" (Ps. xxx. 20). And he himself gives this answer: "They [the saints] shall be inebriated with the plenty of Thy house; and Thou shalt make them drink of the torrent of Thy pleasure. For with Thee is the fountain of life; and in Thy light we shall see light" (Ps. xxxv. 9). "For better is one day in Thy courts above thousands" (Ps. lxxxiii. 11). And what reward our blessed Lord has Himself promised His servants in heaven with these words: "Be glad and rejoice, for your reward is very great in heaven" (Matt. v. 12). And what was the joy of St. Paul when he was deemed worthy to look into the third heaven! He is not able to describe it, therefore he falters the words: "The eye hath not seen, nor ear heard, neither hath it entered into the heart of man, what things God hath prepared for them that love Him" (I. Cor. ii. 9).

The holy fathers of the Church have often taken pains to try to express the sweetness and pleasantness of heavenly joys; but they were not able, as the great thinker St. Augustine himself says, to describe these things as they really are, only in a certain way to feel them. "So great," says St. Augustine, comparingly, "is the glory of heavenly bliss that man, if he had only spent a single day there, would give years of bliss and pleasures of this life for it." "The reward of the saints in heaven," writes St. Bernard, "is so great that man cannot measure it, so rich that man cannot give it utterance, and so precious that man cannot price it." And, therefore, to give us an idea of the joys of heaven, he breaks out in these words: "O joy above all joys! Joy that overreachest every joy, and out of thee there is no joy!" "O gaudium super gaudium! gaudium vincens omne gaudium, extra quod non est gaudium!" "Place," writes a great theologian, "all the many great happinesses which the world has together: the happiness to possess all earthly treasures, the happiness of all power and honors, all the joys and pleasures of a worldly life; multiply these happinesses a hundred, a thousand, a million times, multiply them as much and as often as you can, and they are not to be compared with the never- ending joys of heaven. Compare, as in Holy Scripture, the joys of heaven to a magnificent feast, a brilliant, joyous feast, and you are still immeasurably short of the truth. As here below, trouble and suffering, so there above the elect enjoy bliss and joy on all sides; bliss and joy in their glorified bodies; bliss and joy in the beauty and the glory of the heavenly Jerusalem which they inhabit; bliss and joy in Jesus, their Saviour and their King, whose divine gracious countenance they love to look upon; bliss and joy in Mary, their Mother and their Queen, whose unutterable beauty delights them; bliss and joy at the exalted thrones which they themselves occupy and at the glorious crown which adorns their heads; bliss and joy at the hymns of praise sung by the choirs of heaven; bliss and joy at the sight of the glory of their triumphant brethren." Truly, the prophet is right when he says: "With the stream of Thy glory, O Lord, wilt Thou drown them."

Lastly, the joys of heaven are everlasting. The soul of man is immortal, and everlasting and eternal is the reward for the souls of the just. From the kingdom of God the Son in heaven the angel said to Mary: "And of His kingdom there shall be no end" (Luke i. 33). Our Divine Saviour says Himself of the reward of the just: 'But the just into life everlasting" (Matt. xxv. 46). When Christ spoke to His disciples of His return to the Father, He said also to console them: "So also you now indeed have sorrow, but I will see you again, and your heart shall rejoice; and your joy no man shall take from you" (John xvi. 22). That is to say, it shall last forever. And lastly, St. Paul writes: "For our present tribulation, which is momentary and light, worketh for us above measure exceedingly an eternal weight of glory" (II. Cor. iv. 17).

The eternal joy of heaven! What a glorious reward for the saints for their short renunciation of earthly things, for a short struggle with sin, for a short suffering borne with patience! "A short time," says St. Augustine, "does work in this world last; eternal is the rest in heaven: short is the pain; eternal the glory: short is the suffering; without end the joy" (in Ps.

26). Therefore he sighed for this eternal life and calls out to God: "O Source of Life, when shall I enter into Thy joys, from which no more will be kept away? Oh true, sweet, and pleasant life! O glorious life, without end! There is the greatest certainty, the most sure rest, the most restful happiness, the most joyful sweetness, the sweetest eternity and eternal happiness." And how long have the saints enjoyed this heavenly happiness? For many decades, many hundreds of years. And how much of eternity has passed for them already? Not a moment. And how much longer will they enjoy the happiness of heaven? Centuries? No, forever! Or thousands of years? No, forever! Or millions of years? No, forever! Or for as many years as there are grains of sand on the earth or drops of water in the ocean? No, much longer, much longer—forever! Oh, you saints in heaven, how inexpressibly happy are you!

Now, my dear Christians, what are we going to do after the contemplation of the happiness of the saints in heaven? We all wish to cry out with St. Aloysius: "We want to go to heaven! We want to go to heaven!" And so that we may reach heaven we must place all our thought there, and not on this transitory world. As St. Symphorianus was led to the place of martyrdom, his pious mother, who followed him, to give him encouragement to bear his triumphs steadfastly, repeated these words over and over again: "My child, my child, think of everlasting life!" Dear Christians, when it seems hard for you to renounce the world, to fight against sin, to return to God after sinning, to lead a Christian life and steadfastly walk in the paths of virtue; when trials frighten you, which no one is without; then think of the eternal reward which awaits you in heaven. Consider that for a little trouble you will receive a great reward, for an easy victory a good, and for a momentary trouble an everlasting reward. Undertake, therefore, this light, this little, this short trouble which the way of virtue requires, and you will receive in return a good, a great, and an everlasting reward in heaven. Amen.

ALL SOULS' DAY

"It is therefore a holy and wholesome thought to pray for the dead, that they may be loosed from sin."
II. Mach. xii. 46.

FILLED with holy joy the Church looked up yesterday to those sublime regions where the saints of heaven without number rejoice around the throne of God, and in her gladness of heart, clad in festive garb, she let songs of praise resound in honor of those who, after having ended their life in happiness, have obtained the crown of joy of eternal life.

Tell me, my dear friends, why did the Church, our mother, rejoice yesterday? Why did she clothe herself in festive garments? Why did she join in joyous song as if she had a part in the eternal happiness of the blessed? But do not ask, my friends! The Church, the mother of all Christians, the mother of all those who gained in her bosom that inexpressible bliss of heaven, rejoiced with perfect right that so many millions of her dear children obtained the crown of glory for their faithfulness and are happy and blessed for all eternity. She rejoiced as a mother rejoices when she finds that the greatest happiness has fallen to the lot of her children.

But today her joy has suddenly changed into sorrow; her joyful songs are silenced; she sounds her lamentations in doleful chants; no longer is she attired in festive garments; her vestments are those of mourning.

Oh, do not ask why! The Church, the mother of all Christians, today turns away her eyes from those of her children who exult in the realms above, in the joys of heaven, and looks upon her other children who are still detained in that abode of suffering where they are purified for their sojourn to heaven, and because she loves these no less than those others and longs to see them partake of that divine happiness, therefore she laments and prays:

"Lord, O merciful God, lead these souls also to that abode of eternal happiness which Thou hast deigned to grant to so many millions of Thy children."

It is through us, my dear friends, it is from our lips that the holy Church sends forth these utterances; it is from our tongues that her prayers to the throne of mercy are addressed. This is the reason why she sends us today to the cemetery that we may, over the graves of our parents and deceased relatives, friends and Christian comrades, invoke God's mercy for their souls and entreat with sorrowful heart their deliverance from that purifying fire in which they have to atone for all the sins which have not been expiated by them in this world. And this is why she holds before us today that eternal truth of our faith, that by means of our prayers we may come to the rescue of these suffering souls.

Oh, how mindful our holy Church is, that she may not forget any of her children and ever longs to see every one of them happy and blessed. And you do right, my dear friends, when, rejecting that unbelief which is called "evangelical" truth, that unbelief which does not want to know anything of a purgatory in the world to come and of the efficacy of the prayers for the dead—if you, I say, true to your faith in the holy Catholic Church, come together here on this day, the feast day of the poor souls, and gather round the altar of the Almighty, and through the most holy sacrifice of the Mass, offered by one of your brethren and through your own most fervent prayers, come to the rescue of those poor souls!

This your faith is well founded; therefore fulfill as often as you can these holy acts of charity, and so that you may be encouraged to practice them more and more I will prove to you today the truth of our faith, and assert that—

Firstly, there is a purgatory in the world beyond; and that,
Secondly, we may help the poor souls to their deliverance from said purgatory.

I.

Listen, then. St. John the apostle says in the Apocalypse (xxi. 27): "There shall not enter into it anything defiled." Sin, even the smallest sin, stains the soul of man and defiles it to such a degree that it cannot appear before the face of God and have a share in the kingdom of heaven. But will such a soul which passes into the next world afflicted with such small and venial sins be forever cast into the torments of hell?

Certainly not; for our Saviour himself contradicts plainly such a belief by calling the just man, though he fall seven times,— into small sins,—still a just man, and who, on account of being a just man, though he fall into venial sins, still belongs to the number of the elect. When, therefore, God can, on the one side, not receive into the kingdom of heaven such a just soul which has passed away from this earth afflicted with venial sins, and, on the other hand, cannot condemn a just soul to the tortures of hell, then there must be necessarily some other place set aside where these souls may purify themselves from such defects, so that they may be able to reach the kingdom of heaven, to which, on account of their justness, they have a claim.

Of such a purification of just souls in the world to come the Holy Ghost says in Scripture through the prophet Zacharias: "I will refine them as silver is refined, and I will try them as gold is tried" (Zach. xiii. 9).

If, then, silver and gold are burned in the furnace for no other purpose than that they may be freed from dross, consequently in the same way those souls will be tried and purified in fire by the Lord. Therefore the Holy Ghost says of those souls which the Lord has received into heaven after such trial and purification: "As gold in the furnace He hath proved them" (Sap. iii. 6).

This truth, my dear friends, which has been proclaimed to us by the Holy Ghost has been ever adhered to by God's chosen people as well as by our holy Church.

Therefore we find already under the old law that the Jews brought sacrifices to the temple to deliver the souls of the dead from purgatory. Judas Machabeus, who adhered to the faith of his fathers with such great zeal, sent twelve thousand drachms of silver as a sacrifice for his brethren who had fallen in battle, and Holy Scripture says distinctly in the second book of Machabees, where this occurrence is narrated: "It is therefore a holy and wholesome thought to pray for the dead, that they may be loosed from sin" (II. Mach. xii. 46).

Now, then, my dear people, how can such sacrifices and prayers refer to deliverance of the damned in hell? Never! For this deliverance is impossible. Consequently God must have created some other place from which it is possible to effect the deliverance of the souls of the dear departed.

This faith which is so clearly expressed in the Old Covenant has been confirmed with equal distinctness by our Saviour Jesus Christ himself. He calls purgatory a prison, and says: "Amen, I say to thee thou shalt not go out from thence till thou repay the last farthing" (Matt. v. 26).

In these words Jesus speaks of atonement for sins, of a delivery from the prison, but the punishment in hell is eternal; hence He speaks distinctly of a temporary place of punishment, of a place of purification, where the souls of the just can be freed of unrepented sins and purified for their entrance into the kingdom of heaven. At another time our Divine Saviour says: "But he that shall speak against the Holy Ghost, it shall not be forgiven him, neither in this world nor in the world to come."

Could the Divine Saviour speak more explicitly of a place of purification in the other world than He has in these words? According to Him the pardoning of sins is possible in the other world, but this cannot be done in hell, because the Saviour himself calls hell "eternal fire." And it cannot be done in heaven, for the apostle says: "Nothing unclean can enter the kingdom of heaven." Therefore there must be some other place where it is possible to obtain forgiveness, and it is this other place which we call "purgatory."

In his first letter to the Corinthians St. Paul the apostle states the exact way by which the soul of man may be freed from unrepented sins: "Every man's work shall be manifest: for the day of the Lord shall declare it, because it shall be revealed in fire: and the fire shall try every man's work, of what sort it is."

We must repeat again that the apostle could not have spoken thus of hell-fire, because he would then have contradicted the teachings of our Lord. His words, therefore, refer to a place of purification, from which, according to these words, a delivery is possible, but not otherwise than through fire.

But why should we add further proof? The words in Holy Scripture, the sayings of our Lord and His apostles, are all plain enough, and for that reason has our Church, from the time of the apostles down to our own days, ever steadfastly adhered to and preserved the belief in a place of purification in the world to come.

Dionysius the Areopagite writes during the first century of a place of purification. In the writings of Origen in the year 120 this dogma of the Church is expressly mentioned. Listen to his own words. He says: "When the soul of man brings with it into eternity many good works and only a few sinful deeds, these must be loosened from it like lead by fire, and that what remains is pure gold. The more lead one brings with him, the more one will have to burn (in the fire of purification)." Let us listen to St. Augustine. He calls this place of purification a passing fire and says: "He will be saved, but only as by fire." "One is cleansed not from heavy, but from light sins. The greater the number of our sins, the longer we will have to remain in this passing fire of purification." We therefore find this belief in the earliest days of the Church. She has received it from the apostles and will hold steadfastly to it until the end of time. It is founded upon the revelation of the Holy Ghost and the Gospel of our Lord, and it is therefore proven without any doubt that there is a place of purification, a purgatory in the world yonder, wherein those souls which cannot appear before the face of the Lord on account of minor sins will be cleansed and purified until they are declared worthy of being united to their God.

For the present I will not speak, my dear people, of the pains and tortures which the souls of the departed will have to suffer in purgatory, as the apostle gives us to understand sufficiently the frightfulness of the tortures by the sentence: "They will be cleansed as by fire." Enough for us to feel anxious that perhaps, with arms stretched forth, they call to us and exclaim with the abandoned Job: "Have pity on me, have pity on me, at least you my friends."

Oh, my dear Christians, children or brothers or sisters perhaps of deceased that are lying buried in graves, don't be hard of heart at the sighs and supplications of your parents and relations. Fold your hands, raise them to God, and succor by prayer and good works the suffering souls from their tortures. They cannot help themselves, but we can rescue them by our prayers and good deeds. Of this we will speak now.

II.

St. Augustine, my dear Christians, points out plainly in which way we may come to the rescue of the poor souls in purgatory. "There is no doubt," he says, "that through the prayers of the Church, through the most holy sacrifice, through deeds of charity we may aid the departed." Prayer is, then, a certain means by which we can further the deliverance of the poor souls. The Holy Ghost explicitly states this fact in Holy Scripture. "It is," he says, "a holy and wholesome thought to pray for the dead, that they may be loosed from sin" (II. Mach. xii. 46).

Expressly—listen again—expressly the Holy Ghost says in Holy Scripture that the deceased by our prayers "may be loosened from sin."

I will therefore ask today all those who forget their deceased brethren, what love is this which does not think daily of the deliverance of our deceased fellow-Christians? What love is this that can forget those who in life loved us so dearly? What love is this that can forget those who have done for us so many acts of kindness while they were living? Child, where is your love for your deceased parents? Brother, where is your love for your deceased brother, that you do not pray every day so that those dear ones may be "loosened from their sins"? Have you forgotten your own flesh and blood? Have you forgotten the many acts of kindness they did for you during their lifetime? Have you forgotten those promises you gave them before death closed their eyes? Oh! listen to the groans of your beloved dear ones in that awful prison. Pay by a devout prayer the little mite they are still owing and rescue those who have perhaps waited a very long time for their deliverance.

The saintly Cardinal Hugo exhorts us with impressive words to remember this duty, and says: "To obtain deliverance for the dead, you that are still among the living of this world should remember them in your prayers, so that they may gain through them eternal peace." In a still more urgent manner St. Augustine calls upon us with the words: "Forget not the dead and hasten to pray for them." Yes, make haste! Perhaps you may be able this very day to liberate from that prison by a devout prayer a soul which otherwise might have to sigh and suffer for many a day.

Another means by which we can free the poor souls from their suffering is, according to St. Augustine, the holy sacrifice of the Mass. St. Monica, the mother of this saint, recognized the truth of this, and said on her death-bed to her son: "Don't think of burying my body in magnificent style and of embalming me and where you will bury me. Only think of one thing, I beg of you. Remember me at the altar of the Lord and offer up the most holy sacrifice of the Mass for the benefit of my soul." St. Monica, my dear people, knew very well that there is no better remedy for the souls of the deceased than the most holy sacrifice of the Mass.

When the good Judas Machabeus sent twelve thousand drachms to the temple in Jerusalem as a sacrifice for the benefit of his soldiers who had fallen in battle, so that by virtue of this sacrifice they might be freed from their sins, then tell me, may we not reasonably expect the deliverance of souls from purgatory by the greater virtue of the most holy sacrifice of the Mass?

If the sacrifice of earthly things which have not the least value in the eyes of the Lord, and only obtain value before Him from our good intentions which accompany the sacrifice, is considered efficacious for obtaining deliverance for the souls in purgatory, how much greater must be the efficacy of the sacrifice of the Lord's own body, the value of which no man has ever been able to imagine, to aid the poor souls to their deliverance! And if the bloody sacrifice on the cross, which was able to atone for the curse of God brought upon mankind by the greatest sins of men, and which was able to open up the gates of heaven, which had been closed on account of these sins, may we not expect that the same sacrifice of our Lord, offered bloodlessly on the altar, would be efficacious enough to free the poor souls of a few little sins, small faults which had not changed God's love into wrath, but only dimmed it?

St. Chrysostom expresses a great truth when referring to that sacrifice which Job offered up for the purification of his children. He says: "If Job's sacrifice purified his children, who can doubt that through our sacrifice [of the holy Mass] we can bring consolation to the poor souls?" And therefore St. Anthony is justified in saying: "The most holy sacrifice of the Mass, in which the passion of our Lord is perpetually celebrated, is in itself the finest and best remedy for the souls in purgatory. It is the staff upon which they raise themselves into heaven and eternal rest." By authority of Scripture and the holy fathers the Church pronounces this dogma and says: "The souls in purgatory are aided by the holy sacrifice of the Mass."

According to the opinion of St. Gregory and St. Jerome, the poor souls in purgatory sigh and long for nothing so much as that the most holy sacrifice of the Mass be offered up for them. Listen to St. Gregory's own words: "The offering of the holy sacrifice of the Mass for the poor souls in purgatory is of great benefit to them, and they long for it with grievous wailings."

St. Jerome is of the opinion that the holy sacrifice causes alleviation to the suffering of the poor souls while it is being offered up to the Heavenly Father. These are his words: "The souls who are suffering in purgatory and whom the priest prays for on the altar during Mass do not feel the tortures of purgatory during the time that the Mass lasts. They ask for nothing more, they wish for nothing more than this bloodless sacrifice." Hasten then, my dear friends, to this source of aid for the poor souls as often as you can. Offer up to the Heavenly Father with the priest on the altar the Lamb of God as a ransom for their sins. Offer up the great merits of this holy sacrifice for their faults and shortcomings for which they still may have to suffer, and pray, "O Lamb of God, who takest away the sins of the world, give these poor souls eternal peace!"

A third medium by which we can be of help to the poor souls in their sufferings are works of charity. Do not let us stop to ask for a proof of this. If we can turn the merits of our prayers, the merits of the most holy sacrifice of the Mass, over for the benefit of the poor souls, we can in like manner turn over the merits of our works of charity which we are practicing for the good of suffering humanity, for the benefit of the poor souls. One thing is certain: our acts of charity turn God's anger into mercy, and if we at the same moment at which we have brought forth

God's mercy by a merciful act of our own recommend to the Lord's mercy one or all souls which still have to suffer, He will have pity on those souls.

The Holy Ghost says: "Water quencheth a flaming fire, and alms resisteth sins" (Ecclus. iii. 33).

Therefore St. Augustine is justified in saying: "The alms of a Christian is a sacrifice of propitiation whereby God's wrath is appeased toward the sinner." "Yes," continues St. Chrysostom, "alms does even more. It stands before the judgment seat of God and asks the Lord not only for mercy, but also moves Him to pronounce a merciful judgment."

See, then, O Christian, alms "loosens from sin;" "extinguishes sin;" it appeases God's wrath before the sinner, "it moves Him to pronounce a merciful judgment over the sinner!"

Well, then, a little gift, a small part of your earthly goods, a little something from that which your deceased friends have left you—give it to a needy person and say: "O merciful God, I offer Thee this gift of charity in the person of this poor man. Be merciful to those souls that are separated from You and are still suffering in purgatory. Remit their sins and deliver them from their sufferings. Thou hast said, 'Give, and it shall be given to you.' See, O Lord! I give to this poor person; I give to Thee. Give me for it, I pray you, that soul on whose behalf I offer You this gift, the soul of my father, of my mother, the soul of my brother and sister, and receive it into Your eternal peace!"

Let us, then, my dear Christians, in this manner come to the rescue of those poor souls. Are they not our parents, our brothers, our sisters, our relatives and friends who are perhaps still suffering beyond? They are our parents, our relations; our father to whom we owe our existence; our mother who has borne us under her heart; our brother, our sister, who loved us so dearly; our friends who were so dear to our hearts. Oh! do not let us be hard against our own flesh and blood. Do not let us forget them who call to us every day: "Have pity on us, have pity on us, at least you our friends."

Let us pray for them every day; let us go to the altar for them and receive the most holy sacrament; let us give alms to the poor for them, so that God in His mercy may soon receive them into His eternal peace and heavenly joys. Amen!

FEAST OF THE IMMACULATE CONCEPTION

SANCTIFYING GRACE, THE MOST PRECIOUS GIFT

"Ave, gratia plena."
"Hail, full of grace."
Luke i. 28.

THESE WORDS, with which the Angel saluted Mary, the tender Virgin, in the little room at Nazareth, might have been applied to her before she saw the light of this world. Whilst all other men, in consequence of their descent from Adam and Eve, are stained with original sin, Mary was, from the first moment of her existence, by a special favor of God and the merits of His divine Son, free from original sin, and so adorned with sanctifying grace, which preserved her from sin, that not for one moment of her life was she deprived of sanctifying grace. For this reason the Angel salutes her with the words: "Thou art full of grace." And from this salutation of the Angel's, the holy Fathers conclude that Mary was conceived and born without sin. The sanctifying grace, with which Mary was conceived and born, always increased during her blessed life, and therefore she was "full of grace."

According to the opinion of St. Augustine, the Mother of God was more blessed because she bore the Son of God in her heart, than that she bore Him in her womb; that is to say, more blessed through sanctifying grace, than through the divine Motherhood. What a precious gift from heaven, then, must sanctifying grace be! We have become partakers thereof in holy Baptism, and when we have lost it by a grievous sin, we have obtained it again, by worthily receiving the Sacrament of Penance. Oh! if we only knew how to prize this grace of God; for it is more precious than all that the world offers. It is:

   I. *Our true dignity.*
  II. *Our true wealth.*
 III. *Our true happiness, here, and hereafter.*

Holy Mary, full of grace, stand by us, in today's contemplation, so that we may, for the future, after your example, guard carefully and increase the precious treasure of sanctifying grace, so that we may live and die in the grace of God.

I. Sanctifying grace raises man to the highest dignity, namely, the dignity of a child of God. We became children of God in holy Baptism. When we came into this world we were laden with original sin, and therefore, as the apostle says, "Were by nature the children of wrath" (Eph. ii. 3), objects of God's displeasure. Through holy Baptism, that bath of regeneration, we were cleansed from original sin and adorned with sanctifying grace, and through this grace we became an object of the Divine good pleasure, children of God. As at the Baptism of Jesus, so at the Baptism of a child, the heavenly Father speaks from heaven: "This is my beloved Son, in whom I am well pleased" (Matt. iii. 17). And here the beloved disciple cries out in admiration: "Behold what manner of charity the Father hath bestowed upon us, that we should be called and should be the sons of God" (1 John iii. 1).

Dear Christians! to be a friend of God is truly a great happiness, a great honor. Now, was it not a great honor for Abraham that God spoke to him, as friend to friend? But the honor of a child of God is still greater, for the child belongs to the family and is an heir. And does not the world consider it glorious to belong to a royal family, to be the child of a king, or possibly the heir to the throne? And yet, what is this dignity in comparison with the dignity of a child of God, the King of Kings, and the heir to the Kingdom of Heaven! By this dignity the Christian enters into the family of God, and so into the most intimate fellowship with God (John xvii. 21). And to this high dignity even the beggar is raised through sanctifying grace. If he possesses this, he is a child of God, a son of the Almighty King. Oh! that Christians would think of their high dignity, to which they are raised by Baptism, or if they have lost it, to which they are restored through the Sacrament of Penance. A wise king gave his son this advice: "Wherever you may be, always remember that you are a King's son and behave befitting this dignity." Yes, dear Christian, you too remember that you are a child of God, and bear yourself according to this dignity; avoid everything which is low and mean, avoid conversations and actions which dishonor and offend God, and which are unbecoming a child of God. Be contented with your state, do not envy others, who, are placed higher than you are; remember that earthly greatness and grandeur are vain and transitory. For what brings man respect and dignity? Virtue, according to the words of Holy Scripture: "Oh, how beautiful is the chaste generation with glory! For the memory thereof is immortal; because it is known both with God and with men" (Wis. iv. 1). Sin on the other hand causes disgrace and shame. Therefore this prayer is recommended to all, but especially to Christian young women: "Preserve us from sin and shame." What gives man real greatness? A self-sacrificing love for God and our neighbor. For this reason we honor a St. Martin, a St. Vincent de Paul, and so many others. What gives an undying fame? Briefly: holiness of life, the fruit of grace. Mary was unimportant in the eyes of the world, and in her own eyes, a lowly maiden; but great Was her holiness before God, and in her unto this day are these words fulfilled: "Behold, from henceforth all generations shall call me blessed" (Luke i. 48).

II. As sanctifying grace makes us truly great, so it makes us truly rich. In the Apocalypse (iii. 17) it says: "Because thou sayest: I am rich, and made wealthy, and have need of nothing; and knowest not, that thou art wretched, and miserable, and poor, and blind, and naked." Many in this world are rich, like the rich glutton, but poor before God. Many are poor in this world, like poor Lazarus, but rich before God. For he who has not sanctifying grace is poor, but he who has it is rich before God, rich in real treasures, truly rich.

What the old law says of wisdom is true in the new law of sanctifying grace. "Now all good things came to me together with her, and innumerable riches through her hands" (Wis. vii. 11). Yes, with sanctifying grace come all the other graces. For by sanctifying grace, which is the life of the soul, we are living members of that body, of which Christ is the head. By it we partake of the merits of Jesus Christ and His Saints, partake in all the treasures of grace which Jesus Christ has left to His Church, so that we can say with the Psalmist: "I am a partaker with all them that fear thee, and that keep thy commandments" (Ps. cxviii. 63). We partake in all the prayers and good works of the Saints and the just, because we stand with them in a living communion, which is called the Communion of Saints. Through sanctifying grace we shall be like a good tree, which yieldeth good fruit (Matt. vii. 17), so that the least good action, the cup of cold water, given in the name of Jesus, will bring us a heavenly reward (Mark ix. 40). On the other hand, he who has not sanctifying grace can do nothing meritorious for heaven, not even if he made the greatest sacrifice (I. Cor. xiii. 3.) Therefore, sanctifying grace is a rich source of heavenly treasures, in comparison with which all earthly treasures are to be considered as naught. "What do you possess," cries out St. Augustine, "if you do not possess the only good, which is God?" The possessions of this world cannot satisfy the heart of man, because it is created for God, and therefore can only find rest in God, as the same Saint says: "Thou hast created us for Thyself, O God, and our heart is uneasy until it rests in Thee."

Mary, who was adorned from the first moment of her conception with sanctifying grace, not only carefully preserved it, but by a holy life co-operated with it faithfully, and every moment of her life increased this sanctifying grace, so that she was filled with grace, and also overflowing with merits for heaven; yes, she was not only the fullest in grace, but also the richest in heavenly treasures. We can apply to her the praise of Holy Scripture: "Many daughters have gathered together riches; thou hast surpassed them all" (Prov. xxxi. 29). Let us follow Mary's example. Let us preserve sanctifying grace, as the most precious treasure; let us take care not to commit grievous sin. And should we fall into grievous sin, let us not delay to purify our hearts therefrom in the Sacrament of Penance. And as Solomon prayed for one thing, namely, wisdom, with which all good came to him at the same time, let us pray to God and Mary for one thing, sanctifying grace, with which comes all good.

Our true happiness, in time, as well as in eternity, consists in sanctifying grace. "For wisdom will not enter into a malicious soul, nor dwell in a body subject to sins" (Wis. i. 4). Even so, sanctifying grace, and with it the Holy Ghost, cannot enter and dwell in a soul which is not at least free from grievous sin. Where sanctifying grace is, there is also a good conscience. "For the Spirit himself giveth testimony to our spirit, that we are the sons of God" (Rom. viii. 16). Where sanctifying grace is, there is in addition the hope of eternal life, for the Apostle says: "And if sons, heirs also; heirs indeed of God, and joint heirs with Christ; yet so if ye suffer with Him, that we may be also glorified with Him" (Rom. viii. 17). And this hope fills us with consolation in suffering, as often as we say with the Apostle: "For I reckon that the sufferings of this time are not worthy to be compared with the glory to come, that shall be revealed in us" (Rom. viii. 18).

Yes, sanctifying grace is the surest pledge of eternal life itself; for, if we die in it, we are sure of heaven, and we shall be eternally happy. The world cannot make us happy in time and eternity, only holy religion and sanctifying grace, and all those who claim they make the world happy without religion are false prophets.

How sanctifying grace, joined to the testimony of the conscience, brings consolation, we see in Mary, who, being full of grace, was also full of consolation in the greatest and bitterest sufferings. On the other hand, man, even when the world offers him so many charming pleasures, has no real happiness, if he fails to have sanctifying grace, the testimony of a good conscience. For "there is no peace to the wicked, saith the Lord" (Is. xlviii. 22). And if the wicked have no peace, neither have they consolation in life or death; they are therefore unhappy for time and eternity. It is then sanctifying grace which makes us great before God, truly rich in God, and eternally happy with God. Indeed, he who has found it, has found a precious treasure, more precious than all the treasures of the world, which cannot make us really happy. And we lose this precious treasure by grievous sin. Oh, how foolishly the sinner behaves, who for a vain honor, for a miserable desire, sells this precious gift, his kinship of God, his heirship to heaven, his soul and his blessedness!

Let us then avoid sin, and pray to Mary, the Immaculate Mother of God, for a pure heart. "Ave Maria, gratia plena!" Holy Mary, as you were full of grace on earth, so you are in heaven full of glory, as Queen of Heaven. But you are still full of grace for us poor pilgrims of earth. For thou art, as the Holy Father tells us, the treasurer of heavenly grace. Through thy hands graces are dispensed, which thy divine Son has merited. Thy hands are filled, as thou didst once appear to a Saint with shining jewels, the heavenly treasures of grace. Oh, stretch forth thy merciful hand, enrich and bless us, Mary! and keep us in the state of grace. Pray for us, Mary! Amen.

THE NATIVITY OF OUR LORD

GOD WITH US

"And his name shall be called Emmanuel."
Is. vii. 14.

BELOVED BRETHREN, assembled in the name of Jesus Christ: On the plains of Bethlehem, the angels of heaven brought to the shepherds and to us a wonderful message of joy. "Behold, I bring you good tidings of great joy, that shall be to all the people : For this day is born to you a Saviour, who is Christ the Lord, in the city of David" (Luke ii. 10, 11). Since the world was made no such message of joy had ever been brought to men. Men bring one another messages of joy. How many joyful sounds have already been heard upon earth, how many days of happiness are arranged, how many joyful messages are brought; but the sounds of joy are carried away on the air, to leave behind only slight remembrances, like faint lights; joyful days pass away, and days of visitation follow days of blessing, and joyful chimes are often changed to chimes of mourning. How often is the joy of one the sorrow of the other! How often does it happen that what to one is a cause of jubilation to another is an occasion for tears! And even if the curse of inconstancy and the reverse of earthly happiness did not sadden man's joyful message, it would still be incapable of making the heart of man happy in its deepest depths; it does not send its rays right down to the bottom of the heart; it is hardly able to gild the walls of our soul with its feeble, caressing light. But the angels' message on the plains of Bethlehem was of quite another kind; it did not come from the palaces of earthly kings, or from the halls of pleasure, or from the markets of the earth; it came from heaven, bringing with it heavenly flowers, heavenly blessings, and heavenly graces. The angels, messengers from the choirs of blessed light, bring it on lips overflowing with jubilation; pure and undefiled, without shadow of deception and sorrow, rings out the jubilee down upon the earth, laden with sin, and it reaches into our innermost hearts. It is announced, not to one or the other, but to the beggar and the king, the child and the old man, the poor and the rich. The angels announced to the shepherds that it should be made known to all people, in the east and the west, in the north and the south; it shall ring forth and make joyful through all the ages; it shall never cease, not even when the world shall keep its vigil, and the book of humanity will be closed, and then it will ring on in eternity: a Saviour is born to you, who is Christ the Lord. Oh, who can depict the joy of a Christmas festival! Over our altars floats the joy of this joyful message, from the plains of Bethlehem it sinks into our hearts and breathes consolation and hope into our souls. The Saviour is born for us, a Saviour who will deliver us from sin, and from the thraldom of Satan, who reconciles us to God and opens heaven unto us. What this Saviour is His name tells us, that the prophet Isaias announced: "Behold, a virgin shall conceive and bear a son, and His name shall be called Emmanuel, God with us." Yes, God with us, that is the meaning of the joyful message of the angel: God with us:

I. In His humanity.
II. In His childhood.
III. In His poverty.

This is what we will contemplate, dearly beloved; His name shall be called Emmanuel, God with us.

I.—God with us in His humanity. The angels announced that the Saviour was born, who is Christ the Lord. That is to say, that the second Person of the Trinity had taken a human nature, a human body, and a human soul, the same as we have. He has become one of us. He is like us in all things, with the exception of sin, says the Apostle. That is the first step of the mercy of God, which we devoutly adore, in the crib at Bethlehem.

Sin separated man from God; between man and God there yawned a deep chasm, which man was not capable of bridging over. The Lord God had already given the world proofs of His mercy, before the Incarnation of His Son, but it was on account of the coming Messiah. Without it there was only before us the avenging justice of an angry God, who punishes the sins of the father from generation to generation. Full of longing, the fathers of past ages looked for the day in which the Lord God would pour out the greatness of His compassion upon the sinful fallen generation.

Most beautifully does the prophet Isaias console mankind in their languishing misery: "Say to the faint-hearted: Take courage, and fear not: behold, your God will bring the revenge of recompense: God Himself will come and will save you" (Is. xxxv. 4). God Himself! Who can measure the greatness of this compassion? A prince is certainly merciful if he sends a messenger with gifts to the poor in their forsaken garret. This is what God could have done. He could have sent us a Moses to break the chains of our slavery. He could have sent us a prophet Jonas to preach penance to us. He could have let Elias appear to us again, to bring the word of God like a burning torch. That would have been great mercy, but God wanted to do more than this. The Apostle Paul describes it in these words: "God, who at sundry times and in divers manners, spoke in times past to the fathers by the prophets, last of all, in these days, hath spoken to us by His Son, whom He hath appointed Heir of all things, by whom also He made the world" (Heb. i. I, 2). Now every human heart takes part in the jubilation of Elizabeth, at the visit of the Blessed Virgin: "And whence is this to me, that the mother of my Lord should come to me?" (Luke i. 43). God comes Himself. If a prophet or an angel had come, man's longing for God, for a more intimate communication with God, would not have been satisfied. In every human heart there exists this question, which the psalmist expresses in these words: "Ubi est Deus?" "Where is God?"

Where is my God? says the child at its mother's knee! Where is my God? says the youth, in his striving after happiness. So says the old man, when he is dying. The Apostle St. Paul says that in the times before Christ the people went *quaerere Deum si forte attrectent eum*, looking for God in the valleys, on the summits of the mountains, on the banks of the rivers, and in the depths of the forests, erecting altars, to bring God down to them. All this longing of the people, all this desire of the human heart, was fulfilled in the crib at Bethlehem. God Himself comes.

How will He come? In His majesty? In the brightness of His divine glory? Then we men would not be capable of bearing His look and His presence. Will He come, perhaps, as in a cloud over the ark of the covenant in the temple at Jerusalem? This would not be sufficient for the mercy of God. He wished to be more to us! Will He perhaps come in the semblance of a body amongst us men, as some heretics have supposed? No, God Himself comes, after having taken a real human body and a human soul. So far as His mercy led Him so far has He made Himself like unto nothing. The Apostle describes it with these words: "*Qui cum in forma Dei esset exinanivit semetipsum formam servi accipiens, in similitudinem hominum factus et habitu inventus ut homo.*" "Who being in the form of God, thought it not robbery to be equal with God: but emptied Himself, taking the form of a servant, being made in the likeness of men, and in habit found as a man" (Phil, ii. 6, 7). God Himself comes; He becomes man like one of us. Who can comprehend the greatness of the mercy of God in His abasement? Let the eagle become a worm, and at the same time preserve his eagle nature, you give him the greatest torture, because he can no longer move his wings. Give the lion, with his lion nature, the form of a snail, and he would roar with pain. What a fetter is our body for our soul! But it bears no comparison to the abasement which God laid upon Himself when He took a human body and abased Himself like unto a man. Why this abasement? Because the Son of God wished to come as near to us men as possible. God with us, one of us. There flows from the Incarnate Son of God the blessings of divinity upon all men, the members of the same family, members of the mystical body of Christ. As if the sun sank into a drop of water in the ocean, and through this drop would light up all the other drops in the ocean. As if noble graft was engrafted upon the wild olive tree, all the branches and twigs would partake of the strength of this graft, says St. Augustine, so have we men, since the Incarnation of Jesus Christ, a part in His glory, in His graces, and His merits. God with us, *descendit, ut levaret* (Augustinus). He abased Himself to exalt us. The blessing begins already in the crib. Now the condition of the poor and the sick bed of the sick become meritorious in Christ our Saviour. Now, every tear which is shed by faith, and through contemplating Him, with these is God well pleased. God with us, now is freedom brought to men, for God is a God of freedom. The chains are loosened with which the slaves were fettered. The lowly and the poor have the rights of man restored to them. After the Son of God becoming a brother to the lowliest amongst men, the dignity and equality of man is given by Christ to the world. God with us. What the Incarnate Son of God suffered, the atonement made by Him to the Heavenly Father, is the portion of every man; He is the Redeemer of all. God with us, the Incarnate Son of God, understands the hard lot of man. He prepared Himself a chalice of sufferings to make satisfaction for us. Everything which belongs to us men serves Him for the performance of this work of mercy. The crib, the thorns, the scourge and the spear, are in His hands the tools of our redemption. God with us, then will the Incarnate Son of God go the way of His conquest over this curse-laden earth. In Him the mercy of God travels the way from Galilee to Judea, healing the sick, raising the dead to life, commanding the winds, stilling the waves of the sea, seeking the sinner, like the shepherd going after his lost sheep, and finally taking away the sting from death. God with us, the Incarnate Son of God, will live a life of mercy towards all men, until the day of judgment. In Him and with His incarnate hands the mercy of God flows on the waters, so as to prepare this water as a bath of regeneration for my child in holy baptism. It extends to the olive tree, to prepare from its fruit the holy oil for the Sacrament of Extreme Unction for the sick and for the anointing of the priests. It takes hold of the breath of the priestly mouth, to say to the sinner, bending under the weight of his sins: Go in peace, thy sins are forgiven thee. God with us. The mercy of God will, in His Incarnate Son, pass over the vineyards of this earth, and come into our fields of wheat, to lay hold of the bread and wine, and in their form, by the mystery of transubstantiation, from His body and His blood, to give us food and drink for our souls, so that His mercy may have its triumphant fulfillment, because by Holy Communion we are in Him, and He is in us, God with us; He will also live upon our altars and dwell in the midst of our hearts. His name shall be called Emmanuel: God with us.

II.—God with us in His childhood. The Son of God took another merciful step when He appeared upon earth as a child. The angels announced to the shepherds: You will find an infant. Without doubt, the Son of God might have appeared upon earth as a grown man. But He did not do this. He abased Himself, and lay in the crib as a helpless infant. The heathens have represented Jupiter with lightning in his eyes, falcons at his feet, flaming swords in his hands; no hand free to bless. Our divine Saviour wished to appear very differently. Not a threatening, mighty figure; not armed with lightning. No, He appeared as a child full of love, full of tenderness, full of joy. The child looks at every one; at sight of the child, all fear vanishes. All may approach a child without fear, the high and the low, the learned and the unlearned, rich and poor. How near has God come unto us! When Moses descended from the mountain the majesty of God shone from his countenance, and the mountains shook with thunder and lightning; they smoked and flamed; then the people begged in their fright: "Speak thou to us and we will hear; let not the Lord speak to us, lest we die" (Ex. xx. 19). The prophet Daniel says of the appearance of God: I was afraid and fell down upon my face. St. John says: I saw thy countenance, O God, and fell down at Thy feet as one dead. God has not approached us in such state. *Parvulus natus est nobis*, says the prophet Isaias (ix. 6); a child is born to us. Now we can go to the throne of

His mercy with confidence. At the crib all fear vanishes, the greatest criminal draws near to the child with assurance and confidence. What opens more easily than the hands of a little child? God with us in the form of a child leads us men to God and lets us find mercy. Of a truth, He has given Himself to us in weakness and lowliness. His triumph is a triumph of love, for He, the merciful God, became a child. What is weaker than an infant? Had the Son of God come with the power of this world, to conquer the world, then, perhaps, His victory would have been reckoned amongst the triumphs of earthly lords; He comes as an infant, without the pomp of this world, to vanquish the world. He comes without human help to besiege the hearts of men. What is nothingness in the world He has chosen, so as to put to shame that which is powerful. This infant, so helpless in the crib, holds the world in His arms; by this infant, the Son of God, everything was made that has been made; in Him is life, and the life is the light of mankind. He is the life that animates the Church; in Him is the strength of the martyrs, with which they shed their blood for love of Him; in Him is the virtue of every saint. He works through the priestly office; in Him is the strength, which makes the chief shepherd a rock on which the everlasting Church is founded. What a wonderful triumph Emmanuel celebrates; God with us, in the weakness of an infant, over all obstacles in the world. If I am weak, then am I strong. God with us in the form of a child; what is more humble than a child? The Son of God preaches to us in His infancy from the crib. Unless you become as little children you cannot enter into the kingdom of heaven. The child is not worldly and sensual. The child is unselfish, is humble, and pure of heart. O, when we come to the crib, let us bring our Saviour a childlike, repentant heart, and pray to Him that we may be as little children; that we, as children, may walk in the purity of our hearts, that we may be humble before God and men. There is a beautiful legend which says that a boy encountered the Mother of God in the flight into Egypt and begged for the favor of carrying the Divine Child in his arms. The mother of God accorded him this privilege. When the boy came to a stream and looked into the water and saw his face he noticed that the features of the divine Child were imprinted upon his own. We also will pray the divine Child, that He may imprint the spiritual features of His childish innocence and humility upon our souls, so that we may become as children. How beautiful it is to say of a Christian man: Before the world a man; before God, a child; in the eyes of the world, a man; in the constancy of his opinions and of his faith, a child. A child in his love of prayer, for the child prays; in its love of humility, for the child is humble; in its love of purity, for the child shuns what is impure. Emmanuel, God with us, in His childhood He draws our hearts towards Him, vanquishes the world, and teaches us how to become as children, that we may obtain the kingdom of heaven.

Emmanuel, God with us in His poverty. Out of love for us the Son of God has taken a step further in his mercy. He took unto Himself our human nature. He was born amongst us as a little child, and He appeared amongst us in poverty. The angels announced to the shepherds: You shall find the infant wrapped in swaddling clothes, and laid in a manger. Stable, crib, swaddling clothes, represent the greatest poverty, the poverty of dwelling, the poverty of the way of living. The kings and emperors of this world are born in palaces; heathendom had built for the unknown God whom it sought a temple in all the glory of the world, because it could not make to itself any other idea of God than that He would appear in earthly splendor. The Son of God appears upon earth, and rejects all earthly possessions, all wealth, for He needed them not, as Tertullian says: Had He so desired it, He could have made Himself a house on earth in which splendor and wealth dwell, *gloria et divitiae in domo ejus*. Why did He choose poverty? Undoubtedly He is nearer to us in poverty, more God with us than if He had appeared in wealth. To us poverty is our very existence. How poor and helpless is even the rich man; if he had the disposition of his health, his fate, and his life, he would be perplexed. How poor is the king when he is visited with pain; he may have to go begging for a word of consolation, and a sympathetic heart, and how much poverty is there in the lives of the majority of men. How poor is work, which is the lot of man. Therefore, the Saviour wanted to be nearer to the poor man; that is why He appeared upon this earth in the utmost poverty. When Cyrus had vanquished the Persians by the sword he possessed dominion over them, but when he wished to win the hearts of the Persians he clothed himself as a Persian. That is how our Saviour wished to win our hearts. Therefore, He took upon Himself our weakness, our lowliness, our poverty, so as to approach us as nearly as possible as a poor child. Emmanuel, God with us. Now all hearts feel drawn towards Him, especially those of the poor. The poor have a special right to the love and the association of the incarnate Son of God. Blessed are the poor in spirit, for theirs is the kingdom of heaven; that is the great sermon which our Saviour preached in the poor stable, which He announced from the poor crib. No mother can provide a poorer bed for her child than that provided for the Son of God upon earth in the crib. Now, through Him, the Son of God, poverty is no longer despicable, no longer shameful, no longer mean; through Him is poverty ennobled, exalted, and sanctified. Blessed are the poor in spirit; a rich stream of peace flows from the Saviour's crib into the hearts of the poor of this world. There the poor, kneeling before the crib, are contented with their poverty. The heathen philosophers could not unravel the mysteries of poverty and suffering. The wisdom of this world cannot attempt to make the cross of poverty light, no statecraft of the earth, with all its theories of making the people happy, can draw the thorn of bitterness out of the hearts of the poor. There is only one thing that can content the poor in their poverty: it is Christ, the Saviour, born poor into this world. Since He wandered poor upon this earth, Christendom has contented poor, as Lazarus was contented outside the rich man's palace. Since then Christendom has generous poor, like the poor widow who dropped a penny into the alms box in the temple. Since then Christendom has patient poor, as the poor thief upon the Cross was patient in his sufferings. Blessed are the poor in spirit. How near the poor are to the divine Child Jesus! St. Francis, inspired with the poverty of the divine Infant, chose poverty as his bride, and, as his queen, begged from God for poverty as the partner of his life, and sung its most beautiful praises. O, you, who are poor on this earth, come to the crib of the divine Saviour. He will console you, make you happy, give you peace, so that you may be blessed in your poverty. Blessed are the poor in spirit, that, as St. Bernard says, preaches the stable, that calls to us the crib, that announces as Gospel the tears of the divine Infant. It is enough for all; we learn from the poor child Jesus that it is a delusion of the world that possessions can make us happy; that money can give us liberty, that wealth can redeem us. Let us tear away our hearts from all inordinate attachment to earthly goods, let us use the goods of this world as steps to bring us nearer heaven, by performing works of charity. Let us, by a spiritual renouncement of all inordinate attachment to money and possessions, by overcoming all immoderate desires for wealth, make our heart into a crib, so that we may have a dwelling that we can offer to the divine Saviour, as he seeks and desires a dwelling of poverty, so that He may return into our hearts, He, who is in the most perfect manner our Emmanuel, our God with us, and in us. In this way, if we humble ourselves, will our divine Saviour take possession of us. Then will the angels sing in our hearts, as they did on the plains of Bethlehem, that message of joy and peace to men of good will upon earth.

His name shall be called Emmanuel, God with us, with us in His humanity, in His childhood, in His poverty. To the Blessed Suso was shown the Christ Child on Christmas night, lying on thorns, and he was told that he who wished to have the Christ Child for his own must take him out of the thorns. And we will take the divine Infant out of the thorns of His abasement, out of the thorns of His childlike humility, out of the thorns of His poverty. Then we will beseech Him to renew and strengthen in us the spirit of self-renunciation, the simplicity of our hearts, the love of poverty, so that the divine Infant will make us His own, and be and remain with us through all eternity, our Emmanuel, God with us. Amen!

NEW YEAR'S EVE

"And none of you asketh me: Whither goest thou?"
St. John xvi. 5.

AN OLD Christian proverb says, beautifully and truthfully, "Begin with God and end with God, and yours will be the happiest life." Every one who has honestly striven to verify this has had a thousand opportunities to experience the truth of this pious proverb.

I congratulate you, my dear friends, who have deemed it your sacred duty to begin every day with God. How serenely and with what satisfaction may you not look back upon the course of your life. And those of you also, my friends, I greet with joy, who began this year with God, and are now come here to end it with Him, who not only look up to the Almighty with grateful eyes, but also with a contrite heart, and who are convinced of the truth, that all is vanity except to love God and to serve Him, that we may live for ever more. All of us, my friends, who are gathered together at this holy hour, within these hallowed walls, carry within our souls the firm determination to close the year 1900 with God.

The end of a year is, and always will be, a solemn moment. The departure of a year is fraught with serious admonition. We take leave of father and mother, but in the hope of seeing them again; we leave a place to which we have become attached, which is endeared to us, and connected with indelible memories, but with the hope of one day returning to it; but the year, when it has passed away, is gone forever, and what it has taken away will never more return to us — those three hundred and sixty-five days of our existence have gone forever!

Now, let us look back, my friends, upon the year just ended. Can we look upon it with joyful hearts and a peaceful conscience; and can we welcome the coming year with hearts nerved with courage and without dread of the future? Aye, but there is a strange pang in our soul, full of anxious foreboding and secret dread. The battle of human minds for truth and for falsehood is growing fiercer from hour to hour, and the foundation of human society is trembling and threatens to collapse. And in many a poor human heart there is a private sorrow, and in many a house the light of hope is gone out.

Very well, then, let us ask at this solemn hour, in this sacred place, where we stand in the real presence of Him in the most Holy Sacrament, and try to find out, "Why and how is all this happening so?" And after we have asked this question from the bottom of our hearts and with honest sincerity, then we will try and solve the problem of "What is to be done" to enable us to begin the new year with hope and confidence?

Now join with me in devout prayer. "I will continue, O Lord, in Thy most Holy name, O Lord of all times, Thou wonderful ruler of the fate of men and nations! O Lord Jesus Christ, Blessed through all eternity!"

Jesus Christ, the Son of God, our Saviour and our Redeemer, once addressed His disciples in these significant words: "But now I go to Him that sent me, and none of you asketh me: Whither goest Thou?"

We know whom Jesus meant; His Father by Whom He was sent upon this earth to redeem and to save mankind. Yea, His Father, whose image He was, for doth He not say, "He that seeth me, seeth the Father also"? And to Him He returned after accomplishing His work. "I go to Him that sent me."

We also go to our Father when our mission is fulfilled, and our task on this earth is finished. "We will come to Him, and make our abode with Him," saith Jesus. We also are created to the image and likeness of God, for did not God Himself say, when he created Adam, "Let us make man to our image and likeness"?

And when this temporal habitation, our body, breaks down and returns to the dust from which it came, that image, that likeness, our immortal soul, will also return from whence it came, will return to eternity—to God the Father, and the Son, and the Holy Ghost!

But now, dear friends, to reach the goal that we are striving for, to be sure that we may return to the Father's house with joyful hearts as God's own children, we must above all know the way which will lead us there. The wayfarer who knows where the end of his journey lies will surely and carefully take the right path which will bring him happily to his destination.

It was 1900 years ago when the Word was made flesh and dwelt amongst us. "He, the only begotten of the Father, full of grace and truth" (St. John). "He who laid down His life for us, and offered Himself on the cross as a sacrifice of propitiation," one day said in distinct and solemn tones, "I am the way, and the truth, and the life. No man cometh to the Father but by me." Since then the way lies open before us, and no one can say truthfully, I know it not! let us at his moment raise our eyes to the realm above, and greet with holy reverence the millions of Saints who followed steadfastly and faithfully the way which the Redeemer had shown them. The way is not one of ease and comfort, it demands the entire sacrifice of a God-fearing heart; but it is the only way which leads to the Father, and those who followed it resolutely bedewed it with their tears, dyed it with their blood, and adorned it with the deeds of a living Christian faith. They alone found peace, and now shine in snowy garments with palms and crowns, like stars in heaven, and cry out to the Christian pilgrims the encouraging words, "Look up at us! regard us well! Behold! This is thy reward if thou followest Jesus." But thousands upon thousands leave this path and nobody asketh, "Whither goest thou?"

And herein, my dear friends, we find the first and the last reason for our moral degeneration, the reason for the dreadful errors into which human society plunges. For the wanderer, when once he has left the right path, will never be able to measure the mistakes into which he may be led, and he never knows how to avoid the misfortune which will meet him on the abyss that yawns at his very feet. As the liar is never at a loss to contradict truths with a new lie, nor to add to this another one, or ten others, if need be, even so has the original but ever watchful father of lies, the prince of this world since the days of Paradise, ever stood up, particularly against Christ and His Church. To accomplish his purpose he invented, about eighty years ago, a significant word of falsehood, full of meaning, which has since risen like a password from mouth to mouth. Its name is Progress.

A steadfast adherence to Christ and His Church, a faithful pursuance of the way we are taught, is what we call progress; but to them this is an old-fashioned and ridiculous thing, irreconcilable with the spirit of intelligence, and the exigencies of the spirit of the times, which can only be to the taste of ignorant poor people, or of men whose minds are steeped in monkish fanaticism and superstition.

Now, my dear people, give me your undivided attention. The subject is too serious and too important that we should not try to answer the question, "Whence comes this language which we hear everywhere, day in, day out, in high and low circles, in the houses of the rich, and the workshops of the poor, in mansions, and in huts, on the highways and byways? It certainly did not come to us over night, but it came to us, because millions are heeding the call of untruth and free thought, while nobody asketh "Whither goest thou?"

In the first place and above all it was the puffed up science of the philosophers, full of pride and devoid of faith, which opened up the way to hell. The authority of divine revelation has been set against modern philosophy in order to enkindle the flame of so- called enlightenment. After the foundation of positive Christianity had been undermined and the seed had been sown in the hearts of the young from the lecturer's platform, it was an easy matter to disturb even the historical foundation upon which rests a nation's fame and right.

They have made merry over the most sacred institutions, over the most revered customs and rites in Christian congregations and communities. They called them old-fashioned, and contrary to the spirit of modern progress; they were abolished—new institutions were created, new laws were made—but all without faith, without God, without Christ. For the word which God Himself put into the mouth of the royal psalmist, "Unless the Lord build the house, they labor in vain that build it. Unless the Lord keep the city, he watcheth in vain that keepeth it" (Psalm cxxvi.), this word of eternal truth has been long forgotten, has been scoffed at, and made a mockery of. And so, my dear friends, everything has become modern indeed—government, family life, education, matrimony—all has been modernized; in fact, all our thoughts and deeds have been changed in the progress of modernization. Need we, then, be surprised at what is happening before our very eyes? Is it not the fruit of that tree which falsehood has planted in the place of truth, and of whose fruit the children of the earth eat with such eagerness?

A horse which has thrown its rider and is running away, tries frantically to free itself of bridle and reins. Man, who wants to be free and untrammelled, tears asunder the last bond which holds him in check. Hence "Separation of State and Church," "Separation of School and Church," "Separation of Marriage and Church," separation of everything which stands in the way and might call to your mind the harassing question, "Whither goest thou?" O my dear Jesus, what hast Thou done to mankind that they put Thee aside with such ingratitude and such indifference? What hast thou done to human kind, my beloved Catholic Church, that they turn sullenly away from thee, and clamor for separation? Has not Christ saved the world? Has not Christianity destroyed the barbarity of paganism, spread culture and civilization over the world, sanctified matrimony and family life, taught us to know and practice all those virtues which bring peace to man, and blessings to nations? Is not the Church the continued visible Saviour and Redeemer of the world, since He said explicitly to His apostles: "As the Father hath sent me, so I send you"? Is not the Church the standard-bearer of the conceptions of right, obedience, and love? Does the Church not assure every man his right, does she not demand obedience in the name of God, and by virtue of divine authority, whose first and last command is love?

Let us look at this a little closer. If modern governments imagine that they can govern man solely by their laws, let them take into consideration how long these people, after divesting themselves of all respect for divine authority, will have any respect for human authority. What weight will the oath have which even the modern state uses as the only decisive medium in judicial proceedings; what value, I ask, will the oath have when it is shorn of its terrible consequences in eternity, when the civil government does not concern itself with the question whether man has faith or not? We have no expectation that modern progress will abolish poverty, or diminish the number of the poor; well then, tear out of the heart of the poor his living Christian faith, his belief in Him who was born a child of the poor, in the stable of Bethlehem, and lived all His life a poor man, so that we may learn to respect poverty and learn to suffer poverty with patience; subdue the Church of Christ which, in its chosen members, takes upon itself voluntary poverty, and bears it in humility before the world, and which has at the same time founded those innumerable benevolent institutions and associations for the relief of the sick, poor and the abandoned of this world, where we see them with touching devotion and heroic self- sacrifice soften the sufferings of the poor—yes, deprive the poor of their faith in their poor Jesus, take away from the Church her consoling and benevolent influence, and you will see, you rich and powerful of this world, how you will fare! The lust of the eyes and the lust of the flesh were at all time a source of moral ruin and great misery in this world. How sublime shines that ideal of chastity and virginity through the darkness of night! What a heavenly aroma arises from this sacred flower! Has not Christ taken His flesh from the ever Immaculate Virgin? Has He not Himself called holy virginity the highest gift of an elect soul? Is not the Church the abode and the champion of holy virginity, for, led by her hand, we see that land of saintly youths and maidens, before whom we stand with awe and reverence. Destroy the Church and you will destroy also this sacred ideal!

Then they want to withdraw the school from the influence of the Church; the school, they say, is an institution for instructing the young. But the school is by no means merely a place for instructing, but it is at the same time and pre-eminently the place for the education of the young. Our children take with them to school not only their intellects, but also their hearts and their souls, and the latter must receive quite as much attention as the former. Just as conscientious parents will not be indifferent as to how and by whom their children receive instruction, as regards their intellects, they should also take a great interest in seeing that the right light shall shine into their hearts and souls. And this light is religion. The child's heart is naturally turned towards God, and is grateful to those who will lead it there. Oh, how touching is the sight of a child at prayer, and how close it draws to those who are teaching it to pray. It is, therefore, not only wrong but also ungrateful to try to take away the children from those who are constantly holding before the little ones all that is divine, great, and holy, and who instruct them at the same time in all they need to know for the fulfillment of their duties as good citizens. "I am not a school master, and cannot judge between the different methods of teaching," said the old Duke of Wellington in the House of Lords in London, "but I wish most emphatically to give expression to my firm conviction, that if religion is not made the foundation of teaching it will be your fault if in future the number of clever rogues in the world is largely increased."

In a nation, or a state, or a family, or community, where religion is despised and allowed to perish, there the process of disintegration will invariably occur. It was in the year 1789 when this process was very evident in the State of France. After the holy Catholic faith had been derided and scoffed at for many years, in word and picture, in writings and plays, in public lectures and so-called clubs, and after unbelief and licentiousness had been given full sway, the French revolution broke out. All religion was considered a mortal crime. Priests were killed when they could not flee or hide themselves. Churches were robbed and desecrated; in some places the wickedness went even so far that a lewd woman was placed upon the altar, and mock ceremonies carried on before her as the goddess of reason. When the strong barriers, religion and conscience, which keep man from all wickedness, had been removed throughout the whole country, a new power, as it were, the raging of the devil, broke loose all over the land. Envy, hatred, and cupidity, in a degree as they had never been known to exist before, exercised their power with reckless disregard and wild fury. People were slaughtered by the thousands, by order of their own government, in most cases without their having committed any offence. It was enough to be suspected of an attachment for the murdered royal family, or for the old order of things, or for religion, to be condemned to death on the guillotine. My friends! the world is round and there is nothing new under the sun; it has never been possible to gather grapes from thorns, or figs from thistles. What a man sows, that will he reap. We, also, shall have the same experience, we shall have to suffer for what we ourselves or for what others have sown in fatal self conceit; with us also the same causes will produce like results, and the laws of nature and necessity, bearing the testimony of the history of 7,000 years, will be confirmed in the future as they have been in the past.

Let us then open our eyes; for it is high time that we awake from sleep. The enemy stands before us in full power, and it seems to me as if I could hear our Saviour repeat the words which he once spake in the garden of Gethsemani when he was taken prisoner: "This is your hour and the power of darkness."

We enter into a New Year; with its thousands of highways and byways, paths and roads, it lies before us. Oh! let each one ask himself in earnestness and sincerity today, at this holy hour,

Whither goest thou?

There is only one sure way that leads to the Father, and that is the way which Jesus and His representative on earth, the Church, teach us. Are we really still in the right path, or have we, also, already left it? Have we, perhaps, allowed them to lead us astray by that falsehood which has drawn so many from the right path, namely, that the war which progress has declared against darkness, as it is called, is not directed against Christianity and its Founder, but against the so-called Church?

Many a human heart is empty and desolate and icy cold, and in many a home the beacon of hope has gone out. Why, my dear friends? Let us be candid and do not let us put the blame too much on the world and on other people, but let us beat our own breasts and give a true and sincere answer to the question:

Whither goest thou?

For years you have lived happily with wife and child. The bread which you have had to earn, though by hard labor, you have eaten in the evening in blissful contentment in your family circle. But you have changed. You find too much constraint in your home, and your own are a burden to you. You are looking for distraction outside, and sullenly and with curses on your lips you go to your work. What has happened to cause this change? Be sincere! Have you not deserted your Master, and His way? Have you not fought shy of your Church and your prayers? Do you not pursue other ways now? Stop! Do not let the year glide into the sea of eternity without asking yourself honestly

Whither goest thou?

and tremble, for the end for you may lead to destruction.

And you, sons and daughters! Once you were good children and the joy of your parents! But it is otherwise now. Look! You are afraid of a glance from your father's eye, and you are cold towards your mother, and their teachings you call old-fashioned; in the faces of your parents there are lines of deep sorrow. And what has caused all this? Be sincere! You have left your Master and His way! You neglect your Church and your prayers, for you go quite another way. Bad books, which you know well how to procure; wanton speech, and loose principles in which you have indulged, have kindled the passions which were slumbering in your breast into a blazing flame.

Ah! Whither goest thou?

The New Year is coming, also, for you. Do not begin it in the same way. Return to the right path, which your parents have shown you and which you used to follow with a clean heart and peaceful conscience, so blithe and happy. Follow your Master and your Mother Holy Church.

God's forbearance offers you another year. Will you again be indifferent to this boundless love? Ah! lift up your eyes! Take the bandage from them. See, there is a cemetery, and they are digging a new grave. Perhaps they are digging it for you.

My dear friends! If we are to have peace and gladness in our hearts, in our families, yea, in the whole human society, there is only one sure way, since "the Word was made flesh, and dwelt among us," which leads to this happiness, to peace, and, finally, to the Father. It is the way about which, my dear people, I have preached to you today, and which I will name to you once more with all the strength of my soul. "The way which Thou, O Jesus, hast taught us and Thy Church." Let us, all together, enter upon this way with manly determination, let us raise our right hand for the solemn oath, that indeed we will do it in all sincerity. Upon this ground we will await thee, O New Year, and with courage look forward to all that God in His eternal wisdom may determine upon for us. Amen!

NEW YEAR'S DAY
THE CIRCUMCISION OF OUR LORD

THE TRANSITORY AND THE ETERNAL

"But Thou art always the self-same, and Thy years shall not fail."
Ps. ci. 28.

THERE ARE days and hours when man's views become broader and deeper, when he looks out over the narrow confines of this temporal life into eternity; there are days and hours when man is involuntarily urged, more than usually, to weigh himself and those belonging to him in the scales of eternity. New Year's day is a day of this kind. The New Year reminds us so vividly of the change and the instability of all earthly things, and of our own frailty; the New Year tells us that we have taken another long stride toward eternity; the New Year recalls to our mind these two words, so full of meaning, "Transitory," "Eternal." We will consider these two words today by answering the following two questions:

I. *What is transitory?*
II. *What is not transitory?*

I.—Nothing on this earth is permanent and lasting. There is perpetual coming and going, a continual appearing and disappearing. The life of an individual, as well as that of all mankind, is like the sea, where the waves rise up, to disappear in a short while, altogether; where it is one moment still, and the next stormy; it flows hither and thither, in ceaseless motion. Where are all the myriads of human beings since the time of Adam? They passed away, like shadows on the wall, their bodies to the earth, their souls into eternity Where are all the great and the glorious deeds which they once performed with their power and art? They have disappeared, fallen into decay, and if anything still remains, it is but ruins. Where are the mighty and rich, who made such a display of their power? Their names are still to be found in the pages of history, but they themselves have passed away.

And how uncertain is everything which man possesses? If you are wealthy, happy and well, do not rely upon this too much! For behold! riches, happiness, and health, are like a ball; it requires only the least touch to set the ball rolling, and then your wealth, your happiness and your health are gone. Some people prosper, and others, again, fail; we have a proof of this in the history of every family if you are honored and respected, do not on that account be proud! It can easily happen to you as it did to the Saviour, to whom one day they cried "Hosanna!" and another day "Crucify Him!" Honor, respect and man's favor are like a mirror of Crystal—the least breath, and the mirror is dimmed. And so it is with everything that man possesses; riches, happiness, health, honor, reputation—everything is perishable and subject to continual change, and it is the same with everything that man enjoys. After joy comes sorrow; the chimes of rejoicing are intermingled with the sounds of the death knell. How often can joy be compared to a rose; the leaves fall, and only the thorns remain; happiness departs, and what remains is very often sorrow and a bitter repentance. And if what we possess and enjoy is perishable, is it any different with ourselves? Are we not, all of us, on the way to the grave? Some go quicker, others slower, but each one is on his way to the grave. This is the great pilgrimage of nations, the path of man from the cradle to the grave. Everything, my dear brethren, is transitory—man, and what he has, and what he is. This transitoriness has, however, its consoling, as well as its thrilling aspect, inasmuch as not only do the agreeable and the good pass away, but also all unpleasantness and suffering. The year just departing brought to many people not joy alone, but a great deal of suffering, but with the good days, the bad days passed over, too; the trouble is overcome; tears which flowed have been dried again. And if, perhaps, some of us have to take our old troubles with us into the New Year, let that not discourage us; some day even the greatest sorrow will have an end, when the New Year of eternity dawns for us. Yes, dear Christians, in the beyond all tears will be wiped away, and our sorrow will be changed into joy. All sorrow? Is that true? Unfortunately not. For many people are so foolish as not to bear their troubles with patience and resignation to the will of God. These people make their troubles doubly heavy, and bear them in vain.

The greatest consolation for us is that amongst those things which are transitory, sin, which is the greatest of all evils, will pass away, too. We have indeed a Redeemer, who takes away the sins of the world; we have a Redeemer who has left in His Church the power to forgive sins. Only we must not forget that only the truly repented of, confessed and absolved sins pass away; the others are carried from one year to another by the unrepentant, and from time into eternity. And now, dearly beloved, the second question: What is it that does not perish?

II.—He does not pass away of whom the Psalmist says: "But Thou art always the self-same, and Thy years shall not fail." God does not perish; the Eternal, the Never-Ending, who alone is worthy of our love. It is He whom we must serve during the coming year. Though the years pass away, God remains always the same. He who has been the ruler of the past will be the guide of the future. His hand, which has enriched us with so many benefits in the past, will not be closed to us this year; His love, which He has lavished upon us in the past, He will not deprive us of in the future; His blessing, to which we owe the success of our undertakings, will still flow down upon us. Therefore, we ought to serve God in the coming year, and at all times, because, if all earthly things perish, God remains, who is our eternal reward.

God is Truth. Truth is as imperishable as God Himself. "I am the truth," says Christ. Human opinions change. All lying and deceit in this world are brought to naught, and all the knowledge of the learned disappears. "My words, however, will not pass away." Let this divine truth be our rule of conduct for the coming year, in all our actions; the divine truth which was deposited in His Holy Church by Jesus Christ; let it be our compass to guide the little ship of our life on the sea of the future. And as God is truthful, so let us be truthful; let us detest lies, deceit, and falsehood; let us be upright and honorable. How much quarreling and contention, how much suffering and bitterness, would men spare each other, if they were only upright, honorable and sincere toward one another! Let us, therefore, be truthful, like our Lord and Master; truth alone is durable. Imperishable, also, is the image of God, our souls. No, our souls will never die. Have we, in the years that are passed, known and considered this truth sufficiently? If we had, we should certainly have acted differently; we should have taken more and better care of our souls; we should not have dishonored our immortal souls by making them the servants of our perishable bodies of our sensual natures; we should then have asked ourselves this question of our Divine Saviour, by all our actions: "What doth it profit thee to gain the whole world if thereby thou sufferest the loss of thy own soul?"

If we, perhaps, have, up to the present, forgotten, more or less, the immortality of our souls, and have thereby neglected to care for them, today we will make this our rule of life for the coming year, and for all the future time: "Before performing any actions I will always ask myself, Will this be useful for, or will it injure my soul, my imperishable, immortal soul?" If we do this, dear Christians, our works will not perish, for then our works will be good; good works will last for all eternity. A great many are pleased when at the end of the year they can look back and see that by economy they have been able to take a step forward. Well it is certainly a good thing if our cash account on New Year's Eve shows an increase, and, we ought to take pleasure in this. Only, how few there are who ask themselves at the end of the year: "How do things stand with my account up in Heaven; have I during the past year laid up anything there at interest, or not? In other words: Have I done good works, and amassed a treasure in, and for, Heaven?" If, on New Year's Eve, you can answer this with a "Yes," then you may rejoice, because this treasure is worth more than all the gold and silver and bonds of the whole world. If your cash box here on earth is full to overflowing, what can you buy with it at your life's end? Six boards and a very small portion of land, a coffin, and a grave. Now, you would have obtained all this anyhow, even if you had not had a red cent in your cash box. This world's money has only value and worth as far as the grave; beyond the grave there is another standard; there only the good works which you have performed, and deposited in the treasury of Heaven, will have any value. Therefore we will utilize the time to lay by all the capital we can in heaven, which consists of good works, which are imperishable, and create for us a happy eternity.

My dear Christians! Let us begin this New Year with the serious thought of what is transitory and what is eternal. We will devote the coming year to that which is eternal; we will never again lose sight of that which is imperishable. Let our beginning, our aim and our end be God. May His will rule over us during the New Year! "Lord, not as I will, but as Thou wiliest!" With these words we will leave our future confidently in the hands of God. In this way the New Year will be rich in blessings for us; it will be a step on the ladder of Heaven toward God; and that it may be this is my most sincere New Year's wish for you all! Amen!

THE FEAST OF ST. PATRICK

THE GLORIOUS VIRTUES OF ST. PATRICK
(FROM "THE LIFE OF ST. PATRICK," BY THE VERY REV. DEAN KINANE.)

"God is wonderful in his saints."—Ps. lxvii. 36.

THE BEAUTY and adornment of a soul are its virtues, both theological and moral. As in the heavens, star excels star in brilliancy and beauty, so God from time to time raises up in His Church mighty saints, and places them, so to speak, aloft on a pinnacle, that the lustre of their sanctity and good works may shine upon His people in all ages. Such a saint was St. Patrick, the Apostle of Ireland. God gives grace and sanctity to His servants to fulfil the mission for which they are destined. The higher the missionary, the greater the work; in the same proportion is the abundance of grace granted. St. Patrick's mission was to convert a whole nation from paganism to the most exact observances of the Gospel; hence, all the graces of the Apostolate, in their full plenitude, were showered upon the soul of this glorious Apostle. Every virtue was his, yet some shone out more conspicuously than others. Of these I shall today point out only a few:

    I.—*His faith and confidence in God.*
    II.—*His eminent spirit of prayer; and*
    III.—*His spirit of penance.*

I.

(a) Faith is one of the three theological virtues, because it has God and His divine truths as its immediate object. Faith is the foundation of all religion, and our salvation. "Faith is the beginning of human salvation, the foundation and root of all justification, without which it is impossible to please God, and to come into the fellowship of His Son." (Council of Trent, Lesson VI, Chapter 8). This definition of the Council of Trent is based upon the inspired text which is so clear on this point. The Gospel says:

"Now this is eternal life; that they may know thee, the only true God, and Jesus Christ, whom thou has sent." (John XVII. 3) "Go ye into the whole world, and preach the Gospel to every creature. He that believeth and is baptized, shall be saved; but he that believeth not, shall be condemned. (Marx xvi 15) And St. Paul adds: "Without faith, it is impossible to please God. For he that cometh to God must believe that he is, and is a rewarder of them that seek him." (Hebrews, xi 6). And this is reasonable. How can a traveler reach his goal unless he know something about it? How, therefore, can the soul find God if it know nothing of God? Faith is most pleasing to the Almighty. By faith, proud man submits his intellect and will to God, and believes and adores what he can neither see nor understand. This, my brethren, is the definition of faith: "Faith," writes St. Paul, "is the substance of things to be hoped for, and the evidence of things that appear not." (Heb. xi:1) If I can see or understand a subject, then faith ceases, but submitting my understanding to the infallible authority of God, believing in His unerring word, in divine mysteries, which the human mind can not conceive, that is paying homage to God, and, therefore, pleasing to Him.

This holy faith, so essential for salvation, and so pleasing to God, is dearer to every Christian than life itself. When we look round the world and see countless millions living and dying in heresy, schism, and idolatry, we ought constantly thank Providence for being members of the Holy Catholic Church.

Now, that St. Patrick was a man of faith and lived in faith, I need not at length expound. Born of Christian parents, he drank in the faith with his mother's milk, and it was this faith that he practised throughout his life, and taught, and by which he was able to see the whole isle converted from idolatry to Christendom.

(b) Confidence in God is another of the prominent virtues in the life of St. Patrick. That those who trust and confide in God receive help, is plainly proven both in the Old and New Testaments. "Call upon me in the day of trouble; I will deliver thee." (Ps. xlix. 15.) "Turn to me, and I will turn to thee," saith the Lord of Hosts." (Zach. i. 3.) Christ Himself tells His Apostles: "Whatsoever you shall ask the Father in my name, that I will do: that the Father may be «glorified in the Son." (John xiv. 13.) "Amen, amen, I say to you, if you ask the Father anything in my name, he will give it to you. Hitherto you have not asked anything in my name. Ask, and you shall receive, that your joy may be full." (John xvi. 23.) These promises sank deeply into the soul of our Saint during his studies under the famous masters of the time, and became part, so to speak, of his daily life. Hence we find our Saint in all his great and holy works trusting, hoping, and obtaining all things from God alone. During the six years of his captivity, serving a cruel master, and watching his flock on the mountains of Antrim, the holy youth's confidence in God was unshaken When the voice told him to return to his own country, and that the ship was ready, and when he had traveled southward two hundred miles, and the captain refused to take him on board, saying: "By no means attempt to come to us!" our Saint never doubted God's providence. He soon got his reward, for the captain said to him: "Come, we receive thee in good faith."

When challenged by the pagan priests and magicians to a trial of strength in working prodigies, before kings, princes, and vast unbelieving multitudes, on the Hill of Tara, in Royal Meath; on the plain of adoration, in Cavan; on the capital of Connaught; in every other field of his apostolic labors, St. Patrick's faith and confidence in God rose equal to every occasion. The minister of God took up the challenge, and like the prophet of old, Moses, brought shame and confusion upon the magicians. The kings and priests, princes and bards, with the vast multitude, embraced the Gospel of Christ. You all know of the miracle he worked at Cullen, where he sent two of his disciples to restore to life the son of Elelius. Thus we could continue citing numberless examples of his great confidence in God.

II.

(a) This confidence was but a fruit of his prayer. Our Saint, perfectly acquainted with the necessary means of salvation, too well knew the efficacy of prayer—he understood the meaning of these words of Christ: "Without me you can do nothing." (John xv. 5.) He was aware of the fact that in the supernatural order we can not conceive a good thought, elicit a good act, nor advance one step toward salvation without the grace of God, which, again, is only obtained by prayer. Therefore, St. Paul says: "Not that we are sufficient to think anything of ourselves, as of ourselves, but our sufficiency is from God." (II. Cor. iii. 5.) "For it is God who worketh in you both to will and to accomplish his good will. (Phil, ii. 13.)

(b) He knew the power of prayer. By prayer we can obtain all things from God. God has pledged Himself, so to speak. He has promised to hear our prayers. "Call upon me in the day of trouble, and I will deliver thee." (Ps. xlix. 15.) "Ask, and it shall be given to you; knock, and it shall be opened to you. If you ask the Father anything in my name, he will give it to you." (Matt, and John.) Now, God can not deceive, nor like false man, break His word or promise. "God is not as man, that he change." This virtue of prayer, then, this key to the heart of Jesus, our Saint preeminently used. Our Saint's preparation for his mission, and his whole Apostolate, was a life of prayer, and the most intimate union and familiarity with God. We are told in his life, that during the six years of his captivity on the mountains of Antrim, cold, hungry, and half naked, three hundred times by day, and three hundred times by night, on bended knees, he adored God. Here, without a sacrifice or sacrament, our holy youth lived in intimate union with his Maker.

When refused, as said before, by the captain to sail with him, prayer obtained for him the privilege. To go into the details of St. Patrick's love and spirit of prayer, would be to recite his life; for his whole life was one of prayer. Already before leaving Ireland, our young Saint, by prayer, obtained a high state of perfection. But what must have been his perfection and the odor of his sanctity, after more than thirty years spent in the most famous schools and monasteries on the continent and under masters renowned throughout the Church for their learning and sanctity? Let us only say he was eminently fitted to be the Apostle of a pagan nation. Having got his mission from the Vicar of Christ, who alone has that authority from the Redeemer of the world, our Apostle, armed with the power of prayer alone, set out to evangelize the Irish nation, and with what success you all know. This man of God was marvelously favored with heavenly visions and revelations in prayer. Working of miracles was of almost daily occurrence with him. He gave sight to the blind, and speech to the dumb, cured all manner of diseases, and raised thirty-three persons from the dead in the name of the Holy Trinity.

III.

Now, in addition to his lively faith, his preeminent spirit of prayer, we find his awful austerities. He fully entered into the words of our Redeemer: "Unless you shall do penance, you shall all likewise perish" (Luke xiii. 3), or the other words: "If any man will come after me, let him deny himself, and take up his cross and follow me." (Matt. xvi. 24.) Continually the words of the Baptist were ringing in his ears: "Do penance: for the kingdom of heaven is at hand." (Matt. iii. 2.) He saw the example of the unspotted Lamb of God fasting forty days and forty nights. He knew that a St. Paul had said: "I chastise my body, and bring it into subjection, lest, perhaps, when I have preached to others, I myself should become a castaway." (I. Cor. ix. 27.) All this clearly proved to him that the virtue of penance is as essential for the salvation of the sinner as the waters of baptism for the newly-born babe; or, as an ancient Father writes: "Either penance, or hell's fire." Now, St. Patrick's whole life, from his captivity to the hour of his death, was one constant practice of the most heroic penance, self-denial, and awful austerities. On the snowy mountains of Antrim, day and night, he bore with patience and resignation to God's holy will, cold, hunger, and nakedness.

Here he began to chastise his body, to crucify his flesh, to rid it of vices and concupiscences.

At the famous monastery of Marmentier, founded by St. Martin of Tours, where our young Levite spent some years, he put away all earthly cares and pleasures, and resolved never more to eat meat. At Lerins, the most renowned school of the age for learning and piety, Patrick was the wonder of the masters and pupils for his rigid and austere life. We can not follow our Saint step by step, nor year by year. Carefully handed down tradition tells of the austerity of his life during his mission for the conversion of the Irish nation. Before attacking the great strongholds and centers of paganism, he spent days and nights in prayer and penance. Armed with the spirit of God, and confident of success, he assailed the enemy. Barrier after barrier fell at his touch, and with an easy rush he planted the cross over the ruins of idolatry. The day he spent among them, preaching and baptizing: the night communing with his God. The night he usually divided into three parts. During the first part, he recited one hundred Psalms, making at the same time two hundred genuflections; during the second part, he recited fifty Psalms, immersed in icy cold water, with his hands, his eyes, and heart, lifted up to God. Then he took some hours of repose with a rock or bare ground for his bed, a stone for his pillow, and a rough haircloth for his covering. On the mountain Croagh, ever revered by his people, our Apostle spent the forty days of Lent in prayer and penance. To some minds, profane, and inclined to indulge in a smile at great spiritual things of which they know nothing, all this may appear extraordinary, if not incredible. Yes, it is extraordinary, but quite credible. Remember the words of my text: "God is wonderful in his Saints," and nothing is more natural and in keeping with God's ways to men, than to expect and to find awful austerities, as well as singular miracles in the life of so great a Saint and Apostle as our glorious and beloved St. Patrick. Now, what conclusion are we to draw from all this? Let us praise, bless, and thank God for having so favored our illustrious Saint. Let us venerate St. Patrick for the noble virtues he practised by trying to imitate Him.

Above all, let us never waver in our holy faith, but, like our Saint, hold on to the teachings of Holy Mother Church, especially the Holy Trinity, the incarnation of Jesus Christ and His divinity; which, in our days, is so much assailed, though it is the most consoling article of Holy Faith.

Put all your trust in God; cast your troubles on His shoulders, and you will be relieved. "If God be for us, who is against us?" (Rom. viii. 3.)

"Come to me all you that labor and are heavily laden, and I will refresh you." Follow likewise in the footsteps of our Saint as regards the spirit of prayer and penance. I will not ask of you to practise it as preeminently as our Apostle did, but do not allow a day to pass without having lifted up your mind and heart to God in prayer. Attend the Holy Sacrifice of Mass at least on Sundays, and Holy Days of obligation; unite yourselves from time to time in the most intimate manner with your God in Holy Communion; bear patiently the trials of life, especially those of your state of life to which you have been called; perform the slight penances Holy Mother Church may enjoin upon you, thus imitating, at a distance, at least, our Saint, who, seeing your good will, will intercede for you at the throne of the Almighty, that you be not lost, but saved, for eternity, a blessing that I wish you all. Amen.

Rev. M. N. W., S.T.L.

THE FEAST OF THE ASCENSION

"Rejoice, and be exceedingly glad: because your reward is very great in heaven."
Matt. v. 12.

WITH THESE consoling words, dear brethren, Jesus Christ encourages His Apostles to undertake with fortitude the sufferings and persecutions which were before them. "Yes, my children," this loving Father says to them, "you will be the object of the contempt and hatred of the wicked; you will fall a victim to their rage; the people will hate you and bring you before the princes of the earth, so that you may be condemned to the most dreadful chastisements, to the most cruel and ignominious of deaths; but be not discouraged, rather rejoice, for a great recompense awaits you in heaven." O beautiful heaven, who would not love thee, for thou dost contain so many sublime things! In fact, dear brethren, is it not this thought which makes the Apostles untiring in their apostolical labors, unconquerable in the persecutions which they experience from their enemies?

Animated by the thought of this beautiful heaven, did not the martyrs stand before their executioners with a courage that surprised those tyrants? Was it not the sight of heaven that quenched the heat of the flames which were prepared to consume them, and that blunted the edge of the sword with which they were struck? O how happy they felt to sacrifice their lives, their possessions, for God, in the hope that they would enter into a better life, which shall never end! O blessed inhabitants of the heavenly city, how many tears have you shed, how many sufferings have you endured to obtain possession of your God? They cry out, from the height of their glorious thrones upon which they are seated, to us here below, "O how vastly God has rewarded us for the little good which we have done! Yes, we behold Him, this tender, loving Father; yes, w° praise Him, this most amiable Saviour; yes, we thank Him, this loving Redeemer, throughout all eternity. O blessed eternity!" they exclaim, "what sweetness and joys thou dost give us to taste!"

Beautiful heaven, when shall we behold thee? O happy moment! when wilt thou arrive? Without doubt, dear brethren, we all long and pray for such a great good. So that you may long all the more ardently after it, I will show you, as far as lies in my power:

I. *The happiness which surrounds the Saints, and*
II. *The path which we must take to obtain this happiness.*

I. First of all, the ecstasy of love which takes possession of the hearts of the elect is produced by the sight of the beauty which they experience in the presence of God. No matter how beautiful and charming an object may appear to us in this world, our mind becomes fatigued after a few moments of enjoyment, and we turn away from it—we pass from one thing to another without being satisfied. But in heaven it is different: rather must God grant us His strength, that we may be able to stand the splendor of His beauty and the tender and charming objects which present themselves to our gaze uninterruptedly; a delight which steeps the souls of the elect into such an abyss of sweetness and love. O blessed abode! O lasting happiness! Who among us will enjoy thee?

Secondly, I say, we shall continually perceive the angels, who glorify the magnitude, the rapture and the everlasting duration of these joys by their hymns of praise. No mortal is capable of understanding what the blessed feel at all this.

Thirdly, when we enjoy a pleasure in this world, we feel at the same time the apprehension of losing it, or that of preserving it; this causes us never to be perfectly contented. In heaven it is otherwise: we find ourselves in the midst of pleasures and joys, and we are sure that they will neither decrease nor be taken away from us.

Fourthly, I say, we will enjoy the great and sweet gratification of receiving reward for all the tears which we have shed, and for all our works of penance performed in this life, without one good thought or one good desire being overlooked. O what joy for a Christian who has despised the world and who has mortified his body.

He will behold the steadfastness with which he resisted every bad thought presented by the devil to sully his imagination; he will remember the earnest preparations before going to confession; his ardent desire to nourish his soul at the altar of God; he will behold how often he impoverished himself to assist his poor and suffering fellow creatures. "O my God, O my God!" he will exclaim every moment, "what recompense for such small deeds!" But so as to inflame the love and gratitude of the elect, God will erect His cross in the midst of His court and depict to them all the sufferings which He was driven to undergo out of His great love and in his desire for our happiness. You can picture to yourself how they will be carried away with love and gratitude; how often during the infinite whole of eternity they will lovingly embrace the cross, remembering that God made use of this cross to procure for them so much bliss!

In regard to the happiness of the blessed in heaven, I say that their happiness, their pleasures, their joys, will be in proportion to the sufferings which they endured during this life. If we have had a horror of shameful songs and conversations, in heaven we shall hear the most delightful and entrancing hymns of the angels; if we have been modest in our looks, our eyes will then be occupied with objects whose beauty will accord us continuous rapture without ever feeling the least fatigue; that is to say, we shall be ever discovering fresh beauties, like unto a torrent of love which flows on without ceasing. Our heart, which has sighed and wept in our banishment, will experience such an excess of sweetness that it will be quite enraptured.

The Holy Ghost tells us that chaste souls resemble a person who lies upon a bed of roses, the perfume of which causes them a continual ecstasy. The saints will be nourished and overwhelmed with chaste and pure pleasures through all eternity.

But, you will think, when we are in heaven we all shall be happy alike. Yes, my friend, but there is still a difference. If the damned are miserable, and suffer in proportion to their sins, there is no doubt that the glory of the blessed will be radiant in proportion to the works of penance which they have performed. Nevertheless, it is true that we shall all be very happy and very contented, because we shall be able to enjoy so many delights, so that there will be nothing left to be desired. O beautiful heaven! O glorious dwelling place I when shall we behold thee? O my God! how much longer wilt thou leave us to languish on this imperfect earth in banishment?

II. Now, my friends, you ask me what you must do to obtain heaven. Very well. Pay attention and you shall hear. You must not be attached to the good things of this life; instead of thinking only how to amass money and to purchase property, you must take care to purchase a place for yourself in heaven; instead of working on Sundays, you should keep the day holy by going to the house of God, there to lament your sins, and to implore His grace that you may not fall into the same sins again, and that

He may pardon you; instead of not allowing your children sufficient time to fulfil their religious duties, you must be the first to set them the good example in word and deed; instead of being angry at the least loss, or at a contradiction, you should remember that as a sinner you have deserved far worse, and that God leads you in the surest way toward the goal of your happiness. This, my friend, is what you ought to do in order to reach heaven; but you do not always do it. Do you not envy the blessed inhabitants of the heavenly court? "Ah," you will say, "how I wish I were there; at least I should be free from all the hardships of this life!" But wishing and acting are two different things. If your intention is good, very well; I will tell you what to do. You should, my sister, be more subject to your husband, you should be more complaisant toward him: instead of going about telling what your husband has said or done, you should use that time to ask God to grant you the patience and submission which you owe to your husband; you should ask God to touch his heart and change it. I will tell you what we ought to do to attain heaven. Mothers, pay attention. You should spend more time in attending to your children, to instruct and show them what they should do to get to heaven; you should not spend so much on dress, that you may have more to give in alms, to draw down the blessing of God upon you, or you should lay by something so as to be able to pay your debts; you should put aside vanities, and your whole life should give a good example; morning and night prayer should be carefully said, a devout preparation for Holy Communion and the reception of the Sacraments should be your chief care; your conversation should express contempt for everything worldly and an appreciation of the goods of another life. This should be your occupation and your care; if you act otherwise you will be lost. Reflect upon all this today, tomorrow it will be too late; examine yourself in this respect and then adjust yourself accordingly; weep over your shortcomings and endeavor to behave better, or you may never get to heaven.

What must you do, young people? I will tell you, and I pray you to think it well over. You must not be so solicitous for your body, let it endure a little more; do not think so much about your appearance. You should be more submissive to your parents, remembering that after God it is to them you owe your existence, and you should obey them with a cheerful spirit, without murmuring. Furthermore, you should be more careful of your words, and be modest in your conversations with persons of the opposite sex. This is what God asks of you; if you do this you will attain heaven.

And what do you think of all this, my brother? Toward which side are you inclined? "Ah," you say, "I would much rather go to heaven, because it is so lovely there, than go to hell, where such manifold torments have to be endured, but it is no use to strive to get there; I have not the courage. If one mortal sin suffices to damn us, I, who get angry every moment, can not venture to try." You can not try? Listen to me for a moment and I will prove to you as clear as day that it is not so difficult as you imagine, and that it requires less exertion to please God and to save your soul than it does to lead a life of pleasure and to please the world. Dedicate to God the care and the trouble which you take to please the world, and you will find that He does not expect so much from you as the world does. Your worldly pleasures are at best alloyed with sadness and bitterness, and then follows remorse for having partaken of them. Yes, my friends, by observing all these things you will find how much sweeter it is to serve God than to serve the world. It is only too true that if we would only do as much for God as we do for the world we should all be saints.

Let us resolve, then, today that henceforth we will serve our Lord better than we have done heretofore, so that at the end of our days we may be permitted to partake of the glorious and infinite reward which the Lord has prepared for the faithful. Amen.

CHILDREN'S FIRST COMMUNION

HOLY COMMUNION A MEMORIAL OF THE LOVE OF JESUS TOWARD US

ᖰᑌᐢᎾᐢᎾᐢᎾᐢᎾᑌᖱ

"The bread that I will give, is my flesh for the life of the world."
John vi. 52.

IN A FEW MOMENTS, dear children, you will perform the most holy act which there is possible upon earth, for then you will receive Jesus, the Son of God, with His divinity and humanity. The act is so great, so beautiful, and above all things so holy, that if it were possible the angels of God would gladly change places with you today. If your parents and relatives look upon you today with joyful sentiments, and if the participation in your happiness draws tears from their eyes, who can wonder? And if all those present think, with a mixture of joy and sadness, first of you and then of themselves, who can be surprised? Years ago they, too, stood in your place, to do what you are going to do today. Ah, would that they were all today as they were then! I, too, rejoice with you today, and wish you every happiness. I have every reason to rejoice, for I cherish the conviction that you will prepare a joyful reception for the Son of God in your souls. You are pure, I hope, and when the Saviour comes He will find a believing, a repentant and humble, a pious heart, a heart in which you have kindled the fire of holy charity. One thought only disturbs me. You are pure and pious now, but will you always remain so? You are happy today, but may you not have to confess later, with sighs, that this day was the first, but unfortunately also the only, happy day of your life? Today you receive Communion piously and devoutly, but will you receive Communion afterward with such piety and devotion? O may the love of Jesus never become cold within you! In all your future Communions may the Son of God find you as pure and as holy as you are today! Surely, my dear children, Jesus deserves this, and you owe it to Him on account of the infinite love which He shows to you and to all of us in this holy Mystery. We call it a memorial of love, and it is in fact the work

of the greatest and most disinterested love. So that you may never sin against this Mystery, never dishonor it, never receive it unworthily, I will show you in what this great love consists, which Jesus therein manifests.

I. The Most Holy Sacrament of the Altar is a memorial of God's infinite love toward us. To understand this we must consider what Jesus does and will do for us in this Mystery. He is really and truly present in the same with His divinity and humanity; He is present there:

(a) As the Lamb of God, who takes away the sins of the world. As such he went to Golgotha 1900 years ago, laden with the heavy cross, there to die and to do penance for the sins of men. And behold, in these days, hundreds of priests at the altars every morning to offer up the same Lamb of God. In Holy Mass the adorable Mystery of the Holy Eucharist is celebrated; there the Son of God ascends from the hands of the priest; there He offers Himself perpetually to His heavenly Father. And why does this happen? Out of infinite love. He wishes to make satisfaction for the sins of the world to appease the wrath of God. The world heaps in the most terrible manner sin upon sin, and the Son of God never ceases to appease the wrath of His heavenly Father by the sacrifice of Himself. It is this sacrifice which withholds the avenging arm of justice. We have to thank this sacrifice that God does not chastise the sinful world as it deserves. Every day the Son of God upon innumerable altars stands as a mediator between His Father and miserable mankind; He begs forgiveness for them, and offers up His passion and death in satisfaction for their crimes.

Therefore, my dear children, reflect upon the great grace that this Lamb of sacrifice comes to you today, and as often as you approach in the future the table of the Lord: to be your mediator with His heavenly Father. "Behold the Lamb of God, who takes away the sins of the world:" this is what the priest says to you, holding the sacred Host in his hand, when you are about to receive Holy Communion. O receive it always with becoming love, with the most fervent devotion! Pray thus to Him: "O Thou Lamb of God, who takest away the sins of the world, have mercy upon me!"

(b) In the Most Holy Mystery which you are going to receive, Christ is not only present in the Lamb of God who sacrifices Himself for us, to wipe out our debt of sin and to appease the wrath of God, but at the same time He dwells perpetually among us as our helper and consoler in all our needs.

The church is His abode, the tabernacle His throne, and there He abides day and night in the midst of His faithful, to receive and to console all those who turn to Him in their need. "Come unto Me," He cries out to us, "all you who are sorrowful and heavily laden: I will refresh you: with Me you will find rest for your souls." Did ever a prince speak more gently and graciously to his subjects than the Son of God here speaks to the children of men? Thousands of the oppressed have at all times accepted this invitation; in their sufferings and woes they sought out the church; there they threw themselves upon their knees before the altar, full of confidence, and laid their petitions and their necessities at the feet of the Crucified One, and never did any one go from thence without being consoled. When a danger menaced the Church, the faithful flocked to their Jesus in the Blessed Sacrament. If a plague or pestilence or famine broke out anywhere the faithful took refuge with the divine Saviour. And did these petitions ever remain unheard? Never, my beloved!

Go to Him, too, as often as you are in trouble. To whom can you turn with greater certainty when a cross lies heavy upon you? If you have faith there is no one to whom you can turn with greater confidence than to Jesus in the Most Blessed Sacrament. For behold here present the Lord of all things! "Under the form of bread is that God contained who knows no bounds." Is God's arm not powerful enough to help you? Or is He wanting in love and kindness to wish to aid you? For our sakes He dwells here, not for His sake. Here He hides the riches of His love and mercy, to help all those who come to Him.

(c) It is a great benefit, dear children, for us to have the Most Holy Sacrament always in our midst; we are thereby always near to our God, and God is near us, to give us consolation and assistance. But the love of Christ goes still farther in this holy Mystery, for He is here at the same time as the food of our souls. When any one is invited to a royal table, what a distinction, what an honor for him! But here it is a question of a table more than royal— here is the table of God! The Son of God Himself has prepared it; He, the King of kings, invites every one to it. To whom is this invitation extended? Does He send it to the castles of emperors and kings, of princes and wealthy people? Does He seek out the great and mighty ones of this earth, so as to invite them before the rest of men? Oh, no; no one is shut out from this table; no one is preferred. There the subject kneels beside the prince, the beggar beside the rich man, the laborer and servant beside his master. The most humble is here the greatest. In the world you occupy a small place, perhaps, dear Christian; you have to make ends meet, to worry, to work hard; the world knows and cares as little about you as if you did not belong to their kind. But behold how God honors you! He calls you to His table, and He there gives you the same love, perhaps a far greater love, than He does to the rich and well-to-do.

And the food which God offers us at this table is no perishable bread, but the Bread of Angels, the heavenly manna, the heavenly bread of the faithful; it is the most sacred body and blood of Jesus Christ. "The bread that I shall give you," says the Saviour, "is my flesh for the life of the world." "Take and eat, for this is my body." This is the food which nourishes our souls to everlasting life. "He who eats my flesh, and drinks my blood, he has eternal life, and I shall raise him up at the last day. For my flesh is meat indeed, and my blood is drink indeed." These are our Saviour's own words. When therefore the priest gives the Sacred Host to the communicant, he says: "The body of our Lord Jesus Christ preserve your soul unto life everlasting." But Jesus Christ gives us not only His human nature, His human body as food; He also brings us His divinity. "He who eateth me," He says, "he will live in me."

Dear Christians, what a miracle—what love! The Son of God, Almighty and Infinite, who bears the whole world in His hand, and whom the hosts of angels and saints reverently adore day and night, He deigns to become our food at this wonderful table; He visits us in our unworthy souls; He consecrates us as His temple, as His dwelling. Christians, how stupendous and wonderful is this love! To bear our God within us, to unite our unworthy flesh and blood with His most sacred flesh and blood, how great is this grace! Language has no words in which to express satisfactorily this miracle of divine love. What heart does not feel the most profound reverence and adoration, what head does not bow down humbly into the dust of the earth, what eye is tearless when we are about to approach the table of the Lord? And when the priest stands before the altar, holding the sublime body of Jesus Christ in his hand, saying these words to us, "Behold the Lamb of God, who taketh away the sins of the world," who is not strongly affected then, who does not strike the sinful breast, saying: "Lord, I am not worthy that Thou shouldst enter into my sinful soul!" This is enough, my beloved! He who believes in Jesus here, and does not burn with love, is as hard as stone and rock.

II. I have shown you what Jesus is, and what he does for us in the Most Holy Eucharist. He is here the Lamb of God, who sacrifices Himself for our sins; He is here our constant helper and consoler in all our necessities; He is here the heavenly manna which strengthens and refreshes our souls; and if we consider all this as we ought to, we shall exclaim: "Here, indeed, is the throne of grace; here is manifested the greatest, the purest, the infinite love of God toward us!" And yet you will admire this love still more when I draw your attention to one thing, namely, to the great condescension, yes, even humiliation, of the Son of God in the Holy Eucharist.

The love of a man always appears the more beautiful the greater the sacrifice which is combined with it. If you endure hunger yourself so as to appease that of another, your love is greater and nobler than if you had given him of your abundance. Now look at the Holy Eucharist. Our God is there; but where is His splendor, His majesty and glory? As at the Incarnation, here also He strips Himself of His heavenly splendor. Yes, His humbleness is far greater than then. O look and marvel! He forsakes the glory of heaven and hides Himself under the form of bread, in the form of a little host. Love urges Him to do this. He does it only that He may unite Himself to us. He does it, that no one may be frightened away from His holy table by the splendor of His divinity. Here He foregoes His own honor and glory, that He may save us sinful men and make us happy.

III. And what does He expect in return from men? Do we acknowledge His love and reward it with gratitude? We should think so; but it is not so in fact. Here, where He manifests the greatest love, here He receives the greatest abuse, the blackest ingratitude. Just consider the behavior which men show toward Him, how they dishonor and abuse Him.

During the Holy Sacrifice of the Mass He offers Himself up for our sins to the Father, and He implores His grace and mercy. And what do men do? Many do not think it worth while to attend this act even if they easily can. Others attend, but without thinking what is here done for them. Others even misbehave during the same; laugh, talk, and occupy themselves with other things. Others go so far as to calumniate and ridicule it, and to call it a cursed idolatry. Who does not shudder at this? Our blessed Saviour experiences all this in His work of love, and still He is not prevented by such irreverences from continuing the same so as to appease the wrath of God.

The Son of God dwells in the tabernacle, to be near us in all our necessities, to be the helper of all the oppressed. But what do men do? They have so little confidence in Him that they would rather bear their trouble and their misery for years, or lie bound by their passions, than that they would fall on their knees before their Saviour and pour out their hearts to Him in all humbleness and devotion. And what do those do who are consoled and delivered, perhaps without knowing from whence the help came? Instead of being grateful to Him, they begin to get bolder, and to grieve Him by their sins. And thus is the Son of God misunderstood and sneered at, and yet He never ceases to dwell among us and to prove His love for us. And His love goes so far that He even receives His betrayers and enemies with outstretched arms when at last they come to Him. In the Holy Eucharist Jesus desires to nourish our souls with His most sacred flesh and blood. And what is the reward for such love? Undoubtedly there are many pious Christians who prepare a pure and beautiful dwelling in their hearts for the Saviour, and prepare Him thereby a great joy; but—and this is awful!—many do violence to the Son of God and compel Him to enter into an unworthy soul; into a soul without devotion; into a soul without love; into a soul without contrition and humility; into a soul still steeped in the filth of sin; into a soul more like a filthy, foul sewer than a temple of God. I say they do violence to Him; or is it no violence when they dare to approach the altar in such a condition, when they let the priest hand them the Sacred Host, which they receive in their wicked souls, and thus oblige the Most Holy to enter into this defilement of sin and to dwell there? It is dreadful, and yet the Son of God ceases not to dwell in the Blessed Sacrament in spite of all these insults, so as to impart eternal life to pious souls.

See, my dear children, thus far does the love of Jesus Christ extend to us poor sinners. O appreciate the same, and never be ungrateful toward it! Today you receive for the first time the pledge of this love, and, as I hope and trust, worthily and with consolation for your soul. After this day you will often come to the table of the Lord, so I hope and pray: receive this Holy Sacrament always as you do today. May all the Communions of your whole life be like unto your Communion today, and so may be also your last. As your heart is today so full of faith and love, so full of humility and confidence, preserve it so until your deathbed. Promise this to me, promise it to your God. And that this promise may be kept ever sacred and faithfully, you will renew publicly and solemnly the holy vows which you made to God at your baptism. Answer these questions before God and the assembled congregation ...

Renewal of the Baptismal Vows

You have now made your vows and promises. God grant you the grace to remain faithful to them. The blessing of Almighty God, the Father, Son, and Holy Ghost may descend upon you, and remain always with you. Amen.

After Holy Communion

Dear children, you now hold Jesus within your hearts. The greatest honor which can be conferred upon man has been shown to you. Now prove yourselves worthy of this great grace. Let your thoughts enter the chamber of your heart to pass a few moments at least with the exalted guest who has come to visit you, that you may converse with Him undisturbed. Offer up a devout thanksgiving; recommend yourself to His protection, and carry to Him with confidence all the desires and needs of your heart. Do not leave the church without giving Him once more the sacred promise that you will reward His infinite love with a sincere and lasting love in return. Promise Him, sacredly and firmly, that you will never desecrate by sin your heart, which is His abode; that you will never alienate your soul from Him. Go forth in life with the firm resolution always to remain as pure as you are today, and rather to die than to offend Him by a mortal sin. And, that you may never falter in this resolution, approach the altar frequently to receive the Bread of Angels, the heavenly food of your souls. Happy are you if the bond of love and friendship between you and your Saviour never ceases in this life. You will then be happy in this life, and still greater will be your happiness and your joy in the life beyond. I will take leave of you in the beautiful words of St John: "Be faithful unto death, and God will give you the crown of eternal life." Amen.

TWO JUBILEE SERMONS

"Behold, now is the acceptable time; behold, now is the day of salvation."
II. Cor. vi. 2.

THE ABOVE WORDS are applicable to all those days on which the sources of grace of Holy Church flow more abundantly than ordinarily, as, for instance, to great feasts, to missions, during the forty hours' devotion, but they are especially applicable to the time of a Jubilee, which offers to us the most excellent of all graces which Holy Church places at the disposal of zealous and penitent Christians. For, in the indulgences of the Jubilee, we venerate according to the opinion of the theologians the culmination of divine mercy, the accomplishment of the work of our justification, the completion and fulfilment of our repentance, the all-embracing efficacy of the most precious blood of Jesus Christ, whereby, upon fulfilment of the prescribed conditions, the last barrier is removed which would prevent our entrance into heaven.

The Jubilee indulgence has its origin in the Jubilee year of the Old Law, which was celebrated by divine command every fifty years. It was a year of grace for Israel; then the earth rested, the Israelite enjoyed the gifts of creation, such as did not require manual labor; the slaves were set free, the property forfeited by debt and poverty was restored to its former owner; all debts were remitted, "for it is the year of jubilee." (III. Moses xxv. 10.) The Jubilee year aroused great joy in Israel. It had, however, like so many other institutions of the Old Law, a deep, mysterious meaning. The general immunity from incurred disadvantages and punishments typified the far greater blessings of the remission of the punishment due to sin in the New Law. Our Jubilee brings deliverance from the fetters of the soul, removes its guilt and punishment, and restores to it the full possession of divine grace.

The Christian year of Jubilee has been celebrated for more than 400 years at intervals of 25 years, and is called the Holy Year, or the Great Jubilee. With particular solemnity, however, has the Jubilee been celebrated at the beginning of a new century, as the records show, for the last 600, if not more years. In order that we may perfectly understand the meaning of the Jubilee, and that we may better appreciate its manifold blessings and benefits, I shall endeavor to explain fully to you:

I. *What does the Jubilee grant us?*
II. *What does the Jubilee require of us?*

I.

What does the Jubilee grant us? The Jubilee is an extraordinary indulgence which the Pope grants to the faithful, under the obligation of performing certain works of piety; and during the time appointed for the Jubilee particular authority is granted to confessors to remit certain sins and ecclesiastical punishments, and to release certain vows.

I. What is an indulgence? By indulgence we understand, according to the teaching of the Church in general, a remission of the temporal punishment due to sin which, after the sin itself has been forgiven, is still due—to be accounted for here or in purgatory.

We are speaking here of two entirely different things: of sin and of the punishment for sin. Every sin, venial as well as mortal, leaves, according to Catholic doctrine, a twofold stain upon the soul—the stain of guilt and the stain of punishableness. In mortal sin the state of guilt consists in the complete turning away of the soul from God, in an entire rupture from, and enmity with, God. The mortal offense tears asunder the intimate bond of love and friendship which unites the soul to God by sanctifying grace; this results in punishment by eternal rejection, eternal death, or damnation. The guilt of venial sin is not a complete turning away from God, for this sin does not deprive us of sanctifying grace, but it disturbs and troubles the perfect relation of friendship between God and man; it merits, therefore, not eternal but a temporal punishment, which has to be endured either in this life or in purgatory.

In the case of every sin, then, guilt and punishment are essentials; guilt is the injustice which we do to God, punishment is the exercise of the right, which God has to exact satisfaction from the transgressor of His laws, even after the forgiveness of the guilt.

Now there are two ways by which the temporal punishment of sin can be wiped out: in the first way we either voluntarily undertake works of penance during our earthly life, and make satisfaction founded on the satisfaction of Jesus Christ, or suffer in purgatory after our death; in the other way the grace of indulgence comes to the assistance of the faithful, to deliver them from the temporal punishment due to sins from which they have been purified in the Sacrament of Penance.

Two objections are made to this Catholic doctrine of indulgences. The one is that God never forgives by halves, but that He remits the temporal punishment with the sin. This is not true. As a proof of this we will take two well-known examples from the Bible: When the refractory people of Israel murmured at Moses and Aaron, and Moses besought the Lord for forgiveness, the Lord said to him: "I have forgiven according to thy word . . . ; but yet all the men that have seen my majesty, and the signs that I have done in Egypt, and in the wilderness, and have tempted me now ten times, and have not obeyed my voice, shall not see the land for which I swore to their fathers." (IV. Moses xiv. 20, 23.) The other example is this: After King David had grievously sinned by adultery and murder the prophet Nathan came and upbraided him with his crimes, by reminding him of the great graces and blessings which God had shown him. David acknowledged and confessed, in humility and contrition, the enormity of his guilt. The prophet replied, "The Lord hath also taken away thy sin," but announced to him at the same time the temporal punishment which God would inflict upon him for his sins, namely, that the son conceived in adultery would die, and that other misfortunes would be visited upon his family; and this actually took place. (II. Kings xii. 13, 14.) That a temporal punishment remains after the forgiveness of the guilt of sin also in the New Law is also acquiesced in by the practice of the Church in the first centuries, when most severe penances were inflicted upon sinners. But enemies of the Church overlook this entirely, and they advance the other objection, that, as Christ did complete satisfaction, every punishment which God would impose upon sinners would lessen the merits of the Sacrifice of the Cross. That is as much as to say that Christ had taken away all obligation from us to do penance for our sins according to our own ability. But there is not a word to this effect to be found anywhere in Holy Writ. We do read, however, that Christ, by His example, urges us to walk in His footsteps and to unite our penances with His. Would Christ have been a true Saviour to us if He had not by His humility imposed upon us the obligation to be humble, by His poverty to strip our hearts of all desire for earthly goods, and by His mortified life incite us to mortification and penance? If He is our Saviour and the head of those He redeemed, then we, the members of His mystical body, must be one with our head.

This is what St. Paul understood when he declared (Coloss. i. 24) that he would fill up those things that were wanting of the sufferings of Christ, in his flesh, for Christ's body, which is the Church. And the same great Apostle chastised his body, considering himself unworthy to bear the name of an Apostle because formerly he had persecuted the community of God; and he led a life of penance, to make satisfaction for the sins of his early life, long ago forgiven. Did he do this from motives of pride, or of vanity, or because it pleased him more to do penance than to believe that Christ had left no obligation upon sinners to make satisfaction?

Is it not foolishness to declare that it is only vanity for Catholic Christians to awaken sincere contrition, confess their most secret and debasing sins, mortify their flesh, fast, weep, pray, and give alms to obtain from God the forgiveness of their sins and remission of the punishment? No one performs such severe practices from sheer vanity, but they are done from a feeling of duty.

And when we practise works of atonement, according to Catholic teaching, we do not for one moment believe that they alone will obtain the remission of temporal punishment, but through the power of and in connection with the satisfaction of Christ, who is the true vine, from whom alone we receive the grace to live and to act so as to please God.

If, then, whatever we do in respect to satisfaction is really united with the satisfaction of Christ and essentially connected with it, how, then, is it possible that the satisfaction of Christians should lessen the merits of Christ or bring them into contempt?

The grace of indulgences, therefore, comes to the assistance of the zealous faithful, aids them in rendering satisfaction, makes reparation for the temporal punishment still to be expiated, and removes the last obstacle which bars the faithful from entering into heaven.

II. Now in what way does the repentant Christian acquire assistance in the satisfaction which he should render himself? Whence comes this reparation? Whence come indulgences? Where is their source?

Indulgences are obtained from the boundless and superabundant satisfaction of Christ and the saints. Christ could work a boundless satisfaction by one drop of His blood, in consequence of the infinite merits of any and each of His actions. But in reality He shed all His blood for our salvation. This fact could not increase the already infinite merits of the least of His sufferings; it at least induced God to apply the merits of Christ more abundantly to us. Moreover, Mary and the saints, as well as the holy martyrs, by the power of the merits of Christ, gained far more merits than necessary for their own sanctification and blessedness.

This wealth of satisfaction is now the resource of the Church, which Jesus Christ left her as an inheritance, so that out of the superabundance of merits those who upon earth stand in need of the assistance, might profit of the merits of others.

Now if we ask how the merits of others can be a source of benefit to ourselves, and even become, indeed, our own satisfactions, we have the answer in the doctrine of the power of the keys in Holy Church and of her disposition of the merits of Jesus Christ and the saints. The Council of Trent expresses itself very clearly upon this point: "As the power to grant indulgences was granted by Christ to the Church, and she has used this power given to her by God from the earliest times, therefore the Holy Council of the Church teaches and commands that the use of indulgences, which is very salutary for Christian people, and approved by the Holy Councils, should be retained in the Church, and lays the anathema upon those who declare that indulgences are unnecessary or who deny that the Church has the power to apply them."

This power of the Church is repeatedly confirmed in Holy Scripture. For instance, Christ said to St. Peter (and Peter lives on in the Popes): "Whatsoever thou shalt bind upon earth, it shall be bound also in heaven; and whatsoever thou shalt loose upon earth, it shall be loosed also in heaven." (Matt. xvi. 19.)

As therefore the divine Saviour excludes nothing from this faculty, as a matter of fact the power of binding and loosing in the Church extends over everything, unless removed from her jurisdiction either by the nature of the matter or by special command of Jesus Christ. But no such restriction applies to the remission of temporal punishment. Christ further says: "And to thee will I give the keys of the kingdom of heaven"—that means the power to remove the last obstacles which prevent us from entering into heaven. The last obstacles are the temporal punishments. And on this authority indulgences have been granted until this day.

Indeed, if the divine Saviour gave to His Church the far greater power of remitting eternal punishments (John xx. 23), why, then, should He have withheld from her the lesser power of remitting temporal punishments?

The spiritual merits of others are only applicable to ourselves because we, as members, are in communion with Christ, the head, with the saints in heaven, and with the faithful on earth, as long as we remain in the state of sanctifying grace.

The good works of Christ, and of the saints, are profitable for us because, as in a living body, all the members—through sanctifying grace—are filled with strength and life. If, then, the Church makes use of the boundless treasures which she possesses in the merits of Christ and the saints, if she applies the merits of others to some or to all the faithful, and allows them to make use of these merits, will not God be satisfied in this way, although the satisfaction is not performed personally by the one who really ought to do it? God acts like a creditor who is satisfied if a third party pays instead of the debtor himself, or performs the work the latter should do. Surely it is a great mercy and grace on the part of God that He should accept such a satisfaction by proxy. Has He not accepted the Passion of His only begotten Son, and continually accepts it, for the remission of sins committed by us? That is the fundamental dogma of the Catholic Church. If we did not accept any satisfaction by way of substitution, how could Christ have redeemed us?

God has desired to glorify those who, by sanctifying grace and holiness of life, are living in union with Christ, by accepting their satisfactions as a substitute for that of their weaker brethren.

Through the grace of indulgences our own weakness is supported and makes amends for the temporal punishment for all punishments if the indulgence is a plenary one, for a part only when it is only a partial one.

In this way have indulgences always been used; the Church has granted them, the faithful have endeavored to profit by them, and everywhere the indulgences have born abundant fruits of penance: remarkable conversions, growth in holiness, increase of faith, and of charity, etc., etc. Indulgences bring people to confession, attract them like a heavenly magnet, and are to many eternal salvation.

While the indulgence of the Jubilee is in its essentials not different from any plenary indulgence, still there exists a difference on account of certain conditions.

What is the Jubilee indulgence? The Jubilee indulgence is a plenary indulgence distinguished by a great solemnity, a great power, a great authority.

(a) The Jubilee indulgence is surrounded with great solemnity. For it not only extends to a congregation, a diocese, a country, a certain part of the world, but it extends over the whole earth. From the rising of the sun to its setting the rays of its grace extend.

Moreover, the ceremonies with which it is announced are calculated to give it great authority. From the throne, whereon God Himself has placed him, the Pope raises his voice as shepherd, addresses himself to the whole world, to the bishops, priests, and to the faithful. The proclamation of the graces of indulgences sets the whole of Christendom in joyous agitation. After hearing the voice of the Pope, their shepherd, Christians say: "Behold, now is the acceptable time, now is the day of salvation!" And those who are not of the number of the zealous Christians, will they not be carried away by the extraordinary celebrations which will take place even in the smallest communities—solemnities which, on account of their rarity, make all the greater impression?

(b) The Jubilee indulgence is a great power in itself. This power consists of the prerogatives and particular authority which are granted exclusively during the time of the Jubilee; authority to absolve from certain reserved sins; authority to liberate from ecclesiastical punishments; authority to release certain vows. With this authority not only a few but all confessors are provided, so that if we faithfully fulfil the obligations we may receive this greatest treasure with but little difficulty.

(c) The Jubilee indulgence enjoys the greatest authenticity, particularly the Jubilee which takes place at the change of the century, the history of which reaches back as far as the thirteenth, according to some historians even as far as the seventh century. Thus the Jubilee indulgence is a most valuable and precious gift, the Jubilee year a year rich in graces, a year of revival and penance, a year of expiation and grace, called rightly by the Church the Holy Year; a year which prepares a path to the joys of paradise.

II.
"Prepare ye the way of the Lord: make straight his paths."
Mark i. 3.

The preceding part of this sermon had for its aim to make clear to us the great value of the graces which we may obtain by means of the Jubilee indulgence. In the Jubilee indulgence we venerate the culmination of divine mercy, the accomplishment of our justification, the perfection of our penance, the ransom that Christ Himself paid for us.

But at the threshold of the sanctuary, which holds the wonders of divine grace, we are met by the voice of Holy Church: "Prepare ye the way of the Lord: make his path straight!" Whosoever desire to participate in the reception of the graces offered, let them examine themselves whether they are in the proper condition to receive them.

Let us therefore inquire:
What does the Jubilee require of us?

Holy Church is obliged to speak in this way. She unfolds before the eyes of mankind the whole beauty of divine mercy so as to attract our hearts, but she exacts also purified and devoted hearts. For it is an essential teaching that in the holy work of regeneration, and especially in the accomplishment of sanctification, which the Jubilee indulgence has for purpose, the divine working should be met and sustained by our own exertion and permeate the same. In other words, the great and sublime graces of the Jubilee indulgence must be gained by the faithful on conditions more exacting than would be necessary to obtain ordinary indulgences. "Prepare ye the way of the Lord: make his path straight!" These words will have to be well considered. Whosoever has any idea of the doctrine of the Catholic Church as regards justification can never fall into the error of thinking that the offering of a special grace dispenses with due preparation for the same, and that the announcement of a special indulgence and the invitation to partake of the same can, as a consequence, result in a relaxation or even a cessation of penance. It is the purpose of this sermon to prove that the urgent invitation to partake of the benefits of the Jubilee indulgence does not only not interfere with penance, but that, in fact, there is no greater incentive for penance, and really for most thorough penance, than the prospect of the immense benefit offered by the Church by the authority of God, namely, a complete remission of the punishments incurred by our sins.

The answer, then, to our question, what does the Jubilee require of us, is:

I. *We must be in the state of grace.*
II. *We must duly perform the prescribed works of penance.*

I. We must be in the state of sanctifying grace.

(a) Next to the earnest intention of partaking of the indulgence we must be above all things in the state of grace, for St. Thomas says, "A dead member of the body can not derive any good from the other living members," and he who is in a state of mortal sin is like a dead member. Furthermore, since the granting of the indulgence emanates from the authority of the Church, it can never be the intention of the Church to apply the merits of Jesus Christ and the saints to souls stained with sin. Indulgences are a favor granted to the friends and children of God, certainly not to His enemies. And again, how can the temporal punishment be remitted to those still deserving eternal punishment? As long as the sin itself remains, God does not remit its punishment. It is therefore an indispensable condition, either to have preserved the state of grace or to have again obtained the same by penance.

However desirable it would be now that all the prescribed works for the Jubilee indulgence be performed in the state of grace, it is nevertheless sufficient if we are in the state of grace at that moment in which we complete the last of these prescribed works, because just at that moment the indulgence is gained. Consequently there is no Jubilee indulgence for impenitent and obdurate sinners. They, too, are invited to profit in this time of grace by gaining the indulgence, but the invitation is tendered on the condition that such sinners should repudiate sin, and with repentant hearts and reformed minds they may participate in the benefits of divine grace. Mind this well; there can be no Jubilee graces for you if God does not perceive the image of His Son in your soul, if He does not see that you are grafted on the True Vine, which is Christ, through sanctifying grace, if you can not say: "I live, yet not I, but Christ lives in me."

It is easily understood, therefore, that corresponding conditions are imposed upon the faithful. Sin must be banished from the soul, because sin and grace can no more dwell together than darkness and light, or death and life. The sincere conversion of the heart to God must cover, without exception, each and every sin that has broken the bond of love with God. These obstacles must be removed by a contrite confession, by an earnest and sincere determination to lead a better life.

(b) So that our conversion may be real, we must free ourselves from every disorderly inclination and attachment to sin, as far as our own will is concerned. I mean that our will must break with sin, must abhor it as the greatest of all evils. St. Bernard calls a conversion, where the inclination to sin is not rooted out, an abominable deception. St. Augustine teaches the same, when he speaks of God's commands to Abraham: "Go forth out of thy country, and from thy kindred, and out of thy father's house, and come into the land which I shall show thee." (Gen. xii. 1.) In these words God not only gave Abraham the command to leave his country bodily, which he had already done, but to relinquish all attachment to his former country, and to forsake it in his heart, that he might serve as a model to the sinner.

Is it not a fact that we are not contented with a friend's gifts if we have not his heart? And so God wants our heart. God opens His paternal arms to us, and desires only to see the last barriers fall which prevent our entrance into heaven. But to this end He requires of us the same that we ask of our friends: "Son, give me thy heart! I behold thy tears; I hear thy prayers; I perceive thy good works! but, give me thy heart! Avoid the occasion for sin! Give me thy heart! "

Therefore, in preparation for the gaining of the Jubilee indulgence the first essential condition is the possession of sanctifying grace, the faithful must be purified from every mortal sin, and free from every attachment of the heart or will to the same, and this resolution must be proved by the avoidance of occasions leading to sin. Reason demands this, for even in our courts of law pardon is granted only to repentant and reformed offenders. Religion demands this, for it is written: "But if the just man turn himself away from his justice, and do iniquity, all his justices which he had done shall not be remembered." (Ezech. xviii. 24.)

II. We must perform the prescribed works duly and properly. Above all, the one desiring to gain the Jubilee indulgence must perform the prescribed works in person, as according to the existing rules no one can gain an indulgence for another living person.

The prescribed works must be performed at the appointed times, as also in a spirit of piety and penance, otherwise they would not be in accordance with the intentions which the Pope had in granting the indulgence. 3. As we must strictly conform to the conditions upon which the Church grants the indulgence, not only the voluntary but also the involuntary omission of any of the prescribed conditions, as, for instance, the inability to fulfil the same or ignorance of the same, would prevent your gaining the indulgence, unless the prescribed works are modified by authority of your confessor. 4. If several good works are prescribed, the order of the same is, as a rule, left to the choice of the performer, but the last one of these works, as already stated, must necessarily be performed in the state of grace. 5. A work which the penitent is already obliged to perform can not serve for the gaining of this Jubilee indulgence, for instance, Easter Communion.

The works prescribed for gaining the Jubilee indulgence are in particular: 1. Confession and Communion. Both these sacraments must be received within the time appointed for the Jubilee. 2. Church visits. The churches designated by the bishop must be visited. No one has authority to substitute other churches for those named unless specially authorized by the bishop. Sixty visits altogether must be made. 3. Prayers. The prayers said at each church visit must be offered in the intention of the Holy Father. They must be actually said by moving the lips. Mental prayer is not excluded, but in itself is insufficient. It is considered sufficient to recite in each church visited five times the Our Father, Hail Mary, and Glory be to the Father. Sick and feeble persons and others lawfully incapacitated may have changed the visits of churches by their confessor into some other work of piety.

This, then, is what the Jubilee requires of us. May you all be expected to gain the Jubilee indulgences? Shall we all participate in the benefits of this holy time of grace? Do you understand now why the Catholic Church institutes Jubilees? Is it not foolish and wicked to say that at the time of a Jubilee it is made easy, by a few indifferent acts, to receive forgiveness and grace? This is what the enemies of the Church claim, because they rejoice at a chance to misrepresent her acts. The Church can never do anything to suit them. If she proclaims the forgiveness of sins and the necessity of penitential works, it is said she underestimates the satisfaction of Christ; if she opens the treasury of the expiation of Christ by granting indulgences, it is said that she disturbs the spirit of penance.

It may be convenient for impenitent, obdurate sinners to think so, but the great grace of the Jubilee indulgence, decried by our enemies and scoffed at by impenitent sinners, remains, nevertheless, holy, precious, and propitious, like the golden ray of sunshine falling upon fertile soil.

The good Catholic knows and feels that this is an important and holy season of grace, a time for repentance and contrition, for humility and reform, for the love of God and of our fellow men.

Can you ever hear more impressive words than those of Christ: "The way is steep .... the door is narrow"? When is it ever required of you more urgently to break with sin and to avoid occasion? When are you more earnestly exhorted to combat your evil passions, urged to peaceful reconciliation, to conjugal fidelity, to the restitution of ill-gotten goods, to make good slander?

Thus a holy zeal should be awakened for penance, contrition, and confession. And the Church listens to our sighs .... she beholds our tears .... she comes to our assistance with this Jubilee indulgence. O holy season! How it strengthens our confidence! How it draws men to their merciful God! How light are our hearts, which were oppressed with guilt! Do not ask: "What can the Jubilee indulgence give me after I am made to do all this penance?" Oh, you know not how enormous the punishment is that you have deserved, and compared with that, how insignificant your merits are, how imperfect your works!

Remember that formerly the Church imposed most severe penances, sometimes lasting for years, for one single sin. She certainly possesses the right understanding of our guilt.

Remember how the anchorites did penance; remember St. Peter's tears, shed during his whole lifetime; think of Magdalen's twenty-two years of penance; think of the severe penances of the innocent Aloysius!

O holy indulgence! O precious gift of our Holy Mother Church! Thanks! Eternal gratitude! Amen.

ASSUMPTION OF THE BLESSED VIRGIN MARY

THE GLORIES OF MARY

"Because He hath regarded the humility of His handmaid."
Luke i. 48.

WHEN WE BEHOLD, dear brethren, how the Blessed Virgin in her humility lowered herself beneath all creatures, we behold at the same time that her humility exalted her above everything but God. Not the powers or princes of this earth have raised her to this highest degree of dignity, in which it is our happiness to contemplate her today, no, the three Persons of the Most Holy Trinity have placed her upon this throne of glory. They have proclaimed her the Queen of heaven and earth, and made her the keeper and dispenser of the heavenly treasures. It is safe to say, dear brethren, that we shall never comprehend sufficiently the glories of Mary and the power which Jesus Christ, her divine Son, has given to her; that we shall never fully appreciate the ardent desire she has to make us happy. She sees in us her own children; she rejoices in the power to help us, which God has given her. Yes, Mary is our great helper; she it is, who presents to her divine Son, all our prayers, our tears, and our sighs; she it is, who obtains the graces for us which we need for our sanctification. The Holy Ghost tells us that amongst all creatures Mary is a miracle of might, a miracle of sanctity, and a miracle of love. What a happiness for us, dear brethren, what hope for our salvation! Let us strengthen our confidence in this good and tender Mother by contemplating the glories of Mary.

To attempt to speak of the glories of Mary, means, my dear brethren, to lessen the exalted idea which you should have formed thereof; for St. Ambrose tells us, that Mary is raised to such a high degree of glory, of honor, and of power, that not even the angels can realize it; it is known to God alone. We may therefore conclude, that all that which human creatures might be able to say and to appreciate, would be nothing, or nearly nothing, to that which she really is in the sight of God. The highest praise which the Church gives her, is in the words: Mary is the daughter of the eternal Father, the Mother of the redeeming Son of God, and the Spouse of the Holy Ghost. When the eternal Father chose Mary to be His daughter, what flow of graces must He not have poured into her soul? She received for herself alone more graces than all the angels and saints together. He began by preserving her from original sin, a grace which was granted to her alone. He fortified her in grace with a perfect security, so that she never lost it. Yes, my dear friends, the heavenly Father enriched her with heavenly gifts in just proportion to the great dignity to which she was to be exalted. He erected in her a living temple of the three Persons of the Most Blessed Trinity. Let us say briefly: He did for her everything which it was possible to do for a creature. While the eternal Father took such care of Mary, we see that the Holy Ghost adorned her soul in such a high degree, that already at the moment of her conception she was an object of delight to the three divine Persons. Mary had not only the happiness of being the daughter of the eternal Father; but also that of being the Mother of the Son, and the Spouse of the Holy Ghost. Through this incomparable dignity she now beholds herself made, to form the most adorable body of Jesus Christ. God made use of her to overthrow the dominion of the evil spirit and to annihilate it. She was allied to the three divine Persons therefore to redeem the World, by giving it a Saviour. Can we ever sufficiently comprehend an abyss of such greatness, power and love? Next to the adorable body of Jesus Christ, she is the most beautiful ornament of the heavenly court.

We may say that the triumph of the Blessed Virgin in heaven is the culmination of the graces of the sublime Queen of heaven and earth. Then she obtained the last jewel of her incomparable dignity as Mother of God. After having been subjected for a time to the miseries of this life and the humiliation of death, she enjoys the most glorious, and most honorable existence which a creature could ever enjoy. We wonder sometimes, that Jesus, who loved His Mother so dearly, could have left her so long upon earth after His resurrection. The reason is this: He wished in this manner to still increase her glory, and wanted her also to aid the Apostles, who had need of her presence to encourage and guide them. Mary revealed to the Apostles the greatest mysteries of the hidden life of Jesus Christ.

Mary also elevated the standard of virginity, which made thus known its lustre and its beauty, and showed us the magnificent reward reserved for this holy state. Let us, however, dear brethren, follow Mary up to the moment that she left this world. Jesus Christ desired that before she should be taken up to heaven, she should receive once more all the Apostles. They were all, with the exception of St. Thomas, brought to her side in the most miraculous manner. With the extraordinary humility which she had always practised in such high degree, she kissed their feet and asked for their blessing.

Thus she still increased her virtue, her merits and her reward. Then Mary gave also to the Apostles her blessing. It would be impossible for me to describe to you the sorrow of the Apostles at the loss which they were about to undergo. Was not the Blessed Virgin, after the Redeemer, their entire happiness, their whole consolation? To alleviate their sorrow Mary promised them that she would never forget them before her divine Son. It is thought that the same angel who announced to her the mystery of the Incarnation told her also the hour of her death. The Blessed Virgin is said to have answered to the angel: "O what bliss, and how ardently I desire after this moment!" After these glad tidings she desired to make her last will, which was soon done. She had two robes, which she left to the two maidens who had been in her service for a long while.

Then, when the hour arrived, she felt herself burning with so great a love that her soul could no longer remain in her body. O blessed moment! Can we, dear brethren, contemplate this death, without feeling an ardent desire to live a good life and to die such a holy death? We can certainly not expect to die of love; but we may hope at least to die in the love of God. Mary had no fear of death, for death was to place her in possession of eternal bliss; she knew that heaven was waiting for her, and that she was to be one of its choicest ornaments. Her Son and the whole celestial court were advancing to meet her, the Saints of heaven were waiting to conduct her in triumph into their kingdom. Everything in heaven was ready to receive her; she was to enjoy honors which are above everything which we can possibly imagine to ourselves.

Before leaving this world, Mary was not subject to any sickness, for she was free from sin. In spite of her advanced age, her body was never emaciated, as is the case with other human beings; it seemed, on the contrary, as the end approached, to be rejuvenated. St. John Damascene tells us that Jesus Christ Himself came to call His Mother. This beautiful star which had illumined the world for seventy-two years was about to disappear. Yes, dear brethren, she beheld her Son again, but in an entirely different form than when she saw Him all covered with blood, nailed upon the cross. O divine love! This is the greatest of thy victories, and of thy mercies! Thou couldst do no more, neither couldst Thou do less. O blessed death! O death to be desired! O how greatly is she now compensated for all the humiliations and suffering to which her holy soul was subjected in this mortal life! Yes, she beholds her Son again, but quite different from that day when in His bitter passion she saw Him in the hands of His executioners, carrying His cross, crowned with thorns, without her being able to offer Him the least help. O no, she beholds Him no longer in His great sufferings; she beholds Him resplendent with glory, arrayed in the magnificence which composes the joy and bliss of heaven: she beholds the angels and the Saints who surround Him, who praise Him, glorify and adore Him from the bottom of their hearts. Yes, she beholds again this tender Jesus, free from everything which could cause Him any suffering. O, should we not do everything we possibly can, so as to be able to join the Mother and the Son in this place of eternal happiness? A few moments of struggling and suffering, and such glorious reward. What a blessed death, my friends! Mary had nothing to fear, because she had always loved her God; she had nothing to mourn, because she had never possessed anything but her God.

Do we, too, wish to die without fear? Let us then live like Mary, in innocence; let us avoid sin, which causes our unhappiness in time and eternity. And should we have been so unfortunate as to commit sin, let us, like St. Peter, lament it until our death, and let our remorse end only with our life. Let us descend into the grave weeping, like the holy King David; let us wash our souls in the bitterness of our tears.

Do we wish, like Mary, to die without trouble? Let us then live like her, without attachment to created things; let us do as she did, let us love God alone, let us desire alone Him, let us seek to please Him only in everything that we do. Happy is that Christian who leaves nothing, to gain everything!

Thus let Mary, our beautiful mother, be our guiding star in life and in death. Let us imitate her virtues, her humility, her piety, her charity, so that after the few years in this life we may expect to imitate her also in a happy death, to partake of the glory of her divine Son for all eternity. Amen.

www.ingramcontent.com/pod-product-compliance
Lightning Source LLC
Chambersburg PA
CBHW011128070526
44583CB00023B/2949